Cooperation and Conflict between State and Local Government

Cooperation and Conflict between State and Local Government

Edited by

Russell L. Hanson
Indiana University Bloomington

Eric S. Zeemering
University of Georgia

ROWMAN & LITTLEFIELD

Lanham • Boulder • New York • London

Published by Rowman & Littlefield
An imprint of The Rowman & Littlefield Publishing Group, Inc.
4501 Forbes Boulevard, Suite 200, Lanham, Maryland 20706
www.rowman.com

6 Tinworth Street, London SE11 5AL, United Kingdom

British Library Cataloguing in Publication Information Available

Library of Congress Cataloging-in-Publication Data

Names: Hanson, Russell L., 1953– author. | Zeemering, Eric S., author.
Title: Cooperation and conflict between state and local government / Russell L. Hanson, Indiana University Bloomington, Eric S. Zeemering, University of Georgia.
Description: Lanham : Rowman & Littlefield, [2021] | Includes bibliographical references and index.
Identifiers: LCCN 2020026803 (print) | LCCN 2020026804 (ebook) | ISBN 9781538139318 (cloth) | ISBN 9781538139325 (paperback) | ISBN 9781538139332 (epub)
Subjects: LCSH: State-local relations—United States.
Classification: LCC JS348 .H36 2021 (print) | LCC JS348 (ebook) | DDC 320.80973—dc23
LC record available at https://lccn.loc.gov/2020026803
LC ebook record available at https://lccn.loc.gov/2020026804

Contents

PART II   CONFLICT IN STATE–LOCAL RELATIONS

PART III   COOPERATION IN STATE–LOCAL RELATIONS

Career Profiles

Preface

The contributions to this book, illuminating state–local intergovernmental relations, emerged from the Fifth Annual Deil S. Wright Symposium at the 2018 meeting of the American Society for Public Administration (ASPA). Several of the chapter authors participated at the symposium, where we also engaged in conversations with public service professionals working on the front lines of state and local government. A few additional authors joined the project as we refined the scope and content needed to give students and readers insight into the current landscape of state–local relations in the United States. We thank the contributing authors for framing their work to explain the current conduct of state–local relations across the United States and to spell out the implications for students who seek careers in state and local government.

The Deil S. Wright Symposium, organized by ASPA's Section on Intergovernmental Administration and Management (SIAM), has become a critical venue for sharing research on federalism and intergovernmental relations. We acknowledge and thank current and former SIAM chairs for their investments in the symposium, including David Miller, Christine Kelleher Palus, and now Christopher Hawkins. We thank Carl Stenberg, who organized the event during its formative years and continued to remind us about the legacy of Deil Wright's scholarship. Bill Shields, executive director of ASPA, and Harvey White, former ASPA president, have been friends to SIAM and the Deil S. Wright Symposium, and we thank ASPA for its continued support. Finally, many of us have come to know members of the Wright family who attend the symposium each year. Our lives have been enriched by their participation and their reflection on Deil Wright's legacy. We thank them for their continued engagement in conversations about public service in the U.S. federal system.

After the symposium, we took some time to refine the final content for the volume. We extend our thanks to Traci Crowell at Rowman & Littlefield, who moved the project toward completion at a quick pace to make the timely material accessible to students and readers. The state and local government officials interviewed for the career profiles in this book gave generously of their time to inform students about possible career paths in public service. We extend thanks for their time and investment in future public servants. We also thank Luke Boggs, who supported inquiry into some final details for this project as a graduate assistant at the University of Georgia.

Russ Hanson thanks his mentors at the University of Minnesota, his colleagues in the Department of Political Science and School of Public and Environmental Affairs at Indiana University Bloomington, and his former students everywhere, most especially Eric Zeemering! He is also grateful for the many enjoyable editorial and scholarly collaborations he enjoyed during his professional career.

Eric extends thanks to colleagues in the School of Public and International Affairs at the University of Georgia, who provide a stimulating environment in which to think about the intersection of politics and public administration. Thanks also to Russ Hanson, a valued advisor and now patient writing collaborator. Eric also thanks his family—Kesha, Mason, and Kai—for their patience with late nights of work as this volume moved toward completion.

The authors would also like to thank the reviewers who provided feedback on the proposal: George Hale (Kutztown University), Melanie Bowers (Rutgers University–Camden), Jonathan Winburn (University of Mississippi), Dave Claborn (Howard Payne University), Nicole Shoaf (Missouri Southern State University), John Bertalan (University of South Florida), Erin Richards (Cascadia College), Jeffrey Brauer (Keystone College), and Dave Price (Santa Fe College).

We believe the pages ahead illuminate conflict and cooperation in state–local intergovernmental relations. By learning more about these dynamics, we hope readers will be encouraged to become engaged in our shared governing responsibilities through participation as citizens or through work as public servants in state and local government.

Russell L. Hanson
Bloomington, Indiana

Eric S. Zeemering
Athens, Georgia

About the Editors and Contributors

Editors

Russell L. Hanson is professor emeritus at Indiana University Bloomington, where he taught for thirty-six years after receiving his Ph.D. from the University of Minnesota. With Virginia Gray, he was a former coeditor and contributor to *Politics in the American States.* He also joined William Berry, Evan Ringquist, and Richard Fording in devising dynamic measures of citizens' and legislators' political moods for all fifty states.

Eric S. Zeemering is associate professor and director for the Master's of Public Administration (MPA) program in the Department of Public Administration and Policy at the University of Georgia. He served as chair of the Section on Intergovernmental Administration and Management (SIAM) of the American Society for Public Administration from 2016 to 2018.

Contributors

William Blomquist is professor emeritus of political science at Indiana University Purdue University Indianapolis (IUPUI) and a senior research fellow in the Ostrom Workshop at Indiana University Bloomington. His research interests concern governmental organization and public policy, with a specialization in the field of water institutions and water management. Blomquist received his bachelor's degree in economics, master's degree in political science, and graduate certificate in public administration from Ohio University and his Ph.D. in political science from Indiana University.

Jaclyn Bunch is associate professor in the Department of Political Science and Criminal Justice at the University of South Alabama. Dr. Bunch earned her B.A. in 2009 from Pace University and her Ph.D. in 2014 from Florida State University, where she served as the LeRoy Collins Fellow. Her research primarily falls within the fields of American politics and public policy, with particular interests in state and local relations, federalism, hierarchical dilemmas, political media, and motivation and reasoning. Dr. Bunch's work is published in noted field journals, including *PS: Political Science and Politics, Publius: The Journal of Federalism, Journal of Public Policy, Public Policy and Administration, State and Local Government Review, and Justice Quarterly.*

Erika S. Coe is a graduate student at Indiana University Bloomington studying political philosophy and comparative politics. Her current work explores contentious politics, including the impact of ideology, partisanship, gender, and race in political discourse.

Brian K. Collins is chair and associate professor in the Department of Public Administration at the University of North Texas. His research interests center on puzzles and questions about policy implementation and management. His substantive areas of interest include civic engagement, citizen satisfaction, intergovernmental granting, and performance measurement.

Cali Curley is an assistant professor in the Department of Political Science at the University of Miami. Dr. Curley's research focuses on local government policy tool choices and measuring their effectiveness, typically in the area of sustainability. Her recent research places an emphasis on understanding equity in policy design. She earned her Ph.D. from the Askew School of Public Administration and Policy at Florida State University, and her work can be found in *Urban Affairs Review, Policy Studies Journal, and the Review of Policy Research.*

George W. Dougherty Jr. is assistant professor at the University of Pittsburgh Graduate School of Public and International Affairs. He directs the Master's of Public Policy and Management degree, coordinates the undergraduate public service program, and conducts research in public administration, public policy, and nonprofit management. He holds a Ph.D. in political science from the University of Georgia.

Jayce L. Farmer is assistant professor and graduate director for the School of Public Policy and Leadership at the University of Nevada, Las Vegas. His research interests and expertise include state and local government studies, county finance and administration, and urban studies.

Peter Stanley Federman is an assistant professor in the Paul H. O'Neill School of Public and Environmental Affairs at Indiana University Purdue University Indianapolis. His research focuses on the politics of administration and how bureaucrats engage in political action and behavior. Dr. Federman's recent work looks at the manifest ways these politics impact the policymaking process, particularly in local governments and public safety agencies.

John Kincaid is the Robert B. and Helen S. Meyner Professor of Government and Public Service and director of the Meyner Center for the Study of State and Local Government at Lafayette College in Easton, Pennsylvania. He is an elected fellow of the National Academy of Public Administration. He served as senior editor of the Global Dialogue on Federalism, a joint project of the Forum of Federations and International Association of Centers for Federal Studies (2001–2015); editor of *Publius: The Journal of Federalism* (1981–2006); and executive director of the U.S. Advisory Commission on Intergovernmental Relations, Washington, DC (1988–1994). He is the author of various works on federalism and intergovernmental relations and most recently coeditor of *Identities, Trust, and Cohesion in Federal Systems: Public Perspectives* (2018).

Hannah Lebovits is assistant professor at the University of Texas–Arlington. Her research centers on the ways ideals and mechanisms to enhance social justice, equity, and social sustainability make their way through governing systems. She is also a freelance writer who covers topics related to urban, suburban, and metro politics and policy.

Agustín León-Moreta is assistant professor at the University of New Mexico School of Public Administration. He received a Ph.D. in public administration and policy from the Askew School at Florida State University. His research has appeared in *Public Administration Review, American Review of Public Administration, Urban Studies, State and Local Government Review*, and *Public Administration Quarterly*.

Daniel J. Mallinson is assistant professor of public policy and administration at Penn State Harrisburg. He received his Ph.D. in political science from Penn State in 2015. His research focuses on the dynamics of public policy diffusion in the American states. He also conducts policy-specific research on medical cannabis, opioids, and other health policies.

Ashley Nickels is associate professor at Kent State University. She is the author of the award-winning book *Power, Participation, and Protest in Flint, Michigan* (2019) and coauthor of *Unmasking Administrative Evil*, fifth edition (2019), with Danny Balfour and Guy Adams.

Jay Rickabaugh is currently visiting assistant professor in the Government and Justice Studies Department at Appalachian State University in Boone, North Carolina. He earned a doctorate in public and international affairs from the University of Pittsburgh in 2018.

Thomas Skuzinski is associate professor of public administration at Northern Illinois University and author of *The Risk of Regional Governance* (2018). His research applies a sociological institutionalist lens to understand how rules, norms, and cultural heuristics shape decision making in local governments and metropolitan areas. He is currently using this perspective to explore interlocal cooperation in land use, infrastructure, and affordable housing policies and to investigate the chilling effects of state preemption laws in local governments. Dr. Skuzinski's work has been funded by grants from the Department of Transportation, the Regional Studies Association, and the Commonwealth of Virginia.

Carl Stenberg is the James E. Holshouser Jr. Distinguished Professor at the School of Government, University of North Carolina at Chapel Hill. Previously he served as executive director of the Council of State Governments and assistant director of the Advisory Commission on Intergovernmental Relations. He is an elected fellow of the National Academy of Public Administration, past president of the American Society for Public Administration, and honorary member of the International City/County Management Association. His research interests include federalism and intergovernmental relations, leadership, and local government management. He coedited, with David K. Hamilton, the first book containing presentations from the Deil S. Wright symposia *Intergovernmental Relations in Transition: Reflections and Directions* (2018).

James Svara is senior fellow in the School of Government at the University of North Carolina at Chapel Hill, after teaching at UNC-Greensboro, North Carolina State University, and Arizona State University. His teaching and research have focused on local government, ethics, innovation, and sustainability. He has a special interest in the roles and responsibilities of elected and administrative officials. He is a fellow of the National Academy of Public Administration and an honorary member of the International City/County Management Association. The third edition of his text *The Ethics Primer for Public Administrators in Government and Nonprofit Organizations* has recently been published.

David Swindell is director of the Center for Urban Innovation and associate professor in the School of Public Affairs at Arizona State University. His work focuses primarily on community and economic development, especially public financing of sports facilities, and the contribution of sports facilities to the economic development of urban space. His most recent work examines collaborative arrangements with public, private, and nonprofit organizations for service delivery and citizen satisfaction and performance measurement standards for public management and decision making. His recent book is *American Cities and the Politics of Party Conventions* (with coauthors Eric Heberlig and Suzanne Leland).

Jie Tao is a doctoral candidate in the Department of Public Administration at the University of North Texas. His research interests include intergovernmental transparency, performance management, citizen satisfaction, cooperative public purchasing, information technology, and smart governance. He has published in *Local Government Studies* and *Journal of Public and Nonprofit Affairs*.

Vittoria R. Totaro is a PhD student in sociology at the University of New Mexico, where she received her Master's in Public Administration in 2018. Her research interests lie in local government efforts to adapt to and mitigate the effects of climate change and incorporating social equity into research methodologies.

Shilpa Viswanath is an assistant professor of public administration in the Department of Public Management at John Jay College of Criminal Justice in the City University of New York. She received her Ph.D. from the Rutgers University–Newark School of Public Affairs and Administration. She researches public-sector human resource management with a focus on gender.

CHAPTER 1

Why Do State–Local Relations Need Our Attention?

Eric S. Zeemering, University of Georgia

In Texas, a new law effective in 2019 prevents city governments from regulating lemonade stands operated by children. What prompted state policy makers to limit local government authority to regulate this activity? Four years earlier, the police chief of Overton, Texas, visited the lemonade stand of two young girls and shut down their front-yard business because they lacked the proper permit.[1] The local law enforcement official had the authority to enforce local regulations, but the event sparked national media attention. State lawmakers took action to rein in communities across the state, protecting young entrepreneurs from regulation by local governments. State government action to limit or remove local authority is called *preemption*, and legislatures across the United States are taking aim at more than just lemonade stands. In recent years, states have limited local authority on the regulation of guns, marijuana, and even land use. These preemptions have led some commentators to describe an era of conflict and growing tension in the relationship between state and local government.

Understanding state preemption of local authority is important, but conflict is only one dimension of the relationship between states and their local governments. Many interactions between state and local government are cooperative, with state and local policymakers and administrative officials coordinating action to advance their shared goals. This book provides an overview of the complex landscape of state–local intergovernmental relations today. *Intergovernmental relations* (IGR) refer to the patterns of communication and coordination among public officials from different levels of the U.S. federal system of government.[2] Closely related, *intergovernmental management* (IGM) describes coordination and joint work by local, state, and federal government agencies to implement public policy.[3] The pages ahead introduce IGR and IGM between state and local government, offering examples from across the United States. The contributors have assembled these chapters to help readers enhance their understanding of the importance of state–local relations in the U.S. federal system, to argue for better analysis of the consequences of state–local relations for the quality of policy outcomes, and to introduce readers to public service career opportunities in state and local government.

Local governments are "creatures of the state," an expression found in an Iowa court ruling from 1868 and known as Dillon's Rule. In Dillon's legal interpretation, local governments only hold the authority expressly granted to them by state government. This interpretation of state authority plays a dominant role in shaping state–local IGR. A contrasting doctrine, advocated by Michigan Supreme Court Justice Thomas Cooley, argued local political communities organize their own governance, which must be recognized to balance state power.[4] In some states, home-rule provisions, found either in the state constitution or in statute, provide local governments with a broad grant of authority. Home-rule powers vary significantly across states, but most provide local governments with wide discretion in policymaking and taxation.[5] These contrasting perspectives on local authority are cited when local governments take a proactive role in the intergovernmental arena, defending their prerogatives to make policy and address local problems. According to Richardson, neither concept fully illuminates local government authority. He explains, "Dillon's Rule is a rule of statutory construction, while home rule generally refers to source and/or extent of delegation of authority from the state to local governments. In essence, this type of analysis compares apples to oranges to pears."[6] Because of the complicated legal terrain, Blomquist provides a detailed discussion of these fundamental concepts in chapter 3. The contrasting views of Cooley and Dillon are still today reflected in the words of state and local government officials as they debate policy through IGR. At stake in these debates is the flexibility of local governments to innovate and take action beyond the basic institutional design of local government crafted by the state.

Frequently, litigation is pursued to sort out claims about what state constitutions and statutes really mean for local authority. For example, in the 2013 case *Palm v. 2800 Lake Shore Drive Condo Association*, the Illinois Supreme Court affirmed the power of home-rule municipalities to adopt different requirements than the state, as long as the state has not prohibited such action. In this case, the court upheld a Chicago ordinance requiring the disclosure of condominium association financial records to their members over a state ordinance with more lenient provisions.[7] Joseph Zimmerman explains that the courts have become an important venue for sorting out claims like this because state governments often take a piecemeal approach to preempting local authority rather than collecting all restrictions under one coherent authorization of local authority in the state.[8] Legal battles emerge when state and local officials interpret the law differently or when they have difficulty navigating inconsistencies between authority granted to local government and other aspects of state law. At times, state and local officials avoid legal conflict. Government officials may attempt to negotiate their differences and forge cooperative solutions to the policy challenges that face state and local government together. IGR and IGM are alternatives to legal conflict.

IGR draws our attention to human relationships, explains public administration scholar Deil Wright.[9] State and local government officials interact with one another on a regular and ongoing basis. Elected state legislators engage in policy discussions with local elected officials and hear feedback about state policies and programs. Statewide associations of city, township, or county officials bring their policy concerns to the state capitol by lobbying the legislature and mobilizing local officials to talk with state officials about policy problems facing local government. For example, local government officials have been lobbying in state capitols across the country to retain local regulatory power over the placement of 5G wireless network equipment in their communities. Older cellular and wireless networks used large equipment mounted on high poles or facilities and were easily regulated by local governments. Many municipalities were able to generate revenue by leasing space on public facilities, such as water towers. New 5G technology uses small equipment but requires more units to cover the service area. State governments moved to limit how municipalities could regulate the new technology or placed limits on local fees. As of 2019, forty-four states had taken up or passed 5G legislation.[10] Municipal associations lobbied for more local control of 5G deployment and aided local governments by providing model ordinances to comply with new state laws. While the regulatory tug-of-war continues between state and local governments, the Federal Communications Commission has also considered constraining state and local regulatory powers over 5G. Wireless network infrastructure and technological innovation will continue to be a topic of debate in state–local IGR for the foreseeable future.

Relationships among public administrators are also central to our understanding of IGM. Public administrators, employees within the state and city bureaucracy, interact as they implement policy. This includes state agencies regulating or restricting the action of local governments, such as establishing guidelines for local stormwater management programs. This also includes cooperation and joint work, such as the coordination of state and local programs in workforce and economic development. Morton Grodzins described the county sanitarian, or the public health official, as the quintessential intergovernmental employee, funded by grants and revenues from federal, state, and local government and undertaking work authorized by policy at all tiers of the federal system.[11] Numerous areas of public service delivery are undertaken by local officials with financial support and authority from the state, or are jointly delivered by state and local government officials working side by side. Michigan's ongoing response to water contamination by polyfluoroalkyl substance (PFAS) is one example. PFAS, chemical compounds used in manufacturing, have been identified in water sources in several Michigan communities. This prompted state agencies to enhance coordination with local governments in regulation, research, and public health responses. For example, the state began requiring local governments to monitor PFAS in wastewater pretreatment in 2018 to identify sources of PFAS contamination. The Michigan Department of Health and Human Services received a one-million-dollar federal grant to investigate health impacts of PFAS, which supports work with county health departments who are already studying this problem in local communities.[12] Local governments are also making budget allocations to respond to this public health threat. As the scope and consequences of PFAS contamination gain public attention, state and local government officials will face an ongoing imperative to coordinate their policy response to the complex environmental problem.

Why do state–local IGR require our attention and understanding? W. Brooke Graves argues, "Intergovernmental relations are not a sporadic or specialized type of activity, they are part and parcel of the every-day operation of government."[13] Graves stressed the need for state governments to provide local governments with the administrative and taxing authority to effectively serve the public while maintaining sufficient oversight to ensure they worked efficiently. This establishes a complicated dynamic for state and local governments, as the two sides of the relationship may hold divergent views about the proper balance of local authority and state oversight. "Prompt, vigorous action by governmental units at each level, based upon intelligent analysis of the problems at hand, would go a long way toward solving many of our present interjurisdictional conflicts," argued Graves.[14] At times, state and local officials achieve this balance. Russell Hanson documents examples of successful state–local coordination in an earlier book on this topic titled *Governing Partners*, stressing the possibility of cooperation to address complicated policy problems, including education and environmental quality, through coordinated state and local action.[15] Yet, today, the intense partisan conflict of national politics appears to renew state–local tensions as both sides struggle for policy control, uninterested in the "intelligent analysis" suggested by Graves.

The remainder of this chapter provides a foundation for understanding why state–local IGR is no easy task. The chapters in this book illuminate the dynamics of cooperation and conflict in state–local relations. First, we must consider the institutional landscape in which these relationships unfold. Because local government authority stems from the state, the United States features fifty different systems of state–local relations. Within these systems, elected and administrative officials in state and local government coordinate action and work together to provide services to the public. Some states have carefully analyzed the organization of responsibility in their state–local systems, and new opportunities are on the horizon for a more purposeful discussion about the performance of the U.S. intergovernmental system. Yet conflict also characterizes state–local relations today. Scholars point to partisan polarization in national politics and suggest these forces have consequences for how state and local officials pursue their policy priorities, and in turn how states seek to limit local authority. Finally, diverse and engaging career opportunities await those who hope to contribute to the work of state–local relations in the U.S. federal system. We challenge readers, students in particular, to consider how state–local relations open the door for a variety of careers in public service. The rest of the introduction takes up these challenges and opportunities in more detail.

The Variety of State–Local Relations

Because local government authority is determined by the states, significant variation exists in how local governments approach their work and in what they are allowed to do. States delineate the type and variety of local units, distributing taxing and service provision responsibilities among them.[16] The 2017 Census of Governments illustrates the complexity.[17] Hawaii has only twenty-one units of local government, with county governments serving as the major local service provision units. In contrast, Connecticut operates without county government, reserving those responsibilities for state agencies or devolving them to municipalities.[18] Illinois has 6,918 units of local government, many with overlapping service responsibilities. The state's 1,429 townships play a small role in the local government landscape, providing general assistance (limited poverty relief), maintenance of select roads, and property assessment. Townships in Illinois are frequently, but often unsuccessfully, targeted by reformers advocating government consolidation. States also vary significantly in their use of special-purpose governments—units designed to provide narrow service packages ranging from water utilities to education.[19] Alaska has only fifteen special-purpose units, including regional native housing authorities and regional solid waste management authorities. California reports 2,894, ranging from small cemetery districts to the massive East Bay Municipal Utility District, which provides water to 1.4 million people in parts of Alameda and Contra Costa Counties.[20]

States also provide local governments with the authority to tax and impose fees, and they constrain this authority through tax and expenditure limitations (TELs). California's Proposition 13, passed by voters in 1978, rolled back and limited increases on assessed property value and placed a cap on the maximum tax rate.[21] A response to inflationary pressure that escalated property values and taxes rapidly during the 1970s, Proposition 13 prompted the mobilization of antitax advocates and served as a model for similar campaigns in other states. The stringency of TELs varies across the states, as do the consequences for state and local budgeting. For example, Colorado's Taxpayer's Bill of Rights (TABOR), passed in 1992, slowed the growth of local tax revenue and increased local government reliance on user charges and permit fees.[22] In Colorado and other states, local voters are allowed to override TELs, which may reduce their overall impact on local budgets.[23] Moreover, some evidence suggests local governments exhibit more revenue stability under stringent TELs, which may be a sign that local officials tax at the highest possible level within the state limit rather than adapting local tax rates to changing circumstances.[24] Understanding how home-rule provisions and TELs shape local budget choices is important because during periods of economic recession, constraints on local taxing authority may limit the ability of local governments to respond to increased service needs or reductions in assistance from state government.[25] Most local governments must manage within some form of TEL imposed by voters or state government. Because of this, a familiarity with the taxing tools available to local governments, and caps on revenue or expenditure growth over time, is crucial to our understanding of state–local relations in any given state.

Public employment patterns also vary across the states. The Annual Survey of Government Employment and Payroll from the U.S. Census Bureau sheds light on notable differences.[26] In 2018, state governments employed 4,386,219 full-time equivalent (FTE) employees. Local governments overshadow the states with 12,264,505 FTEs. Employment numbers also illuminate how state and local governments organize responsibility for the delivery of public goods and services. For example, we typically think of parks and recreation as a responsibility of local government, though state governments also run major park systems. California's employment patterns convey the relative importance of local government delivery of parks and recreation services with 4,413 FTEs employed by the state and 39,928 FTEs by local governments. Employment data also illustrate differences in service delivery across the states. For example, public welfare services may be concentrated at the state level, as illustrated by Georgia, where 1,666 FTEs are employed at the local level with 7,072 FTEs in state employment. In contrast, Illinois employs 4,965 FTEs at the local level and 9,320 FTEs at the state level. Functionally, local governments in Illinois play a larger role in the state's system of public welfare service delivery than their counterparts in Georgia. Highway work provides another useful contrast. In highly urbanized New Jersey, 8,526 FTEs are employed by local governments with 6,247 FTEs working for the state. New Mexico's concentrated urban areas and rural landscapes see a different mix with 1,912 FTEs working on highways at the local level and 2,133 FTEs working for the state. These examples stress the need to carefully study government employment patterns to understand the mix of state and local government involvement in public service delivery. In the aggregate, local government employment dwarfs state employment, but patterns of employment in individual service areas vary across the states. Both state and local government play a role in many service areas, creating opportunities for IGM, the coordinated management of state and local programs.

Because of this complexity, an understanding of state–local relations in any particular state hinges on one's study and understanding of state law, systems of taxation, and the organization of the service delivery responsibilities of state and local government. Variation in local government structure and service responsibility is discussed more in chapter 7 by León-Moreta and Totaro. As you begin to explore state–local relations, take time to review pertinent state constitutional provisions and statutes on the authority of local government. Review data from the most recent U.S. Census of Governments to explore the scope and variety of local governments. Compare employment patters for the state reported by the U.S. Census Bureau's Annual Government Employment and Payroll survey. Developing a nuanced picture of state and local government in your state will be advantageous to your understanding of state politics and policy.

Expanding State–Local Conflict

State government engagement in local affairs is nothing new. Analysis of legislation in three states during the late nineteenth and early twentieth centuries shows state legislatures frequently passed bills specific to individual cities or places, with the legislature engaged in many issues of local concern. Burns and Gamm explain, "the relationship between states and their creatures was intimate and utterly routine." Many bills dealt with infrastructure and the organization of specific local government offices, and the legislation seldom showed evidence of an anti-urban bias, as some might suspect.[27] The growth of urban centers and suburbanization during the post–World War II era placed new demands on state and local government, and intergovernmental aid distributed from the federal government to states and cities fostered interdependence in both policy development and implementation.[28] The role of county governments expanded in many states, and state–local partnerships expanded in areas including public health, economic development, and waste management.[29]

Yet, as the twentieth century closed, many federalism scholars pointed to developing fractures in the intergovernmental landscape. As policy responsibility devolved from the federal government to the states, and from states to the local level, resources did not necessarily accompany new demands for action. Kincaid warned of an era of coercive federalism, in which mandates, new responsibilities without accompanying funding, would replace the financial incentives that had been common in the U.S. federal system.[30] Local governments protested unfunded mandates from state governments, just as states complained about mandates from Washington, DC.[31] About half of U.S. states now require some type of financial analysis of proposed state mandates on local government, fostering greater transparency when state legislatures pass costs on to local governments.[32]

The politics of state mandates are complex, and making an argument about the proper distribution of state and local authority can be difficult. For example, in 2019, the Georgia legislature adopted a bill requiring schools to provide daily recess to all children in kindergarten and grades one through five. The bill encouraged elementary schools "to include an average of 30 minutes per day of supervised unstructured activity time, preferably outdoors," and directed school boards to structure policies that provided a break during periods of learning. The legislation passed both chambers with bipartisan support. Proponents argued providing time for recreation is important to address the problem of childhood obesity. Others suggested that children need a break from the pressures of standardized testing. Still, Governor Brian Kemp vetoed the bill, preventing it from becoming law. Kemp's veto message did not argue the merits of recess, instead emphasizing appropriate roles for state government and local school boards. Kemp explained, "While I support expanded recess opportunities for Georgia's students, I am a firm believer in local control, especially in education." The veto attracted national media attention, which focused on recess, not nuanced arguments about state–local relations. Georgia's recess bill shows that state politicians may face criticism or negative attention when opposing popular policy ideas with arguments centered on the proper roles of state and local government.

Tension between state and local governments has also grown due to state preemption of local authority in salient policy areas. Preemption limits local government authority by prohibiting local government from taking action on certain topics or constraining approaches to taxation or administration. For example, in 2011, Florida passed legislation prohibiting local government from regulating firearms or ammunition, unless specifically authorized by state law. The bill also provided penalties for the local government official or agency head violating the law, including a $5,000 fine and removal from office. Both the preemption of local authority and the penalties for local officials are being challenged in state courts by a group of city and county governments.[33] Preemption is a salient concern for local governments across the United States, and chapters 4, 5, and 6 in this volume offer a detailed examination of the scope of preemption by state governments in recent years, the political underpinnings of preemption, and the consequences for local government and policy innovation.

Several states have also developed procedures for state agencies to monitor or take over the administration of local units of government. State takeovers are often triggered by specific indicators of local financial distress or mismanagement. Proponents argue state intervention can help local governments develop a stronger capacity to manage local budgets, while also justifying difficult cuts that constituents might oppose. In some states, an emergency manager is appointed by the state and given broad powers to address financial problems without a vote of the local elected officials. This approach assumes professional managers can do more to enhance government accountability than oversight by elected officials.[34] Scholars studying emergency managers warn the procedure can undermine the representation of local interests and the quality of service delivery by focusing on financial solvency above other indicators of community well-being.[35] Not all states take this approach. For example, Rhode Island provides state financial aid to distressed communities. In other places, narrower efforts have been made by state governments to take control of local infrastructure and services. Georgia has been in conflict with the City of Atlanta over control of Hartsfield–Jackson International Airport. In Michigan, the Great Lakes Water Authority was created to move control of water and sewer services for the Detroit metropolitan region from the City of Detroit to a regionally controlled organization. In chapter 8 of this volume, Nickels, Viswanath, and Lebovitz describe Michigan's emergency manager law and its use in the City of Flint and compare Michigan to models used by other states.

Perhaps the most notable examples of tension in state–local relations are recent efforts to limit the participation of local governments in the political process. Historically, state-level associations of local governments have lobbied their state legislatures to convey the shared concerns of local governments on issues facing the legislature. Large cities, like New York, even have internal staff responsible for government affairs, including lobbying of the legislature and liaison work with state agencies. In some states, the political advocacy of local governments has met resistance from state policymakers. Texas recently debated a ban on lobbying by local units of government, with proponents arguing that taxpayer dollars should not be used to lobby the state. While the bill did not pass the legislature, intergovernmental tension worsened when Speaker of the Texas House of Representatives Dennis Bonnen was recorded attacking local government. In the recording, Bonnen stated, "My goal is for this to be the worst session in this history of the Legislature for cities and counties."[36] The comments drew outrage from local government officials and state legislators. Days after the news broke, Bonnen announced he would not seek reelection.

Utah considered legislation to require local governments to obtain the approval of the legislature before seeking federal land designations. These conservation efforts have been controversial in Utah because federal government involvement in land management and protection may have consequences for state and local government service delivery, including fire management and road maintenance. The final version of the legislature's bill only required local governments to notify the legislature rather than seek advance approval, but the state's effort to stake out a central role in IGR is clear.[37] These recent efforts to curb local government participation in state and federal politics require attention because they represent a significant departure from the established practice of local politicians advocating for their communities' interests with state and federal officials[The actions by Texas and Utah underscore the need for local government officials to maintain regular contact with state legislators who represent their communities to maintain personal intergovernmental ties and to provide direct feedback about the implications of state legislation for local communities.]

Various studies provide evidence state and local government officials view the quality of the state–local relationship differently. Surveys of state and local government officials identify what Ann Bowman and Richard Kearney describe as "perceptional dissonance" on the quality of the state–local relations. Their national survey of state legislators and city managers shows city managers are concerned about the devolution of service responsibility from state to local government without accompanying financial support. City managers also perceive expanded state restriction of local authority. In contrast, state legislators perceive more stability in state–local relations.[38] A survey of mayors by Katherine Einstein and David Glick illustrates a partisan dimension to local views on state–local relations. Mayors in states controlled by Republican legislatures expressed the highest concern about their policy autonomy and state financial support, and Democratic mayors in these states expressed the most negative perceptions about the state.[39] Over time, survey research consistently reveals local officials are concerned about state mandates, preemption, and financial support. These findings raise questions about the extent to which state legislators truly engage in intergovernmental dialogue with local government officials.

With the aforementioned constraints on intergovernmental lobbying and the dissonance between state and local officials on the quality of state–local relations, how will state and local government officials maintain productive IGR? Moreover, can state and local government officials develop a new consensus on the appropriate roles for state and local government? These questions are not easy to answer, and the partisan conflict that characterizes contemporary politics makes them even more challenging. In his recent book *The Increasingly United States*, political scientist Daniel Hopkins provides evidence that state and local campaigns are increasingly contested through the lens of national partisan divisions, and voters take partisan cues from how local officials discuss national issues.[40] Conservative activism at the state level and the sharing of model legislation by organizations like the American Legislative Exchange Council (ALEC) also mean similar legislation preempting local authority can quickly diffuse across the country.[41] These trends may push public policy toward uniformity within a federal system designed to foster distinct governance and policy responses across the states, appropriate to the organization of fifty different systems of state–local relations. Despite these challenges, we have some reason to hope for improved state–local relations in the future.

Opportunities for State–Local Cooperation

Conflict is not the only dynamic characterizing state–local relations today. State and local governments share common goals and interests, including the development and advancement of local economies and the protection of the public during emergencies. In several states, special commissions analyze policy problems from the perspective of both state and local government to improve IGR in the state. A brief overview of state–local cooperation in these areas illustrates how state and local government officials collaborate in the delivery of public services and management of government programs. Indeed, students entering public service careers are now encouraged to develop *collaborative competencies*, or skills to work effectively across organizational boundaries.[42] Public administrators working in state and local government must share information, exchange resources and expertise, and coordinate project implementation to ensure government action achieves policy goals to effectively serve the public.[43]

Constructive state–local relations are critical for successful economic development. State and local government officials frequently collaborate in the development and implementation of policies to match commercial and industrial development with sites that have appropriate access to transportation, infrastructure, and workforce training. Agranoff and McGuire catalog a wide range of state–local collaboration in economic development, including state technical assistance, targeted loans and tax relief, and coordinated marketing and outreach.[44] For example, the Indiana Stellar Communities Program targeted resources from several different state agencies, including the Indiana Department of Transportation and the Indiana Housing and Community Development Authority, to help communities coordinate investments to spur economic growth.[45] States frequently aid communities with strategic planning and consulting to help local government officials better understand the strengths of the local economy and the most logical targets for job growth.[46] State law also structures specific tools for local governments to use to advance economic development, including tax increment financing, business improvement districts, and enterprise zones. Even in a field with significant collaboration, state and local governments may encounter tensions on how to pursue economic development. For example, the State of California eliminated local redevelopment agencies in 2011 due in part to concern about the scope and inefficiency of local redevelopment spending.[47] By 2019, the legislature was considering the revival of these agencies to help address the state's affordable housing needs.[48] Thus, economic development entails significant administrative coordination by state and local government officials, but state law still provides the context for this work.

Emergency management is another field in which state and local officials work together to deliver services to the public. Most state governments provide support to local emergency management professionals through training and technical assistance and operate state command centers to coordinate state and local response during an emergency or natural disaster. An investigation of the response to Hurricanes Katrina and Rita in 2005 by Kapucu, Arslan, and Collins advises states to invest in local emergency management capacity in advance of natural disasters because training and preparation can yield a more effective response during times of crisis.[49] Fostering effective working relationships and trust among emergency responders takes time and repeated interaction. Danczyk, studying responses to fires and earthquakes in California, suggests the leadership of state agency officials plays an important role in fostering cooperative interactions over time.[50] Public service professionals in fields like emergency management foster ongoing communication and coordination across the state–local boundary to provide effective public services.

At times, state and local government officials even work together on the analysis of public policy problems in order to develop shared understanding and plans for action. Given the complex policy challenges confronted by state and local government, we might expect state policymakers to give significant attention to state–local IGR. A few states created special commissions to analyze policy problems at the intersection of state and local government, though their numbers have dwindled over time.[51] These bodies were modeled on the U.S. Advisory Commission on Intergovernmental Relations (ACIR), which advised the U.S. Congress on intergovernmental issues from 1959 to 1996. Typically, the commissions are composed of an appointed group of state and local government officials responsible for commissioning policy analysis from a professional staff. These offices advise the governor and legislature on the possible implications of state policy change for the effectiveness of state and local government and produce reports to inform the policymaking process. For example, the Connecticut ACIR recently began analysis of municipal service sharing in the state. The Tennessee ACIR has recently issued reports on topics including election consolidation, internet sales tax, and access to healthy food. In many other states, these institutions once existed but have been terminated or fallen dormant. Congress has considered reviving the ACIR at the national level to help policymakers better understand the intergovernmental aspects policy problems. Renewing these institutions at the state level may be an important step in fostering improved intergovernmental dialogue between state and local government officials.

In sum, underneath the political conflict between state and local governments, we see a strong foundation of collaboration and partnership, particularly among administrative officials. The public depends on the professional coordination of government services by state and local government officials on a daily basis, and some states maintain venues for constructive dialogue to explicitly reflect on effective state–local relations. By exploring cooperation between state and local governments, and by highlighting the work of elected officials and public administrators who work across the state–local line, we hope this book will help future public servants contribute to constructive and effective state–local relations.

A Guide to Reading

By reading this book, students, public officials, and participants in the American political system will enrich their understanding of the complexity of state–local relations in the United States. Investigating how elected and administrative officials develop and manage their intergovernmental relationships prepares all readers for more effective engagement with American politics. Moreover, the book challenges readers to consider how careful analysis and reflection on the state–local system, and the component roles of state and local government, may help reframe policy debates away from national partisan divisions and toward more thoughtful reflection on the division of responsibilities between state and local governments.

In the pages ahead, readers will learn more about the foundations of state and local government in the United States while also exploring the conflict and cooperation described in this introduction. The first section of the book provides an overview of state power. Chapter 2 by John Kincaid explains why the public expresses the most trust for local government, and compares public opinion in the U.S. to other federal systems. Next, William Blomquist describes the legal terrain of state–local relations, including the importance of Dillon's Rule. Chapter 4 by Jaclyn Bunch and chapter 5 by David Swindell, James Svara, and Carl Stenberg detail the expansion of preemption across the United States and explain the political dynamics underpinning this trend. In chapter 6, Daniel Mallinson reflects on the consequences of preemption for local policy innovation. Agustín León-Moreta and Vittoria Totaro explain variation in local government authority and service delivery responsibility across states in chapter 7.

The second section of the book details conflict in state–local relations and begins with an exploration of state takeover power by Ashley Nickels, Shilpa Viswanath, and Hannah Lebovitz in chapter 8. In chapter 9, Russell Hanson and Erika Coe detail sanctuary policies in local government, exploring how cities work against the policy goals of state and federal governments. Brian Collins contrasts state approaches to the regulation of hydraulic fracturing in chapter 10. The third section of the book continues to illuminate state–local relations, but the dynamic shifts toward cooperation. Jayce Farmer details how state spending spurs local sustainability policies in chapter 11, and Jie Tao and Brian Collins discuss how state laws influence local government transparency in chapter 12. In chapter 13, Russell Hanson and Eric Zeemering consider the complex dynamics emerging from marijuana regulation across states. Chapters 14 and 15 turn our attention to the rescaling of cooperation in the federal system as Jay Rickabaugh and George Dougherty describe regional governing organizations and Thomas Skuzinski explores the balancing of local and regional interests.

Finally, chapter 16 reflects on the trends of conflict and cooperation through the global COVID-19 pandemic. At the end of each chapter, questions for reflection encourage readers to glean the most important lessons for state–local relations from the reading, while also fostering reflection on the reader's own state and community.

Between chapters, readers will encounter career profiles exploring the work of people serving in a variety of positions in state and local government. These public service professionals contributed to this book by describing how their work contributes to state–local relations. The profiles illuminate job opportunities in state and local government that students might consider as they seek out careers related to their course work in political science, public administration, and related fields. Each profile describes how the individual entered a career in public service, details their engagement in state–local relations, and summarizes the professional's advice to students considering careers in public service. Students are encouraged to use these profiles as a guide to develop their own professional networks in state and local government. Student readers might consider identifying related positions in their own state in order to explore job shadow and internship opportunities.

While conflict seems to characterize much of state–local relations today, the work of the public service professionals detailed in this book and the legacy of partnership between state and local administrative officials point to a hopeful future for state–local relations. As readers reflect on these dynamics in their own states and communities, we encourage you to consider how you may contribute to constructive state–local relations as an elected official, as a public administrator, as a citizen, or as a participant in American politics. State–local relations require our attention because constructive problem solving by elected officials at both levels is important to the future of American democracy and effective coordination by public administrators is vital for public service delivery.

■ CAREER PROFILE ■

Cliff Lippard

Executive Director
Tennessee Advisory Commission on Intergovernmental Relations

Cliff Lippard began work for the Tennessee Advisory Commission on Intergovernmental Relations (TACIR) after completing his MPA at Tennessee State University. He later completed a Ph.D. in public administration and moved on to become the commission's executive director in 2016. TACIR is a twenty-five-member group composed of state and local government officials, including two private citizens. Professional staff under Dr. Lippard's direction conduct public policy research requested by the Tennessee state legislature or by commission members. The commission works to analyze, discuss, and contribute to the resolution of intergovernmental policy problems in the state of Tennessee.

TACIR's reports have informed state and local policymaking on issues including education finance, land use, GPS monitoring of domestic violence offenders, and many more. For example, a recent report on broadband access and adoption encouraged collaborative efforts between electric co-ops and private firms or local government to enhance service in underserved areas. The state government targeted grant funds to guide resources to underserved areas of the state, and a library grant program supports technology loans to individuals in underserved areas. The legislature asked TACIR to continue

evaluation of these programs so that policymakers can better understand the impacts of policy change.

Staff working for TACIR come from a variety of academic backgrounds, including psychology, history, economics, public administration and policy, and law. "Any academic background that has a mix of intensive writing requirements along with some level of analytical requirements lends itself to this type of work," explains Lippard. He also advises students to seek out internship opportunities to gain insight into policy analysis done by an agency like TACIR. Finally, he suggests observing government in action. Watch city council meetings and watch the legislature in session to learn how they operate and discuss policy. Also, reach out to participants in the process to learn more about how policy develops.

Interview: August 23, 2019

Discussion Questions

1. Take a few moments to review the U.S. Census of Governments figures for your state. What did you learn about the scope of local government? How would you describe the importance of public services provided by state and local government where you live?
2. Imagine that you serve in a state legislature that has actively pursued preemption of local authority in recent years. How would you discuss this trend with your constituents? How would you discuss the state's ongoing appetite for preemption with local government officials?
3. Economic development and emergency management are two areas in which state and local government officials frequently interact to implement public programs and deliver services. As you continue to explore state–local relations in this book, do you anticipate learning about cooperation in other fields of public policy? Review recent media coverage in your community and identify an area in which state and local government officials are working together.

Notes

[1] Kenneth Dean, "Overton Officials Shut Down Girls' Lemonade Stand, Saying They Lack Permit," *Tyler Morning Telegraph*, June 8, 2015, https://tylerpaper.com/news/local/overton -officials-shut-down-girls-lemonade-stand-saying-they-lack/article_aee67f4f-3cdc-5238-9263 -1d64fda6e0c0.html.

² Deil S. Wright, *Understanding Intergovernmental Relations*, 3rd ed. (Belmont, CA: Wadsworth Publishing Company, 1988).

³ Timothy J. Conlan and Paul L. Posner, eds., *Intergovernmental Management for the Twenty-First Century* (Washington, DC: Brookings Institution, 2008).

⁴ Anwar Hussain Syed, *The Political Theory of American Local Government* (New York: Random House, 1966).

⁵ Dale Krane, Carol Ebdon, and John Bartle, "Devolution, Fiscal Federalism, and Changing Patterns of Municipal Revenues: The Mismatch between Theory and Reality," *Journal of Public Administration Research and Theory* 14, no. 4 (2004): 513–33.

⁶ Jesse J. Richardson Jr., "Dillon's Rule Is from Mars, Home Rule Is from Venus: Local Government Autonomy and the Rules of Statutory Construction," *Publius: The Journal of Federalism* 41, no. 4 (2011): 662–85.

⁷ Adam W. Lasker, "Home Rule Rules, Says the Illinois Supreme Court," *Illinois Bar Journal* 101, no. 6 (2013): 278.

⁸ Joseph F. Zimmerman, *State-Local Governmental Interactions* (Albany: State University of New York Press, 2012), 32.

⁹ Deil S. Wright, "Federalism, Intergovernmental Relations, and Intergovernmental Management: Historical Reflections and Conceptual Comparisons," *Public Administration Review* 50, no. 2 (1990): 168–78.

¹⁰ Mike Maciag, "The Future of 5G: The Bitter Battle for Local Control," *Government Technology*, September 19, 2018; Heather Morton, "Mobile 5G and Small Cell 2019 Legislation," *NCSL Podcast*, July 17, 2019, http://www.ncsl.org/research/telecommunications-and-information-technology/mobile-5g-and-small-cell-2019-legislation.aspx.

¹¹ Morton Grodzins, *The American System: A New View of Government in the United States* (New York: Rand McNally, 1966).

¹² Paula Gardner, "5 PFAS Lessons for Michigan from the Huron River," *MLive*, August 29, 2019, https://www.mlive.com/news/2019/08/5-pfas-lessons-for-michigan-from-the-huron-river.html; Keith Matheny, "Michigan Health Department Gets $1 Million Federal Grant to Study PFAS Health Impact," *Detroit Free Press*, September 24 2019, https://www.frccp.com/story/news/local/michigan/2019/09/24/michigan-grant-pfas-health-impact/2427989001/.

¹³ W. Brooke Graves, *American Intergovernmental Relations: Their Origins, Historical Development, and Current Status* (New York: Scribner, 1964), 927.

¹⁴ Ibid., 705.

¹⁵ Russell L. Hanson, ed., *Governing Partners: State-Local Relations in the United States* (Boulder, CO: Westview Press, 1998).

¹⁶ Jeffrey M. Stonecash, "Centralization in the American States: Increasing Similarity and Persisting Diversity," *Publius: The Journal of Federalism* 13, no. 4 (1983): 123–37.

¹⁷ United States Census Bureau, "Individual State Descriptions: 2017," in *2017 Census of Governments* (Washington, DC: U.S. Department of Commerce, 2019).

¹⁸ J. Edwin Benton, *Counties as Service Delivery Agents: Changing Expectations and Roles* (Westport, CT: Praeger, 2002).

¹⁹ Kathryn A. Foster, *The Political Economy of Special-Purpose Government* (Washington, DC: Georgetown University Press, 1997).

²⁰ East Bay Municipal Utility District, "Service Area," https://www.ebmud.com/about-us/who-we-are/service-area/.

²¹ Christopher Hoene, "Fiscal Structure and the Post-Proposition 13 Fiscal Regime in California's Cities," *Public Budgeting & Finance* 24, no. 4 (2004): 51–72.

²² Franklin J. James and Allan Wallis, "Tax and Spending Limits in Colorado," *Public Budgeting & Finance* 24, no. 4 (2004): 16–33.

²³ Bruce Wallin, "The Tax Revolt in Massachusettes: The Revolution and Reason," *Public Budgeting & Finance* 24, no. 4 (2004): 34–50.

²⁴ Tucker C. Staley, "The Impact of Tax and Expenditure Limitation on Municipal Revenue Volatility," *State & Local Government Review* 50, no. 2 (2018): 71–84.

²⁵ Shu Wang and Michael A. Pagano, "Cities and Fiscal Federalism in the Trump Era: A Discussion," *State & Local Government Review* 49, no. 3 (2017): 184–98.

26 U.S. Census Bureau, "2018 Government Employment and Payroll Tables," https://www.census .gov/data/tables/2018/econ/apes/annual-apes.html.

27 Nancy Burns and Gerald Gamm, "Creatures of the State: State Politics and Local Government, 1871–1921," *Urban Affairs Review* 33, no. 1 (1997): 90.

28 David B. Walker, *The Rebirth of Federalism: Slouching toward Washington*, 2nd ed. (New York: Chatham House, 2000).

29 Benton, *Counties as Service Delivery Agents.*

30 John Kincaid, "From Cooperative to Coercive Federalism," *Annals of the American Academy of Political Science* 509, no. 1 (1990): 139–52.

31 Lawrence Grossback, "The Problem of State-Imposed Mandates: Lessons from Minnesota's Local Governments," *State & Local Government Review* 34, no. 3 (2002): 183–97.

32 Citizens Research Council of Michigan, *Reforming the Process for Identifying and Funding Section 29 Mandates on Local Governments*, Report 355 (Lansing: Citizens Research Council of Michigan, 2009), https://crcmich.org .reforming_process_identifying_funding_section _29_mandates_local_governments-2009.

33 Lisa J. Huriash, "This Mayor Plans Next Challenge to Gun Laws after Recent Legal Win," *South Florida Sun Sentinel*, July 31, 2019, https://www.sun-sentinel.com/news/florida/fl-ne-florida-ap peals-gun-laws-20190731-pmy4tjyev5hw3pw56ubinjtzky-story.html.

34 Shu Wang and Andrew Crosby, "Politics or Professionalism to the Rescue? The Friedrich-Finer Debate in the Context of State Intervention on Michigan," *Public Administration Quarterly* 43, no. 4 (2019): 555–83.

35 Domingo Morel, *Takeover: Race, Education, and American Democracy* (New York: Oxford University Press, 2018); Ashley E. Nickels, "Approaches to Municipal Takeover: Home Rule Erosion and State Intervention in Michigan and New Jersey," *State & Local Government Review* 48, no. 3 (2016): 194–207.

36 James Barragan, "Local Leaders 'Shocked' by Animosity toward Cities, Counties in Secret Bonnen Recording," *Dallas Morning News*, October 16, 2019, https://www.dallasnews.com/news/ politics/2019/10/16/local-leaders-shocked-by-animosity-toward-cities-counties-in-secret-bon nen-recording/.

37 Brian Maffly, "Battle over Public Land Designations Devides Utah Lawmakers, Too, as State Bill Seeks to Usurp Local Control," *Salt Lake Tribune*, February 13, 2019, https://www.sltrib.com/ news/environment/2019/02/13/local-control-is-great/.

38 Ann O'M. Bowman and Richard C. Kearney, "Second-Order Devolution: Data and Doubt," *Publius: The Journal of Federalism* 41, no. 4 (2011): 563–85.

39 Katherine Levine Einstein and David M. Glick, "Cities in American Federalism: Evidence on State–Local Government Conflict from a Survey of Mayors," *Publius: The Journal of Federalism* 47, no. 4 (2017): 599–621.

40 Daniel J. Hopkins, *The Increasingly United States: How and Why American Political Behavior Nationalized*, Chicago Studies in American Politics (Chicago: University of Chicago Press, 2018).

41 Alexander Hertel-Fernandez, *State Capture: How Conservative Activists, Big Businesses, and Wealthy Donors Reshaped the American States, and the Nation* (New York: Oxford University Press, 2019).

42 Heather Getha-Taylor and Ricardo S. Morse, "Collaborative Leadership Development for Local Government Officials: Exploring Competencies and Program Impact," *Public Administration Quarterly* 37, no. 1 (2013): 71–102.

43 Robert Agranoff and Michael McGuire, "Expanding Intergovernmental Management's Hidden Dimensions," *American Review of Public Administration* 29, no. 4 (1999): 352–69.

44 Robert Agranoff and Michael McGuire, *Collaborative Public Management: New Strategies for Local Governments* (Washington, DC: Georgetown University Press, 2003).

45 JoAnna Mitchell-Brown, "Rural Decline and Revival: State and Local Partnerships in Creating 'Stellar Communities' in Rural Indiana," *Journal of Public and Nonprofit Affairs* 1, no. 1 (2015): 43–58.

46 Harold Wolman and Kenneth Voytek, "State Government as a Consultant for Local Economic Development," *Economic Development Quarterly* 4, no. 3 (1990): 211–20.

47 Casey Blount, Wendy Ip, Ikuo Nakano, and Elaine Ng, "Redevelopment Agencies in California: History, Benefits, Excesses, and Closure," Economic Market Analysis Working Paper EMAD-2014-01, U.S. Department of Housing and Urban Development, Office of Policy Development and Research, 2014.

48 Dillon, Liam. "California Lawmakers Move to Reinstate, Revamp Local Affordable Housing Program," *Los Angeles Times*, September 11, 2019, https://www.latimes.com/california/story/2019-09-11/california-legislature-redevelopment-agencies-bill-sb5.

49 Naim Kapucu, Tolga Arslan, and Matthew Lloyd Collins, "Examining Intergovernmental and Interorganizational Response to Catastrophic Disasters: Toward a Network-Centered Approach," *Administration & Society* 42, no. 2 (2010): 222–47.

50 P. Danczyk, "Intergovernmental Interactions in Threat Preparedness and Response: California's Networked Approach," Ph.D. diss., University of Pittsburgh, 2008.

51 Richard L. Cole, "The Current Status and Roles of State Advisory Commissions on Intergovernmental Relations in the U.S. Federal System," *Public Administration Review* 71, no. 2 (2011): 190–95.

PART I

State Power

CHAPTER 2

Which Government Do You Trust the Most
Federal, State, Local, or None?
John Kincaid, Lafayette College

Today's students have never known a time when Americans expressed high levels of trust in the federal government in Washington, DC. Students' grandparents or great-grandparents remember President John F. Kennedy's New Frontier, during the early 1960s, when most Americans reported high levels of trust and confidence in the federal government and believed government could achieve great things, such as ending poverty and landing a person on the moon.[1] Young people were especially attracted to Kennedy's optimism.

An important facet of support for democratic governance and legitimacy is trust—in both government institutions and fellow citizens. Trust is a key component of social capital.[2] Essentially, theories about trust hold that the viability of democracy and legitimacy depends substantially on the ability of political institutions to elicit public trust and reinforce trust within civil society. Trust promotes democracy; withdrawal of trust weakens it.[3]

As we will see below, Americans report low trust in the federal government but much more trust in their local and state governments. This trust is important for helping to maintain democracy in America, especially when trust in the federal government is so low. States and localities are vital arenas of democracy. Trust in these governments can also mitigate state–local conflict and foster more state–local cooperation. It should be kept in mind that while the media often highlights state–local conflict, the lion's share of daily government operations, especially of local governments, which are legal creatures of their states, involves state–local cooperation. By way of contrast with the United States, this chapter also looks at public trust in governments in Canada, Mexico, and Switzerland.

Low Public Trust in the Federal Government

Americans' trust in the federal government dropped after President Kennedy's assassination in November 1963. The proportions of Americans who trust the federal government to do what is right "just about always" or "most of the time" declined continually thereafter to 27 percent by November 1979.[4] Public trust in the federal government perked back up to 45 percent by 1985 under President Ronald Reagan but dropped to 25 percent by the start of President Bill Clinton's administration in 1993 before rising to 44 percent by the end of his second term in 2001.

Since October 2001, when public trust in the federal government reached an aberrant high of 60 percent because of the 9/11 terrorist attacks, trust has been low, averaging only 25 percent since mid-2003 (the last time trust exceeded 50 percent), according to opinion data compiled by the Pew Research Center. Trust reached an unprecedented low of 15 percent under President Barack Obama in October 2011 and stood at 17 percent in March 2019 under President Donald Trump.[5] Most Americans believe the low level of trust is justified. Only 24 percent say the federal government deserves more trust; 75 percent say it does not deserve more trust than it is getting.[6]

Furthermore, about 69 percent of Americans say the federal government deliberately withholds important information from the public that it could safely release, and 64 percent say it is hard to tell what is true and untrue in statements made by elected officials.[7] People aged eighteen to twenty-nine have slightly less confidence in elected officials than do older generations.[8]

Why the Low Trust in the Federal Government?

Urban riots in many cities during the late 1960s, the assassinations of Martin Luther King Jr. and Robert F. Kennedy in 1968, the increasingly unpopular Vietnam War (1955–1975), President Richard M. Nixon's resignation from office in August 1974 due to the Watergate scandal, and President Jimmy Carter's lackluster response to the country's stagflation and unease in 1977–1981 all took a toll on public trust in the federal government.

As a result of events during the 1960s and 1970s, news reporters became much more distrustful of presidents and other government officials and less willing to communicate positive news about government. Two events especially signified this change in journalists' attitudes. One was publication by the *New York Times* and other newspapers of the top-secret Pentagon Papers in June 1971,[9] which exposed many lies by federal government officials about the Vietnam War. The second was the 1972 start of the serial exposé by the *Washington Post* of President Nixon's Watergate scandal.[10] Journalists became more investigative and willing to expose perceived wrongdoings by government officials. Given that bad news sells better than good news, media outlets rarely convey favorable images of government and public officials.

The media's contribution to distrust is reflected in its coverage of the 2016 presidential campaign, during which 77 percent of news reports about Donald Trump were negative, as were 64 percent of news reports about Hillary Clinton.[11] Only about 5 percent of news stories about President Trump's first 60 days in office were positive, compared to 22 percent for George W. Bush, 27 percent for Bill Clinton, and 42 percent for Barack Obama.[12]

News coverage of Congress rises during divided government (i.e., the White House controlled by one party and one or both houses of Congress controlled by the other party) because presidential–congressional conflict is more prevalent under divided government, yet divided governments are as legislatively productive as single-party governments.[13] News coverage of Congress is more negative than positive and emphasizes conflict and deadlock over compromise and resolution.[14] Bills killed in Congress (e.g., gun-control bills) often get more media attention than bills passed by Congress.

The media's role in fostering distrust is compounded by surveys repeatedly showing low public trust in the media. The media is sometimes the least trusted of major institutions. When a 2019 poll asked the public's confidence in the people running the military, law enforcement, universities, Supreme Court, executive branch, Congress, and "the press," about 60 percent expressed "hardly any confidence at all" in the press—the worst ranking of the seven institutions.[15]

Media outlets are not solely responsible for the public's low trust in the federal government. Candidates for Congress and the presidency feed distrust by emphasizing negative aspects of government and of each other. Negative campaign ads prevail on media outlets, and as reflected in the campaign for the 2020 elections, opposing candidates paint dark pictures of the state of government and the country.

Partisanship plays a role, too. Democrats report higher trust in the federal government when a Democrat is in the White House; Republicans express higher trust in the federal government when a Republican occupies the White House. This points to the role of partisan polarization in fueling distrust. The rise of polarization corresponds to the long-term decline of public trust in the federal government. Polarization generates conflict, which citizens dislike.[16] Polarization has given rise to negative partisanship whereby Democrats, Republicans, and even independents increasingly harbor negative feelings about the opposing party and its candidates and elected officials. Additionally, party affiliation has become aligned more closely with ideological, cultural, and social cleavages.[17] A key facet of negative partisanship is that party loyalists are loyal not because they love their party but because they hate the other party. Consequently, even when one's own party controls the White House or Congress or both, one's trust in the federal government rises only moderately.

Some observers contend that distrust of the federal government has been manufactured by attacks on the federal government by big business, wealthy elites, and conservative Republicans. This propaganda has led Americans to forget the federal government's great historical accomplishments and to believe instead, as President Reagan said in 1981, that government is the problem, not the solution, to what ails America.[18] This explanation seems unlikely, however, because public trust in the federal government plummeted continuously from 77 percent in 1964 to 27 percent in 1979 under both Democratic and Republican presidents—although Democrats were the majority party in Congress during 1964–1980. Trust levels have fluctuated since 1980, reaching a post-1980 high of 60 percent shortly after the terrorist attacks of 11 September 2001. A more plausible explanation is that divisive federal politics and policies during the late 1960s and the 1970s produced enduring cleavages and mistrust. Casting further doubt on the elite-manipulation thesis is that even though trust has not rebounded, Americans sometimes reported higher levels of trust in their governments than did citizens in their neighboring federations of Canada and Mexico.[19]

Public distrust persists also because it is a catch-22 for government; citizens want more government services but are unwilling to pay more taxes for services.[20] For example, a national 2019 poll found 60 percent of parents and all adults and 75 percent of teachers saying their community's schools had too little money. Further, 25 percent of all adults said that inadequate financial support is the biggest problem facing the public schools today. However, more than 70 percent of all parents and adults and 61 percent of teachers do not want to pay more taxes for better schools; instead, they want cuts in other government-funded programs.[21]

Yet, when asked about cutting services such as aid to the poor, Social Security, Medicare, Medicaid, environmental protection, and the like, majorities of Americans oppose cuts. Instead, they frequently believe the core problem is government waste. On average, Americans believe the federal government wastes about 51 cents of every tax dollar.[22] If the federal government eliminated waste, they believe, services could be improved without raising taxes. However, even the U.S. Senate's fervid budgetary watchdog, Rand Paul (R-KY), found only $115 million in wasteful federal spending in 2018.[23] This equaled about 0.00004 percent of the total federal budget.

Another contributor to public distrust of the federal government has been the nationalization of many policies historically managed by the states, especially morality policies such as religious practices in public schools, marriage, abortion, firearms, and criminal justice. Prior to nationalization, conflict over these policies was diffused across the 50 states rather than concentrated in the national arena, where they spark polarizing "culture wars."[24] Morality policies involve key values of personal identity and questions of what is fundamentally right and wrong; hence, they often generate us-versus-them politics[25] that drives up distrust among those on both sides of conflicts. The conflicts over abortion in presidential campaigns since 1976 and in U.S. Supreme Court justice confirmations since 1987 are emblematic, as reflected most recently in the 2018 confirmation hearings for Justice Brett Kavanaugh. Indeed, Supreme Court decision making on morality policies contributed to a decline in its public approval rating from 62 percent in 2000 to 51 percent in 2018, although public confidence in the court remains much higher than confidence in Congress and the presidency.

All of these factors have contributed to the persistence of mistrust of the federal government.

High Public Trust in Local and State Governments

One consequence of low trust in the federal government is cynicism about government generally. But what about state and local governments? People often forget about them and don't realize that Americans have high levels of trust in their local and state governments. Even though Americans feel much more emotionally attached to their country, the United States, than to their locality or state,[26] Americans who express a great deal or fair amount of trust in local governments, according to Gallup polls, has never dipped below 63 percent since 1973 and stood at 72 percent in 2018. Trust in state governments has never fallen below 51 percent since 1973 and stood at 63 percent in 2018.[27]

Higher proportions of Americans believe state governments, compared to the federal government, are mostly honest and generally efficient, address people's needs better, can usually work together to get things done, and are careful with the people's money.[28]

There are partisan differences. Although both Democrats and Republicans view state and local governments more favorably than the federal government, Republicans ordinarily view state and local governments more favorably than do Democrats. Republicans and independents report more stable positive views of state and local governments over time; the views of Democrats change more sharply according to the partisan composition of the federal government. For example, in 2018, with Donald Trump occupying the White House, 78 percent of Democrats reported trust in local governments (their highest level since 2001) and 67 percent reported trust in state governments.[29]

In contrast to the 51 percent approval rating of the U.S. Supreme Court, 76 percent of Americans say they have a great deal or some confidence in their state court system.[30] In the case of state courts, however, there are no significant party differences. Democrats, Republicans, and independents are about equally positive.

Compared to the federal government, which Americans believe wastes 51 cents of every tax dollar, people believe state governments waste 42 cents of every tax dollar while local governments waste 37 cents.[31] These perceptions of state and local waste are nonetheless high, although, like perceptions of federal government waste, they are factually incorrect.

On questions such as "which order of government gives you the most for your money" and "which order do you trust most to deliver programs and services important to you," Americans regularly rate local governments the best, followed by state governments and the federal government as the worst.[32] In 2014, for example, 80 percent of Whites, 70 percent of Hispanics, and 56 percent of Blacks believed they got excellent or good value from local government for their local taxes. Some 48 percent of Whites, 34 percent of Blacks, and 32 percent of Hispanics said the quality of public services where they live is determined mostly by local government, while 38 percent of Whites, 47 percent of Blacks, and 38 percent of Hispanics said the quality of services was determined by state government. By contrast, 7 percent of Whites, 10 percent of Blacks, and 17 percent of Hispanics believed the federal government determines the quality of services.[33]

When asked about specific local public services, Americans usually report the most confidence in the police. As of 2017, 57 percent of Americans expressed confidence in the police compared to 36 percent expressing confidence in their public schools, and 27 percent reported confidence in the criminal justice system, compared to 12 percent expressing confidence in Congress.[34] However, as noted in the previous paragraph, levels of confidence vary by race and ethnicity. Generally, Black Americans express less confidence in the police, public schools, and criminal justice system than do Whites and Hispanics. Levels of trust and confidence also vary by such demographic factors as levels of income and education.

Overall, Americans' trust in local and state governments has not varied much over the past forty-five years, but the gap in trust between the federal government and state governments grew from 36 to 45 percentage points from 1975 to 2018 and from 29 to 54 percentage points between the federal government and local governments.[35] Consequently, the seemingly pervasive mistrust of government often highlighted by the news media is directed mainly at the federal government.

Why the High Trust in Local and State Governments?

So state and local governments must be doing something right. Indeed, they provide almost all the public services important to daily life, such as police and fire protection, water and sewage service, streets and highways, and education. However, there is not much research on why public trust in state and local governments exceeds that of the federal government or why the gap in trust has grown over the decades. Explanations are thus more speculative than definitive.

Jennings suggested that trust has two dimensions—instrumental (i.e., performance) and relational (i.e., representativeness and accountability of leaders).[36] The instrumental dimension is more relevant to trust in the distant federal government; the relational dimension influences trust in state and local government. It is often said that citizens feel closer to their local and state governments than to the federal government. The instrumental dimension, however, would also seem to be very important for public trust in state and local governments because citizens more easily see the services provided by those governments, beginning with police, fire, EMS, sanitation, water, sewage, and other front-door services. These services sometimes receive positive media coverage, as when first responders rescue people during a disaster or take down a mass shooter.

A partial explanation may also be that because citizens have less direct experience and interaction with distant governments, such as the federal government, their trust in distant governments is based more on stereotypes and generalized trust.[37] These attitudes are shaped substantially by the mass media and social media. By contrast, citizens can have more personal experiences with local and state government personnel, services, and policies.

To some extent, citizens can choose local and state governments by voting with their feet.[38] If you dislike a particular local or state government, you can move to a different locality or state. If you dislike the federal government, you cannot move to a different one unless you leave the country.

Another partial explanation may be that local and state governments receive less frequent and less penetrating media coverage than the federal government. Compared to presidents and members of Congress, how often do you see your governor, mayor, or state representative on television or other media outlets? Although bad news is often said to be better than no news if one wants to stay in the public eye, for state and local governments, no news may be good news.

Trust in Other Federal Countries: Canada, Mexico, and Switzerland

High trust in state and local governments is not true in every federal country. In Mexico, for example, citizens often trust the federal government the most, partly because they believe state and local governments do not provide effective policing and crime control.[39]

Studying trust in governments across federal countries encounters five obstacles. First, surveys often use differently worded questions with different response choices. The results are not directly comparable. Second, even surveys using identically worded questions are not always conducted at the same time across countries. Cross-country results may be from different years. Third, even if polls with identically worded questions are conducted at the same time, sampling procedures may produce different results. Fourth, each survey is a snapshot in time; survey results are not always available over long time periods. Fifth, most surveys treat all countries as though they are unitary polities; consequently, most surveys ask only about trust in each country's national government, not about state/provincial and local governments in federal countries. The following discussion of Canada, Mexico, and Switzerland, therefore, cannot present comparable and always recent data for the three federations.

Canada

Canada has ten provinces and three territories, including the unique native territory Nunavut. Canada has 37.3 million people, which is smaller than California's population of 39.8 million. Canada is more constitutionally centralized than the United States but more operationally decentralized, with provinces playing large roles in citizens' lives.[40] Canada is predominantly a binational federation of two peoples: English and French speaking, although if one includes Canada's native First Nations, it is a multinational federation. French-speaking Quebec voted on referenda in 1980 and 1995 to declare independence and secede from Canada. In 1995, Quebecers voted against secession by only 50.58 percent. Following Quebec's 1980 referendum, Canada repatriated its constitution with the Constitution Act of 1982, which allows Canada to amend its constitution without approval from Great Britain. This constitution also for the first time enshrined a Charter of Rights and Freedoms. However, Quebec's two referenda and Canada's 1982 act triggered constitutional and political crises that lasted into the early 2000s. For example, Canada was unable to settle the constitutional status of Quebec, and Quebec still has not ratified the constitution.

Consequently, trust in the federal government and provincial governments sometimes dropped quite low during those decades but appears to have rebounded to levels sometimes exceeding trust levels in the United States. Trust in the federal government in Canada declined with the same pattern as the U.S. decline, with only 24 percent of Canadians having trust in 2013 compared to 19 percent of Americans.[41] Also, according to one poll, only 9 percent of Canadians expressed trust in the federal parliament in 2013.[42] However, Canadians' confidence in the federal government based in Ottawa increased to 65 percent by 2017 after the then popular Justin Trudeau became prime minister.

Confidence in the judicial system increased from 57 percent in 2006 to 67 percent in 2017.[43] Unlike the U.S. system of dual federal and state courts, Canada has a single federal court system. In a 2014 poll, 74 percent of Canadians expressed a great deal or some trust in their Supreme Court, 44 percent in their provincial government, 34 percent in the federal Senate, and 51 percent in the federal parliament, although the military was the most trusted institution.[44]

A 2019 poll found that 36 percent of Canadians rated the performance of municipal governments as excellent or good, 27 percent so rated provincial governments, and 23 percent so rated the federal government.[45] Thus, like Americans, Canadians give their local governments their highest rating, although at an apparently lower level than Americans. However, the questions asked in Canada and the United States are worded differently; hence, the results are not directly comparable.

When asked if they believe their state or province is treated with the respect it deserves in the federation, majorities of Americans say yes, and there are no significant differences among states or regions, but in Canada in a 2019 poll, 59 percent of Ontarians said yes while only 36 percent of the respondents in Quebec, 33 percent in New Brunswick, 30 percent in Saskatchewan, 24 percent in Newfoundland/Labrador, and 22 percent in Alberta said yes. Generally, on a variety of evaluative measures, opinions differ much more sharply among Canadian provinces than among U.S. states.[46]

Mexico

Mexico (Estados Unidos Mexicanos) has been a historically centralized federation with thirty-one states plus Mexico City. Mexico has 129 million people. The country was ruled from 1929 to 2000 by the corrupt Partido Revolucionario Institucional (PRI). The emergence of many drug cartels since the early 1980s has contributed greatly to increased government corruption and criminal violence. Among North Americans, Mexicans are the least trusting of their governments.[47] In the last survey in 2009 asking the same question in Canada, Mexico, and the United States, 38 percent of Mexicans expressed a great deal or fair amount of trust in their federal government, compared to 49 percent in Canada and 50 percent in the United States. In turn, 37 percent of Mexicans expressed trust in their state government, compared to 55 percent of Americans and 58 percent of Canadians (for their province). Only one-third of Mexicans trusted their local government, compared to 62 percent of Americans and 60 percent of Canadians.[48] Unlike the United States, though, levels of trust in the state and federal governments vary markedly across Mexico's states and regions depending on levels of corruption and economic opportunities.

When asked in 2009 which government gives them the most for their money, Mexicans picked their federal government first, whereas Americans picked their local governments first and Canadians picked their provincial governments first. When asked which government (federal, state, or local) needs more power, Mexicans said their state governments, whereas Americans and Canadians said their local governments need more power.[49]

More recently, almost 90 percent of Mexicans say that their state government and the federal government are deeply corrupt. Citizens believe corruption is the second most important problem facing their country, after crime and violence.[50] Mexico also consistently ranks at the bottom of Latin American countries regarding citizen satisfaction with democracy, and Mexicans' satisfaction with democracy has been declining. Likewise, Mexicans' trust and confidence in a wide range of institutions—from the police to the Catholic Church, to television news, universities, political parties, Congress, and the president—has declined for many years.[51]

Research on corruption shows that trust in governments and other political institutions is both a cause and a consequence of corruption. As a result of very high levels of perceived corruption and very low levels of trust in governments, efforts to root out perceptions of corruption or improve trust in governments will be extremely difficult.[52] At the same time, because Mexicans tend to trust the federal government more than their state or municipal authorities, recentralizing tendencies may enjoy popular support and further weaken the possibility of state and local governments checking the powers of the federal government.[53]

Switzerland

Switzerland is a much more positive case of trust in governments. It is a federation with twenty-six cantons (Switzerland's equivalent of states) and 8.6 million people. Compared to most European countries, such as France, Germany, and Italy, trust in political institutions is generally high in Switzerland, although, like Americans and Canadians, Swiss citizens display slightly more trust in their local governments first and cantonal governments second. Over time since 1995, trust has increased in local and cantonal authorities as well as in the federal parliament. There is some regional variation though. Trust in local and cantonal governments is highest in German-speaking cantons and lowest in French-speaking cantons, while trust in cantonal authorities is highest for individuals belonging to the Italian-speaking region. Trust in Switzerland may reflect public perceptions that political institutions perform relatively well and that Switzerland has achieved unity while preserving diversity.[54] Switzerland's direct-democracy system may also contribute to high levels of governmental trust because referendums increase citizens' feelings of participation and of belonging to a unified Swiss nation.[55]

Conclusion

Trust is important for democracy and legitimacy in all governments. In federal countries, one must take into account trust not only in the national government but also in state and local governments. Generally, Americans, Canadians, and the Swiss report the most trust and confidence in their local governments followed by their state/provincial/cantonal governments. Mexicans, however, report the most trust in their federal government, though not by much. Mexico remains a fragile democracy with deep public dissatisfaction with all governments and with democracy itself.

Levels and patterns of trust in governments vary by province/state/canton in Canada, Mexico, and Switzerland more than by state in the United States. However, levels of trust in government vary demographically (e.g., race, ethnicity, and class) in the United States. The difference is due partly to the distribution of demographic groups in the four countries. Canada, Mexico, and Switzerland each have a number of demographically distinctive provinces, states, and cantons, such as Italian-speaking Ticino in Switzerland and French-speaking Quebec in Canada. In the United States, demographic differences are more dispersed across the states. Louisiana has a French affinity but is not the Quebec of the United States.

The trust patterns reported here for the United States have been fairly stable for nearly a half century and will likely endure for some time, although growing political polarization introduces uncertainty. Polarization has generated more strains in state–local relations. Various observers have reported an erosion of local autonomy.[56] Under polarization, differences in party control between state governments and major local governments might produce more state preemptions of salient aspects of local authority that could reduce public trust of state governments as citizens resent state intrusions into their local self-governance.

This is hard to predict, however, because we lack longitudinal public-opinion data on state–local relations. Also, scholars focus mostly on state preemptions of high-profile liberal policies such as sanctuary communities, LGBTQ rights, minimum wages, sin and soda taxes, firearm regulations, environmental policies, and fracking bans.[57] These are important issues, but they obscure the fact that preemption has long been a staple of state–local relations that goes largely unnoticed by citizens because most preemptions concern dull technical matters such as code and road specifications. The salient "culture wars" preemptions studied by scholars ordinarily involve Republican state governments preempting liberal Democratic local policies, but the reverse is true too. For example, the predominantly Democratic state governments of Maryland, New York, Vermont, and Washington ban fracking, thereby preempting local communities from employing fracking to stimulate economic development. Many of these are rural and exurban Republican and conservative Democratic communities. Nine Democratic state governments have declared their states to be sanctuary states, thus preempting the authority of Republican and conservative

Democratic localities to cooperate with federal Immigration and Customs Enforcement officials informally as well as formally through the intergovernmental 287(g) and Secure Communities programs.[58] In 2019, New Jersey's Democratic governor declared the Garden State a sanctuary state, but a number of counties, municipalities, and townships reject the policy, and some are suing the state in federal court to block the policy.

Another complicating factor is that the liberal local policies most studied by scholars are present in only small numbers of communities. For example, about 225 cities and counties prohibit "gender identity" employment discrimination.[59] These 225 communities constitute only 0.6 percent of the country's 3,031 counties, 19,519 municipalities, and 16,364 townships. Similarly, there are about 173 sanctuary cities and counties.[60] Of course, the number would be larger were it not for preemptions in some states, such as Texas, but assuming the number might reach 1,000 without preemption, the 1,000 would still be only 2.6 percent of all U.S. general-purpose local governments. Furthermore, these salient liberal policies are found almost exclusively in big cities and urban counties, yet about two-thirds of Americans live in local jurisdictions having fewer than one hundred thousand people.

Another interesting pattern is the number of states in which only one jurisdiction is a sanctuary community. These include Alachua County (home of the university town Gainesville), Florida; Franklin County (home of Columbus), Ohio; Hennepin County (home of Minneapolis), Minnesota; Jackson, Mississippi; Newark, New Jersey; New Orleans, Louisiana; and Washoe County (home of Reno), Nevada. In Illinois, Chicago and its surrounding Cook County are the only sanctuary jurisdictions, as are Clayton and DeKalb counties in the Atlanta, Georgia, metropolitan area.

These geographic dimensions of preemption are consistent with the partisan sorting of voters whereby Democrats are usually concentrated in largely homogeneous cities (in terms of partisanship) while Republicans are more dispersed across smaller, more heterogeneous suburban, exurban, and rural communities.[61] Democratic cities therefore lose many preemption battles because many Democratic votes are wasted in legislative districts where Democrats win by 70 percent or more of the vote, while Republicans, spread across many more heterogeneous districts, win many districts with only slightly more than 50 percent of the vote. This urban–rural divide is accompanied by demographic divides, especially along lines of race and education, that further foster partisan polarization within states and between state governments controlled by one party and local governments controlled by the opposite party.

As such, polarization probably limits distrust of state government to members of the party out of power in the state capital but who regain trust in state government when their party regains control of the state capital. This polarization might also increase party competition as well as voter turnout within states as members of each party increasingly view control of the state government as a high-stakes game. Even so, to circle back to a main point of this chapter, Americans still trust their local and state governments much more than they trust the federal government.

CAREER PROFILE

Simonia Brown
Director of State Legislative Affairs
New York City, Mayor's Office of Intergovernmental Affairs

Some city governments hire lobbyists to advocate for their policy priorities at the state capitol. In large cities, these responsibilities may be carried out by an internal office of intergovernmental affairs. In New York City, Simonia Brown is the director of state legislative affairs (i.e, relations). Her office is responsible for advocating for the city with the legislature and state agencies in Albany. The office also aids local members of the state legislature responding to their constituents in their interactions with state agencies and helps state officials (and agencies) understand the impact of legislation and various demands and problems of city residents. In recent years, this work has included action on speed cameras in school zones, criminal justice reform legislation, protecting funding for universal pre-kindergarten, expansion of discretionary authority over minority- and women-owned business enterprise programs, and design-build authority for critical projects (such as city acquisition of state park land for other public purposes [a process called alienation]), among many other issues.

At times, Brown must advocate for state policies to be adapted to fit the unique needs of New York City due to its size and scope in contrast to other municipalities in the state. At other times, Brown affirms the city's ability to align with programs designed for the rest of the state. "We are similar in many ways to the rest of the state, and where there are opportunities to demonstrate that similarity, we want to take advantage of that too."

Brown was a political science major at the University at Albany, SUNY, and interned with the state legislature during college. After graduating, she worked for the central staff at the state assembly for nearly ten years, honing her skill to analyze the fiscal and operational impact of state legislation. She moved back to New York City to work as associate director of the city's Office of Management and Budget and after several years moved to her current role. Brown explains that having experience in both state and local government was helpful for her current role because these opportunities provided invaluable and different perspectives on state and local policy.

Students interested in lobbying for city government can identify good entry-level positions in state or local government and then take advantage of opportunities to work their way up. Brown advises students to learn from the people around them who have institutional knowledge, observing that "the institutions themselves do not really change; the people change." Learning from experienced public servants and lobbyists prepares students to take on new responsibilities and pursue new job opportunities when people move to new positions. Understanding the backgrounds, motivations, and experiences of other people in government and government lobbyists is also important preparation for working with others constructively in the policy process.

Interview: September 13, 2019

Discussion Questions

1. Why do Americans have low trust in the federal government, and how could public trust in the federal government be improved?
2. Why do Americans have higher levels of trust in their local and state governments than in the federal government?
3. In what ways might polarization between Democrats and Republicans reduce trust in state and local governments?

Notes

1. Arthur M. Schlesinger Jr., *A Thousand Days: John F. Kennedy in the White House* (New York: Houghton Mifflin, 1965).
2. Robert D. Putnam, *Making Democracy Work: Civic Traditions in Modern Italy* (Princeton, NJ: Princeton University Press, 1993), and Francis Fukuyama, *Trust: The Social Virtues and the Creation of Prosperity* (New York: Free Press, 1995).
3. Mark J. Hetherington, *Why Trust Matters: Declining Political Trust and the Demise of American Liberalism* (Princeton, NJ: Princeton University Press, 2005), and Charles Tilly, *Trust and Rule* (New York: Cambridge University Press, 2005).
4. Pew Research Center, "Public Trust in Government: 1958–2019," https://www.people-press .org/2019/04/11/public-trust-in-government-1958-2019/.
5. Ibid.
6. Lee Rainie, Scott Keeter, and Andrew Perrin, "Trust and Distrust in America," Pew Research Center, July 22, 2019, https://www.people-press.org/2019/07/22/trust-and-distrust-in-america/.
7. Pew, "Public Trust."
8. Ibid.
9. Sanford J. Ungar, *The Papers and the Papers: An Account of the Legal and Political Battle over the Pentagon Papers* (New York: Columbia University Press, 1989), and John Kincaid, "Secrecy and Democracy: The Unresolved Legacy of the Pentagon Papers," in *Watergate and Afterward: The Legacy of Richard M. Nixon*, ed. Leon Friedman and William F. Levantrosser, 151–62 (Westport, CT: Greenwood Press, 1992).
10. Carl Bernstein and Bob Woodward, *All the President's Men* (New York: Simon and Schuster, 1974).
11. Thomas E. Patterson, "News Coverage of the 2016 General Election: How the Press Failed the Voters," Shorenstein Center on Media, Politics, and Public Policy, 2016.
12. Amy Mitchell, Jeffrey Gottfried, Katerina Eva Matsa, Galen Stocking, and Elizabeth Grieco, "Covering President Trump in a Polarized Media Environment," Pew Research Center, October 2, 2017, https://www.journalism.org/2017/10/02/covering-president-trump-in-a -polarized-media-environment/.
13. David R. Mayhew, *Divided We Govern*, 2nd ed. (New Haven, CT: Yale University Press, 2005).
14. Stephanie Larson, "Reporting on Congress: The Role of the Media," Dirksen Congressional Center, 2005, https://www.dirksencenter.org/print_expert_media2.htm.
15. Editors, "Poll: How Does the Public Think Journalism Happens?," *Columbia Journalism Review*, Winter 2019, https://www.cjr.org/special_report/how-does-journalism-happen-poll.php.
16. Kevin K. Benda and Justin H. Kirkland, "Legislative Party Polarization and Trust in State Legislatures," *American Politics Research* 46, no. 4 (2018): 596–628.
17. Alan I. Abramowitz and Steven Webster, "The Rise of Negative Partisanship and the Nationalization of U.S. Elections in the 21st Century," *Electoral Studies* 41, no. 1 (2016): 12–22, and

Shanto Iyangar and Masha Krupenkin, "The Strengthening of Partisan Affect," *Political Psychology* 39, no. 51 (2018): 201–18.

[18] Jacob S. Hacker and Paul Pierson, *American Amnesia: How the War on Government Led Us to Forget What Made America Prosper* (New York: Simon and Schuster, 2016).

[19] John Kincaid and Richard L. Cole, "Citizen Attitudes toward Issues of Federalism in Canada, Mexico, and the United States," *Publius: The Journal of Federalism* 41, no. 1 (2011): 53–75, and Richard L. Cole, John Kincaid, and Alejandro Rodriquez, "Public Opinion on Federalism and Federal Political Culture in Canada, Mexico, and the United States, 2004," *Publius: The Journal of Federalism* 34, no. 3 (2004): 201–21.

[20] Pew Research Center, *Beyond Distrust: How Americans View Their Government* (Washington, DC: Pew Research Center, 2015), https://www.people-press.org/2015/11/23/beyond-distrust-how-americans-view-their-government/.

[21] PDK Poll, "Frustration in the Schools," 2019, https://pdkpoll.org/assets/downloads/2019pdkpoll51.pdf.

[22] Rebecca Riffkin, "Americans Say Federal Gov't Wastes 51 Cents on the Dollar," Gallup, September 17, 2014, https://news.gallup.com/poll/176102/americans-say-federal-gov-wastes-cents-dollar.aspx.

[23] Rand Paul, "Chairman Paul's 2018 Festivus Report," December 21, 2018, https://www.scribd.com/document/396160193/Chairman-Paul-s-2018-Festivus-Report#from_embed.

[24] James Davison Hunter, *Culture Wars: The Struggle to Control the Family, Art, Education, Law, and Politics in America* (New York: Basic Books, 1992).

[25] Kenneth J. Meier, *The Politics of Sin* (Armonk, NY: M. E. Sharpe, 1994), and Christopher Z. Mooney, ed., *The Public Clash of Private Values: The Politics of Morality Policy* (New York: Chatham House, 2001).

[26] John Kincaid and Richard L. Cole, "Attachments to Multiple Communities, Trust in Governments, Political Polarization, and Public Attitudes toward Immigration in the United States," in *Identities, Trust, and Cohesion in Federal Countries: Perspectives from Public Opinion*, ed. Jack Jedwab and John Kincaid, 147–80 (Montreal: McGill-Queen's University Press, 2018).

[27] Justin McCarthy, "Americans Still More Trusting of Local Than State Government," Gallup, October 8, 2018, https://news.gallup.com/poll/243563/americans-trusting-local-state-government.aspx.

[28] Pew Research Center, "Growing Gap in Favorable Views of Federal, State Governments," April 26, 2012, https://www.people-press.org/2012/04/26/growing-gap-in-favorable-views-of-federal-state-governments/.

[29] McCarthy, "Americans Still More Trusting."

[30] National Center for State Courts, "2018 State of the State Courts—Survey Analysis," December 3, 2018, https://www.ncsc.org/~/media/Files/PDF/Topics/Public%20Trust%20and%20Confidence/SoSC_2018_Survey_Analysis.ashx.

[31] Riffkin, "Americans Say Federal Gov't Wastes."

[32] John Kincaid and Richard L. Cole, "Public Opinion on Issues of Federalism in 2007: A Bush Plus?" *Publius: The Journal of Federalism* 38, no. 3 (2008): 469–87, and Kincaid and Cole, "Citizen Attitudes toward Issues of Federalism."

[33] Kriston Capps, "Americans Love Local Government—They Just Don't Necessarily Want More of It," *City Lab*, September 11, 2014, http://www.citylab.com/politics/2014/09/americans-love-local-governmentthey-just-dont-necessarily-want-more-of-it/379968/.

[34] Frank Newport, "Americans' Confidence in Institutions Edges Up," Gallup, June 26, 2017, https://news.gallup.com/poll/212840/americans-confidence-institutions-edges.aspx?g_source=confidence+institutions&g_medium=search&g_campaign=tiles.

[35] McCarthy, "Americans Still More Trusting," and Richard L. Cole and John Kincaid, "Public Opinion and America Federalism: Perspectives on Taxes, Spending, and Trust—an ACIR Update," *Publius: The Journal of Federalism* 30, no. 1 (2000): 189–201.

[36] M. Kent Jennings, "Political Trust and the Roots of Devolution," in *Trust and Governance*, ed. Valerie Braithwaite and Margaret Levi, 218–44 (New York: Russell Sage Foundation, 1998).

[37] Mark Lubell, "Familiarity Breeds Trust: Collective Action in a Policy Domain," *Journal of Politics* 69, no. 1 (2007): 237–50.

[38] Charles M. Tiebout, "A Pure Theory of Local Expenditures," *Journal of Political Economy* 64, no. 5 (1956): 416–24.

[39] María Fernanda Somuano and Laura Flamand, "Democracy, Public Safety, and Low Public Trust in Governments in Mexico," in *Identities, Trust, and Cohesion in Federal Countries: Perspectives from Public Opinion*, ed. Jack Jedwab and John Kincaid, 181–222 (Montreal: McGill-Queen's University Press, 2018).

[40] André Lecours, "Dynamic De/Centralization in Canada: 1867–2010," *Publius: The Journal of Federalism* 49, no. 1 (2019): 57–83, and John Kincaid, "Dynamic De/Centralization in the United States," *Publius: The Journal of Federalism* 49, no. 1 (2019): 166–93.

[41] Don Lenihan and Carolyn Bennett, "Rebuilding Public Trust: Open Government & Open Dialogue in the Government of Canada," Canada 2020, April 28, 2015, https://canada2020.ca/open-government-open-dialogue-lenihan-bennett/.

[42] Adam Cotter, "Public Confidence in Canadian Institutions," Statistics Canada, December 7, 2015, https://www150.statcan.gc.ca/n1/en/pub/89-652-x/89-652-x2015007-eng.pdf?st=aDDPPXZs.

[43] Keith Neuman, "Canadians' Confidence in National Institutions Steady," *Policy Options*, August 2, 2018, https://policyoptions.irpp.org/magazines/august-2018/canadians-confidence-in-national-institutions-steady/.

[44] Forum Research, "Canadian Military Most Trusted Institution," news release, May 26, 2014, http://www.forumresearch.com/forms/News%20Archives/News%20Releases/64082_Fed_Trust_News_Release_%282014_05_26%29_Forum_Research.pdf.

[45] Abacus Data, "Everything Is Local: The Role of Municipalities in Canadians' Lives and Opinions about New Funding Tools," Spring 2019, https://data.fcm.ca/documents/reports/GMF/2019/public-opinion-research-report.pdf.

[46] Keith, Neuman, "Confederation of Tomorrow 2019 Survey of Canadians," Environics Institute, March 21, 2019, https://www.environicsinstitute.org/projects/project-details/confederation-of-tomorrow---2018.

[47] John Kincaid, Andrew Parkin, Richard L. Cole, and Alejandro Rodriguez, "Public Opinion on Federalism in Canada, Mexico, and the United States in 2003," *Publius: The Journal of Federalism* 33, no. 3 (2003): 145–62; Richard L. Cole, John Kincaid, and Alejandro Rodriguez, "Public Opinion on Federalism and Federal Political Culture in Canada, Mexico, and the United States, 2004," *Publius: The Journal of Federalism* 34, no. 3 (2004): 201–21, and Kincaid and Cole, "Citizen Attitudes toward Issues of Federalism."

[48] Kincaid and Cole, "Citizen Attitudes toward Issues of Federalism."

[49] Kincaid and Cole, "Citizen Attitudes toward Issues of Federalism."

[50] Luis Gómez Romero, "Mexico Battles Corruption as Trust in Public Officials Plummets," *Wire*, August 18, 2017, https://thewire.in/external-affairs/mexico-battles-corruption-trust-plummets.

[51] Arturo Franco, "Mexico: The Unbearable Cost of Distrust," Mexico Institute, Wilson Center, 2015.

[52] Stephen D. Morris and Joseph L. Klesner, "Corruption and Trust: Theoretical Considerations and Evidence from Mexico," *Comparative Political Studies* 43, no. 10 (2010): 1258–85.

[53] Somuano and Flamand, "Democracy, Public Safety, and Low Public Trust."

[54] Paul C. Bauer, Markus Freitag, and Pascal Sciarini, "Political Trust in Switzerland: Again a Special Case?," in *Identities, Trust, and Cohesion in Federal Countries: Perspectives from Public Opinion*, ed. Jack Jedwab and John Kincaid, 115–45 (Montreal: McGill-Queen's University Press, 2018).

[55] Adrian Vatter, *Swiss Federalism: The Transformation of a Federal Model* (Abingdon, UK: Routledge, 2018).

[56] For example, David R. Berman, *Local Government and the States: Autonomy, Politics, and Policy* (New York: Routledge, 2020).

[57] See, for example, Luke Fowler and Stephanie L. Witt, "State Preemption of Local Authority: Explaining Patterns of State Adoption of Preemption Measures," *Publius: The Journal of Federalism* 49, no. 3 (2019): 540–59.

[58] The Section 287(g) program, named after a part of the U.S. Immigration and Nationality Act (1965), was created under the Illegal Immigration Reform and Immigrant Responsibility Act

(1996). It allows the U.S. Department of Homeland Security to reach agreements with state and local law enforcement agencies whereby state and local officers are trained and deputized to identify, process, and sometimes detain illegal immigrants. Secure Communities began in 2008, was discontinued in 2014, and was reactivated in 2017. The program involves partnerships with state and local law enforcement agencies to increase the apprehension and deportation of "dangerous criminal aliens."

59 Human Rights Campaign, "Cities and Counties with Non-discrimination Ordinances That Include Gender Identity," January 28, 2018, https://www.hrc.org/resources/cities-and-counties-with-non-discrimination-ordinances-that-include-gender.

60 Center for Immigration Studies, "Sanctuary Cities, Counties, and States," 2019, https://cis.org/Map-Sanctuary-Cities-Counties-and-States.

61 Jonathan A. Rodden, *Why Cities Lose: The Deep Roots of the Urban-Rural Political Divide* (New York: Basic Books, 2019).

CHAPTER 3

Local Government Power
The States Give and the States Take Away
William Blomquist, IUPUI

Politics is largely about control—getting it, having it, using it. Just as this is true in familiar political relationships between individuals or political parties or branches of government, it is true of the relationships between governments. In the American states, the politics of the relationships between state governments and local governments involve ongoing processes of argument and adjustment over how much control local governments have, over what subjects and issues, and how that extent of control can be changed.

This continuing dialogue and disputation take place within a cultural and constitutional context. The cultural element includes Americans' long-standing and widely held beliefs that government should be kept close to the people and that local control is preferable to concentration of authority at higher, more remote levels. The idea and the rhetoric of local self-determination have maintained a strong place within Americans' heads and hearts from colonial days onward.

The U.S. Constitution, however, does not recognize local government. You can search the Constitution's 7,591 words for any mention of cities, counties, townships, villages, school districts, and the like, and you will come up empty-handed. Despite our everyday knowledge that American federalism entails three levels of government—national, state, and local—our federal Constitution recognizes only two: "the United States" (that is, the national government) and "the several States."

This turns out to be more than a trivia answer. The fact that our tens of thousands of local governments in the United States have no status in the national Constitution has a defining significance in the legal and political relationship between state and local governments. State governments and the national government are constitutional sovereigns: both have legal status in the Constitution, and neither owes its existence to the other. For local governments, the situation is different—as far as the U.S. Constitution is concerned, they don't exist. For this reason, local governments often have been called "creatures of the state"—legally, they exist only as created under state laws or recognized in state constitutions.

Thus there is a kind of tension—one might even say a contradiction—between our cultural embrace of local self-government and our constitutional disavowal of local governments' existence. The relationship between state and local governments in the Untied States has evolved within the space defined by that tension. The story of that evolution includes the story of what is referred to as home rule—the extent to which local governments have control over their own structures (offices, elections) and can make and enforce decisions over local matters.

State Governments and the Creation of Local Authorities

State governments in the United States, like their colonial predecessors, granted charters of incorporation to local communities. Municipal governments (cities and towns) to this day in most states are formally identified as "municipal corporations." (In some places, you may see the words "Corporation Limit" or "Corp Limit" on signs marking the boundaries of cities or towns, even though our everyday language for these is "city limits.") Most cities and towns in the United States exist legally as local government corporations chartered by the state government.

Counties originated differently. State governments (outside of New England, where the system of townships had already come into existence during colonial days) recognized the need to distribute some public services and facilities throughout their territory. Courts were the most prominent examples, but also surveying of lands and recording of property titles and the construction and maintenance of early trails and roads. State governments therefore subdivided their territory and established county governments over these smaller units, usually with some consideration of placing these important services within attainable reach of residents.

Through much of the 1800s, the establishment and regulation of local governments became one of the largest components of state government activity. This was especially true in the interior sections of the country, away from the Atlantic seaboard. As states were created out of the Northwest Territory, Louisiana Purchase, and other acquisitions, the new state governments were busy establishing counties and chartering municipal corporations within their borders. Over the course of this period, state legislatures in particular became deeply involved in local affairs as they defined and redefined the structures and powers of municipalities and counties, occasionally subdivided counties as populations grew, and in some states experimented with new forms of local governments to specifically address matters such as schooling or drainage and flood control.

By the middle of the 1800s in the eastern half of the United States, a new tension in the relationship between state and local governments became evident—one that has persisted to the present day. On the one hand, state officials generally prefer to have control over local governments; a preference for power is an expected characteristic of people engaged in politics. On the other hand, state governments in the United States in the 1800s were still relatively small operations with few personnel, part-time legislatures, and limited capacity for collecting and archiving, let alone analyzing, information about the residents, resources, and economic activity within their borders. With rapid population growth in much of the United States fostering needs for continual invention and reinvention of local governments, supervising local affairs began to tax much of the time and attention of state officials.

In Indiana, for example, which became a state in 1816 and experienced rapid growth and a proliferation of new local governments (counties and municipalities) by the middle of the century, legislation about local topics became the dominant category of bills in the state legislature, the Indiana General Assembly. In the General Assembly's 1849 session, 91 percent of all bills dealt with local matters, and the vast majority of that was "special legislation," meaning bills that pertained to specific municipalities or counties.[1] Like the Indiana General Assembly, state legislatures throughout the country seemed to be consumed with local affairs.

This phenomenon of state governments spending so much of their time and effort on municipal and county issues illustrates the tension that operates within state governments in regard to their power over local governments. The desire for control runs into the limitations of capacity—that is, the ability of a state government to manage state-level concerns while trying to govern local-level matters too. Occasionally, that tension has risen to the point of triggering reform, as it did in Indiana after that 1849 legislative session—the next year, a state constitutional convention was called, and one of the principal motivations behind the revision of the Indiana constitution was to limit what many criticized as the General Assembly's interference in local issues. One delegate to the state constitutional convention rose "to declare that the primary purpose of this convention is 'to cut down this whole system of local legislation.'"[2] In Indiana and in other states, new state constitutions or amendments to existing constitutions barred state legislatures from passing laws that apply to only one community within the state or required that all state legislation apply uniformly across the state.

Most such reforms were directed at reducing state government activity in regard to local concerns. One might think restricting state interference is the same as enlarging the scope of local control, but that is not necessarily the case. Most nineteenth-century reforms that aimed at curtailing special legislation and limiting state power were not accompanied by broader grants of authority to local governments. That paradox involves another important dimension in the story of state–local relations in the United States—the importance and meaning of Dillon's Rule.

The National Legacy of an Iowa Judge

Two decisions of the Iowa Supreme Court in 1868, both authored by Judge John F. Dillon, articulated in forceful and memorable language the doctrine of state control over local governments (specifically, municipal corporations, i.e., cities and towns). Cities and towns may be some of the oldest forms of government in the United States, but from a legal standpoint, Judge Dillon wrote, they exist merely as entities that have been chartered by the state for state purposes:

> The true view is this: Municipal corporations owe their origins to and derive their power and rights wholly from the legislature. It breathes into them the breath without which they cannot exist. As it creates, so may it destroy. If it may destroy, it may abridge and control. Unless there is some constitutional limitation on the right, the legislature might, by a single act, if we can suppose it capable of so great a folly and so great a wrong, sweep from existence all of the municipal corporations in the State, and the corporations could not prevent it. We know of no limitations on this right so far as the corporations themselves are concerned. They are, so to phrase it, the mere tenants at will of the legislature.[3]

In light of their complete dependence on the state for their existence, cities and towns should be understood as having no powers of their own, only those powers given to them by the state. In the next case, Judge Dillon wrote that a

> municipal corporation possesses and can exercise the following powers and no others: First, those granted in express words; second, those necessarily implied or necessarily incident to the powers expressly granted; third, those absolutely essential to the accomplishment of the declared objects and purposes of the corporation—not simply convenient, but indispensable; fourth, any fair doubt as to the existence of a power is resolved by the courts against the corporation— against the existence of the powers.[4]

That statement came to be known as Dillon's Rule.

Although the two 1868 decisions came in cases about cities and towns, Dillon's Rule was understood and applied in other cases involving other forms of local government (counties, townships, etc.), so it became a broad rule covering local government in general, not just municipalities. Other state supreme courts quickly adopted the same approach to interpreting local government powers in their states. Furthermore, the influence of Judge Dillon's approach did not come solely from his writing of two Iowa Supreme Court decisions— he also wrote the first American legal treatise on local government law, *Commentaries on the Law of Municipal Corporations*, first published in 1872, with several further editions appearing throughout the remainder of his life. Judge Dillon's book repeated almost verbatim the language from the two 1868 Iowa cases and shaped a generation of lawyers' and judges' understanding of the relationship between local and state governments. Dillon's Rule became the general view of the extensive control of the states and the extremely limited powers of localities.

The Emergence of Home Rule
and Its Embrace by Progressive Reformers

Even as Dillon's Rule gained such widespread embrace, however, a contrary position emerged from another state court and another influential late nineteenth-century judge. In *People v. Hurlbut* (1871), Michigan Supreme Court Chief Justice Thomas M. Cooley articulated what he saw as a deeply embedded aspect of American history and culture, namely, that "local government is an absolute right, and the state cannot take it away." To Justice Cooley, an inherent characteristic of the nature of American law and liberty was the authority of communities to make their own governing decision, that is, to enjoy a degree of "home rule." Cooley's "home rule" position held sway in Michigan and a few other states during the late 1800s, despite the prevalence of Dillon's Rule in most states.

In 1875, for example, the Missouri constitution was amended to allow the City of St. Louis to write and adopt its own charter—in other words, to decide on its own form of government. Some other states followed Missouri's lead:

> The California constitutional convention of 1879 . . . proclaimed its efforts to create a "new system of local self-government," by explicitly recognizing the right of local self-government, subject to the terms of general laws, and extending to larger municipalities the authority to formulate home rule charters that were subject to approval or disapproval without amendment by the state legislature.[5]

Thus, at the turn of the twentieth century, the "home rule" idea of local government autonomy had emerged side by side with Dillon's Rule of local government dependency. Dillon's Rule was unmistakably more widely adopted, but it was not unopposed.

Other important trends of the period shaped the contrast and contest between these two approaches. First, it is no exaggeration to say that the size and complexity of cities exploded in the late 1800s in concert with industrialization and immigration. The problem of state governments' limited capacity to actively govern and manage local governments, mentioned earlier, became both more obvious and more problematic. Even though they may have wanted to maintain control and had Dillon's Rule on their side as they tried, state legislatures—still mostly part-time and meeting only every other year—could not keep up with the pace and scale of change at the local government level, especially with regard to cities. Executive agencies of most state governments at this time remained quite limited, and many state courts of the period struggled to stay on top of growing caseloads arising from the new challenges of urban economic, social, and political development. In the ongoing tension between state officials' generally unlimited desire to have control and their acutely limited capacity to actually exercise control, the turn of the twentieth century was one of the times in American politics when the latter appeared to have caught up with the former.

Second, state and local politics of the late 1800s were notoriously, almost flamboyantly, corrupt. Scandal infused everything from the buying of votes to the patronage systems of employment and the crony corruption of government contracts. Party bosses and political machines seemed to run state capitols, county courthouses, and city halls. On the one hand, for the growing number of Americans—especially the more educated and affluent—who began to organize and join reform clubs and movements, Dillon's Rule might have looked like an opportunity to use state government action to wrest control away from a local corrupt political fiefdom. On the other hand, state politics itself was often riddled with graft and incompetence, and political machines were often integrated at the state and local levels, so local reformers did not necessarily stand any better chance with state officials. Also, state legislatures throughout the United States were generally apportioned on the basis of geography (that is, legislators typically represented counties rather than a certain number of residents), so rural legislators substantially outnumbered urban ones and local government reform tended to be a lower priority for them.

The combination of state governments' limited ability to effectively govern local affairs that were growing continually more complex and the exposure of corruption in state as well as local governments created something of a window of opportunity for the reform advocates of greater local government independence—that is, of home rule. For the most part, reformers of the Progressive Era (late 1800s through early 1900s) made greater local autonomy part of their agenda. To these Progressives, state control of cities meant that people who knew little or nothing about cities held power over them. Most Progressives also embraced the idea of government services and functions being provided in a more efficient and professionalized manner; to them, it was difficult to imagine cities being run efficiently without the authority to set their own tax rates, decide what and where services were to be provided, and hire the best available personnel.[6]

Local home rule thus became a vital plank in the Progressive platform. The prominent Progressive reform organization the National Municipal League encouraged urban reformers to seek "home rule" charters from their state legislatures so that city governmental structures and electoral practices could be changed without state approval and cities could be governed with greater insulation from state politics.

In the early 1900s, two decisions from the U.S. Supreme Court made it clear that the campaign for home rule would have to be fought and won state by state. There would be no federal help. Some states followed Judge Cooley's doctrine of home rule, while most states followed Judge Dillon's rule of state control, and when the choice between those approaches made its way to the U.S. Supreme Court, Dillon's Rule prevailed. In *Hunter v. Pittsburgh* (1907), the Court majority wrote:

> The number, nature, and duration of the powers conferred upon these corporation and the territory over which they shall be exercised rests in the absolute discretion of the state. The state, therefore, may modify or withdraw all such

powers . . . expand or contract the territorial area, unite the whole or part of it with another municipality, repeal the charter and destroy the corporation. All this may be done . . . with or without the consent of the citizens, or even against their protest.

Later, in *Trenton v. New Jersey* (1923), the justices referred to a municipality as merely a "department" of the state, and declared, "In the absence of state constitutional provisions safeguarding it to them, municipalities have no inherent right of self-government." At least as far as the federal courts were concerned, Judge Cooley had it wrong and Judge Dillon had it right.

For the Progressive reformers, this meant that home rule would have to be gained and secured through state-level action. Since state legislatures generally were not inclined to willingly forfeit power over local governments, reforms in many states would require alternative routes such as state constitutional amendments or the initiative process (in states that allowed that option). Some constitutional revisions during the Progressive reform movement echoed the earlier effort to restrict state legislatures from enacting legislation that applied only to a specific locality or to a specifically designated situation (e.g., the conveyance of specific parcels of property), requiring them instead to formulate general legislation applicable to all localities in like circumstances. Other revisions were more emphatic, recognizing local governments' authority to make any policies or provide any services that were not forbidden by state or federal law, or to compose their own charters detailing their governmental structures and processes. Eventually, as urban and later suburban municipalities grained greater political influence within states—especially once state legislatures were reapportioned in the 1960s in ways that increased the number of urban and decreased the number of rural legislators—the alternative routes were not always needed, and local autonomy in some states was granted directly by legislative enactments.

The success of the home-rule movement was substantial but not universal. Many states adopted reforms in the 1900s that increased local autonomy and decreased state control. Although often promoted using the "home rule" name, those reforms came in many flavors and varieties.

Home Rule—for Whom, over What, and How Secure?

If you were to do a search for states that recognize home rule and states that still follow Dillon's Rule, you might find the results interesting. Counts of how many "home-rule states" and how many "Dillon's Rule states" there are can vary a lot. Why does such a seemingly straightforward question result in divergent answers? It turns out that states have adopted different types of local autonomy policies applying to varying categories of local governments and, as a result, a simple term such as *home rule* turns out to have multiple shades of meaning. What one researcher treats as a home-rule state another researcher may not, depending on what those researchers are looking for and counting. Here are some of the important differences that can affect those answers.

Home Rule for Whom?

There are approximately ninety thousand local governments in the United States, and the vast majority of them are *not* municipalities or counties. Most local governments in the United States are special-purpose districts such as school districts, sanitation districts, and airport authorities.

Some states have adopted policies that could be defined as home rule but only for cities. Others have recognized home rule for cities and towns. Some have extended home rule to counties as well. Special districts, which make up the majority of local governments, generally do not have any autonomy and have their structure, powers, responsibilities, finances, and so on determined by state legislation or regulations. Therefore, one of the things that varies from state to state is what proportion of their local governments have any kind of home-rule autonomy. As a researcher, would you count a state that recognizes home rule for *any* local governments as a home-rule state even if it is only for cities, or would you reserve the designation of home-rule state for those that grant home-rule autonomy to municipalities and counties? If you choose the latter, you will have fewer states in your home-rule category than if you choose the former, and if you look for states that allow home rule for most of their local governments, your tally will be zero.

Home Rule over What?

After the question of which local governments in a state have home-rule autonomy, the next question becomes what that state's definition of home rule is. Important distinctions can be made among structural, functional, and fiscal home rule.

The idea of local government charters was mentioned above. In states such as California where certain municipalities and counties can adopt their own charters, those localities have what we call structural home rule. For a municipality, for instance, having structural home rule (also referred to as charter authority) could mean being able to make choices such as whether to have a mayor-and-council or a council-and-manager or a commission form of city government, how many city council members or city commissioners to have, whether to have a mix of district-based and citywide ("at large") council members, and so on. Another way of thinking about structural home rule is that is confers on a local government some authority to have its own constitution.

By contrast, functional home rule does not mean being able to create your own local government structure, but it does mean having some autonomy over what public services to provide and how to do so. Functional home rule contrasts directly with Dillon's Rule in this sense: under Dillon's Rule, a local government has the authority to perform some function only if the state has granted that authority, while functional home rule means that a local government can perform a function unless there is a state or federal law that prohibits it. In terms of political power, this is a tremendous difference—you cannot do something unless the state says you can versus you can do anything the state doesn't say you can't.

As if things weren't getting confusing enough, functional home rule has an additional name. It is sometimes referred to as "devolution of authority." In a state that has a devolution-of-authority policy toward any of its local governments, the state recognizes that local government's right to take any action that is not forbidden rather than having to go to the state for a grant of authority first.

Fiscal autonomy for local governments is, at least potentially, a third category of local independence from state control. For local governments, fiscal autonomy would mean being able to determine how to generate revenue (for example, whether to impose a local income tax, sales tax, property tax, excise taxes, or various combinations of the above), spend its revenues, and issue debt obligations such as bonds. Although most local government officials would prefer to have greater control over these essential decisions, states have been more reluctant to grant fiscal autonomy than either the structural or functional kinds.

Although structural, functional (devolution of authority), and fiscal home rule are easy to distinguish, they are not opposites—a state could allow one or two or all three, and to greater or lesser degrees. You can see how this may contribute to the disparities between researchers' counts of which states have home rule and which ones do not. Whether you count a home-rule state as one that allows either structural home rule or functional home rule or only count states that allow both will lead you to substantially different numbers. If you define home-rule states as only those that allow all three forms, you are once again likely to come up with few or none.

How Secure Is Home Rule?

In home-rule states (however defined), it matters a great deal—at least to local government officials—whether and how easily home rule could be taken away. That brings us to another distinction, between constitutional home rule and statutory (or legislative) home rule.

In constitutional home-rule states, the state's grant of local government autonomy is written into the state constitution. In statutory home-rule states, local government autonomy has been established in a law passed by the state legislature and signed by the governor. The difference in the degree of security of home rule is fairly easy to see. If some grant of local government power has been made in an ordinary statute passed by the legislature, that grant could just as easily be repealed by an act of the legislature. The officials of a local government in that state would know that whatever authority and independence they have may be one legislative session away from disappearing.

When home-rule provisions are made part of a state's constitution, they cannot be taken back by the action of a simple majority in the state legislature. Restricting municipal autonomy in a constitutional home-rule state would require another amendment to the state constitution. Although this is possible, in most states it is a fairly long process. Having some kind of home-rule powers in a constitutional home-rule state is therefore a more secure position than having the same powers in a statutory home-rule state.

Mixing and Matching

Combinations of the characteristics described above vary from state to state, and there may be no two states in the United States with exactly the same mix. A state may provide some autonomy to one, several, or none of its types of local governments. That autonomy may be structural, functional, or fiscal, even a combination of structural for some, functional for others, and so on. Last but not least, those grants of autonomy, whatever they may be, may appear in the state's constitution or its statutes or both (some granted in the constitution and others in ordinary laws).

You should not assume that all this variety and complexity somehow makes the subject of home rule or the topic of state and local government authority unimportant. To the contrary, the existence and combination of local and state governments' power and control over where you live, work, or go to school matter a lot, and not only to state and local public officials. The next time you overhear or participate in a conversation about why your city or county or state seems to have plenty of funding for some services and facilities but not others, or why none of your local officials seems to be doing anything about some glaring problem, it is worth asking questions about who is allowed to do what in your state. Understanding these combinations of power and control can also strengthen your ability to recognize blame shifting and buck passing when you hear it—when state officials deflect questions by calling something a local problem or when local officials claim to be handcuffed by the state, they may be right, or they may just be counting on your not knowing the difference.

The Sovereign Strikes Back: Classifications, Preemptions, Mandates, and Takeovers

Home rule may come in many shapes and forms, but there is no mistaking that the home-rule movement (broadly speaking) made substantial progress in many states during the twentieth century, as we have noted already. Like many reform movements, the push for home rule attained just enough success to lose its momentum. By the late decades of the twentieth century, home rule seemed to many to be a victory already won rather than an ongoing fight.

As with the emergence of the home-rule movement at the beginning of the century, there were other trends in American society toward the end of the century that opened a window of opportunity for some retrenchment and retreat. First, many of the older, central cities that had boomed in the late 1800s were shrinking by the late 1900s and were surrounded by multiple suburban municipalities. Metropolitan areas made up of these aggregations of cities and suburbs had sprawled beyond county boundaries too. City governments, suburban governments, and county governments did not always see their interests and concerns as the same or even necessarily compatible. Also during the twentieth century, the number of special districts had proliferated, making the local government landscape everywhere more complex. It became more challenging for local government officials to make common cause against state control, not because they lost their desire for autonomy but because they found it harder to speak with a united voice within their state capitols.

Second, finances were an important factor. By the late 1900s, many older central cities were financially stressed by the combination of aging infrastructure, a smaller and less prosperous population, and diminished tax bases, while suburban and county governments tended to be better off as their populations and economies grew. Some local officials, especially those from inner cities, looked to the state and federal governments for financial help—the language of partnership, of "cooperative federalism," between those local governments and the larger state and federal jurisdictions gained new vigor—but other local governments with more stable financial circumstances retained their preference for autonomy. The share of local government expenditures that came from state and federal sources grew. Financial partnership between larger and smaller governments often has "strings" attached, conditions that receiving governments have to meet in order to satisfy the policy preferences of the governments providing the aid.

Third, changes in state governments expanded their capacity. During the last third of the twentieth century, more states shifted to longer or annual legislative sessions and increased the pay and staffing of their legislatures, and state agencies increased their personnel and expertise (to some extent as a consequence of federal aid). Having fallen behind the pace of development at the beginning of the century, state governments endeavored to catch up at least somewhat toward the end and thus had more ability to fund, regulate, and monitor the activities of local governments than they had before.

* Fourth and finally, some changes in the U.S. economy—the beginnings of what we now simply name globalization—weakened the ties of many businesses and some workers to their local communities. Especially in the 1970s and thereafter, business organizations made greater financial and organizational investments in their ability to effectively lobby at the state and national levels of government in the United States and, having become more accustomed to operating at nationwide and international scales, also became less tolerant of local variations in licensing, contracting, regulations, and taxes. The combination of enhanced ability to influence state and national policymakers and diminished attachment to local communities transformed some business organizations into advocates for greater uniformity of state and federal policy and therefore allies with various interests at the state level (including taxpayer groups) for restrictions on local authority.

These trends did not all advance evenly, at the same time, or to the same degree in every state, but they did nevertheless converge over the last decades of the 1900s to open a new window for the reassertion of state control over local governments. That reassertion has taken multiple forms.

The earliest form, which for the most part precedes the others, is the use of classifications of local governments. As noted earlier, the earliest and most common restrictions that reformers placed on state control over local governments were constitutional prohibitions on "special legislation," that is, state laws affecting only one jurisdiction (municipality, county, etc.) in the state. Even going back to the 1800s, these kinds of reforms often appeared as mandates that state legislation be "general" or "of uniform operation" throughout the state.

With the acceptance of state courts, legislators quickly determined that one way to meet the letter of the mandate was to establish systems of classification of local governments. The most familiar example has to do with cities being classified by population size, so that state law refers to "cities of the first class," "cities of the second class," and so on, with the distinctions between classes of cities tied to population thresholds. State laws might also recognize other municipal government classifications such as "towns" or "villages." Such classification schemes allow a state legislature to make a law that applies, for instance, to "all cities of the first class" or to "all towns," which the courts have accepted as being "general" legislation. By setting (and periodically adjusting) the population thresholds marking these classifications, state legislatures then regained some ability to legislate for specific localities, most commonly when the largest city in a state occupies the lone spot as a "city of the first class." The state can then make policies that apply to "all cities of the first class," meeting the constitutional mandate of general legislation while actually in effect targeting a single municipality. Somewhat more creative license is often required to navigate the "general legislation" mandate for counties, a challenge that state legislators have sometimes met and sometimes failed.[7]

More popular recently have been state restrictions on local control through the passage of preemption statutes.[8] This technique is especially suited to states that allow functional home rule, that is, those with "devolution of authority" language in their statutes or constitutions that grant certain local governments broad authority to make all policies or provide all services that are not prohibited by state law. A preemption statute typically carves out an area of local government authority by adding it to the list of things that are prohibited by state law for that set of local governments. Especially as some local governments in the United States have enacted what would be termed liberal or progressive ordinances such as higher minimum wage laws, bans on single-use plastic bags, or taxes on sweetened soft drinks, businesses and other allies have gone to their respective state legislatures to seek bans on local authority to adopt policies on those subjects. Local power to regulate rents, guns, cellular towers, satellite dishes, and much more has been curtailed through state adoption of preemption laws adding those topics to the list of state prohibitions. The American Legislative Exchange Council (ALEC), which focuses primarily on state legislation and policymaking and produces annual agendas of ALEC-crafted or ALEC-endorsed state legislation, has been especially prolific in championing preemption legislation to eliminate local governments' authority to make decisions ALEC and its members oppose.

In some ways, the opposite of preemption is the mandate. Instead of instructing a local government about what it may not do, a state mandate instructs the local government what it must do. State mandates directed toward municipalities and counties are somewhat less common than mandates directed toward other local governments, in large measure because municipalities and counties are more likely to be covered by functional home-rule policies. But, as mentioned earlier, state grants of local autonomy are rare to nonexistent for other local governments such as special districts. School districts in particular are ripe targets of state mandates, specifying everything from the minimum number of school days per year and what (i.e., how many hours) constitutes a legal school day, to teacher standards and qualifications, required subjects, and so on. The accumulation of state mandates has narrowed the scope of local school districts' authority throughout the United States.

Perhaps the ultimate exertion of state sovereignty over local governments is the takeover. State takeover of a local government may occur under provisions of a state law or constitutional provision setting some thresholds of financial or other local government performance. Usually there is some probationary status into which a local government is placed first upon failing to meet the state requirements, during which the local government may avert a state takeover if its performance rises back above the minimum. Otherwise, the legislature or the governor may direct a state agency, or state-appointed personnel, or a state-approved contractor, to replace the local government with respect to the public services or facilities at issue. While state takeovers of local governments in the United States have been most common with regard to public schools or school districts, by far the most visible and controversial have been state takeovers of municipal services such as occurred with the cities of Detroit and Flint in Michigan. In Flint, of course, the state personnel who displaced the municipal officials made the disastrous decision to replace the city's water source without needed corrosion treatments, resulting in the mobilization of lead in water pipes and the lead poisoning of Flint residents.

Conclusion: Power, Partnership, and Conflict

When it comes to local government power, state governments in the United States can give, and they can take away. In the absence of any protections of local home rule, the default position in the state–local relationship is that the state possesses all the authority and the local governments have only what the state allows them. This legal rule, which came to be known as Dillon's Rule, runs contrary to the rhetoric and expressed values of American political culture, which prizes local control or "home rule." The contradiction between this cultural preference and legal reality has generated a dynamic interaction between local activism in pursuit of greater autonomy and state assertion or reassertion of control.

At times in American political development when state government capacity to manage local affairs was limited or diminished, and when confidence in state government officials' integrity or competence was under substantial attack, the advocates of local government power have had some room to maneuver in pursuit of reforms. The emergence of this home-rule movement, as it came to be known (however accurately or inaccurately), was especially strong during the Progressive Era as Progressives tried to wrest control of governmental administration away from the political parties and machine politics in the name of efficiency and professionalization. At times, state policymakers assisted in these efforts to enact home-rule reforms, although more often they resisted.

Once the impetus behind the home-rule movement ebbed, and at a time when major cities needed more state and federal help, the political dynamic began to shift back toward restrictions on local autonomy. State governments rebuilt some of their capacity and reputation for governing, and a coalition of interest groups led primarily by business interests pushed back against certain kinds of local-level policymaking. The principal vehicle in the twenty-first century for this reassertion of state control and retrenchment of local autonomy has been preemption statutes, but preemption is certainly not the only tool in state officials' kit. As of this moment, the seeds of the next shift in the political tension between state and local government power are not yet visible, and Dillon's Rule has regained much of its stature as the prevailing doctrine of state–local relations.

CAREER PROFILE

Laura Meadows
Director
Carl Vinson Institute of Government, University of Georgia

The Carl Vinson Institute of Government (CVIOG) at the University of Georgia is known across the state for helping state agencies and local governments strengthen their capacities to service the public. "We promote excellence in government," explains Dr. Laura Meadows, the institute's director. "We are a part of the public service and outreach mission of the university that has a special charge to make a difference in the lives of all Georgians." CVIOG was established in 1927, and its programs help state and local government agencies enhance the efficiency and effectiveness of their work. This includes conducting training programs for new local elected officials, which is required by state law. Other programs serve government employees working in fields ranging from budgeting to code enforcement. The Certified Public Manager program provides a practical management curriculum to help government managers enhance their management skills. CVIOG also engages in applied research with individual local governments or state agencies, such as conducting an evaluation of a local government's employee classification and compensation plans. Other tasks include strategic planning, group facilitation, and fiscal and economic analysis. For example, CVIOG is one of two university units that analyze all new municipal incorporation proposals in Georgia considered by the legislature.

Meadows became the director of CVIOG in 2012 after serving in various government positions, including as commissioner of the Georgia Department of

Community Affairs. She holds an Ed.D. in higher education administration from the University of Georgia and an MPA from Brenau University. Faculty and staff at the institute come from a variety of fields, including law, public administration, and adult education. "Most people have government experience themselves," explains Meadows. Experience in the field helps CVIOG bridge the gap between the important organizational insights that emerge from research and the practical challenges faced by managers and policymakers in the field.

"People in the public administration field have to do a lot of things. They have got to be great listeners; they have got to

be able to think on their feet; they have got to be able to negotiate conflict." Meadows explains that the development of technical skills is important, but critical thinking and interpersonal skills are critical to advancing in public service careers. Developing both specialized knowledge and the ability to work broadly is important, explains Meadows. She encourages students to dig into the work of public service and explore what their personal interests will be. CVIOG facilitates this student exploration by supporting graduate assistants from the University of Georgia's MPA program and employing other student workers.

Interview: September 17, 2019

Discussion Questions

1. If you were a local government official, what types of home rule would you prefer and why? What about if you were a state government official?
2. Why does the federal government have little or nothing to do with the relationship between state and local governments in the United States? Do you think this is good or bad, and why?
3. Can you think of reasons why state government officials might favor home rule even though it means giving up some power? Can you think of reasons why local governmental officials might favor Dillon's Rule even though it limits what they can do?
4. In what ways might preemptions and mandates represent a return to Dillon's Rule, even in home-rule states?
5. Do you see Dillon's Rule as consistent or inconsistent with keeping government to a minimum in people's lives and why?

Notes

[1] Frank E. Horack, "Special Legislation: Another Twilight Zone Parts I and II." *Indiana Law Journal* 12, no. 2 (December 1936): 115.
[2] Ibid.
[3] *City of Clinton v. Cedar Rapids and Missouri River Railroad Co.* (1868).
[4] *Merriam v. Moody's Executors* (1868)
[5] Vincent Ostrom, Robert Bish, and Elinor Ostrom, *Local Government in the United States* (San Francisco, CA: ICS Press, 1988), 34.
[6] Dennis R. Judd, *The Politics of American Cities: Private Power and Public Policy*, 3rd ed. (Glenview, IL: Scott Foresman, 1988), 102.
[7] See, e.g., Jon Laramore, "Indiana Constitutional Developments," *Indiana Law Review* 37 (2004): 932–38.
[8] Lori Riverstone-Newell, "The Rise of State Preemption Laws in Response to Local Policy Innovation," *Publius: The Journal of Federalism* 47, no. 3 (Summer 2017): 403–25.

CHAPTER 4

Preemptions and Partisanship in America
Jaclyn Bunch, University of South Alabama

E arly in its history, the United States was primarily a dual federal system in which the federal government and state governments wielded the power regarding the rule of law. Over the last half a century, however, we have observed cities and counties pushing for increased autonomy from their states at an exponential rate. These demands for increased autonomy have resulted in conflicts between the state and local levels and has led to a trend of states passing "preemption laws" in order to maintain control. Preemption laws are "the use of state law to nullify a municipal ordinance or authority."[1] The state will pass a law either in advance of or in response to an ordinance passed by a city or county. This new preemption invalidates the city or county ordinance.

Throughout this chapter, we will be exploring some of the conflicts between state and local governments that occur in areas such as employment law, immigration law, and discrimination law. We will discuss situations in which states pass laws to preempt local ordinances as well as when cities and counties challenge a state law. Finally, we will also discuss the effect partisanship has in these areas. By addressing this emergent trend, we may better understand the nature of conflict and power between the local and state units within our federal system.

Federalism and the Rise of Local Autonomy

The American government has undergone a steady transformation,[2] moving from what was predominantly a two-part dual federal system, including the federal government and state government as key players, to an intergovernmental network that includes empowered localities and other "third" parties such as nongovernmental organizations (NGOs). This transformation has changed the landscape of the United States. Localities (units of government below the state, such as counties, cities, and townships) now play an intricate and important role in the American federal system. Spurred by growth and accelerating demand for public services, the last third of the twentieth century has brought about considerable social and economic change for localities.[3] Today, more than three thousand counties, nineteen thousand municipalities, sixteen thousand township governments, thirteen thousand school districts, and three thousand special districts[4] account for more than half of all government activity in the United States.[5] However, this was not always the case; instead, localities primarily served as the "arm" of the state government, whose main role was collecting taxes for the state. Since the 1980s, localities have increased service delivery exponentially and, as a result, have demanded additional levels of authority.[6] Localities now provide a myriad of governmental services, from simple roles such as trash collection to more complex institutional roles in education and health care. Moving from merely recipient governments, localities are now recognized as dominant players in intergovernmental networks.[7]

Due to this shift and the pressing demands of local governments, it is unsurprising that large-scale devolution has occurred throughout much of the United States. Devolution is the delegation of political authority from a higher level of government to a lower level. Given our current system's functionality, devolution is often thought to be a desirable feature embedded in our system of federalism.[8] The "devolution revolution" of the 1990s increasingly allowed for greater state flexibility and experimentation in the implementation of public policy and services. This trend often trickled down to the local level as a form of second-order devolution.[9] Thus, devolution has allowed local expertise and preferences to guide public policy and services—rather than implementing a one-size-fits-all solution on the state level. Despite this, some states have been reluctant to extend this same flexibility and experimentation to their localities.[10]

Advocates for good municipal government have argued that the institutional arrangements associated with devolution can produce smaller and more efficient local government than under traditional institutional means.[11] However, states continue to steer the policies and capabilities of local governments through the use of mandates and preemptions.[12] Preemption occurs when the law at a higher level of government is used to overrule authority at a lower level. State law can be used to preempt local ordinances, and federal law can be used to preempt state law.[13] Through much of American history, localities have pushed their state governments, demanding more authority and greater financial resources.[14] One of the most notable ways that localities have won additional authority and autonomy has been through the attainment of home rule. Home rule "refers to a state constitutional provision or legislative action that provides a city or county government with a greater measure of self-government,"[15] often via a state constitutional amendment or legislative action.

In the United States, home-rule status is not consistent across states and is even inconsistent within states. Some states make home rule available to selected local units, although generally counties and municipalities are the primary focus. For example, New Jersey and Ohio guarantee home rule within their constitution. Others, like Florida, Oregon, and South Dakota, allow counties or cities to adopt home rule via government charters.[16] Home rule provides a higher degree of autonomy over policy outputs to local governments and may serve to attenuate the pressures of state mandates and grounds to combat preemptions.[17] The most common form of home rule gives local governments the right to make decisions on local matters.[18] Other forms of home rule can grant fiscal or structural advantages, including the opportunity to enact local taxes or restructure local governments.[19] Thus, three potential types of processes delineate home-rule government. These include (1) the ability to pass self-governing legislation, (2) the ability to impose additional revenue generating activities, and (3) the ability to impose judicial jurisdictional authority.[20] For county governments, these expanded abilities could provide enumerated authority to better serve and meet the growing needs of a population.[21] Discretion permitted to a locality through home rule depends not only on state constitutions or laws but also on judicial interpretation of how legislators have chosen to implement it.[22] State court interpretations of local authority may vary widely due to this; however, the state constitution is the final authoritative source in interpretation.[23]

Despite the growth in authority and the prevalence of home rule throughout the United States, local power is not guaranteed. While home rule gives local governments the ability to enact local legislation, it does so only when it does not interfere with state government.[24] Home rule, especially as granted by constitutional provision, gives a locality power over certain policy domains; "if a state wants to reclaim power it must first show a conflict between state and local ordinances."[25] Through the use of preemptions, local power can be superseded regardless of home-rule status—thus, in this chapter, we turn our attention not to whether a state can take power but to when.

Conflicts of Power: The Federal Struggle

For the remainder of this chapter, we will focus on the struggle for power between state and local units of government. Recent literature has begun to question under what circumstances we observe increased use of preemptions to neutralize local ordinances. The typical argument put forth in the media suggests that political affiliation guides preemptive efforts. The expectation is that within the United States more conservative Republican governments are most likely to preempt more liberal Democratic localities.[26] Although understudied, academic research tends to support this hypothesis. Kogan contends that conflicts between state and local rule are a product of electoral politicking.[27] He asserts that liberal mayors in large localities may purposefully seek out and support policies that cause conflict with their state legislatures to boost their own reelection prospects. In a similar vein, Bulman-Pozen argues that partisan politics, aided by national interest groups, motivate preemptions; they find that Republican-controlled state legislatures seek to preempt the policymaking authority of democratically controlled city governments.[28] Literature has found the policy type itself can motivate the preemptions, with more liberal-leaning policies such as climate change policy,[29] oil and gas policy,[30] or LGBT+-related ordinances preempted frequently.[31]

However, it is not partisanship alone that determines the likelihood of preemptive action. Scholars have most recently argued that while preemption is more common based on Republican control of state government, legislative professionalism, political culture, and home-rule status also all play a role in whether or not preemptions will take place.[32] Perhaps the most thorough exploration of local preemptions to date was undertaken by Swanson and Barrilleaux, who construct an original data set of 404 local governments that had local ordinances challenged in state courts.[33] They find that local governments with citizen ideological preferences that differ from the state are less likely to have an ordinance preempted by the courts when the level of local autonomy given by the state is high—suggesting that while partisan divide between local and state government increases the likelihood of preemptions, the existence of home rule and other autonomy-granting institutions reduces the likelihood of it occurring. The likelihood of preemptions can go beyond institutional arrangements or partisanship. Einstein and Glick found that one reason for the increase in state preemptive efforts may come from a conflict in preferences between mayors and state officials; specifically, mayors report being unsatisfied with state regulations and funding, leading to conflict.[34] This only fuels the observed partisan divide, as urban centers are far more likely to elect Democrats, whereas a state at large may be more Republican. Thus, we are likely to observe Republican-dominated states exhibiting tension with urban centers over various policies and ordinances that go beyond the state status quo.

Despite the identification of other attenuating factors, a factor that appears to come up repeatedly is the existence of a partisan divide, whereby the local government is primarily made up of one political party while state government, either predominantly or wholly, is composed of the opposing party. Studies have suggested that the conservative dominance of state legislatures has provided the political opportunity to preempt or forestall progressive, often liberal-leaning local ordinances.[35] This trend is observable across numerous policy areas, including preventing minimum wage ordinances, preempting local nondiscriminatory policies such as LGBT rights ordinances, and environmental conflicts such as local fracking bans. Findings such as these lend credence to the argument that partisan division may be the primary cause of state preemptive actions. To explore the application of partisan conflict, this chapter will conclude by discussing three of the most common areas for partisan-driven preemptions in recent U.S. history: employment law, discrimination policy, and environmental issues.

A Closer Look: Employment Law

Employment law includes areas such as minimum wage, paid time off, and fair scheduling. These laws dictate what employers are and are not allowed to do to ensure fair treatment of employees. In this section, we will cover minimum wage and paid leave laws, as these are some of the most commonly relevant areas of employment law.

Minimum wage law refers to a state or federal imposed standard of payment, indicating what the minimum pay for an employee may be set to within a jurisdiction. This is a topic of interest for millions of employees across the United States. In 2009, the federal government passed a law that compelled states to increase their minimum wage to at least $7.25 per hour.[36] The intent of this federally required increase was to ensure that employees in the United States were paid a fair wage, relative to the cost of living. However, over a decade later, there have been no additional minimum wage increases by the federal government despite a steadily increasing cost of living. This has led to many city and county governments creating ordinances to increase the minimum wage, in many cases even above the minimum wage of the state they reside in.

These minimum wage increases have not gone unnoticed by state governments. As an increasing amount of local governments work to enact ordinances to increase the minimum wage, states have maneuvered to pass ordinances that block such local legislation. In cases where a local government previously had an ordinance in place, the state laws have sought to invalidate that local ordinance. Perhaps the most well-known example of a bill that preempted local government comes from North Carolina. The 2016 Public Facilities Privacy and Security Act, while best known for the controversy it created regarding bathroom use, also banned local municipalities from increasing the minimum wage within their borders. A second example can be seen in Iowa, which passed a state law in 2017 preempting cities and counties from raising the minimum wage.[37] At that time, Republican Representative John Landon stated, "Allowing cities and counties to set standards for employment matters and commerce creates an inconsistent playing field that hinders economic growth and business interests." Representative Landon was one of fifty-six Republican representatives in Iowa who voted in favor of the bill. The result of its passage was the nullification of existing minimum wage laws in Johnson, Linn, Polk, and Wapello Counties.[38] This stance on preemption is not unique to the minimum wage debate. As will be covered in the next section of this chapter, preemptions often take the form of "uniformity" or "business equality" bills—legislation with the stated intent and purpose of creating unified state measures, or measures that protect business interests. However, "uniformity" in this case hardly takes the form of reaffirming local legislation and raising state standards, but instead often nullifies local ordinances.

As of July 2019, twenty-five states have enacted statutes that prevent localities from raising the minimum wage.[39] In some cases, states are passing these laws in advance, to stop localities from even attempting to raise the minimum wage. In December 2016 the governor of Ohio signed legislation that blocked a special election planned to take place in 2017. The special election was intended to include a vote on whether to raise Cleveland's minimum wage to $15 per hour.[40] To date, twelve cities and counties in six states have approved local minimum wage increases only to have them invalidated by state statute. Of note, in Missouri a minimum wage preemption law was passed in 2015; however, an exemption was included to protect St. Louis's existing minimum wage ordinance. In 2017, an amendment was made to the preemption law that removed this protection.[41]

We can see that partisanship appears to have a strong relationship with successful passage of preemption laws. Figures 4.1 through 4.3 show the political affiliation of the state governor and state legislature when a minimum wage preemption law was passed. In the majority of cases, the state-level government

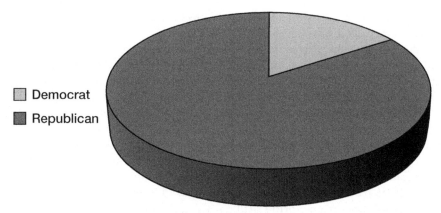

Figure 4.1 State Governor Political Affiliation When Minimum Wage Preemption Law Passed

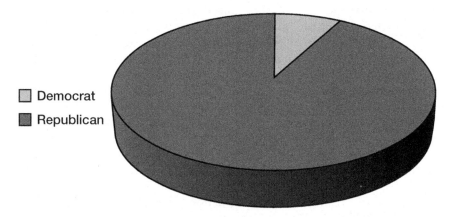

Figure 4.2 State House Political Affiliation When Minimum Wage Preemption Law Passed

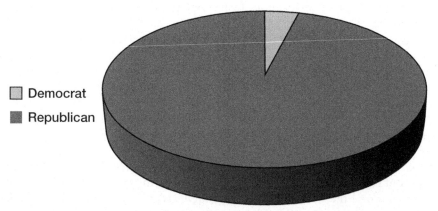

Figure 4.3 State Senate Political Affiliation When Minimum Wage Preemption Law Passed

was predominantly Republican, with cities and counties often being liberally led.

Based on these three figures, we observe that when a state preemption law was passed, the state governor and legislature were Republican in nearly every case. In the future, we may see some of the established preemption laws struck down. As of 2019, bills have been introduced in at least eleven states to repeal past minimum wage preemption laws. Colorado has already repealed an existing law prohibiting localities from raising the minimum wage.[42]

Another area of employment law in which preemptions are common is paid leave. Currently, there is not a federal paid sick leave requirement. This means that if the state, city, or county has no paid sick leave requirement, an employer is not required to provide paid sick leave time to employees. Since 2011, twenty-two states have passed laws that prevent cities and counties from requiring local employers to offer paid sick leave. In many cases, these state laws preempt ordinances passed by cities and counties, invalidating existing or preventing the creation of new laws that provide paid leave. One example of where preemption occurred was in Arkansas. The *Arkansas Times*, in an article regarding employment law preemptions, acknowledged the tendency for the red state to regularly preempt: "Arkansas is among the leaders in state preemption laws . . . a state that preempts any local regulation of firearms and is attempting under court challenge to preempt protection of civil rights laws for LGBT people."[43]

Similar partisan division can be found in the case of paid leave laws. Figures 4.4 through 4.6 show the political affiliation of the state governor and state legislature when a paid leave preemption law was passed.

Like minimum wage, we observe that these preemption laws are usually passed when a Republican governor and state legislature are present, although in some cases a Democratic governor or state legislature are present. Of note, when the governor and state legislature were Democratic, the preemption law that was passed also required employers statewide to provide paid sick leave while prohibiting cities/counties from establishing their own paid sick leave

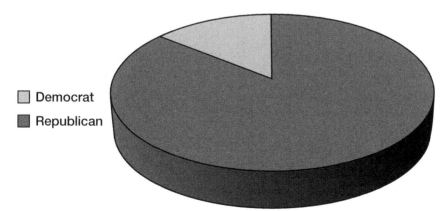

Figure 4.4 State Governor Political Affiliation When Paid Leave Preemption Law Passed

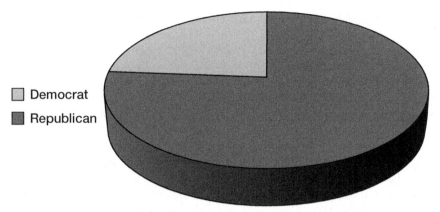

Figure 4.5 State House Political Affiliation When Paid Leave Preemption Law Passed

laws.[44] In these cases, the state law "preempted" local legislation but upheld the initiative and often expanded it statewide. Using the examples of minimum wage and paid leave, we see that preemptions regularly occur between the state and local levels. We also observe that partisanship plays a significant role, not only in when a preemption law is passed but in what the effects of that law are on the local governments. Employment law will likely remain a highly salient area of concern, and therefore it is likely that in the future more laws and ordinances will be proposed, passed, and possibly preempted.

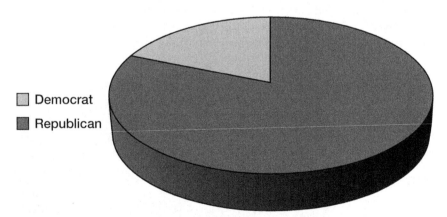

Figure 4.6 State Senate Political Affiliation When Paid Leave Preemption Law Passed

A Closer Look: Discrimination Policy

One area in which there has been a great deal of local innovation and passage of local measures is discrimination policy. Over the last decade, the United States has seen a rise in antidiscrimination policies across all levels of government. Historically, discrimination policy has been dominated by federal and state statutes, but the topics of gender and gender identity have sparked policy movement on the local level. As of 2019, at least 225 cities and counties have passed ordinances prohibiting "gender identity" discrimination in employment.[45] Local governments are taking the lead in policy innovation, leaving states to react to these developments; states are often moving to counteract these ordinances, by enacted preemptions that allow discrimination based on religious beliefs. For example, Arkansas and Tennessee both have similar preemption laws explicitly banning cities from passing local antidiscrimination regulations protecting LGBTQ individuals.[46]

Given the recent surge in these local ordinances and the lack of previous state innovation on this topic, discrimination policies pertaining to gender identity provide a perfect case study to understand the preemption process in the United States. The recent wave in proposed and passed preemptions typically takes three forms. The first we can classify as "expansion" or "uniformity" bills. The stated goals of such legislation is to prohibit local governments from passing laws that extend beyond or "expand" rights and privileges over that which is provided for in the state statute or constitutional provision. Oftentimes the preemptions are framed as uniformity measures, evoking the argument that businesses should be treated equally across all jurisdictions and not subject to differing discrimination ordinances in different localities.

The second form largely observed is "business discrimination" bills that permit forms of discrimination made by a business in specific manners. These include a range of legislation, such as Mississippi's Religious Liberty Accommodations Act HB 1523, which expressly allows businesses and public employees to discriminate against LGBT+ individuals in the protection of their religious beliefs.[47] Another similar law included under this category is the Tennessee Unemployment Compensation Bill of 2015, which prevents government agencies from examining a business's antidiscrimination policies when deciding whether to hire that business for a taxpayer-funded contract. Often these bills are presented to the public as better business legislation or coupled together with other statutes that also preempt local authority in another manner.

The final group of preemptive legislation covers the media-dubbed "bathroom bills." On the local level, these ordinances primarily allowed for individuals to utilize public restrooms in accordance with the gender they identify with or have transitioned to. State preemption largely overturns this measure, prohibiting local ordinances that permit access to bathrooms on the basis of gender identity. Perhaps one of the most well-known bathroom bills is North Carolina's Public Facilities Privacy and Security Act (HB 2) of 2016. The bill amended state law to preempt any antidiscrimination ordinances passed by localities and compelled public facilities to only permit bathroom entrance based on gender assigned at birth. Interestingly, the bill also preempted other local ordinances by giving the state exclusive rights to determine the minimum wage. The bathroom bill received widespread criticism both within and outside of the state, as the bill prevented transgender people who did not or could not alter their birth certificates from using the restroom consistent with their presently assigned gender. The prohibition of local antidiscrimination protections was widely criticized, as there were no state-level protections for sexual orientation or gender identity. Ultimately, after a change in executive office, Governor Cooper signed HB 142, which repealed HB 2 but imposed a three-year moratorium on local nondiscrimination ordinances and prohibited ordinances related to bathroom access. While this bill overturned a preemption, it did not revert the state entirely to its previous condition. Rather, the bill preempted local efforts for a fixed amount of time while the moratorium was in place. A collection of these proposed and often passed preemptions can be found below in table 4.1.

Given the nature of the policy movement, it is unsurprising that the partisan divide is so evident. In nearly every case study of preemptions that permit some form of discrimination, the prevailing partisan theology of the state has been Republican. Nearly every governor at the time of proposed preemption identified as Republican. There do exist a few exceptions, and in each case, the proposed preemption failed to become law. For instance, one notable exception is the case of HB 2782 of Washington, whose governor was Jay Inslee, a Democrat. Not only did the bill fail to reach his pen for veto, but by April 2017 Governor Inslee penned a memo instituting a travel ban prohibiting nonessential state-funded travel to North Carolina, citing the North Carolina bathroom bill as discriminatory. Governments with split partisan dominance, either in the legislature or across the legislative and executive branches, appear to be far less likely to pass or even present preemptive proposals regarding the LGBT+ community. It is also largely the case that proposed preemptions adversely affect Democratic-led localities. Take, for example, the Texas bathroom bill SB 6, which failed to pass in 2017.[48] The bill was largely a reactionary measure responding to local ordinances passed in Austin, Dallas, Fort Worth, Plano, Rockwall, and San Antonio, the mayors of which were all Democrats at the time except for Rockwall (Republican) and San Antonio (Independent). There are cases in which both the state and the locality are Republican led, such as local ordinance 5871 of Fayetteville, Arkansas; however, these are few and far between and often follow a judicial order rather than a proposed legislative reactive measure. In the Fayetteville case, the city had passed an ordinance in 2015 that barred discrimination on the basis of either sexual orientation or gender identity. However, by 2017, the local law was challenged, and the Arkansas Supreme Court overruled it, citing that it expanded protected classes beyond state law.[49]

By and large, in the case of LGBT+ policy and preemption actions, there appears to be a local movement to expand protections and statewide movement to limit those expansions. Localities as innovators have led to reactionary movements on the state level. For discrimination policy regarding the LGBT+ community, these movements appear to be partisan driven, with largely

TABLE 4.1   Preemption Legislative Proposal Examples

State	Proposed Legislation/Year	Party Affiliations	Purpose of Bill	Type
Arkansas	Intrastate Commerce Improvement Act, SB 202 (2015)	Governor: Republican Legislature: Split	Prohibits localities from passing nondiscrimination laws that are more expansive than the state's	Expansion or Uniformity
Florida	Preemption of local government regulations, HB 3 (2019)	Governor: Republican Legislature: Republican	Prohibit localities from imposing and adopting new regulations on businesses	Expansion or Uniformity
Texas	HB 2899 (2017)	Governor: Republican Legislature: Republican	Prohibit localities from passing nondiscrimination laws	Expansion or Uniformity
Tennessee	Equal Access to Intrastate Commerce Act (2011)	Governor: Republican Legislature: Republican	Prohibits localities from passing nondiscrimination laws that are more expansive than the state's	Expansion or Uniformity
Texas	Intrastate Commerce Improvement Act, HB 4097 (2017)	Governor: Republican Legislature: Republican	Prohibits localities from passing nondiscrimination laws that are more expansive than the state's or adopting new regulations on businesses	Expansion or Uniformity

(continued)

TABLE 4.1 *(continued)*

State	Proposed Legislation/Year	Party Affiliations	Purpose of Bill	Type
West Virginia	Local Government Labor and Consumer Marketing Regulatory Limitation Act (2019)	Governor: Republican Legislature: Republican	Prohibits localities from passing requirements regulating certain areas of the employer-employee relationship and the sale or marketing of consumer merchandise	Expansion or Uniformity
Arkansas	Upheld Act 137 (2015)	Governor: Republican Legislature: Republican	The Arkansas Supreme Court struck down Ordinance 5871, a 2015 Fayetteville ordinance barring discrimination on the basis of sexual orientation or gender identity.	Expansion or Uniformity
Florida	Preemption of Local Regulations (2019)	Governor: Republican Legislature: Republican	Prohibits localities from imposing and adopting new regulations on businesses	Expansion or Uniformity
Tennessee	Unemployment Compensation (2019)	Governor: Republican Legislature: Republican	Prevents government agencies from examining a business's antidiscrimination policies when deciding whether to hire that business for a taxpayer-funded contract	Business Discrimination
Mississippi	Religious Liberty Accommodations Act, HB 1523 (2015/2016)	Governor: Republican Legislature: Republican	Permits private associations to choose to provide or withhold services discriminatorily in accordance with the three "deeply held religious beliefs or moral convictions" specifically outlined in the bill	Business Discrimination

State	Bill	Government	Description	Category
Florida	Preemption of Conditions of Employment (2019)	Governor: Republican Legislature: Republican	Prohibits localities from regulating businesses conditions of employment by an employer	Business Discrimination
Texas	Bathroom Bill, SB 6 (2017)	Governor: Republican Legislator: Republican	Prohibits local ordinances requiring access to bathrooms on the basis of gender identity	Bathroom Bill
North Carolina	Public Facilities Privacy and Security Act, HB 2 (2016)	Governor: Republican Legislator: Republican	Prohibits local ordinances requiring access to bathrooms on the basis of gender identity	Bathroom Bill
Tennessee	Students in Public Schools (2017)	Governor: Republican Legislature: Republican	Requires "that a student use student restroom and locker room facilities that are assigned for use by persons of the same sex as the sex indicated on the student's original birth certificate"	Bathroom Bill
Washington	Concerning the Use of Facilities Segregated by Gender (2016)	Governor: Democrat Legislature: Split	Prohibits local ordinances requiring access to bathrooms on the basis of gender identity	Bathroom Bill

Republican-dominated states and Democratic-led localities. In states where there has been Democratic state dominance, the policies have largely been LGBT+ friendly and do not overturn local-led legislation. One example of this is Illinois, which expanded its Human Rights Act with an amendment, signed by Democratic Governor Rod Blagojevich, that prohibits discrimination on the basis of an individual's sexual orientation. Prior to this state-level expansion, a number of localities already prohibited discrimination based on sexual orientation. The amended act, in this case, did not preempt but rather expanded protections to all cities and counties statewide. Furthermore, Illinois was not alone, with fourteen other states at the time prohibiting discrimination based on sexual orientation statewide. In most of these instances, the state served as the first mover, with little to no local ordinances to preempt.

By surveying the existing cases of state preemption regarding LGBT+ policies, we can see that partisanship seems to play a major role in the likelihood of preemptive action. In nearly all cases in which localities were preempted, the state government largely consisted of a unified or majority Republican presence. Conversely, the localities that passed local ordinances that were preempted tended to favor liberal or Democratic governance. The partisan conflict appears to be a driving force behind preemption in the United States.

A Closer Look: Environmental Policy

State preemption of environmental law is a relatively recent phenomenon.[50] In recent years local governments have taken a lead in the proposal and execution of many environmental policies across the United States. Since a large number of environmental issues are "place specific," localities tend to be more knowledgeable on issues as well as aware of the needs of local citizens in that area, leading decentralists to argue that local policies should handle these issues. However, arguments for centralization to the state or federal government exist, such as the increased capacity of the larger forms of government. It is often the case that states create or impose expressed preemption by establishing minimum air, waste, and other standards that preempt local laws. Implied preemptions such as these are typically used in courts to rule in the states.[51]

Perhaps one of the most notable hotbeds for environmental policy preemptions surrounds the issue of fracking. Fracking is the process of drilling into the earth before a high-pressure mixture of water and chemicals is directed at shale rock deposits in order to release the gas inside. Along with the rise in the extensive use of fracking in the United States has come a host of environmental concerns. Fracking uses enormous amounts of water, which must be transported to the site of drilling at significant environmental costs. Opponents also charge that the process itself may cause earth tremors and argue that potentially carcinogenic chemicals may escape during drilling and contaminate groundwater around the fracking site.[52] Numerous local governments throughout the United States have attempted to enact local ordinances to prevent fracking within their jurisdictions, citing fears of water table contamination or environmental disruption.

Since 2016, there have been two major instances of state–local conflict that have risen to national attention. Each time the local government has moved to prevent fracking in its jurisdiction. In each of these cases, the state courts have ruled or remanded in favor of the state regulation and fracking was permitted.[53] While these contentions were not merely partisan in nature, they fall in line with the typical partisan divisions of "big business versus environment." One of the first instances of state fracking preemption occurred in Colorado. In 2016, the Colorado Supreme Court struck down a five-year moratorium on fracking in Fort Collins and a fracking ban in Longmont in May 2016.[54] The court ruled that the cities' fracking regulations were unenforceable because the state has an interest in creating uniform regulations. Attorneys for the cities had argued that the state's constitution includes an inalienable rights provision under which citizens' rights preempt state law. Energy companies' representatives argued that state officials should have the ability to mediate disputes between local officials and fracking operators without the complications of local regulations. Ultimately, the governor of Colorado came out in favor of fracking, his website stating that "Governor Hickenlooper recognizes that fracking provides thousands of jobs, more than one billion dollars in tax revenue, and clean energy to Colorado." As observed with other preemption policy disputes, the theme of uniformity and expansion continues here. In the case of most home-rule jurisdictions, localities have the right to innovate and create new ordinances to govern their jurisdiction, but that power is limited in that it must not conflict with existing state statute or constitutional provision. In cases such as Colorado's fracking or LBGT+ policies covered in this chapter, preemption occurs not when there is a conflict with the existing statute but when ordinances expand beyond. When a local ordinance expands protections or regulations above that of the state, the state's primary mode of response is to preempt through state law to cause a conflict or challenge in court as a form of preemption.

A similar dispute occurred in Louisiana that same year. In June 2016, the Louisiana Supreme Court voted 4–3 against hearing an appeal of the district and circuit court rulings upholding the issuance of a state drilling permit to the company Helis Oil & Gas.[55] St. Tammany Parish had attempted to use zoning ordinances to block the Helis project. The lower courts found that the parish's ordinances were preempted by state oil and gas regulations. St. Tammany Parish filed suit against the Helis project in June 2014 due to concerns that it would pollute the area's water supply and adversely affect property values. The case study is yet another example of when preemption will occur—when local ordinance conflicts with existing state statute or when local ordinance expands beyond statute, causing states to act. While not as clearly partisan driven as policies such as the antidiscrimination and employment laws covered in this chapter, issues of environment tend to follow the same formula. Local governments seek to extend protections but are preempted by state regulations or state priorities, in this case through judicial interpretation.

Conclusion

Over the past three decades, localities have pushed for increased autonomy from their parent state or federal government. While we have looked at employment law, discrimination, and environmental policy, these are hardly the only areas in which federal, state, and local governments attempt to exert authority. The trend of localities attempting to exert their influence is likely to continue as they offer additional public services to their constituents. Unsurprisingly, the data shows that the passage of laws that preempt local governments are increasing as well. This struggle between federal, state, and local governments is unlikely to end as each level of government seeks to protect its sovereignty. In the case of state and local relations, the fight for authority is more tenuous. Localities largely exist at the leisure of the state, as they have no pre-prescribed rights in the U.S. Constitution and thus are only given rights via state statute or constitutional amendment. While there has been a great deal of authority granted to localities, especially in the form of home rule, this power does not extend to cases where local ordinances conflict with state law. As seen throughout the chapter, conflicts of these nature lead to either preemptive laws that induce conflict to nullify the local ordinance or in some instances resolution through the court system so that an interpretation can be made on where governmental powers lie.

A predominant theme we observed across the issues examined is the role of partisanship in state and local conflict. In nearly all the examples we examined, partisanship appears to play an important role in the likelihood of preemption laws, but also in how preemption laws were implemented. For example, in the case of minimum wage, the data shows that when preemption laws are passed to block cities and counties from raising the minimum wage above that of the state, a Republican governor and state legislature are present. Another example can be seen when examining paid leave laws. In these cases, there are both Republican and Democratic governors and state legislatures in place when these preemption laws are passed. However, the data shows the difference is that when the governor and state legislature are Democratic, the preemption law that is passed also required employers statewide to provide paid leave.[56] This trend is also observed in the case of LBGT+ discrimination policy. For nearly every preemption, the local legislation came from a Democratic-led locality within a Republican-dominated state. In the rare case where states had been majority Democratic, the policies have largely been LGBT+ friendly and do not overturn local-led legislation and perhaps expand them, such as in Illinois, which expanded its Human Rights Act with an amendment.[57]

The recent surge in preemptive state action likely has a myriad of causes, but it is difficult to turn a blind eye to the role of partisanship. Conflict in governance appears to be notably prevalent since the turn of the twenty-first century. In the case of the United States, this may largely be because many of the locally driven policies lean liberal. In this chapter, we discussed local-level innovation for typically Democratic-dominated topics such as the environment and discrimination laws. While local innovation for more conservative-leaning policies does exist, it simply does not reach the salience levels observed with the liberal-leaning laws, and perhaps the lack of attention given to these movements in part explains why the partisan plight appears one directional.

CAREER PROFILE

Emanuel "Chris" Welch
Partner, Ancel Glink
State Representative, Seventh District, Illinois General Assembly

State constitutions and statutes provide a foundation for understanding state–local relations. Because of this, attorneys play an important role helping local governments understand state law or litigate when conflicts emerge. Emanuel "Chris" Welch is a partner with Ancel Glink, an Illinois law firm that is well known for its expertise in municipal law. Welch also serves in the state legislature, representing the seventh district, which includes parts of several suburban communities west of Chicago. Working in a law firm that specializes in serving local government provides a variety of work, explains Welch, ranging from human resource and collective bargaining issues to litigation when local governments are sued. Helping local governments understand their authority under the Illinois home-rule statutes is another important task.

Welch completed an undergraduate degree at Northwestern University and a J.D. at the University of Illinois at Chicago's John Marshall Law School. He also worked as a weekend assignment editor at WGN news, an experience that

Welch credits with helping him better understand policy issues facing the community. He bought a home in his hometown and ran for the school board, where he served for three terms before running for the state legislature. Welch credits his law experience and work for local government clients as assets that prompted others to encourage him to run for state office.

How can students prepare for a career in municipal law? "Keep your head down and work hard. Don't be afraid to do a bunch of different things because those experiences all matter," advises Welch. Also, read as much as possible and go to local meetings to understand what is going on in your own community. Finally, be aware that changes in the economy and state political environment will impact the specific issues faced by local government at any given time. Welch points to recent budget challenges in Illinois and explains these state-level challenges impact communities and the issues faced by firms working in municipal law.

Interview: September 5, 2019

Discussion Questions

1. What are preemptions, and what are the most likely causes of them? Are certain policy areas more prone to preemptions? Why or why not?
2. What role does home rule play in the face of preemptions?
3. Can you think of an example where the state may not wish to preempt local legislation? Why do you think that is the case?

Notes

[1] Nicole Dupuis, Trevor Langan, Christiana Mcfarland, Angelina Panettieri, and Brooks Rainwater, "City Rights in an Era of Preemption: A State-by-State Analysis; 2018 Update," National League of Cities, February 2018, 4, https://nlc.org/sites/default/files/2017-03/NLC-SML Preemption Report 2017-pages.pdf.

[2] Donald F. Kettl, "The Transformation of Governance: Globalization, Devolution, and the Role of Government." *Public Administration Review* 60, no. 6 (2000): 488–97, https://doi.org/10.1111/0033-3352.00112.

[3] Paul Peterson, *The Price of Federalism* (Washington, DC: Brookings Institution, 1995).

[4] David R. Berman, *Local Government and the States: Autonomy, Politics and Policy.* (Armonk, NY: M.E Sharpe, 2003), 12.

[5] G. Ross Stephens and Nelson Wikstrom, *American Intergovernmental Relations: A Fragmented American Polity* (Oxford: Oxford University Press, 2007).

[6] Edwin J. Benton and Platon N. Rigos, "Patterns of Metropolitan Service Dominance: Central City and Central County Service Roles Compares," *Urban Affairs Review* 20, no. 3 (1985): 285–302.

[7] Robert Agranoff and Michael McGuire, *Collaborative Public Management: New Strategies for Local Governments* (Washington, DC: Georgetown University Press, 2003).

[8] Jeffrey Swanson and Charles Barrileaux, "State Government Preemption of Local Government Decisions through the State Courts," *Urban Affairs Review* 56, no. 2 (March 2020): 671–97.

[9] Amanda Sheely, "Devolution and Welfare Reform: Re-evaluating 'Success,'" *Social Work* 57, no. 4 (2012): 321–31.

[10] Jon Russell and Aaron Bostrom, "Federalism, Dillon Rule, and Home Rule," ACCE White Paper, January 2016, https://www.alec.org/app/uploads/2016/01/2016-ACCE-White-Paper-Dillon-House-Rule-Final.pdf.

[11] Michael Craw, "Taming the Local Leviathan: Institutional and Economic Constraints on Municipal Budgets," *Urban Affairs Review* 43, no. 5 (2008): 663–90.

[12] Jaclyn Bunch, "Does Local Autonomy Enhance Representation? The Influence of Home Rule on County Expenditures," *State and Local Government Review* 46, no. 2 (2014): 106–17.

[13] DuPuis et al., "City Rights in an Era of Preemption."

[14] Berman, *Local Government and the States.*

[15] Jesse J. Richardson Jr, Meghan Zimmerman Gough, and Robert Puentes, "Is Home Rule the Answer? Clarifying the Influence of Dillon's Rule on Growth Management," Brookings, January 1 2003, https://www.brookings.edu/research/is-home-rule-the-answer-clarifying-the-influence-of-dillons-rule-on-growth-management/.

[16] Stephens and Wikstrom, *American Intergovernmental Relations.*

[17] Garrick L Percival, Martin Johnson, and Max Neiman, "Representation and Local Policy: Relating County-Level Public Opinion to Policy Outputs," *Political Research Quarterly* 62, no. 1 (March 2009): 164–77.

[18] Berman, *Local Government and the States.*

[19] Frank P. Sherwood, *County Governments in Florida: First in a Series on Local Government* (New York: iUniverse, 2008).

[20] Ibid.

[21] Bunch, "Does Local Autonomy Enhance Representation?"

22 Berman, *Local Government and the States.*
23 Jesse J. Richardson Jr., "Dilon's Rule Is from Mars, Home Rule Is from Venus: Local Government Autonomy and the Rules of Statutory Constructions," *Publius: The Journal of Federalism* 41, no. 4 (October 2011): 662–85.
24 Russell and Bostrom, "Federalism, Dillon Rule and Home."
25 Jaclyn Bunch, "Give and Take: The Case of Home Rule Infringements in the United States," *PS: Political Science & Politics* 51, no. 1 (2018): 31–32.
26 David Graham, "How St. Louis Workers Won and Then Lost a Minimum-Wage Hike," *Atlantic*, August 29, 2017, https://www.theatlantic.com/business/archive/2017/08/st-louis-minimum-wage-preemption/538182/.
27 Vladimir Kogan, "Means, Motives and Opportunities in the New Preemptions Wars," *PS: Politic Science & Politics* 51, no. 1 (2018): 28–31.
28 Jessica Bulman-Pozen, "State-Local Preemption: Parties, Interest Groups, and Overlapping Government," *PS: Political Science & Politics* 51, no. 1 (2018): 28–29.
29 Dorothy M. Daley, "Climate Change and State and Local Covernments: Multiple Dimensions of Intergovernmental Conflict," *PS: Political Science and Politics* 51, no. 1 (2018): 33–34.
30 Jonathan M. Fisk, "Boom and Bust Federalism: Intergovernmental Politics during the Shale Renaissance," *PS: Political Science & Politics* 51, no. 1 (2018): 34–35.
31 Jami K. Taylor, Donald P. Haider-Markel, and Daniel C. Lewis, "Tensions over Gay and Transgender Rights between Localities and States," *PS: Political Science & Politics* 51, no. 1 (2018): 35–37.
32 Luke Fowler and Stephaniee L. Witt, "State Preemption of Local Authority: Explaining Patterns of State Adoption of Preemption Measures," *Publius: The Journal of Federalism* 49, no. 3 (2019): 540–59.
33 Swanson and Barrilleaux, "State Government Preemption."
34 Katherine L. Einstein and David Glick, "Cities in American Federalism: Evidence on State–Local Government Conflict from a Survey of Mayors," *Publius: The Journal of Federalism* 47, no. 4 (2017): 599–621.
35 Lori Riverstone-Newell, "The Rise of State Preemption Laws in Response to Local Policy Innovation," *Publius: The Journal of Federalism* 47, no. 3 (2017): 403–25.
36 Kai Filion, "Fact Sheet for 2009 Minimum Wage Increase—Minimum Wage Issue Guide," Economic Policy Institute, July 20, 2009, https://www.epi.org/publication/mwig_fact_sheet/.
37 Andy Mitchell, "Johnson County's Symbolic Minimum Wage to Increase in July," *Daily Iowan*, April 10, 2019, https://dailyiowan.com/2019/04/10/johnson-countys-symbolic-minimum-wage-to-increase-in-july/.
38 Ibid.
39 Jared Bernstein, "Cities Would Like to Raise Their Minimum Wages, Too, but States Keep Blocking Them," *Washington Post*, July 18, 2019, https://www.washingtonpost.com/outlook/2019/07/18/cities-would-like-raise-their-minimum-wages-too-states-keep-blocking-them/?noredirect=on.
40 Jermery Pelzer, "Gov. John Kasich Signs Bill Blocking Cleveland's $15 Minimum Wage Proposal," Cleveland.com, December 19, 2016, https://perma.cc/G9MK-25TN.
41 Laura Huizar and Yannet Lathrop, "How Workers Have Lost Billions in Wages and How We Can Restore Local Democracy," National Employment Law Project, July 3, 2019, https://www.nelp.org/publication/fighting-wage-preemption/.
42 National Employment Law Project, "Colorado Legislature Approves Landmark Bill to Repeal Preemption of Local Minimum Wage Laws," news release, May 16, 2019, https://www.nelp.org/news-releases/colorado-legislature-approves-landmark-bill-repeal-preemption-local-minimum-wage-laws/.
43 Max Brantley, "Arkansas a Leader in Laws against Better Working Conditions," *Arkansas Times*, November 19, 2017, https://arktimes.com/arkansas-blog/2017/11/19/arkansas-a-leader-in-laws-against-better-working-conditions.
44 William Hayden and Benjamin Nucci, "Federal Preemption of State and Local Paid Sick Leave Laws," JD Supra, August 3, 2018, https://www.jdsupra.com/legalnews/federal-preemption-of-state-and-local-76797/.

45 Human Rights Campaign, "Cities and Counties with Non-discrimination Ordinances That Include Gender Identity," January 28, 2018, https://www.hrc.org/resources/cities-and -counties-with-non-discrimination-ordinances-that-include-gender.

46 See, for example, State of Arkansas, Senate Bill 202, Act 137, 90th General Assembly, Regular Session 2015, http://www.arkleg.state.ar.us/assembly/2015/2015R/Acts/Act137.pdf.

47 Mississippi Legislature, House Bill 1523, 2016 Regular Session, http://billstatus.ls.state.ms.us/ documents/2016/html/HB/1500-1599/HB1523SG.htm.

48 Madison Park, "Bathroom Bill' Fails to Make It out of Texas Special Session," CNN Politics, August 16, 2017, https://www.cnn.com/2017/08/16/politics/texas-bathroom-bill-dead/index .html.

49 State of Arkansas, Senate Bill 202.

50 Paul S. Weiland, "Federal and State Preemption of Environmental Law: A Critical Analysis," *Harvard Environmental Law Review* 24, no. 1 (2000): 237–86.

51 Ibid.

52 "What Is Fracking and Why Is It Controversial?," *BBC News*, October 15, 2018, https://www .bbc.com/news/uk-14432401.

53 Justin Miller, "Why It's So Hard to Regulate Fracking," *American Prospect*, June 24, 2015, https://prospect.org/environment/hard-regulate-fracking/.

54 National Employment Law Project, "Colorado Legislature Approves Landmark Bill."

55 C. Pech Hayne Jr. and Paul Simons, "Louisiana Supreme Court Denies Writs." *Drill Deeper*, June 30, 2016, https://www.gamb.com/louisiana-supreme-court-denies-writs/.

56 Hayden and Nucci, "Federal Preemption of State and Local Paid Sick Leave Laws."

57 Equality Illinois, "Federal 'Equality Act,'" news release, October 28, 2015, http://www.equality illinois.us/issue/federal-equality-act/.

CHAPTER 5

State Preemption
and the Ghost of Judge Dillon

David Swindell, Arizona State University
James Svara, University of North Carolina at Chapel Hill
Carl Stenberg, University of North Carolina at Chapel Hill

The U.S. Constitution is silent on the authority of local governments, as the two-tiered federal system only recognizes the nation and the states. But citizens live in local jurisdictions too, which have responsibilities for service delivery, public safety, and land use regulation. Where do these responsibilities come from? Are they granted or restricted by state governments? Under what circumstances are local governments able to do what they want unless prohibited by state or federal statute? The answers to these fundamental governance questions are not completely clear and have evolved over time. This chapter illustrates the changing nature of this governance challenge, provides a framework for assessing local autonomy, and identifies options local leaders can take to capitalize on opportunities to exercise and deal with constraints on their authority.

Two general competing local governance approaches emerged in the later part of the nineteenth and early twentieth centuries. The initial legal doctrine established the principle that local governments are basically administrative subdivisions of their state and could undertake no actions without express permission from the state.[1] This principle became known as Dillon's Rule, named for the Iowa Supreme Court chief justice who first set down this precedent in 1868 (*City of Clinton v. Cedar Rapids and Missouri Railroad Company*, 24 Iowa 455, at 461). Dillon's Rule states that the powers of a local government are limited to

> First, those granted in express words; second, those necessarily or fairly implied in or incident to the powers expressly granted; third, those essential to the accomplishment of the declared objects and purposes of the corporation—not simply convenient, but indispensable. Any fair, reasonable, substantial doubt

concerning the existence of power is resolved by the courts against the corporation, and the power is denied.

In 1903, the U.S. Supreme Court issued a decision confirming Dillon's Rule as the law of the land and underscoring that municipal corporations are auxiliaries of the state with powers that could be restricted, enlarged, or withdrawn by the state legislature (*Atkins vs. Kansas,* 191 U.S. 207, at 220–21).

Nevertheless, other local practitioners resisted the position that local governments are "creatures of the state" and have no independent sovereignty. They pushed for state constitutional changes or legislative grants of authority to allow local jurisdictions to operate with greater autonomy from their state governments. This effort gave rise to "home rule," also known as Cooley's Doctrine, named for the Michigan Supreme Court judge who championed the idea of a locality's inherent right to self-determination.

Dillon's Rule states and "home rule" states are not the only two options, and in fact neither actually exists in its purest sense. Rather, all states have elements of both. As a result, Bowman and Kearney argue that these classifications have limited explanatory power. Many of the states that have adopted Dillon's Rule as their explicit approach to local government have also granted local autonomy or various home-rule provisions.[2]

Typically, these provisions apply to different kinds of local jurisdictions. For instance, home rule may be limited to larger cities while excluding counties. Even under Dillon's Rule, greater flexibility has also been permitted by allowing local officials to petition the state to enact local bills that allow the specified local government to exercise a power not available to other local governments. However, regardless of the form of local autonomy a community might pursue, it does not change the fundamental legal principle that local governments are still creatures of the state. Rather, as Frug and Barron note, these local autonomy options are grants of authority.[3] Some of these grants are quite substantive, while other powers remain completely denied to local governments.

While the debate continues, today the pendulum appears to be moving in the direction of less local autonomy and greater state control. State legislatures are increasingly interceding in local affairs with limitations, requirements, and penalties affecting local units in both Dillon's Rule and home-rule states. Examples include bathroom access restrictions, gun control prevention, preemptions on issues ranging from plastic bag bans to fracking bans, penalties for elected officials in "sanctuary cities," and requirements to provide private companies access to public rights-of-way and utility infrastructure for small cell deployment at below-market rates.

As a result, local government leaders face a complex and uncertain environment in which to address new issues that arise in line with their citizens' preferences. For instance, 2015 saw an extensive increase in the number of recreational unmanned aircraft systems (i.e., drones). Many local governments wanted to regulate and protect airspace over their jurisdictions.[4] However, the lack of federal or state guidance initially created confusion until states (and subsequently the federal government) preempted local action in this policy area.

A similar situation has surrounded the introduction of automated vehicles on local roads. This type of governance complexity can often lead to a hesitancy to act, which can stifle policy initiation and innovation critical for local governments to address new situations.

The Arguments

Local government advocates and scholars have devoted attention to the issue of local autonomy, particularly to the practice of state preemption that controls local authority in advance of policy formulation and implementation rather than waiting for the courts to resolve a challenge to local actions. This section summarizes some of the common arguments heard to support both viewpoints.

Perhaps the most common argument in support of state control is that statewide policy, particularly in terms of the regulation of businesses, creates a better economic climate. Consistent requirements and regulations across an entire state lowers uncertainty and bureaucratic hurdles for businesses, thereby making them more profitable and supporting the economy of the state.

Many local officials have heard this argument and have responded by calling attention to the role that private-sector lobbyists for these companies have played in helping get these laws drafted, adopted, and implemented. Business interests may use state control as a means to circumvent local preferences regarding how businesses operate in a community or restrictions on practices supported by industries, effectively using the state to get an exemption from local regulations. For instance, several state legislatures are prohibiting local governments from regulating home sharing services like those provided by Airbnb in response to lobbyists targeting a single legislative body instead of dealing with a multitude of individual local governments. This is an acute problem in a state like Florida, where residents in coastal communities face very different challenges with home sharing than more interior communities in the state.

While standardizing the state's business climate and regulatory regime is the common argument in support of greater state control, other arguments have emerged as well. According to these arguments, Dillon's Rule

- allows for the technical expertise of state employees to be brought to bear to solve local problems having regional consequences that spill over local jurisdictional boundaries
- allows states to grant authority to local governments to be the lead agencies on local-scale issues (e.g., planning, zoning, financing, etc.) and to "test drive" and experiment with new approaches at minimum risk to other jurisdictions
- facilitates state redistributive policies providing assistance for central cities, suburbs, and rural communities that individual jurisdictions could not or would not choose to achieve
- provides for a more efficient service delivery system as opposed to the state setting a standard and having a multitude of delivery systems that need to be established and coordinated in order to meet that standard

- gives local officials "cover" for not acting on the desires of the community when what the community wants is not in the jurisdiction's best interests
- allows state governments to curb the worst aspects of irresponsible, corrupt, or uncooperative local governments
- enables states to protect individual rights that could too easily be trampled by the parochial nature of local communities

There is also a broad array of arguments in favor of local autonomy. From public officials like former New York City mayor Michael Bloomberg to scholars like Bruce Katz, there is broad consensus that cities and their urban areas are economic engines and the originators of innovative ideas involving economics, technology, architecture, governance, and art.[5] The argument goes that local diversity should be encouraged in order to create robust innovation laboratories.

As noted by Robert Shalhoub, president pro tem of the town of Lake Clarke, in response to the State of Florida's efforts to pass a super-preemption bill, "It's been touted that they [the legislators] know better than we do. Wrong. Absolutely wrong. We know what's best for our neighborhoods. We know what's best for our constituency. We live it every day."[6] This view reflects the idea that local autonomy can facilitate faster and better responses to public problems since local officials are more familiar with the situation and available resources than are distant state legislators and governors. Different communities have different needs, and a one-size-fits-all approach by a state government that is home to a diverse set of communities is not likely to meet the needs, values, and priorities of most jurisdictions. This is especially likely when the state legislature is dominated by representatives elected from rural areas and small communities.

Additional arguments in favor of greater local control include the following:

- Empowering local governments to run their own local affairs means the state government will be free to focus on state-level matters, which will improve overall efficiency and effectiveness of government throughout the state.
- Citizens will be more engaged in local affairs as they can see the effects of their participation, which strengthens the civic fabric of communities and reduces the sense of disaffection many citizens feel toward government.
- Arguments that state governments can address issues more effectively, consistently, and efficiently presume that the states are taking steps to do so. But this is often not the case, thus leaving local governments to handle issues in the absence of state action.
- Creating a default presumption of local autonomy (instead of a strict construction like Dillon's Rule) will reduce the need for judicial interference in local affairs and free the courts to focus on other issues.

These arguments for state control and local autonomy are not mutually exclusive, and individuals could hold positions drawing on both perspectives.

A Framework for Assessing Local Government Autonomy

While most states provide some degree of autonomy to local governments, issues emerge that fall into a gray area in terms of whether a local government has the authority to act on its own. Sometimes local officials will proceed and act in good faith, believing that their existing arrangement for local autonomy provides the authority to do so. And in some of those situations, their state government will take exception to those local government activities and will intervene in some manner to reverse or prevent those actions rather than allowing the courts to resolve whether the local government has the authority to act.

States act toward local governments in specific ways that fall into three broad categories: permit local action, restrict local action, and require local action. The exact form of these approaches may differ in Dillon's Rule and home-rule states, but they can all occur in all states.

Permit Local Action

States must authorize local governments to act. Home-rule states *permit* action by a broad authorization to all or selected cities. In non-home-rule states, cities have the express powers that are included in their charter approved by the state or in state laws that grant specific powers. An important element to recognize is that the availability of authority does not mean it will be accepted and utilized by local governments. Table 5.1 illustrates variations in permitted actions.

If a state permits "local legislation," as is the case in twenty-one states, a legislature can grant an authorization of power to a specific local government.[7] Although a local bill can represent state intrusion into the affairs of a local government, in the past such actions were often used to provide local choice and encourage experimentation. Local government officials asked their state

TABLE 5.1　Types of State Actions: Permit Local Actions

Type of Permission	Type of State–Local Legal Relationship	
	Dillon's Rule States	Home-Rule States
Broad or specific authorization*	Express powers granted to city in charters or in state law	Broad authorization to all or to designated municipalities plus specific authorization in laws
Limited or targeted authorization	Local bill granting power to a specific city (if local legislation is allowed) or group of cities	Use of classification to permit some cities to act

* Cities and counties must agree to use the authority. Only one city in Utah, for example, uses a home-rule charter.

legislative delegation to introduce these local bills on behalf of the local government. When the delegation unanimously supported the local bill, the legislature as a whole typically would approve it under the norm of legislative courtesy. This process does not work as smoothly when there are partisan differences, such as between an urban area requesting the change from a rural legislative majority. The request may simply be denied. Alternatively, some local officials might fear that the request will be altered by the legislative majority to impose an unwanted change on the local government. In recent years, local governments have needed to be more cautious in requesting local legislation.

Restrict Local Action

Restrictions on local government action come in many forms (see table 5.2). Given that powers have to be authorized by the state in broad or specific language, omitting a power from those specifications or refusing to grant a power is a major limiting factor. New York City attempted to replicate the traffic control measures adopted in London and other large cities abroad, but its grant of limited home rule in the state constitution did not override a prohibition on setting charges and fees for the use of public highways.[8] During Mayor Bloomberg's administration, city officials requested authorization from the legislature to set

TABLE 5.2   Types of State Actions: Restrict Local Actions

Type of Permission	Type of State–Local Legal Relationship	
	Dillon's Rule States	Home-Rule States
Omission	Fail or refuse to grant express power*	Fail to include in general authorization
Targeted restriction	Intervene in single jurisdiction (if local legislation allowed)	Use classification to prevent some cities from acting
Nullification	Nullify local policy/program/ practice that is not expressly granted or fairly implied	Nullify local policy/program/ practice in conflict with state laws
Prohibition	Forbid local action that is not consistent with state law**	Forbid local action that is not consistent with state law
Penalization	Impose sanctions for specified actions***	Imposed sanctions for specified actions
Preemption	Preempt the authority of local government to act in specified areas	Preempt the authority of local government to act in specified areas

* Iowa provides home rule in the state constitution but does not permit local fiscal autonomy.

** For example, forbidding "lunch shaming" programs.

*** For example, penalties for "sanctuary cities."

a congestion charge, but the legislature denied the request. Subsequent similar requests have also run into continued opposition within the regional delegation to the New York statehouse.

Local legislation can be used to restrict as well as to allow local action. Restrictions may be imposed selectively when applied to certain classes of cities in home-rule states. For example, Orange County, North Carolina, was denied the power to charge impact fees on developers to provide funds for the education system (a county responsibility in North Carolina) because legislators believed the county was charging excessive fees. Other local governments in North Carolina still have the expressly granted power to impose these fees.

Local governments' powers are subject to challenge in state courts and are therefore subject to nullification. For home-rule governments, the basis for the challenge may be inconsistency with state law. In Dillon's Rule states, judges use the rule as a guideline to determine whether to permit or overturn an established power. In addition, the legislature can intervene in a single jurisdiction to overrule a practice to which it objects.

The broadest form of restriction is preemption. States may preclude local governments from acting in selected areas of policy. This is different from "floor preemptions" (requirements to provide a basic level, but permission to provide more if local preferences warrant) and "ceiling preemptions" (permission to provide up to a certain level but no more).[9] The number of state preemptions has risen in the past decade. This reflects differing political perspectives in state government and demonstrates a strong assertion that states have the right to control policies within local jurisdictional boundaries. Unlike nullifying or overriding an existing local law, preemption occurs before local governments can approve a policy in the targeted area. As Governor Greg Abbott asserted in March 2017, as opposed to a state having to take multiple rifle-shot approaches at overriding local regulations, "I think it would be far simpler . . . if the state of Texas adopted an overriding policy to create certain standards that must be met."[10] He has advocated passage of a broad-based law that says, across the board, the state is going to preempt local regulations. Based on a recent report by the National League of Cities, home-rule status is not a full protection against state preemption, but non-home-rule states appear to be more vulnerable.[11]

The American City County Exchange (ACCE)—a conservative, free-market organization under the umbrella of the American Legislative Exchange Council (ALEC)—strongly advocates for and helps draft model preemption and regulatory (and deregulatory) laws that have been adopted in several states.[12] ACCE has assisted in advancing the practice of preemption by writing bills in a wide range of areas, including minimum wage ordinances, pesticide and GMO restrictions, public broadband, internet taxation, rent control, gun control, cell phone regulation, and charter school authorization.[13] According to one observer, "Thanks in part to ALEC's promotion of the concept, preemption has become the most powerful statehouse tactic of our time."[14]

One of the most controversial preemption examples in terms of recent national attention emerged from North Carolina. In 2016, Charlotte's city council passed a local ordinance in which the city banned discrimination against

LGBTQ individuals and provided for transgendered individuals to use the bathroom of their choice. The state legislature responded in great haste with HB 2 (aka, the "Bathroom Bill"), which not only nullified Charlotte's local ordinance but also preempted all local governments in the state from passing any other nondiscrimination ordinances. The bill went on to preempt the state's municipalities from establishing minimum wages that exceeded the state minimum wage level. Students in all schools (K–12 as well as higher education institutions) had to use the bathroom that matched the student's gender as specified on their birth certificate.[15] The bathroom element of the bill was repealed in part in March 2017, in response to considerable pressure from the community and business groups.[16] But the repeal left in place the preemption of local governments from legislating issues of bathroom access, nondiscrimination regulation, and establishing minimum wage levels higher than the state level.

Preemption can be particularly disruptive of the relationship between state and local governments because the prohibition of involvement covers all local governments in the state, and because of the nature of preemption itself. The established pattern in Dillon's Rule states was that local governments would initiate a new policy or program with the possibility of a later challenge in court. Preemption overrides this process and does not permit local governments to experiment in new areas. Furthermore, the decision about the appropriateness of local government action is being made by the legislature with no criteria for what local governments will be permitted to do in place of the cautious but clear tests of compliance with state law or express authorization. This development has been called "blanket" or "super" preemption.[17]

With the rise of tensions between cities and their states over these practices, there is a significant concern when states impose penalties for noncompliance by local governments. Such penalties now include reductions in state aid as well as exposure of local officials to personal liability in third-party lawsuits. For example, Arizona's Senate Bill 1487, passed in 2016, allows any legislator to request the attorney general (AG) to investigate local government actions in light of state law. During that investigation, state revenues that are owed to the local government are withheld and forfeited if the AG finds against it. The local government would also be charged the court fees if it were to lose a court challenge to the AG ruling. This happened to Tucson in 2017 when the city wanted to destroy the firearms confiscated by police in the commission of closed crimes. A legislator requested an investigation, the AG found that the city's actions would violate a state law prohibiting the destruction of guns (and now requiring the resale of them), the city took the decision to court, and the state supreme court ruled against the city. This kind of preemption with penalties has been called the "new preemption" and "preemption plus" in the public health field.[18]

Require Local Action

The third area of interaction is state requirements of action by local governments (see table 5.3). States set limits or impose responsibilities that affect autonomy. According to the National League of Cities, forty-two states have

TABLE 5.3   Types of State Actions: Require Local Actions

Type of Permission	Type of State–Local Legal Relationship	
	Dillon's Rule States	Home–Rule States
Requirements	Set standards that all governments must meet*	Set standards that all governments must meet
Mandates	Require all governments to act (e.g., unfunded mandate) or comply with requirements	Require all governments to act (e.g., unfunded mandate) or comply with requirements

* For example, requiring local governments to apply the same property tax rate to all property owners regardless of income.

some sort of tax and expenditure limitation on their local governments, including all ten states they classify as home-rule states. The autonomy that is supposed to be available to these local jurisdictions is constrained by the limited capacity to raise or spend resources.

Additionally, states may require local governments to provide services with expenses covered from the local budget. These "unfunded mandates" require commitments of funds that are not available for other purposes. Recently, the federal and some state governments have required that local governments cooperate in specific ways with federal immigration authorities in identifying and turning over persons who are undocumented. Many local governments object that they cannot be incorporated into the federal government enforcement process because they have to fulfill their own responsibilities to protect the safety and well-being of all local residents. Furthermore, if residents cannot trust local law enforcement, jail, and court officials to protect their identity, they will fear cooperating with officials to combat any criminal activity they observe or of which they are victims. Some state governments such as Arizona have passed legislation threatening sanctions for local governments they consider to be providing "sanctuary" to undocumented residents—an example of "penalties" (as outlined in table 5.2).

Where Is the Pendulum Now?

As noted previously, there has been a marked increase in the number of legislative actions interfering in some manner with local autonomy in recent years. But how much? What do local government officials and citizens think about the increased centralization of local authority moving to state control? Recent surveys provide some indications.

Einstein and Glick report the results of the 2015 Menino Survey of Mayors conducted in cooperation with Boston University and the U.S. Conference of Mayors.[19] Even taking partisan identity of the responding mayor and the dominant political party in their state legislature into account, mayors reported consistent frustrations with the intrusions of their state governments into local affairs, particularly in terms of financial controls and regulation. While Democratic mayors were more inclined to these positions, Republican mayors also exhibited similar frustrations, even when their party was in control of the statehouse.

Of course, politics and partisanship play a role in the state–local tug-of-war.[20] The idea of local control and moving decision-making authority closer to the individual and away from "the government" has traditionally been a philosophical foundation stone of the modern Republican Party. More state legislatures and governorships are dominated today by Republicans. As will be seen, most of the preemption efforts to centralize authority in state government and away from localities is happening in Republican-dominated legislatures. This is particularly acute in the relations between "red" statehouses and "blue" central cities.[21]

A recent study of Michigan's local government administrators illustrates how their opinions are even more sharply critical of the state government. A large majority of Michigan's local officials (70 percent) believe that state government takes too much local decision-making authority away. However, that belief varies depending on the policy area. A majority of the respondents did not think the state took away too much authority on issues related to antidiscrimination, social justice, business, environment, and natural resources. They were more prone to this belief on issues related to local economic development, public financing, and taxes, suggesting a more nuanced appreciation for how local authority should be balanced relative to the state.[22]

Local governments continue to maintain greater trust among citizens than the states or federal government. So one may not be surprised that surveys of citizens tend to favor greater local control. Schneider, Jacoby, and Lewis report results from a subsample of the 2006 Cooperative Congressional Election Study and found that respondents strongly favor giving power to local governments in order to solve community problems.[23] More recently, a survey by ALG Research found that regardless of political party affiliation, residents agree that local government better reflects their community's values than their state government.[24]

In addition to opinion data, recent scholarship has also begun to focus on the rise in legislation limiting local autonomy, the change in the basic purpose of such legislation, and an increase in the punitive consequences for noncompliance. Research has found a steady increase in preemption bills across the country from 2011 to 2016.[25] Also, the 2018 survey by the National League of Cities found that forty-one states had preempted local authority in ride sharing, twenty-eight had done so regarding minimum wage, twenty-three had preempted paid leave policy, and another twenty had restricted municipal broadband authority.[26]

Preliminary Findings

To understand these changing dynamics in terms of both restriction and empowerment of local governments, this research effort undertook a nationwide electronic review of state legislative actions in eight pilot states (Arizona, Pennsylvania, Georgia, North Carolina, Colorado, Iowa, Tennessee, Utah) covering any issue involving a limitation or expansion of local authority. The research team examined these from 2001 to mid-2017. Once the pilot phase was complete, the team examined the legislative actions of the remaining states but with a more limited focus on two specific policy areas: minimum wage policy and broadband issues.[27]

Our preliminary findings revealed that during this period legislatures in twenty-seven states passed at least 167 laws focused on expanding or limiting local autonomy covering a wide range of economic, social, health, and environmental policy areas. Figure 5.1 illustrates the clear and consistent increase in this legislative activity over this period. While only a fraction of all state legislation, figure 5.1 illustrates that the number of actions taken per year has increased since 2006, at the rate of about 0.7 additional state laws limiting or expanding local power each year. Regionally, nine southern states (especially Texas, Louisiana, and Arkansas) took twenty-two preemptive actions, eight midwestern states took twelve actions, and three western states took six actions.

The vast majority of these legislative actions represent some form of limitation on local governments (70.3 percent), and another sizeable portion imposed additional requirements on local governments (18.6 percent). Most of the state actions involved preemption of local authority in very specific fields (e.g.,

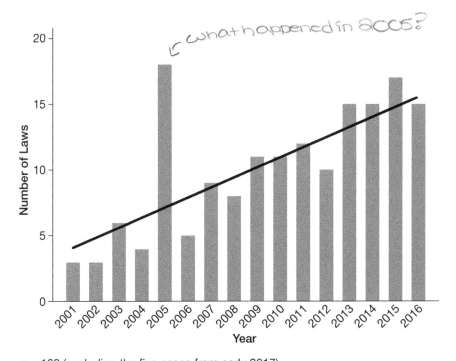

n = 162 (excluding the five cases from early 2017)

Figure 5.1   State Actions Aimed at Local Government Authority: 2001–2016

regulation of firearms and ammunition, sale and use of consumer fireworks, pest management, livery vehicles, taxis, and limousines) and not involving core services. Only 11.0 percent expanded local autonomy in any way. Figure 5.2 illustrates this distribution by type of action. In most cases the team reviewed during this period, there was no clear event that triggered state action.

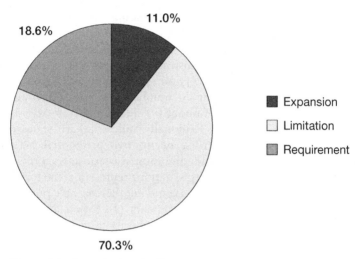

11.0%

18.6%

- Expansion
- Limitation
- Requirement

70.3%

Figure 5.2   State Actions by Type

Figure 5.3 highlights the number of state law interventions by partisan control of the state governments. Republican "trifectas" enacted just over half (52 percent) of state actions (meaning Republicans controlled both state legislative chambers and the governorship). Democratic trifectas passed just under one-quarter (24 percent). These results suggest that party orientation is not as important as state control being dominated by one party. States are more likely to pass legislation regarding local government powers when one party controls both the executive and legislative branches of state government. For example, of the fifteen states that passed minimum wage legislation, thirteen limited local ability to regulate the minimum wage, one placed a requirement on localities, and one expanded local authority. Republican trifectas enacted 77 percent of the minimum wage legislation.

The research team's initial review of state legislative enactments revealed other actions in addition to preemptions. These included *bans* (e.g., plastic bags, breast-feeding in public), *restrictions* (e.g., local election dates), and *requirements* (e.g., allow use of sign walkers, prohibit driving on unpaved surfaces that are not streets or roads, American flags that are displayed by local governments must be manufactured in the United States, and distribution of information pamphlets prior to an election on bond, sales, or property tax measures). While distinguishing the type of limitation the state had imposed was sometimes

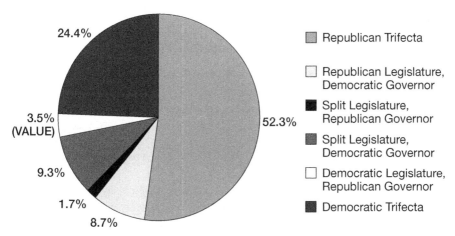

Figure 5.3   State Actions by Party Control

difficult because of vagueness of statutory language, the next phase of the project will address this challenge.

States also have passed laws protecting local regulatory authority and allowing for more stringent local regulation (e.g., time limits of idling automobiles, elevator safety, building codes, open containers, low-efficiency plumbing features and water conservation). Furthermore, some laws declared an area to be an issue of statewide interest or concern but did not preempt local authority (e.g., regulation of massage therapy, internet sweepstakes cafés, poison control services, trap grease, wireless facilities).

Options for Local Governments to Take Action

Local officials react to preemptions, restrictions, and penalties in a variety of ways. These include informal negotiations with state agencies and legislators, various forms of disobedience and "work-arounds," as well as lawsuits.

If a community is considering a new approach to address a local goal or need, then local officials can use the factors in tables 5.1, 5.2, and 5.3 as checklists of opportunities and constraints to assess the prospects for being able to proceed into new policy areas or service responsibilities. The opportunities or constraining factors may differ depending on the policy being considered. Along with this assessment of opportunities and constraints, local officials can consider how they might move forward to accomplish the change. Table 5.4 provides a summary of optional approaches.

Use Legal Powers and Test the Limits

The first option is to determine whether the local government can make a plausible case that it has the authority to act. Being the first government in a state to enter a new area of policy does not necessarily mean that an action is not

TABLE 5.4 **How Local Governments Can Take Action**

Type of Action	Type of State–Local Legal Relationship	
	Dillon's Rule States	Home-Rule States
Defiance	Resist preemptions and limitations	
Testing of legal limits	Initiate local legal action within granted powers	Initiate local legal action within broad powers; take advantage of home-rule option if available
Referendum	Change state policies	
Work-around	Find method that circumvents restrictions by using other legal authority	Find method that is consistent with state law
Request for additional powers	Seek specific authorization from legislature for all local governments or request targeted local bill to permit action	Seek broad legislative authorization for all cities concerning previously ungranted power
Advocacy and voluntary efforts	Raise awareness through partnerships with nongovernmental organizations to promote preferred policy outcome	

permitted. Furthermore, it is possible that the constraint is not the lack of legal authority but the presence of other requirements or expectations that interfere with setting a clear policy commitment. The approach needed may be to untangle constraints and develop a clear commitment to act in the needed policy area.

This general approach may include testing the legal limits of local government action. Seattle has established an income tax of 2.25 percent for individuals with an income over $250,000 per year. Opponents argue that there are constitutional and legal obstacles to this tax. Seattle's actions will determine what Washington law will permit. The tax was declared illegal in a court ruling in November 2017. Now the city faces the question of whether to expend resources to put the new tax in place while it awaits a final decision from the state supreme court.

This general approach may include testing the legal limits of local government action, but it must be done in a reasonable way, taking state law into consideration. Claiming or exercising a power that is clearly beyond the scope of expressed powers cannot only be nullified by court or legislative action, but the action may lead to penalties and needless court costs. Since 2011 in North Carolina, a judge may award attorney's fees and court costs to challengers who prevail in suits against local governments if the judge finds that the local government "acted outside the scope of its legal authority."[28]

As noted with the North Carolina "Bathroom Bill" example, testing the limits can also provoke state intervention to nullify one local government's actions and then go further by passing a preemption measure limiting all other local governments in the state. Furthermore, there may be the opportunity to seek remedy from federal courts.

Request Additional Powers

Second, the local government can seek authorization either through a grant of power that would apply to all cities or counties or by requesting local authorization. A consequence of this approach is that it clearly signals the local government's hope to enter the new policy area and is an acknowledgment that the power is not currently available to use. In North Carolina, four municipalities have obtained authority through a local bill from the legislature to create and operate their own charter schools and give enrollment preference to residents. Although there are more than 170 charter schools in North Carolina, none are run by a municipality. In these four prosperous communities, there is allegedly dissatisfaction with overcrowding in traditional schools run by the Charlotte-Mecklenburg system and the practice of busing students from municipalities elsewhere.[29] The request aligned with the legislature's strong support for charter schools, explaining the success of this request.

Work around the Limits

Third, a local government can seek to find a method of action that is consistent with state law in home-rule states. In other states, the local government could attempt to find a way to pursue the policy by a method that complies with restrictions but circumvents them using other legal authority. Some municipal leaders are even taking advantage of local governments' economic status to act as contractors and press on locally important issues like net neutrality.[30]

One example is a recent action in Durham, North Carolina, to offset sharp increases in property appraisals and tax bills in gentrifying neighborhoods. North Carolina law requires that properties be appraised based on the market value of nearby properties, and all property owners are required to pay the same property tax rate. City revitalization efforts and changing market conditions have increased the attractiveness and elevated the housing prices in neighborhoods close to downtown, with adverse effects for long-term, low-income homeowners.

The city sought to provide some form of tax relief to low-income families who do not qualify for the existing state relief programs aimed at elderly and disabled homeowners. Although the city cannot change the appraisal or tax rate for a low-income homeowner, it used its community development and housing improvement powers to provide housing stabilization assistance to low-income homeowners in neighborhoods with escalating property values. Using what one council member (who is now mayor) referred to as a "Durham work-around," the city council approved neighborhood stabilization grants to the residents of three neighborhoods equivalent to the amount of their recent tax increase. This work-around approach creates a local tax relief program while efforts continue to broaden the state relief programs. Creativity and determination are required to find such approaches.

There are many other examples of work-arounds local governments are employing. For instance, Orange County, California, along with several of its municipalities, is resisting the state government's position as a "sanctuary state" by publishing the release dates of undocumented individuals they have in custody in case Immigration and Customs Enforcement officials want to pick them up at that time. Hennepin County, Minnesota, circumvented the possibility of a "Bathroom Bill" issue like North Carolina's by replacing the group bathrooms in their county offices with individual bathrooms for anyone. And when Memphis's application to the Tennessee Historical Commission for a waiver from the Heritage Protection Act to enable it to remove Confederate monuments from two city parks was denied, the city transferred ownership of the properties to a nonprofit organization, Memphis Greenspace, which removed them. In response, state legislators cut $250,000 from the appropriation for Memphis's 2019 bicentennial celebration.[31]

Direct Democracy on the State Ballot

There are three additional approaches that can be taken in most states regardless of the legal position of local governments. The most ambitious of these is to change state policies and legal stipulations through a state ballot initiative (available in twenty-one states) or ballot referendum process (available in twenty-six states). A successful example of this is the movement in Arizona to raise the minimum wage. This effort in 2016, which survived court challenges in 2017, raised the state minimum wage to ten dollars in 2017 and then incrementally to twelve dollars by 2020. The efforts in several cities to raise the minimum wage that were being threatened with state nullification became a uniform approach statewide. Similar efforts were successful in Colorado, Maine, and Washington in November 2016. This approach is a major undertaking that would obviously require a collective effort by local governments in a state, probably coordinated by the state's league of cities and counties or other similar organizations.

Defy State Restrictions

Local governments can defy state restrictions and approve programs/actions that counter state law. Kansas City voters approved an increase in the minimum wage on August 8, 2017. It ran into the state limit of $7.70 an hour that took effect on August 28. The action, though largely symbolic, may help to activate the groups that started a petition drive to put an initiative on the ballot for voters throughout the state to set a higher limit.

Advocacy and Voluntary Approach

If establishing a new policy in law is not possible at least in the short run, governments can be advocates for change and seek to promote their policy objectives through their own internal policies and voluntary action in their communities. Efforts can focus on raising awareness and forming partnerships with nongovernmental organizations to promote preferred policy outcomes. As part of the effort, the government can look at its own practices to ensure they are consistent with the policy objective(s). For example, regarding higher wages, the government can make certain that it pays all of its employees a living wage, including those who are part-time or seasonal. It can support efforts in the community to adopt living wages and help draw attention to employers that pay wages at this level. Assembling a network of nongovernmental organizations to promote the desired outcome can expand the scope of support and broaden understanding of the issue.

Conclusion

In navigating the sometimes-troubled waters between autonomy and preemption, local governments are subject to greater scrutiny and have more limits placed on their freedom of action than in the past. They should not allow these conditions to deter them from dealing with emerging policy issues and addressing the distinctive opportunities and problems that are present in their communities. City and county officials should not assume that they are powerless to move into new areas of policy. If there are substantial restrictions, they should identify them and look for ways to counter them. When all other options are ruled out, they should consider advocacy and networking with other governments and nongovernmental organizations in their community to gain support.

■ CAREER PROFILE ■

John Olszewski Jr.

County Executive
Baltimore County, Maryland

Known to the community as "Johnny O," the current Baltimore County executive has observed state–local relations from both sides. Olszewski began his public service as a student member of the Baltimore County Board of Education. After completing a bachelor's degree at Goucher College, he worked as a high school teacher and ran for the Maryland State Assembly, where he served two terms. Along the way, he completed a master's degree at George Washington University and a Ph.D. in public policy at the University of Maryland, Baltimore County. In 2018, he was elected county executive. He is the chief executive for a local government serving over 850,000 residents.

With no municipalities inside its borders, the Baltimore County government provides all local government services to its residents. Maryland's local government structure also gives the county funding authority for the public schools, though their governing board is separate. As a county leader, Olszewski must interact with the state frequently. He explains, "We view the state as an important partner in the work that we do." For example, the county is working with the legislature to secure additional funding for school building and renovation efforts. Experience in state government aids Olszewski's understanding of the nuances of the state policy process. Continuing relationships from his time in state government facilitate discussions when the county and state must work together on regulatory compliance or policy implementation.

Olszewski encourages students to have conversations with state and local government policymakers in order to learn about their work. These informal conversations can turn into internships and future work opportunities. Service at both levels of government require similar skills, such as strong interpersonal skills. Olszewski also recommends joining relevant professional organizations. The Maryland Association of Counties, for example, provides networking opportunities and insights into how other county governments are facing shared challenges. Finally, Olszewski encourages students to develop depth and expertise in a specific policy area so they become a go-to resource, but also take time to understand the policy process broadly so they can pivot and engage new problems and ideas.

Interview: October 10, 2019

Discussion Questions

1. What is the basis for Dillon's Rule? What is the basis for home rule? Which one overrides the other and on what basis?
2. The state legislature is considering bills to preempt local authority from regulating (1) broadband, (2) minimum wage, and (3) plastic bags. Which of the arguments for state control over local autonomy would you advance?
3. In what ways, and for what reasons, do local officials view state legislators as their (1) partners and (2) adversaries?
4. Think of an issue or service in your community that you believe should be handled by your local government. What is the nature of this issue or service that leads you to believe it belongs in the purview of local control?
5. Give an example of how a municipality could work around a state restriction on local authority.

Notes

The Alliance for Innovation commissioned a white paper for its BIG Ideas conference hosted in Raleigh, North Carolina, on October 6–8, 2017, on which portions of this chapter are based. The authors would like to thank graduate students Vanessa Shaw and Heather Curry for their assistance in gathering the background legislative information.

[1] G. Frug, "The City as a Legal Concept," *Harvard Law Review* 93, no. 6 (1980): 1059–1154.
[2] A. Bowman and R. Kearney, "The Legislative Transformation of State-Local Government Relations," in *Intergovernmental Relations in Transition: Reflections and Directions*, ed. C. Stenberg and D. Hamilton, chap. 11 (New York: Taylor & Francis, 2018).

3 G. Frug and D. Barron, *City Bound: How States Stifle Urban Innovation* (Ithaca, NY: Cornell University Press, 2008).
4 K. Desouza, D. Swindell, K. Smith, A. Sutherland, K. Fedorschak, and C. Coronel, "Local Government 2035: Strategic Trends and Implications of New Technologies," Brookings, May 29, 2015, https://www.brookings.edu/research/local-government-2035-strategic-trends-and-implications-of-new-technologies/.
5 B. Katz and J. Nowak, *The New Localism: How Cities Can Thrive in the Age of Populism* (Washington, DC: Brookings Institution, 2017).
6 A. Keller, "How State Preemption Became a 'Serious Problem' for Local Governments in Florida," *Route Fifty*, August 20, 2017, https://www.routefifty.com/management/2017/08/florida-state-preemption-local-government/140364/.
7 D. Krane, P. Rigos, and M. Hill, eds., *Home Rule in America: A Fifty-State Handbook* (Washington, DC: Congressional Quarterly Press, 2001).
8 Frug and Barron, *City Bound*.
9 W. Buzbee, "Asymmetrical Regulation: Risk, Preemption, and the Floor/Ceiling Distinction," *NYU Law Review* 82, no. 6 (2007): 1547–1619.
10 D. C. Vock, "The End of Local Laws? War on Cities Intensifies in Texas," Governing.com, April 5, 2017, http://www.governing.com/topics/politics/gov-texas-abbott-preemption.html?utm_term =Th.
11 N. DuPuis, T. Langan, C. McFarland, A. Panettieri, and B. Rainwater, "City Rights in an Era of Preemption: A State-by-State Analysis; 2018 Update," National League of Cities, 2018, http://nlc.org/sites/default/files/2017-03/NLC-SML%20Preemption%20Report%202017-pages.pdf.
12 M. Jackman, "ALEC's Influence over Lawmaking in State Legislatures," Brookings, December 6, 2013, https://www.brookings.edu/articles/alecs-influence-over-lawmaking-in-state-legislatures/.
13 M. Bottari and B. Fischer, "The ALEC-Backed War on Local Democracy," *Huffington Post*, March 30, 2015, https://www.huffingtonpost.com/mary-bottari/the-alec-backed-war-on-lo _b_6961142.html; cf. M. McIntire, "Conservative Nonprofit Acts as a Stealth Business Lobbyist," *New York Times*, April 22, 2012, https://www.nytimes.com/2012/04/22/us/alec-a-tax-exempt-group-mixes-legislators-and-lobbyists.html.
14 H. Grabar, "The Shackling of the American City," *Slate*, September 9, 2016, http://www.slate .com/articles/business/metropolis/2016/09/how_alec_acce_and_pre_emptions_laws_are_gutting _the_powers_of_american_cities.html.
15 D. Graham, "North Carolina Overturns LGBT-Discrimination Ban," *Atlantic*, March 2016, https:// www.theatlantic.com/politics/archive/2016/03/north-carolina-lgbt-discrimination-transgender -bathrooms/475125/.
16 J. Hanna, M. Park, and E. McLaughlin, "North Carolina Repeals 'Bathroom Bill,'" CNN, March 30, 2017, https://www.cnn.com/2017/03/30/politics/north-carolina-hb2-agreement/index.html.
17 R. Florida, "City vs. State: The Story So Far," *Route Fifty*, June 13, 2017, http://www.routefifty .com/management/2017/06/city-vs-state-story-so-far/138652.
18 R. Briffault, "The Challenge of the New Preemption," *Stanford Law Review* 70, no. 6 (2018): 1995–2027; cf. J. Hodge, A. Corbett, K. Weidenaar, and S. Wetter, "Public Health 'Preemption Plus,'" *Journal of Law, Medicine, and Ethics* 45, no. 1 (2017): 156–60.
19 K. Einstein and D. Glick, "Cities in American Federalism: Evidence on State–Local Government Conflict from a Survey of Mayors," *Publius: The Journal of Federalism* 47, no. 4 (2017): 599–621.
20 L. Richardson and J. Milyo, "Giving the People What They Want? Legislative Polarization and Public Approval of State Legislatures," *State and Local Government Review* 48, no. 4 (2016): 270–81.
21 Einstein and Glick, "Cities in American Federalism"; cf. L. Riverstone-Newell, "The Rise of State Preemption Laws in Response to Local Policy Innovation," *Publius: The Journal of Federalism* 47, no. 3 (2017): 403–25.
22 D. Horner and T. Ivacko, "Improving Communication, Building Trust Are Seen as Keys to Fixing Relationships between Local Jurisdictions and the State," *Michigan Public Policy Survey*, May 2017, http://closup.umich.edu/files/mpps-state-local-relations-2016.pdf.

[23] S. Schneider, W. Jacoby, and D. Lewis, "Public Opinion toward Intergovernmental Policy Responsibilities," *Publius: The Journal of Federalism* 41, no. 1 (2011): 1–30.

[24] National Employment Law Project, "Poll Results: Groundbreaking New Polls on Local Democracy, Home Rule, Minimum Wage," press release, March 1, 2018, http://www.nelp.org/news-releases/poll-results-groundbreaking-new-polls-on-local-democracy-home-rule-minimum-wage.

[25] Riverstone-Newell, "Rise of State Preemption Laws."

[26] DuPuis, Langan, McFarland, Panettieri, and Rainwater, "City Rights in an Era of Preemption."

[27] The team spent the summer of 2017 collecting these data through an extensive search of qualitative records. Using Boolean searches on LexisNexis and state legislature websites, bills that were successfully signed into law were added to the data set. The data set included other characteristics about the new laws, such as the legislative name of the bill, the state statute affected by the law, a categorization of the law (expansion, limitation, or requirement), the targeted policy area, the breadth of affect (targeted or comprehensive of all local governments), the party in power at the time of passage, and the triggering event leading to the bill's origination. Search terms included variations and combinations of "municipal," "county," "restriction," "limits," "require," "prohibit," and "preempted" (though the last term generated very few hits in the legislative records as that term rarely appears in the legislation). The team tested the initial coding for interrated reliability, and later borderline cases were discussed before inclusion in the data set. The data set does not include *all* bills or laws passed, as the intent here is to measure the increase in the number of laws passed specifically to expand or limit local autonomy.

[28] F. Bluestein, "Is North Carolina a Dillon's Rule State?," *Coates' Canons: NC Local Government Law*, October 24, 2012, https://canons.sog.unc.edu/is-north-carolina-a-dillons-rule-state/.

[29] Associated Press, "Charter School Creation for 4 Towns Gets Final Approval," WUNC, June 6, 2018, http://wunc.org/post/charter-school-creation-4-towns-gets-final-approval#stream/0.

[30] N. Flatow, "Cities Launch Plan to Protect Net Neutrality," *CityLab*, March 12, 2018, https://www.citylab.com/equity/2018/03/net-neutrality-executive-orders-fcc-mayors-bill-de-blasio/555344/.

[31] D. Lohr, "This Is Why Another Confederate Statue Won't Come down in Tennessee," *Huffington Post*, June 7, 2018, https://www.huffpost.com/entry/tennessee-confederate-statues_n_5b0f1b77e4b05ef4c22a7796.

CHAPTER 6

Quarantining the Spread of Policy Innovations Using Preemption

Daniel J. Mallinson, Penn State Harrisburg

T his chapter will discuss how the act of state preemption fits into a broader understanding of how state and local governments innovate. The research on state policy diffusion often focuses on instances where states learn from each other, as well as from their local governments. But American federalism is not only cooperative, it is also conflictual. States compete for economic advantages. They also conflict with the federal government over policy priorities and design. Finally, local and state governments conflict over policy and who has the right to establish those policies. This chapter will begin by briefly describing the study of policy diffusion. It will then present the concept of diffusion quarantine, that is, the use of preemption by states to prevent the spread of policy innovations among local governments. Finally, the chapter will discuss how diffusion theory can help us better understand preemption activity.

The Diffusion of Policy Innovations

For fifty years, political science and public policy scholars have studied how policy innovations spread among the American states.[1] Scholars study why diffusion occurs by examining patterns of adoption geographically and over time. We find, for example, that while some states tend to be more innovative than others, even generally noninnovative states can take the lead on certain policies.[2] We also know that some states make an effort to reinvent and change innovations when they adopt them, while others simply copy the bills of earlier states or interest organizations.[3] Sometimes, states even copy typos in previous laws.[4]

There are five recognized mechanisms of policy diffusion.[5] Each of these mechanisms implies the forces and actors that are engaged in the diffusion of a specific policy innovation. Figure 6.1 categorizes these mechanisms based on two dimensions. The first dimension, direction, separates the mechanisms based on whether a policy is being pushed into the state by outside forces or pulled in

What does it mean by actors (handwritten, left margin, vertical)

Level of Analysis

		Macro	*Micro*
	Push	Coercion (Drinking age of 21)	Elite Socialization (Voter Identification) Social Contagion (Public smoking bans)
Direction			
	Pull	Competition (Lotteries)	Learning (Electric Deregulation)

Figure 6.1 Mechanisms of Policy Diffusion

by state actors. The second dimension, level of analysis, separates them based on whether the specific forces behind the innovation's spread are happening broadly at the macro level or are primarily affecting individual actors at the micro level.

Coercion refers to a higher level of government (federal or state) taking some action that prompts a lower level of government (state or local) to enact an innovation. This can come through financial resources, mandates, or even just paying attention to specific issues and thus raising their importance.[6] The force of coercion is pushing a policy and is likely having a broad impact on all states. Social contagion, on the other hand, occurs when policy ideas spread among citizen networks that cross state lines, specifically between a state with an innovation and one without.[7] As public opinion changes, legislators in the state without the innovation become more receptive to passing it. This is happening on a micro level but is still serving to push an innovation onto state officials. Elite socialization is similar but occurs among elected officials. It can occur through professional or ideological networks.

In the cases of competition and learning, ideas are being pulled into states, often by legislative staff.[8] In the case of competition, states innovate so they can keep up with their peers. This can lead to a "race to the bottom" where states outcompete each other on things like lowering taxes or environmental regulations. It can also lead to a "race to the top," as with the eponymous program in the Obama administration.[9] States are responding to broader competitive pressures, be they regional or national. Learning occurs at the personal level, as legislators or their staff seek out information for solving public policy problems. Of course, more than one mechanism can be at play during an innovation's spread. But understanding the mechanism helps us also understand which forces are influencing the spread of an innovation and whose voices are being heard by state government.

Traditionally, scholars have thought about policy diffusion through the lens of internal, external, and policy determinants of adoption decisions.[10] In 2010, however, Graeme Boushey proposed a rethinking of how diffusion is conceptualized. Building on punctuated equilibrium theory that explains both rapid and slow changes in issue attention,[11] he did so for the purpose of better understanding why policies spread at different rates. Boushey presented an epidemiological conceptualization of diffusion that views policies as infectious agents, states as hosts, and interest groups as vectors of transmission.[12] Each has characteristics that condition whether innovations spread quickly or slowly. Boushey uses the term "policy outbreak" to describe "a process characterized by a positive feedback cycle leading to the extremely rapid adoption of policy innovations across states."[13] Thus, while some policies spread slowly, others break out rapidly due to a confluence of favorable agent, host, and vector characteristics. This is like how a confluence of factors, such as overcrowded tenements, lack of fresh water, and failed quarantining, led to the 1849 outbreak of cholera in New York City.[14]

While Boushey's epidemiological model explains both rapid and slow adoption, as well as elevates the role of interest groups as vectors of policy transmission, it fails to account for the main purpose of epidemiological modeling: containment. Public health officials do not simply seek to understand why contagion occurs; they want to stop it. This is quite different from how policy diffusion is traditionally viewed. Innovations are typically viewed positively, often with references to Supreme Court Justice Louis Brandeis's reference to states as "laboratories of democracy." The laboratories are supposed to be experimenting for the purpose of solving public problems. Thus, the failure to examine the place of quarantine in Boushey's model is understandable. But policy innovations are not always positive.[15] Or, at least, they are not always viewed positively by all actors across the federal system. In fact, there is a great deal of conflict within American federalism, including during policy diffusion.[16] Marijuana liberalization is a good example of this dynamic, where states are defying the federal government in the creation of a new policy.[17]

This shortcoming is apparent in our limited understanding of vertical policy diffusion between local governments and states. One study found two pathways for the adoption of state smoking restrictions due to local pressure: the snowball effect or the pressure valve effect.[18] In the case of a snowball effect, states take up innovations when a critical mass of local governments has previously adopted them. In the case of a pressure valve, states act, at least in nominal ways, to appease local governments, even if the state government is not entirely supportive of the policy. These are important insights into how states emulate local governments, but the model does not address a third potential option: suppressing local action through state power. I refer to this option as diffusion quarantine. Before discussing how and why states quarantine local policy innovations, it is first necessary to establish the original meaning of the terms *quarantine* and *cordon sanitaire*.

Quarantine and Cordon Sanitaire

Quarantining the sick to protect the healthy extends deep into human history, but the procedure and terminology were formalized during the Black Death in Europe in the fourteenth century.[19] At the time, the Great Council in the Mediterranean city of Ragusa adopted a requirement of isolating outside visitors for thirty days before allowing them admission to the city. By extending the isolation to forty days, the policy of *quarantino* was formally established.[20] Cordon sanitaire is commonly attributed to the French sending thirty thousand troops to the Pyrenes in 1821 to prevent the spread of a plague from Spain. While often used interchangeably, the terms have important distinctions. Quarantine involves the physical removal or siphoning of known or potential infecteds to a remote location, often to protect a domestic population from outside disease. Cordon sanitaire involves separating communities from each other for the purpose of allowing a disease to run its course in one population for the sake of protecting another. In the case of France and Spain, this meant preventing the movement of people across a national border. Or, as in the case of the 1899 outbreak of bubonic plague in Honolulu's Chinatown, segments of an urban population can be isolated with a cordon of police, military, or public health officials.

The key feature shared between both tactics, and that is relevant to our present discussion of preemption, is the decision to separate a "healthy" population from one that is infected. Regardless of whether it is removal to isolation or the physical separation of communities, governments are using state power to protect healthy populations. Thus, the practices of quarantine and cordon sanitaire by public health officials form the conceptual foundation for innovation quarantine.

In fact, applying the concept of quarantine to policy diffusion is not a stretch of the imagination if one considers the use of epidemiological language in describing the spread, and containment, of ideologies. Western Europe and the United States sought to contain the Soviets/Bolsheviks, the United States "quarantined" Cuba in the 1960s, and today there are efforts to contain the spread of far-right/fascist ideology in Europe and the alt-right in the United States.[21] Thus, like ideological cordons, diffusion quarantine is the use of state power to prevent the spread of innovations that a state government finds undesirable.

State–Local Relations, Preemption, and Diffusion Quarantine

While the structure of the American federal system is relatively clear regarding the sovereign existence of the states and the federal government, the United States Constitution does not provide for, nor does it regulate, local governments. In fact, in 1907, the United States Supreme Court, in *Hunter v. Pittsburgh* (207 U.S. 161), held that "municipal corporations owe their origin to, and derive their powers and rights wholly from, the [state] legislature. [The state] breathes into [municipalities] the breath of life, without which [they] cannot exist." Thus, states, which establish the conditions for municipal incorporation under their own constitutions or by statute, have a say in local governance. The landscape of state–local relations, however, is complicated.

Dillon's Rule, named for Chief Justice of the Iowa Supreme Court Forest Dillon, holds that local governments may only do what state governments explicitly allow. This is different than the relationship between the states and federal government because states have sovereignty and both the states and the federal government have reserved and enumerated powers under the Constitution. Ten states reject Dillon's Rule, but the remaining forty apply it to some or all municipal incorporations (see figure 6.2).[22] This grants the states a great deal of power over local policy and sets the stage for potential conflicts.

The forty Dillon's Rule states, however, have either constitutional or statutory provisions for home rule in certain municipalities. The difference in perspective between Dillon's Rule and home rule may be best described relative to the direct role of the state in local affairs. Under Dillon's Rule, municipalities may not act unless explicitly authorized by state legislatures. Under home rule, municipalities may act until they are explicitly or implicitly prevented from doing so by the state. Thus, home rule does not change the fact that states have the power to set the boundaries on municipal incorporation, but it does shift the onus for preemption from state inaction (under Dillon's Rule) to state action. This means that a given state must expend legislative resources weighing in on local issues, which competes with other demands on crowded state agendas. This is akin to the resource trade-off states face when adopting innovative policies.

Traditionally, state preemption legislation set the floor for local government regulations, meaning they set a minimum standard for local governments.[23] Recent "maximum preemption" laws, however, have prohibited local government action or set ceilings on local government actions.[24] It is these cases of maximum preemption that fall under the concept of diffusion quarantine, meaning states are using their power, and legislatures their policymaking resources, to prevent the spread of a policy innovation among their local governments. Some states even "weaponize" preemption by holding local officials personally responsible for violations of state preemption laws. In Florida, local officials can be removed from office. In Mississippi and Arizona, local officials are subject to fines up to fifty thousand dollars. The growing use of extreme approaches to preemption threaten to chill local government action.

Preemption is not the only choice for quarantining local governments, as states try other mechanisms short of explicit preemption to implicitly prompt local governments to restrain their policy options. Though ultimately struck down in state court due to single subject rule violation, Pennsylvania tried to expose local governments to lawsuits should they adopt stricter restrictions on firearms. The Uniform Firearms Act in Pennsylvania is a collection of statutes that prevents local governments from adopting gun restrictions stricter than state law. To give the act more teeth, Pennsylvania adopted the nullified statute in 2014 that allowed for direct suits against municipalities adopting restrictive

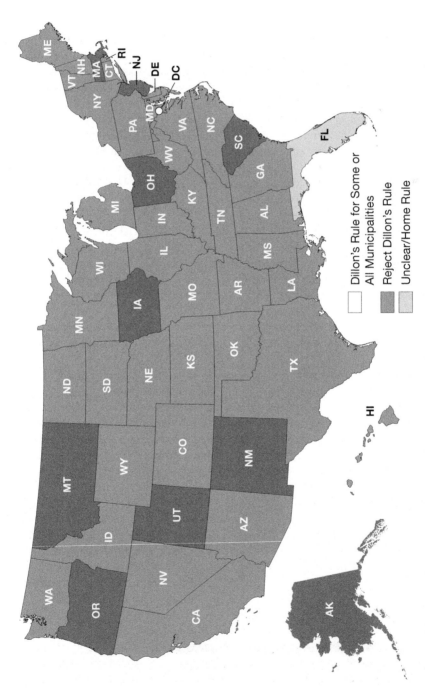

Figure 6.2 States That Use and Reject Dillon's Rule

Dillon's Rule for Some or All Municipalities

Reject Dillon's Rule

Unclear/Home Rule

gun ordinances, without the requirement of proving injury. Thus, the state was allowing outside actors to sue local governments to enforce state law.

States also utilize their power of the purse to prevent local government defiance. Not unlike the current threats to "sanctuary cities" by the Trump administration, states threaten defiant local governments with the loss of revenue. In 2016, Arizona's legislature and Governor Doug Ducey threatened local governments with losing state funding if they raised their minimum wage, only to have voters approve a November ballot measure increasing the state's minimum to ten dollars per hour. Also in 2016, Arizona passed laws barring local governments from adopting regulations that substantially burden business and allow state legislators to lodge formal complaints with the state attorney general when a local government violates state law. In response, the local government must either repeal the violating statute or the attorney general will instruct the state treasurer to withhold state funds from the municipality. Each of the tools outlined above has a common factor—states are expending scarce legislating resources in the effort to stop the spread of local policy innovations that they view as undesirable.

There is substantial variation in when and for what issues state governments are engaging in preemption. While not restricted to Republican state governments, many of the states that have been more heavily engaged in preemption have been conservative. Figure 6.3 demonstrates this variation within one policy domain: workers' rights. Local governments have passed a variety of measures to support workers, only to have states preempt some or all of them. The Economic Policy Institute tracks the advancement of preemption legislation in states for six specific policy areas: minimum wage, fair scheduling, project labor agreements, prevailing wage, paid leave, and gig economy.[25] Figure 6.3 presents a map of U.S. states shaded based on how many of the six areas were preempted by state law through 2018. The practice started in Louisiana in 1997 but increased rapidly between 2013 and 2017. The question becomes, how can we explain this variation in when and which states adopt preemption measures?

Why Do States Quarantine Policy?

A healthy body of literature surrounding the politics of preemption is developing, but I argue that the study of policy diffusion offers a theoretical framework upon which to build a theory of state preemption activity.[26] In fact, many of the suppositions currently offered for the emergence of increased and stricter preemption activity fit well within what we have learned over the past fifty years about the diffusion of policy innovations. The standard model of policy diffusion contains the following general elements: internal characteristics of the states, external influences, and characteristics of the innovation.[27] Each broad category contains a wide variety of diffusion predictors. This section presents common explanations offered for state preemption, identifies the linkage between each explanation and policy diffusion theory, and then leverages diffusion theory to offer additional explanatory factors that go beyond observations of single acts of preemption.

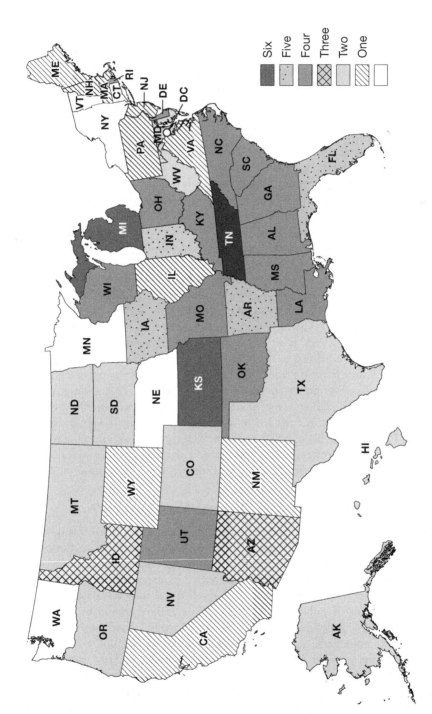

Figure 6.3 States Adopting Workers' Rights Preemptions

Internal Characteristics

The first explanation for recent preemption efforts most commonly cited among scholarly and journalistic writers is Republican control of state governments.[28] As of January 2017, Republicans had single-party control (i.e., control the legislature and governor's office) of twenty-four states, whereas Democrats control 78 percent of the country's forty largest cities.[29] The potential for state–local conflict is thus heightened and is apparent in state efforts to punish cities for adopting progressive prerogatives, like sanctuary status. In fact, while so much attention has been paid to the Trump administration's threats against local governments over immigration, the groundwork for conflict was arguably laid during the Obama administration. Facing gridlock in Congress and a wave of Republican wins in statehouses, the Obama administration sought to bypass states and work directly with local governments, particularly cities, to enact a progressive agenda.[30] Thus, partisan composition of state, local, and even the federal government contributes to increased preemption activity. The opportunity for adoption of innovations opened by unified party control is not foreign to the study of policy diffusion.[31] That said, it is unlikely that partisan control is the only explanatory factor for the increase in preemption activity and weaponization of preemption, given that Democratic mayors have dealt with Republican state capitols in the past. In fact, preemption fights are ever present in the American federal system.[32]

Political polarization, likely in concert with partisan splits across all three levels of government (federal, state, local), may also pay a role in the growing use of preemption legislation. Fay points out that there is little incentive for Republicans in Congress to listen to Democratic mayors.[33] Further, given the role of cities as lobbyists of their state governments,[34] it is likely that Republicans in states with high political polarization are equally likely to ignore the needs of cities. Polarization influences both policy and political learning in diffusion.[35]

The role of interest groups in lobbying for and promoting preemption model legislation is another common explanation offered for recent preemption activity. This should not be a surprise, given that interest groups are offered as *the* vector of transmission in Boushey's epidemiological model. Policy entrepreneurs and interest groups are often involved in coordinating the transfer of policy between states.[36] The American Legislative Exchange Council is often cited in recent cases of preemption, due to its adoption and promotion of model preemption bills that fight local increases in the minimum wage and paid family leave.[37] Broadly speaking, ALEC is receiving increased scholarly attention as a facilitator of diffusion for conservative policy innovations.[38] The organization employs a two-tiered lobbying approach when it comes to local policy. ALEC promotes preemption legislation at the state level while its sister organization, the American City County Exchange (ACCE), targets local governments directly. Counterbalancing, the progressive State Innovation Exchange (SIX) promotes progressive policies, like increasing the minimum wage, which conservative states preempt. Other interest groups like the National Rifle Association and the tobacco lobby have also long been involved in promoting preemption of local gun and tobacco restrictions, including threatening local governments through litigation. Such lobbying is a "power play" whereby "an industry uses it superior influence to preempt state or local authority."[39] Thus, interest groups remain an important vector for preemption legislation.

Local governments also welcome state leadership on certain issues. A survey of local officials in Michigan found that while "70% of Michigan's local government officials believe the State government is taking away too much decision-making authority from local governments," pluralities or majorities supported state policy leadership in the following areas: antidiscrimination, social issues (e.g., public welfare, homelessness, gun control), business issues (e.g., minimum wage, plastic bag bans, Uber, Airbnb), and environmental issues (e.g., water, solid waste, agriculture, and forestry).[40] Local officials desired control over land use and planning, zoning, permitting, local finance and tax policy, local government operations, and economic development. Thus, the degree of resistance/opposition to state preemption varies across local governments and policy domains. Much attention is paid to cities due to the partisan split with Republican state governments, but other municipalities may not share their perspective.

Legislative term limits may also play a role in the extent to which state governments are willing to preempt localities. Term limits predictably increase turnover in legislative membership, which can affect representation of local governments in two ways. First, it eliminates institutional memory that is important to local governments, particularly among legislators who previously held local office. Second is the concern of a "Burkean shift" toward feelings of trusteeship instead of parochialism among term-limited legislators.[41] This means that while high turnover opens opportunities for local government officials to move up and influence state policy, it also makes state government more of a stepping stone to higher office, which require less of a focus on local interests.[42] Studies from several states find that the imposition of term limits did in fact increase the representation of local-level officials within the legislature.[43] Thus, the consideration of preemption by state legislators offers another means for testing the effects of term limits in state governance.

Diffusion Mechanisms

An important question to consider for preemption legislation is by which diffusion mechanism is it most likely to spread (see figure 6.1)? In this case, states are likely responding to actions both by their own local governments, particularly cities, and by those in nearby states. The influence of neighboring localities could come through competition, whereby states with neighbors who have large populations on the border compete with each other.[44] In the case of diffusion quarantine, however, states are not acting in competition with their peers but to block the influx of policy ideas from neighboring cities. In fact, Fay argues that the regional effect of states adopting constitutional bans on same-sex marriage reflected lawmakers "protecting" their states from the spread of marriage equality.[45] Thus, it may not be actions by neighboring states that facilitate a regional pattern of preemption adoption but actions by urban centers that are geographically close to the state's borders. The influence of neighbor states is often characterized as a learning process, but preemption is a negative form of learning. Meaning, instead of learning for the purposes of solving a problem, states are observing the potential for "infection" of their localities by policies in local governments from neighboring states.

Given the potential for diffusion quarantine being driven, at least in part, by ideological differences between state and local governments, it is impossible to ignore the possibility of an ideological pathway of diffusion.[46] Minimum wage and paid family leave preemption model legislation promoted by ALEC serves as a useful example. It is likely that such conservative legislation only diffuses among a subset of more conservative states. This is like the liberal ideological diffusion of medical marijuana.[47] Thus, instead of an increasing pressure among all states for adopting preemption statutes over time, there is more likely a division of states based on ideology, whereby preemption is spreading among ideologically similar states that are not necessarily contiguous.

Policy Characteristics

The final major category of diffusion predictors are the characteristics of policy innovations. Policy attributes influence both the likelihood and speed of innovation adoption.[48] Of the five attributes identified by broader innovation diffusion theory—relative advantage, compatibility, complexity, observability, and trialability—I contend that relative advantage, compatibility, and observability are likely the most relevant to preemption adoption.[49]

Relative advantage is the degree to which a given innovation is superior to the status quo (often based on cost–benefit analysis). In the case of preemption, states should be more likely to preempt if there is a perception that the local policy will hurt the state in some way. What is important here is *perception*.[50] While there may be ways to identify the effects of a policy, legislators form their perception of its threat to the state from a variety of sources. Thus, relative advantage is challenging to measure, but it could be easier for some policy domains for which there is direct competition between the state and local governments or between urban and rural local governments. Take minimum wage, for instance. If a conservative state has an eight-dollar minimum wage and a large city within that state wants to raise it to fifteen dollars, it is possible that the state government will push back on ideological grounds and also because suburban or rural local governments resent competition from a nonuniform minimum wage. Commentators have noted growing urban–rural resentment, which likely plays a role in preemption cases where city action disadvantages rural municipalities.[51]

Compatibility is a relatively straightforward concept and easier to measure. For example, one could directly compare the ideology of localities adopting an innovation with the ideology of state legislatures. The greater the ideological distance between state and local governments, the more likely local policy innovations will be viewed as a threat by the state. Finally, observability, often called salience by political scientists, should increase the perception of the infectiousness of an innovation. For example, high public attention to a fifteen-dollar minimum wage may prompt swift action from state legislatures if local governments try to increase their own minimum wages. Likewise, the spate of gig economy preemptions comes with rapidly increasing attention to services like Uber, Lyft, and Airbnb.

Localities Fight Back

Just as states can defy the federal government, and even do so in ways that foster innovative policies,[52] local governments have tools for resistance. This is especially the case for large cities whose size and economic power are influential in state politics.[53] In fact, preemption by the state can have the opposite effect of that intended, at least in the short term. Local governments fight back simply by adopting conflictual policies in the first place.[54] For example, when North Carolina considered preempting local tobacco restrictions, local governments rapidly adopted such restrictions in the lead-up to state preemption.[55] Over the past year, mayors in cities across the United States have positioned themselves as part of the "resistance" against the Trump administration. Mayor of Charlottesville, Virginia, Mike Singer called his city the "capital of resistance."[56] Such defiance can be either symbolic or substantive.[57] Thus, localities may respond to state threats of preemption with outright defiance and continue innovating, perhaps even at an increased rate.

Local governments also challenge state preemption in the courts. Granted, this option proves costly, though cities often do so with the support of sympathetic state legislators.[58] For example, over thirty Arizona state legislators joined with representatives of local government in suing the state to block its preemption of local paid sick leave ordinances. Additionally, the two primary names on the 2016 Pennsylvania gun control case discussed above, *Leach, D. et al. v. Turzai, M. et al.*, are state Senator Daylin Leach (D-Montgomery and Delaware) and Speaker of the House Mike Turzai (R-Allegheny). In both cases, however, the suits are about technicalities, not the fundamental question of whether the state's preemption action was lawful. In *Leach v. Turzai*, the legal challenge was based on the state's single subject rule. In the Arizona case, the point of contention was whether the state law supersedes a 2006 ballot measure without the requisite three-quarters vote in the legislature. This leads to another potential source of local defiance, at least in some states: ballot initiatives.

There is mixed evidence that the availability of ballot measures serves as a "gun behind the door" to reticent legislatures, but ballot initiatives can be used as a check on unpopular legislative action.[59] After Arizona's state government threatened municipalities over efforts to increase the minimum wage, the state's electorate passed Proposition 206, raising Arizona's minimum wage to ten dollars per hour in 2017 and twelve dollars by 2020. The proposition also declared that paid sick time is a right of workers. This was not the only minimum wage bill that appeared on state ballots during the 2016 election. Colorado, Maine, and Washington also adopted increased minimum wages through ballot measures. Thus, initiatives can serve as a means for pushing back against state preemption and for driving the spread of innovative policies.[60] Further, local-level ballot initiatives, such as those banning hydraulic fracturing of natural gas, can also thrust local governments into a position of defiance. Preliminary evidence suggests that partisanship and proximity to negative focusing events are part of the story for why local populations support fracking ban ballot measures.[61]

Another possibility for local governments is to behave as lobbyists. Local governments can lobby their own states, but evidence from big cities suggests that their position can be undermined by disagreement among their delegates.[62] Alternatively, local governments can lobby the federal government for resources, especially when their preferences diverge from those of the state legislature. Goldstein and You found increased federal lobbying by cities between 1999 and 2012, as the state–local gap also increased.[63]

In sum, state acts of preemption and local level defiance, that is, a conflictual federalism, can be destructive (in respect to local policy innovations), but it can also be creative. State–local struggles over local policy initiatives thus fit within the concept of defiant innovation[64] and, therefore, the broader theory of policy diffusion. Furthermore, the above demonstrates how policy diffusion theory, and the concept of diffusion quarantine, helps us better understand state–local conflict.

Conclusion

This chapter presents policy diffusion theory as a means for helping us better understand when and why states choose to preempt local governments. By appropriating the concept of quarantine from epidemiology, students of state and local government can understand not only positive innovation that occurs in American federalism but also conflictual acts like preemption. It is likely that both circumstances internal to the states (especially partisan divergence between state and local governments, interest group presence, term limits, and availability of the initiative) and external (proximity to neighboring cities and ideological cues) and characteristics of the innovations themselves (observability, compatibility, and relative advantage) shape preemption decisions by state governments. Much research is still required to test these ideas, but fleshing out the concept of diffusion quarantine can be useful to both scholars and those who work in public service. Both need to better understand how and why conflict emerges in American federalism.

Scott Jensen

Director, Department of Labor and Training
State of Rhode Island

Scott Jensen was appointed director of the Rhode Island Department of Labor and Training by Governor Gina Raimondo in 2015, to launch Real Jobs Rhode Island, a workforce development grant platform. "We needed to rethink the way we match workers who need jobs with employers who need employees. Real Jobs Rhode Island has fundamentally changed the way we 'do workforce development' by letting employers shape the training networks that lead to their jobs," explains Jensen. This approach to workforce development is a "sector strategy" placing business at the center of workforce development and developing training networks that involve state government, education institutions, labor organizations, and nonprofit organizations.

Jensen's background illustrates that people enter public service through diverse paths. He completed a B.A. in history from Illinois State University and a M.A. in liberal education from St. John's College. He worked toward a doctoral degree in philosophy and taught for three years, but other opportunities emerged and opened doors to his current work. He ran for and won a position on the city council in Easton, Maryland. He explains that local elected office drew on skills he had developed in education, as he engaged in policy discussions in the community. His work as a union organizer also engaged him in state-level policy discussions and political campaigns. Eventually, he was called to state service. Before moving to Rhode Island, Jensen was the deputy secretary for labor in Maryland.

Students interested in public service should carefully identify the area of government in which they hope to engage. For Jensen, this was leadership in labor policy at the state level. He also encourages students to understand their motivations for public service. "Be able to discern an agenda that helps people through government. There is no sense of being in government unless your primary motivation is to achieve public good." Jensen also emphasizes the development of skills that will be used on a regular basis. "The most practical skill set is interest-based negotiations and dispute resolution," he explains. Each day, people in government leadership positions must negotiate solutions. Developing negotiation skills will be relevant to work in public service broadly but is particularly important for students who seek jobs that require coordination with other levels of government and nonprofit organizations.

Interview: October 21, 2019

Discussion Questions

1. Why might a state preempt a local government? Are there times when pre-emption seems inappropriate? Discuss when and why preemption occurs.
2. What are the implications of state preemption of local governments for representation of citizen's interests? How should state governments weigh statewide versus localized interests and demands?
3. What are the advantages and disadvantages of having a single policy across the state? Likewise, what are the advantages and disadvantages of allowing a policy to vary throughout the state? How should state government decide when to make a policy uniform and when to allow it to vary?

Notes

[1] Jack L. Walker, "The Diffusion of Innovations among the American States," *American Political Science Review* 63, no. 3 (1969): 880–99.

[2] Frederick J. Boehmke and Paul Skinner, "State Policy Innovativeness Revisited," *State Politics & Policy Quarterly* 12, no. 3 (2012): 303–29; Virginia Gray, "Innovation in the States: A Diffusion Study," *American Political Science Review* 67, no. 4 (1973): 1174–85; Walker, "Diffusion of Innovations among the American States."

[3] Henry R. Glick and Scott P. Hays, "Innovation and Reinvention in State Policymaking: Theory and the Evolution of Living Will Laws," *Journal of Politics* 53, no. 3 (1991): 835–50; Scott P. Hays, "Influences on Reinvention during the Diffusion of Innovations," *Political Research Quarterly* 49, no. 3 (1996): 631–50; Joshua M. Jansa, Eric R. Hansen, and Virginia H. Gray, "Copy and Paste Lawmaking: Legislative Professionalism and Policy Reinvention in the States," *American Politics Research* 47, no. 4 (2019): 739–67.

[4] Walker, "Diffusion of Innovations among the American States."

[5] Erin R. Graham, Charles R. Shipan, and Craig Volden, "The Diffusion of Policy Diffusion Research in Political Science," *British Journal of Political Science* 43, no. 3 (2013): 673–701; Julianna Pacheco, "The Social Contagion Model: Exploring the Role of Public Opinion on the Diffusion of Antismoking Legislation across the American States," *Journal of Politics* 74, no. 1 (2012): 187–202; Charles R. Shipan and Craig Volden, "The Mechanisms of Policy Diffusion," *American Journal of Political Science* 52, no. 4 (2008): 840–57.

[6] Andrew Karch, "Vertical Diffusion and the Policy-Making Process: The Politics of Embryonic Stem Cell Research," *Political Research Quarterly* 65, no. 1 (2012): 48–61; Priscilla M. Regan and Christopher J. Deering, "State Opposition to REAL ID," *Publius: The Journal of Federalism* 39, no. 3 (2009): 476–505; Susan Welch and Kay Thompson, "The Impact of Federal Incentives on State Policy Innovation," *American Journal of Political Science* 24, no. 4 (1980): 715–29.

[7] Pacheco, "Social Contagion Model."

[8] Andrew Karch, *Democratic Laboratories: Policy Diffusion among the American States* (Ann Arbor: University of Michigan Press, 2007).

[9] Charles R. Shipan and Craig Volden, "Policy Diffusion: Seven Lessons for Scholars and Practitioners," *Public Administration Review* 72, no. 6 (2012): 788–96.

[10] Daniel J. Mallinson, "Identifying and Explaining Instability in the General Model of Policy Innovation Diffusion," Ph.D. diss., Pennsylvania State University, 2015.

[11] Frank Baumgartner, Bryan D. Jones, and Peter B. Mortensen, "Punctuated Equilibrium Theory: Explaining Stability and Change in Public Policymaking," in *Theories of the Policy Process*, ed. Paul A. Sabatier and Christopher M. Weible, 59–104 (Boulder, CO: Westview Press, 2014).

[12] Graeme Boushey, *Policy Diffusion Dynamics in America* (New York: Cambridge University Press, 2010).

[13] Ibid., 5.

[14] Sonia Shah, *Pandemic: Tracking Contagions, from Cholera to Ebola and Beyond* (New York: Sarah Crichton Books, 2016).

[15] Shipan and Volden, "Policy Diffusion."

[16] Jessica Bulman-Pozen and Heather K. Gerken, "Uncooperative Federalism," *Yale Law Journal* 118, no. 7 (2009): 1256–1310; A. Lee Hannah and Daniel J. Mallinson, "Defiant Innovation: The Adoption of Medical Marijuana Laws in the American States," *Policy Studies Journal* 46, no. 2 (2018): 402–23.

[17] Hannah and Mallinson, "Defiant Innovation."

[18] Charles R. Shipan and Craig Volden, "Bottom-Up Federalism: The Diffusion of Antismoking Policies from U.S. Cities to States," *American Journal of Political Science* 50, no. 4 (2006): 825–43.

[19] Philip A. Mackowiak and Paul S. Sehdev, "The Origin of Quarantine," *Clinical Infectious Diseases* 35, no. 9 (2002): 1071–72.

[20] Ibid.

[21] Jan Erk, "From Vlaams Blok to Vlaams Belang: The Belgian Far-Right Renames Itself," *West European Politics* 28, no. 3 (2005):493–502; Wouter Van Der Brug and Meindert Fennema, "Protest or Mainstream? How the European Anti-Immigrant Parties Developed into Two Separate Groups by 1999," *European Journal of Political Research* 42, no. 1 (2003): 55–76; H. H. Fisher, *The Famine in Soviety Russia* (New York: Macmillan, 1927); James Matthews, "Battling Bolshevik Bogeymen: Spain's Cordon Sanitaire against Revolution from a European Perspective, 1917–1923," *Journal of Military History* 80, no. 3 (2016): 725–55; Myres S. McDougal, "The Soviet-Cuban Quarantine and Self-Defense," *American Journal of International Law* 57, no. 3 (1963): 597–604; Joost Van Spanje and Wouter Van Der Brug, "The Party as Pariah: The Exclusion of Anti-immigration Parties and Its Effect on Their Ideological Positions," *West European Politics* 30, no. 5 (2007): 1022–40.

[22] There is a debate as to whether Florida is the eleventh state to reject Dillon's Rule.

[23] Marni von Wilpert, "City Governments Are Raising Standards for Working People—and State Legislators Are Lowering Them Back Down," Economic Policy Institute, August 28, 2017, https://www.epi.org/publication/city-governments-are-raising-standards-for-working-people-and-state-legislators-are-lowering-them-back-down/.

[24] Lori Riverstone-Newell, "The Rise of State Preemption Laws in Response to Local Policy Innovation," *Publius: The Journal of Federalism* 47, no. 3 (2017): 403–25.

[25] For the Economic Policy Institute's interactive map, see http://www.epi.org/preemption-map/.

[26] See Christopher B. Goodman, "State Legislative Ideology and the Preemption of City Ordinances: The Case of Worker Rights Laws," *SocArXiv*, February 1, 2019, https://doi.org/10.31235/osf.io/2mnws.

[27] Mallinson, "Identifying and Explaining Instability."

[28] William D. Hicks et al., "Home Rule Be Damned: Exploring Policy Conflicts between the Statehouse and City Hall," *PS: Political Science & Politics* 51, no. 1 (2018): 36–38; Riverstone-Newell, "Rise of State Preemption Laws."

[29] Sophie Quinton, "Expect More Conflict between Cities and States," *Stateline*, January 25, 2017, http://www.pewtrusts.org/en/research-and-analysis/blogs/stateline/2017/01/25/expect-more-conflict-between-cities-and-states.

[30] Daniel C. Vock, "How Obama Changed the Relationship between Washington, the States and the Cities," *Governing*, June 2016, https://www.governing.com/topics/politics/gov-obama-federalism.html.

[31] Frances Stokes Berry and William D. Berry, "State Lottery Adoptions as Policy Innovations: An Event History Analysis," *American Political Science Review* 82, no. 4 (1990): 395–415.

[32] Riverstone-Newell, "Rise of State Preemption Laws."

[33] D. L. Fay, "Moves and Countermoves: Countermovement Diffusion of State Constitutional Amendments," *Policy Studies Journal* 46, no. 2 (2018): 354–77.

[34] Rebecca Goldstein and Hye Young You, "Cities as Lobbyists," *American Journal of Political Science* 61, no. 4 (2017): 864–76.

[35] Daniel J. Mallinson, "Who Are Your Neighbors? The Role of Ideology and Decline of Geographic Proximity in the Diffusion of Policy Innovations," *Policy Studies Journal* (forthcoming).

[36] Donald P. Haider-Markel, "Policy Diffusion as a Geographical Expansion of the Scope of Political Conflict: Same-Sex Marriage Bans in the 1990s," *State Politics & Policy*

Quarterly 1, no. 1 (2001): 5–26; Debra Horner and Thomas Ivacko, "Michigan Local Leaders' Views on State Preemption and How to Share Policy Authority," Center for Local, State, and Urban Policy, June 2017, http://closup.umich.edu/michigan-public-policy-survey/62/michigan-local-leaders-views-on-state-preemption-and-how-to-share-policy-authority/.

[37] Riverstone-Newell, "Rise of State Preemption Laws."

[38] Alexander Hertel-Fernandez, Theda Skocpol, and Daniel Lynch, "Business Associations, Conservative Networks, and the Ongoing Republican War over Medicaid Expansion," *Journal of Health Politics, Policy and Law* 41, no. 2 (2016): 239–86; Jansa, Hansen, and Gray, "Copy and Paste Lawmaking."

[39] M. Pertschuk, J. L. Pomeranz, J. R. Aoki, M. A. Larkin, and M. Paloma, "Assessing the Impact of Federal and State Preemption in Public Health: A Framework for Decision Makers," *Journal of Public Health Management and Practice* 19, no. 3 (2013): 2.

[40] Horner and Ivacko, "Michigan Local Leaders' Views on State Preemption."

[41] John M. Carey, Richard G. Niemi, Lynda W. Powell, and Gary F. Moncrief, "The Effects of Term Limits on State Legislatures: A New Survey of the 50 States," *Legislative Studies Quarterly* 31, no. 1 (2006): 105–34.

[42] Michael B. Berkman, "State Legislators in Congress: Strategic Politicians, Professional Legislatures, and the Party Nexus," *American Journal of Political Science* 38, no. 4 (1994): 1025–55.

[43] John C. Green, Christopher Z. Mooney, Richard J. Powell, and John C. Green, eds., *Legislating without Experience: Case Studies in State Legislative Term Limits* (Lanham, MD: Lexington Press, 2007); Mark P. Petracca, "A Legislature in Transition: The California Experience with Term Limits," Institute of Governmental Studies, UC Berkley, 1996.

[44] William D. Berry and Brady Baybeck, "Using Geographic Information Systems to Study Interstate Competition," *American Political Science Review* 99, no. 4 (2005): 505–19.

[45] Fay, "Moves and Countermoves."

[46] Lawrence J. Grossback, Sean Nicholson-Crotty, and David A. M. Peterson, "Ideology and Learning in Policy Diffusion," *American Politics Research* 32, no. 5 (2004): 521–45.

[47] Hannah and Mallinson, "Defiant Innovation."

[48] Todd Makse and Craig Volden, "The Role of Policy Attributes in the Diffusion of Innovations," *Journal of Politics* 73, no. 1 (2011): 108–24; Daniel J. Mallinson, "Building a Better Speed Trap: Measuring Policy Adoption Speed in the American States," *State Politics & Policy Quarterly* 16, no. 1 (2016): 98–120; Sean Nicholson-Crotty, "The Politics of Diffusion: Public Policy in the American States," *Journal of Politics* 71, no. 1 (2009): 192–205.

[49] Everett M. Rogers, *Diffusion of Innovations*, 5th ed. (New York: Free Press, 2003).

[50] Makse and Volden, "Role of Policy Attributes in the Diffusion of Innovations."

[51] David A. Graham, "Red State, Blue City," *Atlantic*, March 2017, https://www.theatlantic.com/magazine/archive/2017/03/red-state-blue-city/513857/.

[52] Hannah and Mallinson, "Defiant Innovation."

[53] Gerald Gamm and Thad Kousser, "No Strength in Numbers: The Failure of Big-City Bills in American State Legislatures, 1880–2000," *American Political Science Review* 107, no. 4 (2013): 663–78.

[54] Ann O'M. Bowman, "The State-Local Government(s) Conundrum: Power and Design," *Journal of Politics* 79, no. 4 (2017): 1119–29.

[55] E. Conlisk, M. Siegel, E. Lengerich, W. Mac Kenzie, S. Malek, and M. Eriksen, "The Status of Local Smoking Regulations in North Carolina Following a State Preemption Bill," *JAMA* 273, no. 10 (1995): 805–7.

[56] Nora Neus, "Charlottesville Mayor Holds Rally to Declare City Capital of Resistance," NBC29, January 31, 2017, http://www.nbc29.com/story/34389763/charlottesville-mayor-holds-rally-to-declare-city-capital-of-resistance.

[57] Jonathan M. Fisk, "Fractured Relationships: Exploring Municipal Defiance in Colorado, Texas, and Ohio," *State and Local Government Review* 48, no. 2 (2016): 75–86.

[58] Lori Riverstone-Newell, "Bottom-Up Activism: A Local Political Strategy for Higher Policy Change," *Publius: The Journal of Federalism* 42, no. 3 (2012): 401–21.

[59] Edward L. Jr. Lascher, Michael G. Hagen, and Steven A. Rochlin, "Gun behind the Door? Ballot Initiatives, State Policies, and Public Opinion," *Journal of Politics* 58, no. 3 (1996): 760–75.

60   E.g., Hannah and Mallinson, "Defiant Innovation."

61   Jonathan M. Fisk, Yunmi Park, and Zachary Mahafza, "'Fractivism' in the City: Assessing Defiance at the Neighborhood Level," *State and Local Government Review* 49, no. 2 (2017): 105–16.

62   Gamm and Kousser, "No Strength in Numbers."

63   Goldstein and You, "Cities as Lobbyists."

64   Hannah and Mallinson, "Defiant Innovation."

CHAPTER 7

What Can Local Governments Do?
Variation across States

Agustín León-Moreta, University of New Mexico
Vittoria R. Totaro, University of New Mexico

This chapter presents a synthesis of theory and research about the functional roles (responsibilities) of municipal government in the American states. The chapter examines state and local factors contributing to differences in the functional responsibilities of municipalities. It highlights the importance of a broad assessment of state–local governance, with special consideration of state policies that regulate the functional responsibilities of municipal government.

Municipal government is an incorporated type of local government that provides a wide breadth of services to its communities. While other governments play relevant roles, tangentially or otherwise, municipal governments are in charge of fundamental local functions. This particularly is the case for functions derived from the general policing powers of municipalities (Spitzer 2000). Those functions can be broad in metropolitan areas where municipal governments are in charge of delivering core services, like public safety, emergency services, economic development, parks and recreation, solid waste management, transit, and the like. The specific roles of municipalities vary, however, across states. Some municipalities provide minimal services, whereas other municipalities provide a broad range of services. What functional roles do municipalities serve in the states? What factors account for different delegations of functional autonomy—the ability to determine what scope of services will be provided—from the state to their municipal governments?

These questions are critical for study and policy analysis for multiple reasons. First, municipal governments are the main type of general-purpose government as they spend more money and hire more employees than other local governments in the United States (US Census Bureau 2012). Second, municipal governments have functions, such as policing powers, that other local governments do not. Using those powers, municipalities carry out law enforcement, zoning, land use planning, and other regulatory functions that are employed to protect the public health, safety, and "morals" in their communities (Spitzer 2000). Using those general powers, municipal governments can regulate and intervene in private-sector actions in a way that other local governments cannot. Third, the functional responsibilities of municipal governments vary sharply across states, and those sharp variances merit attention.

Functional responsibility is defined as the breadth or scope of responsibilities carried out by municipal governments. The concept of functional responsibility has been employed in research for examining differences in the functionality of municipal government across states. The concept of functional responsibility accounts for the capacity of governments to deliver services to their communities. Understanding differences in functional responsibilities is central to discussions of what the role of local government should be in state–local systems (León-Moreta 2019; Jimenez 2014). To this effect, we look at the influence of local capacity, state rules, and coordination mechanisms that affect municipalities' ability to support and extend services in governmentally fragmented regions.

The chapter summarizes scholarship on the functional responsibilities of local government, focusing on the functional differentiation of governments—municipalities in particular—across the states. We further analyze factors that shape differences in the scope of functional responsibilities across municipalities. Broadly speaking, factors of influence may be categorized as economic and institutional factors. Economic factors include social and economic influences on local governments. Institutional factors include governmental and policy processes affecting the functional roles of municipal government in states. Importantly, the state–local system is the central framework for governance and service delivery at the local level.

Service and Policy Preferences

The demand for services is a basic factor influencing the functional responsibilities of municipal government (Fisher 2018). Local demand for services prompts local governments to extend their provision of services. Some services respond immediately to a growing demand for services, for example, utilities, assuming that municipal government has the capacity to increase the production of services upon demand. The demand for services is the primary factor that determines the functional scope of municipal government. As a provider of services, a municipal government will adjust its productive capacities to the demand for services in the community.

The functional responsibilities of governments reflect the demand for services in communities. There must be sufficient demand for services for a municipal government to begin the political process of determining the level of provision of services. As the political process results in decisions for service delivery, municipal governments will carry out functional programs to meet preferences for services. Still, a foundation of local capacities must be available for municipal governments to produce and deliver functional services to residents.

Community characteristics will shape the demand for services. Some basic factors underlying the demand for services include the population, demographic diversity, and wealth of the community (Honadle, Cigler, and Costa 2003). Differences in those factors will result in preferences for certain services rather than others. As a result, the functional programs of government reflect in part those underlying social and economic conditions in municipalities.

Metropolitan areas contain diverse populations whose preferences for services will differ substantially. The decentralized organization of governments in metropolitan areas facilitates the provision of services according to that diversity of preferences (Tiebout 1956). Mobile residents will be able to shop around for a municipal jurisdiction that offers them a preferred package of taxes and services. Tiebout (1956) noted that residents in a metropolitan area vote with their feet, moving across municipalities via residential relocation. Municipal fragmentation allows residents to choose those service packages across municipalities. As a consequence, fragmented regions tend to show wider differences in the functional responsibility of governments. In a fragmented region, some municipalities will offer limited services while other municipalities will offer broader packages of goods and services. In metropolitan regions, the central city typically offers a comprehensive range of goods and services while smaller municipalities offer fewer services. Metropolitan areas enable such a market for public goods and services whenever a multiplicity of municipalities is present.

Ideology may affect certain functional responsibilities of municipal government since it predicts the public preferences for the role of government in a democratic system. In more conservative municipalities, local services might be delegated to the private sector. In principle, ideology would affect the functional responsibilities of municipal government in a way similar to the effect of ideology at the state or federal levels. Research shows, however, that the effect of ideology is rather nuanced. Ideology explains the provision of services such as law enforcement, but it fails to explain the provision of other local services (Gerber and Hopkins 2011).

The influence of ideology thus hinges on the type of good or service. While conservatism is often interpreted as limiting the role of government, conservative ideology may actually result in governments increasing their spending in functions such as law enforcement. Ideology may not have the typically assumed effect: conservatism with smaller government, liberalism with larger government. Ideology has different effects on municipal functions, in fact altering the allocation of resources to particular programs (Tausanovitch and Warshaw 2014). Thus the assumption that conservatism and liberalism predict smaller and larger government may not hold at the local level. Ideology influences the allocation of resources between functions rather than the overall size of municipal government.

The State–Local Systems

The state–local framework is the central factor affecting the functional roles of municipal government. Specifically, home-rule and related legislation determine the ability of municipal governments to carry out their functions (Krane, Rigos, and Hill 2001). The state will enable or restrict the ability of municipal governments to govern, regulate, and deliver services. The state–local framework thus is the starting point for explaining and eventually adapting the functional responsibilities of municipalities. When a municipality wants to broaden its functions, it generally has to look to the state for authority to take on broader functional responsibilities. The state–local relationship, however, can be a turbulent one as the state preempts or overrides local policies.

Preemption is an action by which the state government adopts policies that override local policies, typically in an antilocal direction. Some municipalities have adopted ordinances dealing, for example, with controlled substances, immigration, employment, and other areas traditionally regulated by federal and state laws. Local ordinances can be in conflict with federal and state policies, then raising questions of federal and state preemption of those ordinances. Some states have explicitly prevented local governments from regulating areas such as gun control and minimum wages. Preemption is relevant to our analysis since it restricts a local government's ability to carry out its functional responsibilities (Shipan and Volden 2012). The states generally have the power of preemption. However, there is growing concern that state–local conflict has increased due to ideological polarization. Conservative legislatures have prevented cities from adopting progressive policies (Riverstone-Newell 2017). Though preemption targets specific policies, it gradually reduces the functional autonomy of municipal government.

Home rule offers municipal governments one line of legal defense. Based on home-rule provisions, municipal governments might be able to dispute the state preemption of local policies (Briffault 2006; Kean 1975). Even though the states have plenary control over their local subdivisions, home-rule legislation could give municipalities a degree of immunity against state intervention in local areas of responsibility. Under some circumstances, local governments may challenge state preemption of local policies before the courts. State courts may be willing to uphold certain powers of local government. Contesting state preemption through the courts can help local governments keep basic powers that local governments require. Although the states have general authority over their political subdivisions, home rule affords municipalities some degree of functionality and discretion that may be promoted for their governments.

In most cases, state courts will be deferential to the preemptive power of the states. But, in certain cases, the state courts can be supportive of functional autonomy for municipal governments. Home rule, especially constitutional home rule, may encourage the states to uphold a degree of substantive autonomy for municipalities. This will be less likely, however, in states that have a strict Dillon's Rule tradition. Dillon's Rule doctrine asserts that local governments derive their powers strictly from state delegation of authority. Under that doctrine, a local government may only provide those services explicitly authorized or enabled by a state grant of authority. Due to restricted functional autonomy, municipalities in Dillon's Rule states, for example, West Virginia, perform fewer functions than municipalities in other states (Gillette 1991; Krane, Rigos, and Hill 2001). To enhance the functional capacity of local governments, some states have adopted home-rule provisions. Alternatively, municipal governments can attempt to persuade state lawmakers for specific grants of functional autonomy. In effect, functional autonomy represents a delegation of authority by the state to local governments (Richardson 2011).

Local Capacities of Government

Structural capacity is a foundation of municipal functional responsibility. Structural capacity represents the ability of local governments to reorganize their governmental foundations. Structural capacity implies the ability of local governments to pursue proceedings of annexation, consolidation, secession, dissolution, or reorganization. It further involves changes in the legal basis and form of government (Boyne 1992). Structural capacity matters because, if this capacity increases, local governments will be able to adjust or enhance their structures to provide functional programs. Municipal governments can enhance their functional programs if they are able to reorganize their organizational structures. Structural capacity ultimately deals with institutional constraints on, or sources of, local government capacity.

Organizational capacity is the ability of local government to organize or reorganize its working processes for delivering functional programs. Under this general definition, greater organizational capacity allows a municipality to support or extend its services. Some municipalities have substantial capacities of reorganization with which to enhance their service programs, such as the ability to modify internal processes or, in an extreme situation, the ability to reorganize an entire government under proceedings of bankruptcy. In such a situation, a municipal government can stop its service delivery or even terminate some functional responsibilities on a permanent basis. The City of Highland Park, Michigan, had drastically reduced emergency services—911, for example—because of insolvency (Anderson 2014).

The capacity of reorganization allows municipalities to broaden or restrict their offering of functional programs as needed. In many cases, stronger organizational capacities allow governments to accommodate preferences for services through more or improved services.

Workforce capacity is another type of capacity that shapes the functional roles of municipal government. This capacity is a specific dimension of organizational capacity. If the workforce capacity of municipalities increases, the functional responsibilities of municipalities will increase as well (Burgess 1975). The state–local system can restrict a government's ability to employ a workforce. Some authors argue, for example, that California's collective bargaining requirements have affected the financial position of local governments (Lewin, Keefe, and Kochan 2012). Workforce capacity implies that municipal governments that have an ability to expand their workforce will be able to broaden their functional responsibilities as well. For this reason, the functional role of municipal governments depends on their capacity to employ personnel for delivering services. Workforce capacity reflects the ability of municipal governments to fulfill their responsibilities by employing human resources.

Fiscal capacity is another critical capacity since it relates to the ability of governments to fund their programs. It is both an economic and an institutional capacity. Fiscal capacity first depends on a local economic base so that the local government can tap that base for generating revenue. As well, fiscal capacity depends on an institutional or legal ability of governments to raise that revenue. Thus, it is equally important that the local economy has taxable resources and that the local government has an ability to resort to those resources by taxation. A municipal government should be able to raise the necessary resources to support its functional responsibilities. Higher fiscal capacity will generally result in an improved ability to deliver services.

Functions: Governmental and Proprietary

Since governments have diverse responsibilities, we may distinguish their responsibilities by their theoretical types. A broad classification can be made between governmental and proprietary functions. The governmental–proprietary distinction of functions is useful to differentiate the functions that the states delegate to local governments. With different governmental and proprietary responsibilities, municipal governments also have different capacities for delivering those different responsibilities.

Governmental functions include the traditional functions of municipal government such as police, fire, and regulation. Governmental functions are typically delegated by state law to municipalities (Reynolds 2015). Regulatory functions are generally related to the policing powers of municipalities. Municipal governments typically retain their regulatory functions and almost never delegate them to other entities (Fischel 2009). Regulatory functions, based on policing powers, include functions such as zoning and land use regulation. This and other regulatory functions are powers valued highly by both local officials and voters. Land use regulation in particular deals with the very nature of community composition and growth.

Proprietary functions, on the other hand, are business-like services that municipalities opt to provide (Reynolds 2015). Some municipal governments opt to provide, for example, golf courses or parking lots. These types of functions, though permissible by state law, need not be provided by municipalities. Because business-like functions may be optional for municipalities, it is often easier for them to contract out those functions. Proprietary functions are not necessarily required of municipalities. Municipalities opt to provide proprietary functions because they can improve the accessibility of services. Proprietary functions tend to be self-funded through business-like income. Typically funded by user fees and charges, these services are by definition proprietary functions. For this ability to tap business-like income, proprietary functions can be easier to deliver via alternative providers. One example is the municipal utilities supported by their own revenue sources. Utilities may be alternatively provided by contracting with other public or private entities.

Municipal governments differ in their functional roles, as above implied, because of differences in their proprietary functions. While most municipalities deliver governmental functions, they will differ in their choice of proprietary functions. Municipalities differ sharply in their methods of service delivery for services that are business-like in nature. Some municipalities offer a full range of proprietary services, whereas other municipalities rely on alternative providers for obtaining such services (Auby 2017).

Types of Municipalities

The types of municipality under state law are an essential foundation of their functional responsibility. Whereas some states offer localities much discretion for choosing a type of jurisdiction that suits their needs, other states offer less discretion (Berman 2020). We focus on municipal types of jurisdiction for understanding differences in the scope of functional responsibility among municipalities. The type of jurisdiction is a fundamental factor shaping the functional role of governments. If the state restricts their functional autonomy, municipalities have responsibilities limited to a narrow range of functions. But if the state allows for greater autonomy, municipalities are more likely to adapt their functional responsibilities to the demand for services. We consider the functional responsibilities of municipal governments in light of the types of municipalities that state law allows for.

Municipalities are classified by population in some states. In these states, population is the essential criterion in state law underlying the functional responsibility of governments. Population thresholds define the type of municipal structure available to communities (Frederickson 2016). The municipal structure will affect the functional responsibility of municipal governments. Large cities typically have the ability to design their own charters. They may adopt home-rule charters, in particular, granting them expansive functionality. By contrast, smaller municipalities, such as towns and villages, tend to have less functional autonomy.

The type of municipal jurisdiction is important because different jurisdictions have different organizational, fiscal, and workforce capacities (Bowman and Kearney 2017). Large cities have broader capacities in those areas. Smaller towns and villages, by contrast, have limited capacities as the state law differentiates local powers by types of municipalities. While our discussion relies on the census types of municipality (cities, towns, and villages), we note that state laws can differ from that generic census typology. Some states allow for even more types of municipality, while the State of Hawaii does not have any independent municipal jurisdiction.

City-county consolidation is one example of structural reorganization that affects the functional responsibilities of government. A consolidated city-county has power over a broad range of functions since it has to provide both city and county functions as a result of consolidation (Brierly 2016). For this reason, consolidated city-counties have more functional responsibilities than other municipalities. In most cases, consolidated city-counties will deliver a full range of policies and services. Research shows that most consolidated city-counties in effect absorb municipal and county functions after consolidation (Savitch and Vogel 2004). The encompassing functionality of consolidated governments is one of the reasons why proponents promote initiatives for city-county consolidation.

Finally, the type of municipal jurisdiction is also related to the geographic position of municipalities. Older cities tend to be located in central districts of the metropolitan area, whereas towns and villages tend to be located in outer areas. This might be a generalization as cities, towns, and villages can develop into idiosyncratic patterns. But that general pattern reflects the typical configuration of municipalities in metropolitan areas. Due to their geography and history, central cities will offer a broader range of functional programs than municipalities from outer areas of the greater metropolitan area (Barnett 2018).

Alternatives to Functional Restrictions

Intergovernmental cooperation can be an effective alternative to functional restrictions on municipalities. State–local or interlocal cooperation may be instrumental for providing functional services if a local government is unable to provide services itself (Hanson 2018; Carr and Feiock 2004). The local government can contract with other governments to obtain those services. For example, some municipalities procure their police services from a county government. In this case, a municipal government pays the county government for the extension of services to the municipality. In principle, municipalities can collaborate with other governments for a variety of functional areas. But these collaborations are more frequent in particular functions, such as emergency services, and functions in which scale economies are important for the economy of service production.

Extraterritorial jurisdiction is a legal foundation that a local government can employ to extend services to other municipalities. Extraterritorial jurisdiction involves the ability of a municipality to exercise its governmental powers in other jurisdictions (Krane, Rigos, and Hill 2001). Extraterritorial authority depends on lawful grants of authority from the state to municipalities. There are agreements between municipalities for extraterritorial policing authority as well. If state law allows for such agreements, police officers from one jurisdiction may exercise law enforcement actions in another one. In other cases, extraterritorial jurisdiction may be a legal foundation for extending services from one jurisdiction to another one. The power of extraterritorial jurisdiction can be useful in general for sharing services between municipalities. If powers of extraterritorial jurisdiction support interlocal cooperation, some municipalities may have less direct responsibilities for services. In such a way, a local government delegates part of their functionality to another municipality.

one service pulled together between county
B
city

Partial consolidation of functions is an alternative to the consolidation of
governments. Some municipalities have attempted the consolidation of specific
services, such as public safety (Krimmel 1997). As, for another example, in Florida, the City of Tallahassee and Leon County have merged their planning functions in a consolidated department. Partial consolidation is more viable than
the complete consolidation of governments. As different from complete consolidation, partial consolidation minimizes political conflict since it concerns only
one function. Other functions are not consolidated and remain under the control of each municipality. Some partial consolidations have been attempted for
certain functions provided by city and county governments as well (Leland and
Thurmaier 2014). As approved by their governing bodies, proposals for partial
consolidation can be more expedient than full consolidation. Partial consolidation allows multiple governments to attain scale economies in the provision of
the consolidated function. If consistent with both state law and local policies,
partial consolidation can be a promising approach for mitigating functional
fragmentation in metropolitan areas.

Intergovernmental cooperation is also possible across state and local levels. One cooperative system is the distinct programs of grants-in-aid available
in states. The states can provide functionally restricted or unrestricted aid to
municipalities. Functionally restricted aid involves categorical grants in which
the funding supports a specific function. Some categorical grants come with
matching requirements that make them even more restrictive as the municipality must show a willingness to match the funding before the state grant can be
used. Categorical grants support a variety of functional programs, but these
grants can sometimes complicate the management of those programs. Categorical grants are often subject to revision, reduction, or expiration (Dilger and
Cecire 2019).

On the contrary, general grants are a form of unrestricted aid that can be
allocated to any functional purpose. From a local government's standpoint,
general grants are preferred over restricted grants since the general grants can
be expended for any purpose (Fisher 2018). General grants give municipalities
substantial leeway as to how a municipality can spend the funds. A municipality will likely employ general grants-in-aid to fund functional programs favored
by its constituents. For example, some municipalities will allocate general aid to
law enforcement while other municipalities will allocate it to economic development. However, a substantial portion of these grants tends to be allocated to
core governmental functions (Léon-Moreta 2019).

Alternative providers of services are one alternative to functional restrictions on municipalities. In the public sector, counties and special districts can
supplement or even substitute for the role of municipal government (McCabe
2016). If those other governments play substantial roles, a municipal government will serve fewer functional roles. Particularly in urban areas, municipal
government is the public entity playing a central role in the delivery of services.
Yet, for several reasons, communities may opt for counties or special districts
to obtain services. This may be the case when municipal governments are constrained by functional restrictions or, simply, when it is easier for the county or

special districts to deliver services in lieu of municipal government. For example, special districts are in charge of water sourcing and management in California and other western states (Mullin 2009). In that case, a municipal government will have a rather limited presence. In unincorporated areas, lacking a municipal government, the county government will deliver most services.

Alternative service delivery includes the nonprofit sector. The nonprofit sector can provide services in lieu of municipal government (Feiock and Jang 2009). Some nonprofits have a long history in delivering local services. Other nonprofits are incorporated to deliver services by contracting with local governments. A government pays for the services while procuring its production from nonprofits. Some nonprofits deliver, for instance, social work and welfare services on behalf of municipalities. In this instance, a municipal government does not produce services but is responsible for funding them. Nonprofit organizations cannot substitute municipalities in general, but those organizations can play supplemental roles.

In addition, private contractors may supplement the delivery of local services. Municipal governments may opt to provide services by relying on private contractors at any stage of the service cycle (Warner and Hefetz 2008). Some private contractors assist municipalities in the early stages of service production. Other private contractors assist municipalities in the last stage of service delivery. The functional responsibilities of governments continue, but in any case, municipal governments opt to contract with private vendors for a certain stage of the service cycle. Thus, in theory, private contractors reduce the need for direct service delivery by municipalities. In reality, private contractors can serve a rather complementary role in the provision of services. The use of private contractors is especially attractive in urban areas where a market of alternative providers exists.

The last alternative to functional restrictions of municipalities is the self-provision of services. The lack of institutional providers, public or private, may make self-provision of services the only option. In other situations, self-provision may be the preferred service arrangement. For example, in Poinciana, Florida, the Poinciana Villages' homeowners association provides a variety of community and recreational services. Self-provided services also depend on collaborative mechanisms within communities. Self-provision must be permissible or consistent with state law. Where these conditions are present, communities may opt to provide services themselves. As a result, if the self-provision of services is feasible, the functional roles of municipal government may decrease.

A Specific Example: Functional Roles of Municipal Government in New Mexico

We illustrate the proposed concepts, using municipal government in New Mexico as an example. Although large in land area, the state of New Mexico is relatively small in terms of population or economic size compared to other states. New Mexico has 103 municipalities according to recent census data.

When compared to other states, municipalities in New Mexico appear to have broader functional autonomy. Larger cities in particular have home-rule powers granting them substantial capacities of service and policymaking.

The Constitution of New Mexico grants municipalities a significant extent of functional autonomy. Municipal governments, chartered ones in particular, enjoy broad functional home rule. Due to a constitutional provision adopted in 1991, municipalities have "maximum local self-government." Under this provision, municipalities in New Mexico can adopt or amend their own charters. This provision gives municipalities substantial functional and structural autonomy, but their fiscal capacity still is centralized at the state level. Based on that home-rule provision, municipal governments in New Mexico perform similar or broader functions than municipal governments in other states.

New Mexico statutes once classified municipalities by population: over 3,000 for cities; 1,500 to 3,000 for towns; and under 1,500 for villages. Current statutes no longer define those population thresholds for types of municipalities, but in reality, most municipalities still use those thresholds to define their official names (Krane, Rigos, and Hill 2001).

Municipalities may adopt home-rule charters. New Mexico statutes grant all municipalities substantial functional responsibility, but a home-rule charter would grant a municipality broader functional capacity. For instance, cities enjoy extraterritorial powers that allow them to regulate land uses up to five miles beyond the city's boundaries. These extraterritorial powers further expand the functional authority of municipal governments, particularly in urban areas.

For example, the City of Albuquerque adopted a home-rule charter in 1974. The city offers a range of municipal services: police, fire, public works, sewer and sanitation, transportation (including a major airport), planning, housing and community development, economic development, environment, libraries, culture, parks and recreation, and others. Compared to similar cities in the Southwest, for example, Tucson, the City of Albuquerque offers wider functional programs. Several factors explain Albuquerque's wide range of programs. Albuquerque is older than other municipalities in the region. It is the largest city in the greater metropolitan area, and in effect, Albuquerque delivers both governmental and various proprietary functions. Consequently, Albuquerque itself is the dominant provider of services in the region.

In 1959 and 2003, the consolidation of the City of Albuquerque and Bernalillo County was proposed to the voters. Those consolidation proposals were partly advocated on the potential benefits of functional consolidation of services. On both occasions, the voters rejected the consolidation proposals. More recently, city and county officials have discussed options for consolidating or coordinating specific services.

Functional responsibilities vary across municipalities in New Mexico. As compared to Albuquerque, smaller municipalities have fewer functional roles. Some municipalities rely on the county government or special districts for obtaining services, particularly services that require economies of scale for their effective provision. Many municipalities rely on special districts for the provision of utility services such as gas, water, and power. Some municipalities rely on the county government to receive police services. So, to a certain extent, the functional roles of governments vary according to their size, geographic position, and ultimately their legal foundation. Their functional responsibilities continue to evolve as the communities' demand for services evolve over time.

Discussion

The functional responsibilities of municipalities reflect their role in state–local systems. When those responsibilities are broad, they reflect a substantial role of government. When those responsibilities are restricted, they reflect a limited role of government. Those municipal roles of government are an area of high interest for public administration theory and practice in the states. The functional responsibilities of local governments are evolving and will continue to evolve. This evolution reflects the changing context of metropolitan areas and the changing assignments of responsibilities to municipalities by the states. The evolving roles of municipal government matter for the quality of governance in states. It matters if decisions are made at the most local (municipal) level of democracy, as opposed to a higher level. While other levels of government play relevant roles, municipal government is the level of government closest to the people. So, theoretically, it better reflects local preferences for public goods and services in a federal system.

We describe the incentives that public officials face when making decisions on the scope and production of services, emphasizing intergovernmental arrangements for service delivery. Since municipal governments have different scopes of responsibilities, we outline a framework for explaining factors that affect the functional responsibilities of governments and approaches that public officials can employ to deliver functional programs. Our framework encompasses both explanations of the functional scope of governments and policy approaches as to how public officials can support service delivery in their communities. In particular, our discussion stresses coordination mechanisms that local governments can employ to support and extend services in fragmented regions.

Local capacities matter because local officials make decisions for service delivery based on those capacities. Both elected officials and public managers serve important roles in that decision making. Elected officials shape the level and scope of services by approving functional spending allocations. Public managers implement programs and use those allocations in the day-to-day delivery of programs. Public managers are crucial actors in decisions, for example, regarding interlocal arrangements for delivering services. Thus we emphasize the need for working relationships between elected and administrative officials in decisions regarding the provision of functional programs in municipalities.

Certain implications can be derived for policy or administrative decision making. One implication concerns the central role of the state–local system in the functionality of municipal governments. The implication for policy is that states should recurrently evaluate the appropriateness of the legal framework for local government autonomy. From a localist perspective, greater autonomy is useful for municipal governments to deliver services in ways that satisfy the diverse preferences for services in their communities. Since states constrain that autonomy in different ways, it is necessary to broaden the discussion on what the proper role of municipal government should be in state–local systems. Whenever possible, state legislation should promote larger autonomy for municipal governments unless that autonomy is in conflict with more general principles of policy and governance in the states.

Another implication concerns the foundations of institutional capacities. Consider fiscal capacity, for example. Fiscal capacity is one distinct but influential foundation of service functionality. A municipal government depends on the basic ability to raise revenues and spend them through its functional programs. The practical implication is that local governments should seek expanded fiscal authority from their state government whenever feasible. If municipal governments can justify the benefits of autonomy, they may be able to obtain greater authority from the state. This of course requires proactive approaches to persuade lawmakers about the importance of enhanced fiscal authority. Local governments could work together to find that authority from their state. They could appeal the state government or perhaps seek alternative options if state policymakers are skeptical of granting local governments greater autonomy. Local governments may also work together to apply for and administer grant funds for their programs.

Note the distinct roles of state–local and interlocal factors influencing the capacities of local governments. Even though the functional responsibilities of governments can be supported either by interlocal cooperation or assistance from the state government, substantial gaps in service capacity may ultimately call for federal government assistance. The municipal experience in states thus yields those various insights for a comparative analysis of the functional role of municipal government, and its foundations.

Conclusion

The ability of local governments to deliver public goods and services depends on their functional capacity. If that capacity is robust, local governments will be able to fulfill the demand for public goods and services. But if that capacity is limited, local governments might be unable to fulfill those demands and the broader aspirations for self-governance that a federal system is based on. The quality of governance may be affected if local governments lack sufficient capacities, and citizens will likely demand action by the federal or state government to meet those aspirations. Functional autonomy will continue to be a critical agenda of policy and research, particularly for municipalities that are recently incorporated or those whose minimal capacity encumbers their ability to deliver their services responsibilities in the federal system (Anderson 2014; Bowman and Kearney 2017).

The state–local system is a foundation for a descriptive and prescriptive analysis of the functional autonomy of municipal government in the federal system. The essential takeaway of the chapter is that the functional responsibilities of municipal governments depend on the autonomy granted to governments by the state. The fundamental factor underlying the functional responsibilities of governments is the state–local legal framework for municipal government. State–local factors, such as home-rule and related legislation, have the potential to confine or expand the scope of responsibilities of municipal governments. This also calls attention to the role of Dillon's Rule versus home-rule legislation in states. Those alternative traditions of functional autonomy will continue to have a differential impact on the functional role of municipal governments.

To conclude, the functional role of municipal governments may be explained in part as an outcome of institutional capacities. Those capacities have an internal foundation, yet the intergovernmental framework of the states will determine whether municipal governments are able to use those capacities to meet their functional responsibilities. The state–local framework has the potential to either enable or constrain the ability of governments to fulfill those responsibilities. So we emphasize the importance of both internal and intergovernmental elements. Internal and intergovernmental contexts are essential both for explaining functional differences between municipalities and for discussing how their functional autonomy could be promoted. If internal and intergovernmental contexts support their functional capacities, local governments will be able to meet the demands for public goods and services in their communities.

CAREER PROFILE

Courtney Long
Food Systems Program Manager
Iowa State University Extension

Agriculture is important to many states and local communities. Courtney Long with Iowa State University Extension supervises a team that engages communities and stakeholders in food systems development. This work connects to everything from growing and processing to managing food waste, thinking systematically about the process of food growth and use. "Our focus is really about how food systems connect with community development . . . and looking at ways of encouraging equitable spaces, building businesses, and creating civic areas." This

work links Long and her team with communities across Iowa and nationally as they provide educational courses about food systems and as they engage with community groups to map and understand the local links between food systems and community development.

"Everyone eats, but not everyone always has access to food," explains Long. "Figuring out ways of engaging in that system, engaging in those areas of community, is really an important and needed role for community development." Long notes many businesses intersect with food, from growing to processing. Understanding this adds value to a community and allows new innovations in the food sector. This entails coordination with city, county, and state government, as well as community organizations. Long explains relationship building is critical to this work, and identifying gatekeepers for access to food discussions in different communities is critical to the development of successful initiatives.

Long completed a bachelor's degree in landscape architecture and an M.S. in sustainable agriculture, is a certified health coach, and is currently pursuing her Ph.D. in sustainable agriculture. She emphasizes the development of skills including facilitation, group dynamics, strategic planning, and evaluation in order to effectively engage in discussions with stakeholders. Long worked in local government and on farms to develop experience and learn about work environments in different organizations, and she advises students to find internships to learn more about this work. Contacting professionals who work in organizations related to food systems, or in university positions that support food systems, and arranging job shadow opportunities can shed light on the strengths and challenges associated with different types of jobs.

Interview: September 10, 2019

Discussion Questions

1. How does the state–local system affect the functional responsibilities of municipal government?
2. What alternative approaches can localities consider to mitigate functional restrictions on municipal governments?
3. How is local government structured in your state? Take a look at recent news coverage. Do you see evidence of local governments arguing that services are constrained by what the state allows?

References

Anderson, Michelle. 2014. The new minimal cities. *Yale Law Journal* 123:1118–1227.

Auby, Jean-Bernard. 2017. Contracting out and 'public values': A theoretical and comparative approach. In *Comparative administrative law*, 2nd ed., ed. Susan Rose-Ackerman, Peter L. Lindseth, and Blake Emerson, 552–65. Northampton, MA: Edward Elgar.

Barnett, Jonathan. 2018. *The fractured metropolis: Improving the new city, restoring the old city, reshaping the region.* New York: Routledge.

Berman, David. 2020. *Local government and the states: Autonomy, politics and policy.* 2nd ed. New York: Routledge.

Bowman, Ann, and Richard Kearney. 2017. *State and local government.* 10th ed. Boston: Cengage.

Boyne, George. 1992. Local government structure and performance: Lessons from America? *Public Administration* 70 (3): 333–57.

Brierly, Allen. 2016. Issues of scale and transaction costs in city-county consolidation. In *City County consolidation and its alternatives: Reshaping the local government landscape*, ed. Jared Carr and Richard Feiock, 55–86. New York: Routledge.

Briffault, Richard. 2006. Home rule and local political innovation. *Journal of Law and Politics* 22:1.

Burgess, Philip. 1975. Capacity building and the elements of public management. *Public Administration Review* 35:705–16.

Carr, John, and Richard Feiock. 2004. *City-county consolidation and its alternatives: Reshaping the local government landscape.* Armonk, NY: M. E. Sharpe.

Dilger, Robert, and Michael Cecire. 2019. Federal grants to state and local governments: A historical perspective on contemporary issues. Congressional Research Service.

Feiock, Richard, and Hee Jang. 2009. Nonprofits as local government service contractors. *Public Administration Review* 69 (4): 668–80.

Fischel, William. 2009. *The homevoter hypothesis: How home values influence local government taxation, school finance, and land-use policies.* Cambridge, MA: Harvard University Press.

Fisher, Ronald. 2018. *State and local public finance.* New York: Routledge.

Frederickson, George. 2016. *The adapted city: Institutional dynamics and structural change.* New York: Routledge.

Gerber, Elisabeth, and Daniel Hopkins. 2011. When mayors matter: Estimating the impact of mayoral partisanship on city policy. *American Journal of Political Science* 55 (2): 326–39.

Gillette, Clayton. 1991. In partial praise of Dillon's Rule, or, Can public choice theory justify local government law. *Chicago-Kent Law Review* 67 (3): 959–1010.

Hanson, Russell. 2018. *Governing partners: State-local relations in the United States.* New York: Routledge.

Honadle, Beth, Beverly Cigler, and James Costa. 2003. *Fiscal health for local governments.* Burlington, VT: Elsevier.

Jimenez, Benedict. 2014. Separate, unequal, and ignored? Interjurisdictional competition and the budgetary choices of poor and affluent municipalities. *Public Administration Review* 74 (2): 246–57.

Kean, Gordon. 1975. Local government and home rule. *Loyola Law Review* 21:63–79.

Krane, Dale, Platon Rigos, and Melvin Hill. 2001. *Home rule in America: A fifty-state handbook.* Washington, DC: CQ Press.

Krimmel, John. 1997. The Northern York County police consolidation experience: An analysis of the consolidation of police services in eight Pennsylvania rural communities. *Policing: An International Journal of Police Strategies & Management* 20 (3): 497–507.

Leland, Suzanne, and Kurt Thurmaier. 2014. Political and functional local government consolidation: The challenges for core public administration values and regional reform. *American Review of Public Administration* 44 (4 suppl.): 29S–46S.

León-Moreta, Agustín. 2019. Functional responsibilities of municipal government: Metropolitan disparities and instruments of intergovernmental management. *Urban Studies* 56 (12): 2585–2607.

Lewin, David, Jeffrey Keefe, and Thomas Kochan. 2012. The new great debate about unionism and collective bargaining in US state and local governments. *Industrial and Labor Relations Review* 65 (4): 749–78.

McCabe, Barbara. 2016. Special districts. In *City county consolidation and its alternatives: Reshaping the local government landscape,* ed. Jared Carr and Richard Feiock, 131. New York: Routledge.

Mullin, Megan. 2009. *Governing the tap: Special district governance and the new local politics of water.* Cambridge, MA: MIT Press

Reynolds, Osborne, Jr. 2015. *Local government law.* St. Paul, MN: West Academic.

Richardson, Jesse. 2011. Dillon's Rule is from Mars, home rule is from Venus: Local government autonomy and the rules of statutory construction. *Publius: The Journal of Federalism* 41 (4): 662–85.

Riverstone-Newell, Lori. 2017. The rise of state preemption laws in response to local policy innovation. *Publius: The Journal of Federalism* 47 (3): 403–25.

Savitch, Hank, and Ronald Vogel. 2004. Suburbs without a city: Power and city-county consolidation. *Urban Affairs Review* 39 (6): 758–90.

Shipan, Charles, and Craig Volden. 2012. Policy diffusion: Seven lessons for scholars and practitioners. *Public Administration Review* 72 (6): 788–96.

Spitzer, Hugh. 2000. Municipal police power in Washington State. *Washington Law Review* 75:495–518.

Tausanovitch, Chris, and Christopher Warshaw. 2014. Representation in municipal government. *American Political Science Review* 108 (3): 605–41.

Tiebout, Charles. 1956. A pure theory of local expenditures. *Journal of Political Economy* 64 (5): 416–24.

US Census Bureau. 2012. *Census of governments.* Washington, DC: Department of Commerce.

Warner, Mildred, and Amir Hefetz. 2008. Managing markets for public service: The role of mixed public-private delivery of city services. *Public Administration Review* 68 (1): 155–66.

PART II
Conflict in State–Local Relations

CHAPTER 8

When States Intervene—or Don't
Local Fiscal Distress, Municipal Takeovers, and the Complexities of Local Control

Ashley Nickels, Kent State University
Shilpa Viswanath, John Jay College of Criminal Justice, CUNY
Hannah Lebovits, University of Texas–Arlington

A municipal takeover occurs when a state declares a local government—or municipality—to be in a fiscal emergency, places it under state receivership, and appoints an "emergency manager" or a receiver to manage its affairs.[1] Takeovers are not common; only a handful of states allow for this type of intervention. In fact, state responses to local fiscal crises vary considerably, ranging from nonintervention to aggressive interventions, such as municipal takeover.[2] As one might imagine, any intervention is complex. And, in the case of municipal takeover, which is ostensibly aimed at addressing local fiscal conditions, the trade-offs between intervention and local control are often central to the conflict.

A major criticism of municipal takeover policies is that they produce winners and losers within a municipality, with residents and city employees losing the most.[3] In this chapter, we begin by outlining the legal history of municipal takeovers. We highlight how state approaches to municipal financial distress evolved over time, illustrating that the tensions between state intervention and local control have deep roots. We then use three case studies to show how these tensions play out in the local arena. In the first two cases—Flint, Michigan, and Atlantic City, New Jersey—we illustrate how municipal takeover placed significant burdens on community stakeholders, specifically residents and city employees. We also present a counterfactual—or alternative perspective—a city in significant decline and distress in a state that does not allow for this type of strong state intervention. The third case—East Cleveland, Ohio—adds insight to our discussion through the use of an alternative perspective. Unlike Michigan and New Jersey, the state of Ohio does not engage in direct municipal takeovers. We use this case to describe the tensions that can also exist when a takeover is not possible and the slow and steady decline of a community is compounded by issues related to race and class. We end with a discussion about the complexities of state intervention, highlighting that both municipal takeovers and less aggressive intervention practices are political decisions, with complex sociopolitical implications for the people living and working in their respective cities.

History, Law, and Local Context

The roots of municipal takeover date to the late nineteenth century. Beginning in the 1850s, local governments took on significant public debt to build railroads and develop real estate, resulting in a flood of local government defaults that was instrumental in creating the economic depression of 1873.[4] As a response to such crises, Missouri created a process for state-imposed receivership—allowing a state to take on the role of custodian or receiver of the local governments' assets and operations—in the mid-1870s.[5] Going a step further, the first state-imposed takeover took place in Memphis, Tennessee, in 1880. The intervention was "so controversial that it resulted in a challenge to the state receivership law" that was eventually taken up by the U.S. Supreme Court.[6] In *Meriwether v. Garrett* (1880), the court ruled that the state, via the court, had a right to force the city into receivership, adding "the receiver appointed by the court was invested with larger powers than probably any officer of a court was ever before intrusted [*sic*] with." Particularly important here is the court's statement on municipal governments, affirming the right of a state to repeal a city's charter and thus affirming the subordination of the municipality to the state.

Eight years prior, Judge John Dillon wrote what is now a famous opinion on municipal power and its subordination to the state: "Municipal corporations owe their origin to, and derive their powers and rights wholly from, the legislature. It breathes into them the breath of life, without which they cannot exist. As it creates, so it may destroy."[7] Dillon's Rule, as it is now known, was highly influential in the *Meriwether* case. His comments were derived in part from the public perception that local governments were irresponsible and wasteful, as evidenced by the large upsurge of municipal defaults on loans in late nineteenth-century America.[8] Under Dillon's Rule, Lyle Kossis argues, "City policymaking was legal *only* if it was expressly authorized by local charter, incidental to express powers in the local charter, or essential to accomplishing the declared objectives of the city."[9]

By the mid-1930s, municipal defaults had become a national problem. In response, the federal government passed the Municipal Bankruptcy Acts of 1934 and 1937 to provide mechanisms for orderly debt adjustment for municipal governments.[10] While the new legislation offered federal support to local governments, states continued to intervene. Some states took complete control of local governments that were in fiscal distress, continuing to place them under receivership, including legislation that allowed state courts to place municipalities that defaulted on their bond payments under receivership.[11]

World War II and the affluence of the postwar period reduced concerns about municipal defaults; however, the 1970s brought another cycle of urban fiscal crises. Large cities such as New York, Chicago, and Philadelphia faced fiscal crises and were placed under financial oversight by their respective states, renewing discussions over the benefits of strong state interventions via fiscal emergency laws. Many states developed local financial emergency laws in a proactive attempt to cope with the consequences of local financial emergencies.[12] Still, there remain significant differences in how states deal with local financial emergencies.[13] In his 2014 work, Eric Scorsone identified some of the characteristics that municipal fiscal emergency laws share. In addition to outlining the fiscal conditions that "trigger a crisis," such laws typically include language on what governing bodies should do "once the crisis is established" (for example, practices for intervention) and define "exit" strategies, such as how and when to return control back to local government.[14] He also noted the variation between states when it comes to enforcement.

Nineteen states have some form of intervention laws on the books.[15] Of these, Connecticut, New York, and Massachusetts are special legislation states that address local fiscal concerns on a case-by-case basis. The remaining sixteen have general legislation in place to monitor and address local fiscal conditions.[16] Moreover, some states are more aggressive than others in how they intervene; some simply monitor fiscal conditions, while others allow for stronger forms of state intervention. Anthony Cahill and Anthony James noted that "the most extensive form" of such intervention gives state officials the power to "supplant local decision-making authority."[17]

Fiscal Distress, State Interventions, and Local Control

Much of our understanding of state intervention policy and practice draws on the fields of economics and public budgeting and finance and is typically focused on efficiency and stability.[18] From a state's perspective, it is critical to intervene in local fiscal crises.[19] Local fiscal distress can be a drain on state resources, such as through long-term state aid. Failure to address crises can lead to municipal bankruptcies or downgraded credit ratings of other localities and the state, what is sometimes referred to as the "spillover effect."

Cities are limited by their legal subordination to state government. While many states have adopted home-rule protections to support local autonomy and community control, addressed in more detail below, cities are not totally free of state intervention under home rule.[20] Proponents of municipal takeover contend that states have extensive fiscal *oversight* responsibility over local and municipal governments, thus warranting municipal takeover when local fiscal distress threatens the economic or fiscal stability of the region or state.[21]

Cahill and James argued that, "in the interest of efficiency," state interventions are desirable, yet the authors recognized that such policies are at odds with the political value of local control, "which holds that municipalities have significant roles and functions in the political system and that their existence should be supported, not supplanted."[22] These authors concluded, like many of their colleagues, that from a "rational" fiscal and economic perspective, municipal takeovers look like the best alternative when compared to municipal bankruptcy or doing nothing.[23] Moreover, states have a fiduciary responsibility to local governments, meaning that states have a legal and moral responsibility to ensure that municipalities meet their public service obligations.[24]

The dominance of this way of thinking captures what Deborah Stone refers to as the "rationality project," which views policies as rational, systematic, and scientific, eschewing politics as "an unfortunate obstacle . . . to good policy."[25] In the case of municipal takeovers, such examinations often fail to consider the role of politics, and the values of the "polis" (including democracy), in the policy process. And, as Ashley Nickels argues, the focus on "rationality" often disregards the potential long-term sociopolitical ramifications of municipal takeover policy. In times of crisis, austerity and democracy can be at odds with each other.[26] The activities of the state-appointed emergency manager can squelch local democratic and participatory control. Existing relationships and agreements, important components of internal organizational workings, might be ignored or sidelined in an effort to stabilize. The city as a system, as a unit in a larger network of the region, will undoubtedly be impacted by the state's actions. In this chapter, we dig deeper into these concerns, moving past the "rationality" perspective to understand some of the broader political impacts of state responses to fiscal crisis—illustrating that state intervention is premised on trade-offs—trade-offs that create new and lasting politics.

Municipal takeovers, by definition, suspend local control and representative democracy by removing or superseding the powers of local elected officials.[27] Most criticisms of municipal takeovers focus on this element and pay scant attention to the deeper, longer-lasting impact on local politics.

Theoretically, municipal takeovers are intended to be temporary and limited: once the fiscal crisis is abated, the city is supposed to return to its *ex ante* political status. Yet those that decry municipal takeovers as an affront to local autonomy draw our attention to the many value conflicts inherent in municipal takeover: fiscal stability versus local control, emergency management versus deliberative participation, efficiency versus equity. As such, it is important to think critically about the trade-offs between state intervention and local control—and what that means for local politics more broadly.

Legal scholarship emphasizes this threat to local control. Michelle Wilde-Anderson referred to municipal takeover policy as a form of "democratic dissolution," emphasizing, for example, how the Michigan law "empower[s] Emergency Managers to replace all officials elected to govern the city."[28] She continued, "[the law] allows the [state-appointed Emergency Managers] to literally lock local officials out of city offices, email accounts, and internal information systems, if needed to minimize disruption of 'the Emergency Manager's ability to manage the government.'"[29] Wilde-Anderson's argument is primarily a normative one, claiming that municipal takeovers do little to address a city's structural deficit while undermining democracy in the process. Municipal takeovers, from this perspective, are a threat to local control[30] and popular sovereignty. These are important critiques but do little to illuminate long-term political impact. To further illustrate the impact of state action, and inaction, on localities, we offer three short case studies. These examples illustrate the tensions—and politics—at play in three fiscally distressed cities in three different states: Flint, Michigan; Atlantic City, New Jersey; and East Cleveland, Ohio.

Local Fiscal Distress
and State Intervention in Practice

Two Rounds of Takeovers in Flint, Michigan

Michigan has one of the most aggressive policies for addressing local fiscal crises. It is also a home-rule state. First passed in 1988 to address financial issues in the city of Hamtramck, the policy has been revised several times, most recently in Public Act 436 in 2012. Over the past three decades, nine Michigan municipalities have seen the power of local elected officials usurped by the state for varying periods of time. The experience in Flint, however, has placed the municipal takeover practice under great scrutiny due to its connection to the ongoing Flint Water Crisis. Flint's takeovers were implemented from the top down to address the city's ongoing fiscal woes. While some in the community welcomed the state's intervention, many were ambivalent or outright opposed to the policy.[31]

In 2002, Flint residents pursued a recall election to oust the then-mayor Woodrow Stanley, setting off a series of events that ultimately led to Flint's first takeover in July of that year. Stanley had served as mayor for more than a decade, from 1991 to 2002, after serving eight years as the second ward city councilor. In 2002, Stanley faced criticism for his handling of the city's finances and his ineffective attempts to address the city's ongoing economic condition. As a result, on March 5, 2002, Stanley was recalled by voters: 15,863 to 12,336. Darnell Earley, who served as city administrator during Stanley's time in office and would later go on to serve as one of Flint's emergency managers (EMs), was appointed interim mayor. In an interview with the *LA Times*, Stanley indicated that he had been "made the scapegoat for the downturn created by GM's painful withdrawal" and that the election had "reopened deep racial wounds in a place where Blacks live north of the Flint River, the Whites to the south."[32] In response to the mayor's recall and the pending financial crisis in the city, Earley noted, "the city should have made tougher decisions sooner."[33]

Not long after, State Senator Bob Emerson (D-Flint) sought a preliminary review of the City of Flint's financial condition under the Local Government Fiscal Responsibility Act, known as PA 72. The subsequent findings compelled the governor to appoint a financial review team to conduct an assessment of the city's fiscal situation. On July 8, 2002, the Financial Assistance Loan Board appointed Ed Kurtz, former president of Flint-based Baker College, as Flint's emergency financial manager (EFM). The following day, the City of Flint filed an appeal, which began a months-long legal battle between the city and the state regarding the legality of PA 72 and the use of EFMs. Actions undertaken by Kurtz included conducting a salary and wage study of top officials; implementing new procedures for hiring, travel, and spending within the city; closing city community centers and the city ombudsman's office; laying off city employees; and raising water rates by 11 percent. He also negotiated pay and contribution cuts with unions and the city retirement board, respectively.

The appointment of Kurtz was met with mixed reviews. The *Flint Journal*'s editorial board praised the state for stepping in to address the city's fiscal concerns. The Mackinac Center, a conservative Michigan-based think tank, also supported the action, while criticizing the policy for not going far enough to address the issues facing Flint.[34] Lawrence Ford, then president of the Chamber of Commerce, noted that he would have "preferred no takeover but that he will work with whomever."[35] Others living and working in the city, however, were more skeptical of the policy. They leveled their criticism at Kurtz directly, suggesting that his appointment was "fueled by a larger power base that included the business community, the [C.S.] Mott Foundation and the *Flint Journal*."[36] City Council Vice President Johnnie Coleman seconded this criticism, concluding, "The White elite group has picked this receiver and their only concerns are downtown and City Hall, not the neighborhoods . . . they literally took away our rights as citizens."[37]

The state continued to monitor the city's finances until 2006. Kurtz, before his exit as EFM in July 2004, was able to engineer a transition from a $26.6 million general fund deficit to a $6.1 million surplus by June 30, 2005.[38] However, by the end of 2010, the city was again in a budget deficit of $14.6 million.

The city's property tax revenue, income tax revenue, and state-shared revenue had decreased significantly between 2006 and 2010, while expenditures kept increasing.[39] Three of the city's special purpose funds were also in a deficit position: the building department fund, parks and recreation, and garbage collection. In 2011, Mayor Dayne Walling's administration asked the Michigan Department of Treasury's permission to issue $20 million in a twenty-five-year stabilization bond in order to maintain operations but was only authorized $8 million.[40] Unfortunately, this was insufficient.

After the state was notified of the city's fiscal condition by then finance director Michael Townsend, the Department of Treasury began yet another review of Flint's financial condition. The preliminary review confirmed that the city had incurred cumulative deficits in many of its funds, had not followed its own deficit elimination plan, and had consecutive years in which expenditures exceeded revenues. Based on the findings of the review, the Treasury Department reported on September 12, 2011, that "probable financial stress existed in the city of Flint and recommended the appointment of a financial review team."[41]

On September 30, 2011, Governor Snyder appointed an eight-member Financial Review Team, key among them was Darnell Earley, former Flint city administrator, and Bob Emerson, former state senator (D-Flint) and former state budget director. The review team met during October and November 2011 to review the financial statements and reports from the city, as well as conduct interviews and meetings with local officials and outside experts.

On December 1, 2011, the state-appointed EM took office in Flint, thereby placing the city under state control. The EM eliminated the positions of seven political appointees, cut the salaries and benefits of the mayor and city council, and took control over city governance. Community responses to emergency management in Flint were more nuanced than a simple support/oppose. Of the forty-eight community leaders interviewed by Ashley Nickels regarding Flint's municipal takeover, there was great variation in how people felt about and made meaning of the takeover, mirroring residents' reactions.[42] There were leaders who fully supported the intervention but also many others who voiced concerns about the policy. These community leaders felt that it was a "necessary evil," acknowledging that something had to be done to address Flint's dire fiscal situation but voicing discomfort with the suspension of local democracy.

Municipal Takeover and Local Government Employees in Atlantic City, New Jersey

Like Michigan, New Jersey is a home-rule state. The current state constitution, adopted in 1947, outlines limits on legislative interference, textually promotes local autonomy, and enumerates the specific rights of local governments. Further, New Jersey is *not* a "right-to-work" state, which means that in New Jersey state laws do *not* prohibit union security agreements or union representation, and labor unions can negotiate contracts with the government.[43] Despite these qualifying characteristics, New Jersey also allows for strong state intervention in the form of municipal takeover. And, despite protections, takeovers result in disenfranchisement of local government employee rights. In other words, the expansive fiscal involvement of the New Jersey state government in its municipalities and the current circumstances in Atlantic City illustrate the consequences of state receivership on local government employees, despite legal protections for those same employees.

Although the state adopted home-rule provisions, New Jersey has experienced steady erosion of those same protections.[44] Legislative restrictions on municipal power predate the New Jersey Constitution. The Local Government Supervision Act, adopted in 1947, authorizes the state to "make provisions for the imposition of special restraints upon municipalities in, or in danger of falling into, unsound financial condition and in this way to forestall serious defaults upon local obligations and demoralize finances that burden local taxpayers and destroy the efficiency of local services."[45] The state used this idea to address municipal fiscal failings throughout the state, eventually creating a basis in law for complete municipal takeover. The City of Camden was subject to a municipal takeover in 2002, the first in the state.[46]

Atlantic City's history is full of booms and busts. Beginning in the eighteenth century, New Jersey experienced municipal split-offs—the process of smaller municipalities separating from larger municipalities to form new municipal entities—which were provoked by private real-estate developers whose interests conflicted with the farming and industrial interests of the larger region;[47] the creation of Atlantic City was no exception. The city was incorporated in 1854. That same year, the city of Camden was established, and the Atlantic Railroad train service began bringing visitors to Atlantic City.[48] From the 1880s until the 1940s, Atlantic City was a major East Coast vacation resort.

However, with the advent of cheap air travel to Florida and the Caribbean in the 1950s, Atlantic City's popularity as a resort destination began to decline.[49] In 1976, New Jersey voters approved a referendum legalizing gambling in Atlantic City, leading to the opening of the first casino.[50] The city's tax base skyrocketed from $316 million in 1976 to almost $7 billion in 2007.[51] Until 2007, property values increased, and between 2005 and 2006 Atlantic City had the highest percentage increase (25.9) in average home value in the United States, while most of the country showed little or no home value appreciation.[52] However, the Great Recession in 2007 caused casino revenue to fall, resulting in the closing of four of Atlantic City's twelve casinos. Two more declared bankruptcy. The fall of the casino industry, coupled with high unemployment and falling property values, caused significant fiscal distress in the city.

The state first intervened in 2010, putting a state monitor in charge of Atlantic City's finances and taking over management of its tourism districts. Then, in 2012, Hurricane Sandy further devastated the city, with historic levels of storm surge and beach erosion. After the storm, the city continued to face budget deficits and low revenue, and in 2015 Standard & Poor's Ratings Services slashed Atlantic City's credit rating deeper into junk territory, implying a very high risk of default.[53]

Early in 2016, Atlantic City was placed in state receivership under the New Jersey Department of Community Affairs (DCA). The Municipal Stabilization and Recovery Act (MSRA) was introduced on February 29, 2016, in the New Jersey legislature and ultimately gave the state broad authority to fix the city's finances, including the ability to unilaterally break union contracts and sack local government employees. Public-sector union contracts are often a target of emergency action. The state's argument rests on the presumption that the contracts are too expensive and that unsustainable and underfunded union-won pension plans are undermining the finances of cities and states. Yet, in response to the takeover, the Atlantic City Police Department PBA Local 24 and the Atlantic City Professional Firefighters Local 198 filed lawsuits against the State of New Jersey. As such, two consequences of the takeover were, as Shilpa Viswanath argued, the infringement of both substantive and due process rights of local government employees and undermining of collective bargaining rights of local government employee unions.[54] The case of Atlantic City also reveals the "intermediary" role of the office of the governor in interpretation of state and local relationships. The New Jersey governor's decision to place Atlantic City in state receivership and subsequently break union contracts to reach debt settlements displays the power of the governor in shaping legislative policy and public policy at the local levels of government.

The constraints of local employment contracts also relate to broader concerns about the quality of democracy. For instance, the passing of the Municipal

Stabilization and Recovery Act resulted in layoffs, elimination of leave, increased work hours, salary cuts, and elimination of civil services in hiring new employees within the police and fire departments; all these consequences of the takeover legislation can also directly impact service delivery, in this case, disruption of law, order, and safety in Atlantic City. The municipal takeover of Atlantic City, therefore, shows the ways state intervention not only undermines the legal rights of local government employees but also has significant implications for local governing capacity.

Fiscal Distress and State Avoidance in East Cleveland, Ohio

Like Michigan and New Jersey, the state of Ohio monitors the fiscal health of municipalities and steps in when an emergency status is triggered. In 1978, the state adopted a set of laws to regulate the City of Cleveland's financial irregularities, then expanded those laws in 1996 to include townships and counties.[55] However, while the state might take over a failing school district, Ohio does not engage in a complete takeover when a city enters into a state of fiscal crisis. Unlike New Jersey or Michigan, Ohio will not place the fate of the locality in the hands of a single manager. Instead, cities in a state of fiscal emergency will be monitored by a state-appointed commission, mostly made up of local- and state-level actors, with oversight from the state auditor's office.[56] Ohio's revised code outlines the exact requirements for a municipality to enter into a state of emergency, and once in that state, the chief executive of the municipality (mayor or manager) must submit a plan to move toward recovery within three months, which can then be extended based on the city's progress and specific needs.[57] As the state does not engage in a direct takeover, it is up to the city to right itself. But sometimes, that doesn't happen.

Founded as a village in 1866 and incorporated in 1911, the city of East Cleveland was initially envisioned as a suburban retreat for the wealthy elite.[58] Like many other early suburban cities, East Cleveland was intentionally built outside of the municipal boundaries of Cleveland, preferring to maintain an independent municipality, complete with a council–manager governing system. The first few decades of the city were marked by population and industry growth, along with rapid housing development. However, beginning in the 1960s, the city quickly diversified as White residents moved further from Cleveland's growing Black community and regional economy spiraled downward. In the decades following, the city became a new type of suburb: a predominantly Black and poor one.

In 1985, the residents of the city voted to change the form of government from manager to strong mayor. Shortly thereafter, the city was declared to be in a state of fiscal distress, and a state-appointed commission began to monitor and manage the city's finances. While the State of Ohio did not engage in a municipal takeover, the commission, formed in 1988, was tasked with working with the city to stabilize the finances.[59] Exchanges between the commission and the city leadership included threats of state funding cuts, should the city not comply with the commission's demands. However, the council and mayor remained responsible for the day-to-day governing of the city, including the management of funds. In East Cleveland, the commission included the treasurer of state, or a designee; the director of budget and management, or a designee; the mayor of East Cleveland; the president of city council; and three members appointed by the governor from a list submitted by the mayor of East Cleveland.[60] However, in the decades following the creation of the commission, the various adopted financial plans were not followed.[61] Without an emergency manager to take on the effort, the commission continued to provide guidance and demand certain activities but had little direct control over the city's actions.

Since the 1988 declaration of fiscal emergency, East Cleveland has spent only five years outside of state oversight. As a predominantly residential city in a state that supports local income taxes, the city services were heavily reliant on personal wealth in the form of property and income. For decades following the initial declaration of a state of fiscal emergency, the city's population continued to decline. Poverty rates increased. The mayor made headlines for grievances that were both illegal and abhorrent.[62] Still, through meticulous budgeting efforts, the city inched its way back from the financial brink. Finally, in 2006, the state announced that the city was no longer in fiscal crisis, after whittling away its debt and completing several years in the black. Only six years later, however, with the constant resident out-migration, the financial and housing crisis of 2007–2008, and the 2011 closing of a key economic stakeholder—a Cleveland Clinic extension called Huron Hospital—the city was once again declared to be in a state of fiscal emergency. A year after Huron closed, the city lost almost a million dollars in revenue due to the governor's cuts to local government funds.[63]

Three years after it returned to fiscal distress, East Cleveland still struggled to pay for basic services. In 2015, city residents and politicians began to discuss, in earnest, the idea of a merger with the nearby city of Cleveland. Then mayor Gary Norton urged residents to consider a merger proposition. At the time, the city owed $3.2 million in payments and had a yearly budget of only $11 million.[64] Many residents, however, were more interested in recalling the mayor, stating concerns that his mismanagement led to the crisis. Feeling overwhelmed by a tax burden with little apparent payoff, one resident noted, "We're paying taxes like it's a suburb but it don't look like a suburb."[65] Meanwhile, the state auditor's office referred to the city's books as "inauditable."[66] With errors in the budgets, incomplete information, and audits that were years behind, the city engaged in a seemingly irrational practice of increasing spending in 2012, despite the loss of the local hospital.[67] Norton's predecessor, Eric Brewer, told local media that council told Norton to reduce spending and he refused to listen.[68] With fewer and fewer quality services, residents tried to fill in the gaps on their own. But no single or collective effort can fill every pothole or replace every streetlight.

In April 2016, while still awaiting a decision on a Cleveland–East Cleveland merger, Norton petitioned the state for bankruptcy protection, allowing the city to restructure without losing its tax base.[69] Four months later, the idea of merging East Cleveland with the city of Cleveland died quickly when the

Cleveland City Council president summarily dismissed it.[70] By the end of the year, Norton was recalled and had been fined over $110,000 by the Ohio Elections Commission for campaign finance reporting errors.[71]

Today, East Cleveland remains under fiscal watch. In early 2019, the city showed significant progress, with fewer than $250,000 still in debt. However, the city did not maintain adequate accounting records, which might influence when and whether it can move out of a state of fiscal distress.[72] Additionally, despite local efforts to encourage growth and stabilization, the city is not a prime development location and was entirely overlooked when the state chose local census tracts for the federal Opportunity Zones initiative.[73] Poverty rates remain high, and the city has not bounced back from the foreclosure crisis. Should the city continue to cut its spending, fix its books, and move out from under state supervision, who can say how long it will be before the financial weight of the city and the mismanagement in city hall draws the city right back into fiscal emergency.

Discussion

Municipal takeovers are a policy of last resort, used when both local government and the local economy are unstable and crisis prone. They are designed to be temporary and limited solutions to fiscal crises. Yet changes to city governance and the manner in which community members interpret the takeover have a long-term political legacy. In many ways, the use of municipal takeover is a policy paradox that centers on short-term fiscal stability versus long-term political change, and economic rationality versus democratic principles.

Within this broader topic, two key components highlight the impact that state decision making can have on various stakeholders at the local level. First, it is clear that there can be significant costs attached to state decision making when it comes to municipal fiscal distress. In these cases, the costs came in the form of employee rights violations and lawsuits against the city, the restriction of democratic systems, and the lengthy decline of a once-thriving community. Additionally, it is clear that political and legal systems play an important role in what might ostensibly be seen as a "purely" administrative issue.

In Flint, municipal takeover had the capacity to restructure local politics by "defining who belongs in the political community, specifying how and when citizens can participate in politics, redistributing resources among individuals and social groups, and determining the balance of power and influence among citizens."[74] Takeover policies, like all policies, are "political forces that [have the capacity to] reconfigure the underlying terms of power, reposition actors in political relations, and reshape political actors' identities, understandings, interests, and preferences."[75]

To the extent that takeovers reorder governance and local policymaking, they also create new opportunities or pathways for citizens and interests that were dissatisfied with the previous arrangement. Policy implementation is like a "coordination game," in which distributive issues, such as who gets what and how, depend on the "relative power of the actors."[76] Moreover, how political actors respond to these changes depends, in part, on whether or not they are included in the new—albeit temporary—power structure. Despite politician's claims to the contrary, municipal takeovers have significant consequences outside of the "rationality" framework. In Flint, the state's intervention not only suspended the authority of local elected officials in the short term but reshaped the local political landscape. Some community interests gained influence, while others lost influence. Moreover, the implementation of the policy by a series of state-appointed managers interrupted politics as usual.

Similarly, the Atlantic City case study helps conceptualize and link macrostructures of state legislative policy (municipal takeover) to microlevel consequences of local government employee rights. The case also shows that the interplay of legislative policy and administrative policy cannot be studied in isolation from the role of the governor. The governor played an important role in shaping the outcomes of the takeover at the local level. Given the fact that governors in the United States can serve two consecutive terms of eight years in office, they can exercise remarkable power over the legislative branch in their state. This is especially true in the case of New Jersey and the governor's decision to place Atlantic City in state receivership and subsequently break union contracts in order to reach debt settlements. This case study reflects the formal tools (budget-cutting discretion, power of veto, gubernatorial appointments) a governor can use in order to shape both legislative policy and public policy at the micro levels of public administration. Furthermore, the Atlantic City case also reflects that the superior courts of New Jersey had a pivotal role in interpreting the Municipal Stabilization and Recovery Act and in blocking the state from going ahead with some of the personnel decisions.

The events in East Cleveland highlight a different trend: the abandonment by the state and region of a city undergoing significant racial, social, and economic changes. Politics is not only evident in action but in inaction, neglect, and activities that are so implausible they are guaranteed to fail. However, like the other two cases, East Cleveland's current state was not only tied to local, internal issues but to state- and federal-level policies. While the fiscal oversight of East Cleveland only began in 1988, the White flight that so negatively impacted the city began decades earlier, encouraged by federal policies that supported segregation efforts.[77] The practice of "blockbusting" added to this pattern as well. The real-estate tactic involved persuading entire blocks of homeowners to sell their homes for cheap out of the fear that undesirable people were moving into the neighborhood. These homes would then be sold to African American families at a significantly higher price point. Additionally, the inability of the state and county to contain sprawl encouraged the wealthy to leave the city and inner-ring communities. Moreover, in the years since the second round of fiscal oversight, the state has further cut its allocation of local government funds—redistributed resources that are dispersed to individual communities. Lastly, in East Cleveland's most recent attempt to gain some additional investment—the Opportunity Zone credits—the state ignored their ask. These historic and current actions added tremendously to the decline of the city. In East Cleveland we can observe the events that occur when strong state-level support for fiscal stability is missing.

As these cases highlight, strong tensions exist between state and local governments when it comes to local fiscal distress. Sometimes this happens in the form of a state engaging in a direct takeover and ignoring the democratic and contractual obligations of the city. Other times, the state might provide inadequate support to a struggling municipality. In both scenarios, it is evident that state practices do not do enough to center the concerns of the municipality and local actors and environments. Additionally, these cases further illuminate the need to systematically and intellectually reengage with the study of federal and state law, and its interpretations and implications for local actors and activities.

▰ CAREER PROFILE ▰

Jamie Benning
Water Quality Program Manager
Iowa State University Extension and Outreach

Across the United States, cooperative extension services link the U.S. Department of Agriculture with state universities organized under the Morrill Act of 1862, which established land-grant universities. In turn, these university extension organizations work with communities across the state in the areas of agriculture and natural resources, 4-H and youth development, human sciences, and community and economic development. Jamie Benning is the water quality program manager for Iowa State University Extension and Outreach. This work brings Benning into contact with groups across the state with different levels of expertise and interest in water quality. She provides a variety of water-quality programming, from one-hour community information sessions on water science, informing the public about nutrient loss and the impacts of runoff on water quality in the Gulf of Mexico, to focused professional development events for agriculture and conservation professionals. Through collaboration with other groups in the state, Benning helped to organize a watershed academy that develops the skills of watershed coordinators who work with landowners and farmers on conservation practices to improve water quality.

In Iowa, one hundred soil and water conservation districts are geographically aligned with county governments. These local boards elect commissioners to attend to local conservation priorities. Benning works closely with these local government officials to share best practices and provide updated scientific information to help these units in their planning and decision making. Benning explains, "Protecting and enhancing natural resources is the foundation of a healthy, productive society. Agriculture is a major contributor to our economy in Iowa, but that is based on having some of the highest-quality soils in the country and the world." Through Benning's work with other state agencies, local governments, and communities across the state, water, soil, and environmental quality are preserved to help maintain the state's natural resources.

Students interested in this career field need to be able to help people think through goals that are sometimes in conflict, such as economic productivity and environmental conservation. "Those skills of facilitation and consensus building are really important for a position like this," explains Benning. Students can look to their own state's land-grant university to learn more about extension services. Benning holds a bachelor's degree in agronomy and a master's degree in soil science from Iowa State University but notes many other backgrounds are relevant to work in water and soil quality. "I suggest exploring natural resource areas of study, being involved in campus organizations such as the Soil and Water Conservation Society student chapters . . . so that you learn leadership skills and make connections with other students." Internship opportunities are also important, explains Benning, because they give students an opportunity to "test-drive" different types of jobs in order to better understand their own goals and interests.

Interview: September 11, 2019

Discussion Questions

1. Identify the legislative framework in your own state. Is it a home-rule state? Does it allow for state intervention or municipal takeover?
2. As these case studies illustrate, democratic ideals of participation and citizen-driven governance can be threatened in cases where a state engages in a municipal takeover, as well as when the state leaves a community to flounder. What protections do you think should be put in place to ensure that the residents within a community retain their voice—their power—when the governmental system is failing? Which governance levers can be used to protect the power of the people and basic democratic ideals?
3. In Flint and Atlantic City, the takeover efforts resulted in significant crises related to local control. But East Cleveland is still floundering despite decades of low-intensity state oversight. Can and should we attempt to justify short-term limits on democratic and participatory governance when a long-term outcome, such as stabilization, seems worthwhile?

Notes

Portions of this chapter appear in *Power, Politics, and Participation in Flint, Michigan: Unpacking the Policy Paradox of Municipal Takeover* (Philadelphia: Temple University Press, 2019). We would also like to acknowledge Anna Hutcheson for her assistance on this project.

[1] Ashley E. Nickels, "Approaches to Municipal Takeover: Home Rule Erosion and State Intervention in Michigan and New Jersey," *State and Local Government Review* 48, no. 3 (2016): 194–207.

2 Ibid.
3 Ashley E. Nickels, *Power, Participation, and Protest in Flint, Michigan: Unpacking the Policy Paradox of Municipal Takeover* (Philadelphia: Temple University Press, 2019).
4 Eric H. Monkkonen, *The Local State: Public Money and American Cities* (Stanford, CA: Stanford University Press, 1995).
5 Lynne A. Weikart, "Monitoring the Fiscal Health of America's Cities," in *Handbook of Local Government Fiscal Health*, ed. Helisse Levine, Eric A. Scorsone, and Jonathon B. Justice, 387–404 (Burlington: Jones & Bartlett Learning, 2013).
6 Lyle D. Kossis, "Examining the Conflict between Municipal Receivership and Local Autonomy," *Virginia Law Review* 98, no. 5 (2012): 1117.
7 As cited in David R. Berman, "Takeovers of Local Governments: An Overview and Evaluation of State Policies," *Publius* 25, no. 3 (1995): 56.
8 Kossis, "Examining the Conflict"; Monkkonen, *Local State*.
9 Kossis, "Examining the Conflict," 1113, emphasis added; see also Gerald E. Frug, *City Making: Building Cities without Building Walls* (Princeton, NJ: Princeton University Press, 1999).
10 Henry W. Lehmann, "The Federal Municipal Bankruptcy Act," *Journal of Finance* 5, no. 3 (1950): 241–56.
11 Berman, "Takeovers of Local Governments"; Kossis, "Examining the Conflict."
12 Philip Kloha, Carol S. Weissert, and Robert Kleine, "Someone to Watch over Me: State Monitoring of Local Fiscal Conditions," *American Review of Public Administration* 35, no. 3 (2005): 236–55; Eric A. Scorsone, "Municipal Fiscal Emergency Laws: Background and Guide to State-Based Approaches," Mercatus Center Report 14-21, July 2014, http://mercatus.org/sites/default/files/Scorsone-Municipal-Fiscal-Emergency.pdf.
13 Anthony G. Cahill and Anthony J. James, "Responding to Municipal Fiscal Distress: An Emerging Issue for State Governments in the 1990s," *Public Administration Review* 52, no. 1 (1992): 88–94; see also Pew Charitable Trusts, "The State Role in Local Government Financial Distress," July 2013, and Scorsone, "Municipal Fiscal Emergency Laws."
14 Scorsone, "Municipal Fiscal Emergency Laws," 11.
15 Pew, "State Role in Local Government Financial Distress."
16 Pew, "State Role in Local Government Financial Distress"; Scorsone, "Municipal Fiscal Emergency Laws."
17 Cahill and James, "Responding to Municipal Fiscal Distress," 91.
18 Berman, "Takeovers of Local Governments"; Cahill and James, "Responding to Municipal Fiscal Distress"; James E. Spiotto, A. E. Acker, and L. E. Appleby, *Municipalities in Distress? How States and Investors Deal with Local Government Financial Emergencies* (Chicago: Chapman and Cutler LLP, 2012).
19 Spiotto, Acker, and Appleby, *Municipalities in Distress?*
20 Frug, *City Making*.
21 Pew, "State Role in Local Government Financial Distress"; Spiotto, Acker, and Appleby, *Municipalities in Distress?*
22 Cahill and James, "Responding to Municipal Fiscal Distress," 91–92.
23 Cahill and James, "Responding to Municipal Fiscal Distress"; Kloha, Weissert, and Kleine, "Someone to Watch over Me"; Charles C. Coe, "Preventing Local Government Fiscal Crises: Emergency Best Practices," *Public Administration* 68, no. 1 (2008): 759–67.
24 Kloha, Weissert, and Kleine, "Someone to Watch over Me."
25 Deborah Stone, *Policy Paradox: The Art of Political Decision Making*, 3rd ed. (New York: W. W. Norton, 2011), 10.
26 Christina Flesher Fominaya, "European Anti-austerity and Pro-democracy Protests in the Wake of the Global Financial Crisis," *Social Movement Studies* 16, no. 1 (2017): 1–20.
27 Nickels, "Approaches to Municipal Takeover"; Ashley E. Nickels, Amanda D. Clark, and Zachary D. Wood, "How Municipal Takeovers Reshape Urban Democracy: Comparing the Experience of Camden, New Jersey and Flint, Michigan," *Urban Affairs Review* (2019).
28 Michelle Wilde-Anderson, "Democratic Dissolution: Radical Experimentation in State Takeovers of Local Governments," *Fordham Urban Law Journal* 39, no. 3 (2012): 587.
29 Ibid.

146 Ashley Nickels, Shilpa Viswanath, and Hannah Lebovits

30 See also Kossis, "Examining the Conflict."

31 Nickels, *Power, Participation, and Protest.*

32 R. Frammolino, "Mayor Is Ousted in a Town Divided: Voters in the Debt-Ridden City Recall a Three-Term Incumbent," *Los Angeles Times*, March 7, 2002, http://articles.latimes.com/2002/mar/07/news/mn-31628.

33 As cited in Danny Hakim, "For Flint, Mich., Takeover Adds to the List of Woes." *New York Times*, July 10, 2002, http://www.nytimes.com/2002/07/10/us/for-flint-mich-takeover-adds-to-the-list-of-woes.html.

34 M. D. LaFaive, "Mayoral Recall May Foreshadow Flint Bankruptcy," Mackinac Center for Public Policy, March 7, 2002, https://www.mackinac.org/article.aspx?ID=4106; M. D. LaFaive and H. L. Schimmel, "State Should Reform Public Act 72 of 1990," Mackinac Center for Public Policy, January 10, 2011, http://www.mackinac.org/14290.

35 As cited by C. Machniak, "The Story of Flint's Takeover: Recall Pushes Senator to Act," *Flint Journal*, July 14, 2002, A01.

36 Ibid.

37 As cited in ibid. Moreover, as Mayor Stanley's comment suggests, the city is highly segregated. The reference to White elites and downtown development is juxtaposed with a reference to the "neighborhoods," which can be read as nonelite and non-White neighborhoods throughout the city, but especially on Flint's north side.

38 Eric A. Scorsone and Nicolette Bateson, "Long-Term Crisis and System Failure: Take the Fiscal Stress of America's Older Cities Seriously, Case Study: City of Flint, Michigan," Michigan State University Extension, September 2011, https://www.cityofflint.com/wp-content/uploads/Reports/MSUE_FlintStudy2011.pdf.

39 Ibid.

40 Ibid.; Kristen Longley, "City of Flint Hopes to Avoid State Takeover of Finances by Borrowing $20M," *MLive*, January 10, 2011, http://www.mlive.com/news/flint/index.ssf/2011/01/city_of_flint_hopes_to_avoid_s.html; Kristen Longley, "Special Flint City Council Meeting to Consider $8 Million Bond," *MLive*, March 23, 2011, http://www.mlive.com/news/flint/index.ssf/2011/03/special_flint_city_council_mee.html.

41 Michigan Department of Treasury, "Report of the Flint Financial Review Team," 2011, https://www.michigan.gov/documents/treasury/Flint-ReviewTeamReport-11-7-11_417437_7.pdf.

42 Nickels, *Power, Participation, and Protest.*

43 National Labor Relations Board, "Employer/Union Rights and Obligations," https://www.nlrb.gov/rights-we-protect/rights/employer-union-rights-and-obligations.

44 Nickels, "Approaches to Municipal Takeover."

45 Local Government Supervision Act of 1947, P.L.1947, c.151 (C.52:27BB-1 et seq.).

46 Nickels, Clark, and Wood, "How Municipal Takeovers Reshape Urban Democracy."

47 A. J. Karcher, *New Jersey's Multiple Municipal Madness* (New Brunswick, NJ: Rutgers University Press, 1998).

48 Robert Strauss, "Judge Nelson Johnson: Atlantic City's Godfather," *NJMonthly.com*, August 16, 2010, https://njmonthly.com/articles/jersey-living/atlantic-citys-godfather/.

49 T. R. Winpenny, "The Engineer as Promoter: Richard B. Osborne, the Camden and Atlantic Railroad, and the Creation of Atlantic City," *Essays in Economic & Business History* 22 (2012): 301–12.

50 James F. Clarity, "Its 'Place Your Bets' as East's First Casino Opens," *New York Times*, March 27, 1978, https://www.nytimes.com/1978/05/27/archives/its-place-your-bets-as-easts-first-casino-opens-its-place-your-bets.html.

51 State of New Jersey, Casino Control Commission, 2012, https://web.archive.org/web/20120707230726/ http://www.state.nj.us/casinos/.

52 Ibid.

53 "S&P Cuts Atlantic City's Credit Ratings," *Press of Atlantic City*, August 3, 2015, https://www.pressofatlanticcity.com/news/s-p-cuts-atlantic-city-s-credit-rating/article_2753fc06-3a39-11e5-9943-bf669a35f327.html.

54 Shilpa Viswanath, "Public Sector Collective Bargaining during Municipal State Takeovers: Towards a Theory of Local Government Employees," Rutgers University-Graduate School-Newark, 2019, https://rucore.libraries.rutgers.edu/rutgers-lib/61668/PDF/1/play/.

55 Scorsone, "Municipal Fiscal Emergency Laws"

56 Ibid.

57 Ibid.

58 Information on East Cleveland was retrieved from an online databased via Case Western Reserve University at https://case.edu/ech/articles/e/east-cleveland.

59 Betty Montgomery, "City of East Cleveland, Cuyahoga County, Single Audit," Auditor of the State of Ohio, February 7, 2005, http://www.auditor.state.oh.us/auditsearch/Reports/2005/City_of_East_Cleveland_01-Cuyahoga.pdf.

60 Ibid.

61 Ibid.

62 Alberto Salvato, "Ohio Mayor Convicted of Seeking Bribes," *New York Times*, September 1, 2004, https://www.nytimes.com/2004/09/01/us/national-briefing-midwest-ohio-mayor-convicted-of-seeking-bribes.html.

63 Nick Castele, "The Numbers behind East Cleveland's Financial Predicament," *Ideastream*, March 27, 2015, https://www.ideastream.org/news/the-numbers-behind-east-clevelands-financial-predicament.

64 Ibid.

65 Ibid.

66 Ibid.

67 Ibid.

68 Ibid.

69 Maria Scali, "East Cleveland Petitions State for Bankruptcy Protection," *Fox8.com*, April 28, 2016, https://fox8.com/2016/04/28/east-cleveland-petitions-state-for-bankruptcy-protection/.

70 Cleveland City Council, "Council President Rejects East Cleveland Merger Proposal," press release, August 26, 2016, http://www.clevelandcitycouncil.org/news-resources/press-releases/2016/08-august/council-president-rejects-east-cleveland-merger-pr.

71 Vince Grzegorek, "East Cleveland Mayor Gary Norton Fined $114,100 by Ohio," *Cleveland Scene*, November 25, 2016, https://www.clevescene.com/scene-and-heard/archives/2016/11/25/east-cleveland-mayor-gary-norton-fined-114100-by-ohio-elections-commission.

72 Nick Castele, "East Cleveland General Fund Starts 2019 in Positive Territory," *Ideastream*, April 5, 2019, https://www.ideastream.org/news/east-cleveland-general-fund-starts-2019-in-positive-territory.

73 Nick Castele, "Cuyahoga County Won Dozens of Opportunity Zones: Now What," *Ideastram*, December 10, 2018, https://www.ideastream.org/news/cuyahoga-county-won-dozens-of-opportunity-zones-now-what.

74 Tracy Burch, *Trading Democracy for Justice: Criminal Convictions and the Decline of Neighborhood Political Participation* (Chicago: University of Chicago Press, 2013), 4.

75 Donald P. Moynihan and Joe Soss, "Policy Feedback and the Politics of Administration," *Public Administration Review* 74, no. 3 (2014): 321.

76 Peter Hall, "Historical Institutionalism in Rationalist and Sociological Perspective," in *Explaining Institutional Change: Ambiguity, Agency, and Power*, ed. James Mahoney and Kathleen Ann Thelen (New York: Cambridge University Press, 2010), 215.

77 R. Rothstein, *The Color of Law: A Forgotten History of How Our Government Segregated America* (New York: Liveright, 2017).

CHAPTER 9

State Laws and Local Sanctuaries

Russell L. Hanson, Indiana University
Erika S. Coe, Indiana University

O ver the past two decades, national politics has become increasingly polarized, but so, too, have state politics. It is now commonly the case that one party controls both chambers of the legislature and enjoys the support of a like-minded governor. Moreover, governors and legislators are acting programmatically, as national lobbying organizations, such as the conservative American Legislative Exchange Council and its liberal counterparts, promote their policy agendas nationwide.

This has aggravated tensions between red state legislatures and blue city councils, and blue state legislatures and red city councils, on such issues as minimum wages, clean energy, and land uses. An obvious example is cities characterizing themselves as sanctuaries for immigrants, in ways that conflict with state laws. The standoff between Austin, Texas, and the Texas state legislature that meets in Austin is a prime example of this localized effect of the polarization of state legislatures, which is explored in this chapter.

However, it is important to remember that cities, which often enjoy home rule, are different from counties, which typically are treated as subordinate units of state government. Hence county councils, and perhaps even more noticeably, county sheriffs, who are independently elected in the United States, may oppose local ordinances, or even state laws, they find objectionable.

Gun controls are a flashpoint for these controversies. Whereas some cities and urban counties have defied state legislatures by declaring themselves "sanctuaries" for immigrants, a substantial number of county sheriffs have declined to enforce state laws, or even voter initiatives, on gun control. In effect, hundreds of county sheriffs have declared their counties "sanctuaries" for gun owners, who might otherwise vote incumbent sheriffs out of office in favor of someone who advocates gun rights or who promises not to enforce state policies that encroach on them.

In the end, few if any of these declarations of "sanctuary" status are likely to be approved by state supreme courts, which typically uphold state sovereignty over local concerns. It is important to understand, though, that different units of local government react differently to state mandates, reflecting the differences in their electoral bases. A city council member answers to a limited area within a city; in most cases, the county sheriff answers to a combination of rural and urban constituencies. Consequently, the council member and sheriff may not agree on the most appropriate response to a state mandate, or for that matter the absence of a mandate.

In other words, it is not simply red state versus blue city, or vice versa. It is red state versus blue city in a red county, and vice versa, as this chapter analyzes. The politics are complex, not binary. This is most evident in metropolitan areas where a population center that extends to several counties declares itself a sanctuary city, while the rural areas of included counties consider themselves gun sanctuaries.

Urban–rural differences are prominent within states and within state legislatures, although the declining populations of rural areas means they are less well represented in state legislatures. But sheriffs are elected within counties, and that colors their view of what is acceptable to voters in the county where they wish to be the preeminent enforcer of state and local law.

Immigrant Sanctuaries

There is a long history of private organizations offering sanctuary to immigrants in the United States. These sanctuaries may be churches, schools, nonprofit organizations, or other spaces that welcome those who need assistance, resources, or a safe place to stay. The term *sanctuary* has been used for hundreds of years and has referred to a place for people seeking political asylum. It was even used in the United States for young people seeking refuge from the Vietnam War draft.[1]

What is new are formal declarations by state, county, and city governments declaring themselves "sanctuaries," often with support from local police forces and county sheriffs, who decline to cooperate with Immigration and Customs Enforcement (ICE). Six states have barred local officials from cooperating with ICE.[2] Vermont severely limited cooperation by state and local law enforcement with federal authorities but stopped short of declaring itself a sanctuary. "This law has been carefully crafted through a consensus-building process to confirm Vermont remains compliant with federal law, that we would not be establishing a sanctuary state," Vermont Governor Phil Scott said before the signing.[3] Similar legislation failed in New Mexico in 2019.

In the absence of state action, some counties declared themselves sanctuaries by refusing to sign a 297(g) agreement, which promises cooperation with federal authorities on the enforcement of section 287(g) of the U.S. Immigration and Nationality Act. It outlines a relationship between the federal government and counties that in effect deputizes local police to aid immigration enforcement and become an extension of ICE. Most of these sanctuaries are concentrated on the Pacific Rim, where immigrant labor is an important, and potent, political force. But there are cities, too, that include significant numbers of immigrants who, by virtue of their electoral might, affect public policy.

A map of officially declared sanctuary cities, counties, and states is shown in figure 9.1. Immigrant sanctuaries are shaded darkest, gun sanctuaries next darkest, and counties that are sanctuaries for both lightly shaded. Most counties are neither; they are shown as white.[4]

Sanctuary cities, counties, and states often rely on immigrant workforces for economic as well as humanitarian reasons; eight of the eleven million undocumented immigrants are estimated to be participating in the workforce. "Unauthorized immigrants represent about 24 percent of all workers in farming, fishing and forestry and 15 percent of those employed in construction, which is the industry that uses the most undocumented immigrant workers overall, at 1.35 million. Nearly one quarter of restaurant workers in 2016 were foreign-born compared with 18.5 percent for all sectors."[5] The integral participation of undocumented immigrants in the workforce complicates the issue in some areas, forcing communities to face the possible economic consequences of losing their immigrant neighbors if they cooperate with federal authorities.

Moreover, sheriffs working in conservative counties inside of Democratic-controlled states must worry about the budgetary consequences of cooperating with ICE. In Josephine County, Oregon, Sheriff Dave Daniel abandoned the county's long history of cooperating with ICE. After an economic downturn caused by limits to the logging industry, ICE stepped in to help fund the county jail in exchange for housing detainees. According to Oregon Public Broadcasting, "Just three years ago, the ICE contract made up 20 percent of the jail's revenues. . . . The ICE contract remains a notable part of the jail's 2017–18 projected budget. The county estimates it will receive $36,500 for housing ICE detainees this year."[6]

Several lawsuits targeting counties that detained immigrants who qualified for release under state law persuaded Sheriff Daniel to let Josephine county's contract with ICE expire in May 2018. "This decision," said Sheriff Daniel, "had nothing to do with any sanctuary issue or designation provided by state law.

> Three counties suffered lawsuits stemming from ICE detainees. Columbia County and Clackamas County have both paid out to detainees as a result of lawsuits. NORCOR in Wasco County currently has two pending lawsuits and is now the only county correctional institution in Oregon holding ICE detainees. Another factor in terminating the contract was as a result of the passage of the Corrections Levy in May of 2017. Detainees were filling beds and as a result taking beds away from our local inmate population. The Josephine County Jail can now serve the county better by holding more of our own. Lastly, risk versus reward. In the fiscal year 2016–17 the Sheriff's Office received $45,000 in revenue from ICE which is not worth the risk of a lawsuit, difficulties in classification as detainees cannot be housed with anyone with a violent history and in addition, the contractual benefits detainees receive are above the local population. The decision to terminate the ICE contact was not for political reasons, it was a business decision to reduce liability, increase operations and to better serve Josephine County citizens.[7]

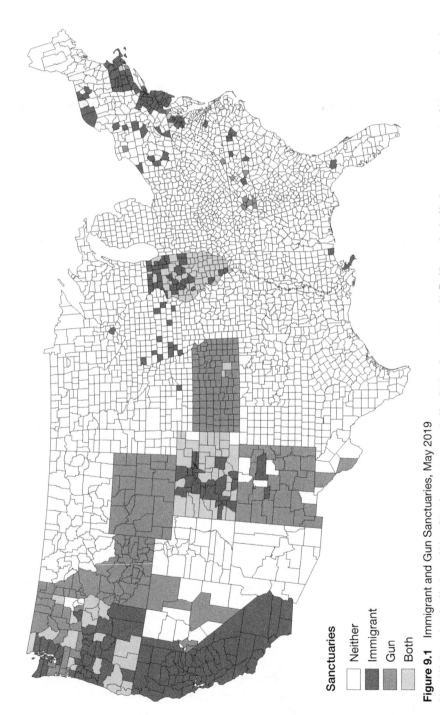

Sanctuaries

- Neither
- Immigrant
- Gun
- Both

Figure 9.1 Immigrant and Gun Sanctuaries, May 2019

Note: We have data for Alaska and Hawaii but have not succeeded in plotting those states with R. All counties in Alaska are gun sanctuaries; none are immigrant sanctuaries. There are no sanctuaries of any sort in Hawaii. Data on immigrant sanctuaries are from the Center for Immigration Studies, as of April 18, 2019. CIS is a conservative organization, and as such may be expected to keep close tabs on immigrant sanctuary declarations.

Sheriff Daniel took pains to separate himself from the immigrant sanctuary issue order to avoid upsetting his conservative constituency. On the other hand, the sheriff's office needed to be realistic about avoiding expensive risks that the lawsuits could potentially bring. And while Sheriff Daniel did share his support of the 2018 motion to repeal Oregon's sanctuary-status law, he said that he would ultimately defer decision making on the matter to Oregon voters.[8]

Another concern with the immigration debate is that it compromises the relationship between immigrant communities and law enforcement. Many police chiefs and sheriffs decline to cooperate with ICE because it would seriously impact public safety.[9] A survey of Mexican nationals found that if San Diego was cooperating with ICE, "60.8 percent said they are less likely to report a crime they witnessed, and 42.9 percent said they are less likely to report being a victim of a crime."[10] If fewer people are reporting crimes or willing to be witnesses, local police will have to work harder and spend more money to solve crimes. Immigrants who are less likely to call the police are also more likely to be victims of crime, though a study done by the Marshall Project concluded crime has been on a steady decrease in some areas and remained the same in others, regardless of rising or falling immigrant populations.[11]

Multnomah, Oregon, is a prime example of a sanctuary county operating within a blue state. Oregon was one of the first states to pass a law restricting cooperation with federal agencies like ICE; its passage was in response to an incident where a sheriff and three deputies approached two men eating in a restaurant and interrogated them about their citizenship status. This incident prompted a lawsuit and revealed a clandestine relationship between ICE and the county, whereby ICE would routinely ask for information and give instructions to the county. Almost ten years later, former Oregon governor Neil Goldschmidt signed ORS 181.850 into law, which stated that "no law enforcement agency of the State of Oregon or of any political subdivision of the state shall use agency moneys, equipment or personnel for the purpose of detecting or apprehending persons whose only violation of law is that they are persons of foreign citizenship present in the United States in violation of federal immigration laws."[12] The law was uncontroversial; it passed in the state senate on a 29–1 vote and in the state house by 58–1.[13]

In 2017, deputies in Multnomah County admitted to giving ICE information about six immigrants that led to their deportation. Their actions violated Sheriff Mike Reese's policy against cooperating with ICE. State law prohibited these deputies from using money or personnel time toward this matter, but a federal law prevents local jurisdictions from restricting government employees from communicating with ICE about a person's immigration status. This led to an investigation surrounding the actions of these deputies, who were cleared of wrongdoing on the basis that five of six of these deported men had prior felony convictions and so were not protected under the 181.850 law.[14]

Since this controversy, Sheriff Reese has been under scrutiny from residents who argue that the sheriff's office is cooperating with ICE more than is required by law. Reese has had to balance local versus federal priorities, arguing that his policy against cooperating with ICE respects community sentiment, but he does cooperate when issues of national security, like trafficking or terrorism, come into play.[15] In 2018, Oregonians for Immigration Reform obtained enough signatures to force a vote on measure 105, which aimed to repeal law 181.850. About 63 percent of Oregon voters voted against the antisanctuary measure out of 1.6 million Oregon constituents.[16] Sheriff Reese advertised his dislike for the bill through preelection advertisements, maintaining that measure 105 would affect law enforcement's ability to do their job and eviscerate what trust remained between their office and the immigrant community.[17]

In response to President Trump's threat to defund cities that do not cooperate with ICE in 2016, Mayor Ted Wheeler announced that Portland would remain a safe place for immigrants. "We will always see ourselves as a sanctuary city, and we will continue to be welcoming to everyone. President-Elect Donald Trump will be the president of all of America, and that requires an understanding of the values that drive Portland and other cities. These are our values."[18] This kind of rhetoric had large consequences, as Trump signed Executive Order 13768 in 2017, which aimed to cut off large portions of federal grant funding for local law enforcement agencies in sanctuary cities. Multiple lawsuits challenged this executive order, and most recently Oregon won a U.S. district court case in 2019. The judge argued that the president does not have the authority to place stipulations on grant money that was given to states by Congress and that states should know of those stipulations before accepting grants. Changing the conditions afterward would not be fair.[19]

President Trump's executive order also brings up a large constitutional issue; the U.S. Supreme Court has ruled that the Tenth Amendment forbids federal "commandeering" of state governments to help enforce federal law. Most of the support for this anticommandeering principle originated from conservative justices such as the late Antonin Scalia.[20] This means the federal government cannot compel states to enforce federal law, complicating President Trump's executive order.

During this legal conundrum, police chiefs and sheriffs are left in a difficult position. They may not be compelled to enforce certain federal laws, but they may lose federal funding meant to induce their cooperation. Executive Director of the National Sheriff Association Jonathan F. Thompson argues that while ICE cannot "just pick up the phone and say, 'Please hold an individual," he does support releasing crime reports of any immigrants who were released before ICE could detain them. Sheriffs must consider these conflicting orders.[21]

Portland is a blue city in a blue state. Austin represents an example of a sanctuary city operating within a Republican-controlled state. Austin's demographic makeup is over one-third Latino, and it is also one of the top twenty US cities with the highest populations of undocumented immigrants, with estimates being around one hundred thousand in 2016.[22] Because Austin and Travis County are liberal areas in a more conservative state, the stage is set for conflict surrounding the issue of how to deal with illegal immigration.

In response to President Trump's inauguration in early 2017, Austin Mayor Steve Adler expressed his commitment not to cooperate completely with ICE. Travis County Sheriff Sally Hernandez also shared plans to change her predecessor's policy of cooperating completely with ICE detainer requests. Under the old policy, jails would potentially hold suspected undocumented immigrants until ICE could pick them up, even if local law entitled them to be released unless charged with a crime that would keep them in jail.

Sheriff Hernandez's policy was that the Travis County jail would only "comply with detainers on murder, aggravated sexual assault and human trafficking charges. For other crimes, Hernandez said she would keep suspects jailed when there is a court order or judicial warrant issued."[23] These officials in Austin argued that increased cooperation with ICE would be a detriment to public safety. If undocumented immigrants fear the police and deportation, they will be less likely to report crimes and be witnesses, enroll their children in school, or avail themselves of public services. ICE detainer requests, most not signed by judges, may also be unconstitutional under the Fourth Amendment, further complicating the scope of federal versus state and local jurisdictions. Austin and Travis County's commitment does not fully comply with ICE's definition of a sanctuary city or jurisdiction, which hinges on willingness to sign a so-called 287(g) agreement.

In response, Texas Governor Greg Abbott eliminated one and a half million dollars of state funding allocated for Austin's criminal justice division to help support veterans and women experiencing domestic violence and their children, few of whom are immigrants. Furthermore, that same year the Texas legislature passed Senate Bill 4 (SB4), which authorizes police officers to ask for immigration and residency status of anyone they arrest or detain. These acts of preemption were meant to show the state government's disapproval of Austin and Travis County's local policies and to force them into complying with state law.

Different police departments responded by expressing concern that SB4 would be putting extra stress on officers to do the job of federal agencies. Houston is in Harris County, and its sheriff, Art Acevedo, immediately spoke out against the law, arguing that this kind of law takes authority away from sheriffs. "If all the sudden I have a police officer who decides 'I'm going to go play ICE agent all day and harass day laborers at Home Depot,' explain to me, when I lose my authority to tell my officers they can't do that, how does that enhance public safety?"[24] The law does not require police to ask for residency status; however, it gives them legal standing to do so, prompting more confusion and disunity within departments.

Sheriff Hernandez subsequently altered her policy to comply with all future detainer requests—because of the ambiguity in the Fifth U.S. Circuit Court of Appeals, which ruled that most of the immigration enforcement legislation can remain in effect.[25] The ruling elaborates: "The 'comply with, honor, and fulfill' requirement does not require detention pursuant to every ICE detainer request. Rather it mandates that local agencies cooperate according to existing ICE detainer practice and law."[26] Immigrant activists argued that this part of the ruling left room for different interpretations that Hernandez could have used to modify her policy to a less extreme extent.

In response, a few Texas cities brought lawsuits against Texas and SB4, but presiding judges allowed most parts of the law to go into effect. The battle of jurisdictions is still raging as Austin and Travis County have asked the U.S Fifth Circuit Court to rehear the case and repeal certain parts of SB4. However, the only part that has been halted is the provision that would punish local law enforcement for "adopting, enforcing or endorsing policies that prohibit or limit enforcement of immigration laws."[27]

To bypass the new law and signal support to the immigrants in their midst, Austin modified its declaration of being a sanctuary city, now calling itself a Freedom City. In 2018, the Austin City Council passed Resolution 73, calling for an end to discretionary arrests, meaning that police will no longer arrest people in cases where they can just give them a citation. Resolution 74 calls for officers to respect residents' constitutional rights to remain silent regarding answering questions about their residency status.[28] Sheriff Hernandez has received a lot of criticism for cooperating with ICE, but she says her hands are tied by SB4. Since the passage of SB4, there has reportedly been a 12 percent decrease in reporting serious crimes to the police in Austin.[29]

Cuban-born Houston Police Chief Art Acevedo has told Houston residents that SB4 gives police legal standing to ask for residency status; however, he maintains that his department had only done this twice as of March 2018. "From an operational standpoint, from a policy standpoint, [SB4] will have no impact. The problem is the perception problem that it creates, that local police officers are going to be more interested in immigration enforcement of people who don't bother anybody."[30] Houston Mayor Sylvester Turner joins Acevedo in this sentiment, arguing that local police should not be forced to act as ICE officers. In July 2019, Turner received advance notice of possible ICE raids and encouraged residents not to open their doors and to know their rights of due process.[31] They see these raids as part of a political strategy by conservatives and President Trump rather than a response to concerns of public safety.

Gun Sanctuaries

The Second Amendment to the U.S. Constitution asserts that "a well-regulated Militia, being necessary to the security of a free State, the right of the people to keep and bear Arms, shall not be infringed." It has been a frequent subject of federal litigation, but in the absence of federal legislation, it has also become a field for state action, particularly in recent years, as mass shootings have proliferated.

In response to mass shootings, states have reacted differently to this injunction. Four states preempted local regulations concerning firearms early on: Alaska and Wyoming in 2010, Kansas in 2013, and Idaho in 2014. These states prohibited counties and local governments from regulating the purchase and use of firearms.

Since then, several rural counties in other states have declared themselves gun sanctuaries, echoing designations of immigrant sanctuaries in urban counties. For example, Effingham County, Illinois, Board Member David Campbell supported a gun resolution passed in a neighboring county but wondered on YouTube if the language could be made "a little more provocative." He hit on

(handwritten margin note: modified sanctuary city to freedom city)

the idea of alluding to some cities' policies on cooperating with federal authorities on immigration enforcement. "I said, well, they're creating sanctuary counties for illegals up in Chicago, why don't we just steal their word and make Effingham County a sanctuary county for firearms?"[32]

This was partially in reaction to Washington State Initiative I-1639, which passed into law by a vote of 59 to 41 percent in a public referendum on November 6, 2018. The initiative made several amendments to state law: the minimum age to purchase semiautomatic rifles was raised from eighteen to twenty-one, the extent of mandatory background checks for semiautomatic weapons purchasers was expanded, and requirements for home storage of firearms were established. The restrictions created by the legislation did not extend to single-shot or bolt-action rifles and the new regulations generally mirrored those already in place for handguns. According to the *Seattle Times*, it was the most "ambitious" gun control legislation in the history of the state.[33]

In King County, home to Seattle, 76.42 percent of voters supported the measure. So did 54.41 percent of voters in Pierce County, site of Tacoma, as did 59.89 percent of voters in Klickitat County on the border with Oregon; so did 50.89 percent of voters in Spokane County. The heavy urban vote in favor of I-1639 swamped rural opposition to the measure.

Sheriffs representing less than a fifth of the state's population initially declined to enforce the proposition. Indeed, Republic County's Washington Police Chief Loren Culp proposed on the police department's Facebook page and later to the city council what he called a "Second Amendment Sanctuary City Ordinance" that would consider I-1639 null and void by the city of Republic. Culp also said, "As long as I am Chief of Police, no Republic police officer will infringe on a citizen's right to keep and bear arms, PERIOD!"

Other sheriffs from rural counties in Washington expressed opposition to the initiative and stated they would not be enforcing it, including sheriffs in Spokane, Chelan, Stevens, Douglas, Benton, Adams, and Lewis Counties.

In response, Washington Attorney General Bob Ferguson (D) issued an open letter to sheriffs and police chiefs who said they would not enforce I-1639:

> Like all laws passed by the people of Washington and their representatives, Initiative 1639 is presumed constitutional. No court has ruled that this initiative is unconstitutional. Local law enforcement officials are entitled to their opinions about the constitutionality of any law, but those personal views do not absolve us of our duty to enforce Washington laws and protect the public. If you personally disagree with Initiative 1639, seek to change it. Or file a lawsuit challenging it. But do not substitute your personal views over that of the people. As public officers, our duty is to abide by the will of the people we serve, and implement and enforce the laws they adopt. I encourage you to do so.[34]

Opponents of I-1639, including the National Rifle Association and the Second Amendment Foundation, filed lawsuits against the State of Washington and Attorney General Bob Ferguson in U.S. District Court in Seattle on November 15, 2018. The plaintiffs alleged that the measure violates the right to bear arms and wrongly regulates interstate commerce, which is under the jurisdiction of the federal government. The lawsuit specifically challenged the provisions relating to (1) the increased age requirement and (2) sales to people from out of state. Plaintiffs sought to have the above-mentioned provisions ruled unconstitutional and to block enforcement of the entire measure unless and until those provisions are deemed severable and are blocked.

But these issues aside, Klickitat County Sheriff Bob Songer vowed not to enforce the law. "Even if it was a legal law, you have discretionary power," Songer told VICE News. "Unfortunately for the governor and the attorney general, they're not my boss. My only boss is the people that elected me to office," Songer said.[35] That is certainly true in a political sense, but it is not true in a constitutional sense, under Dillon's Rule.

In a related vein, one that echoes the rural–urban divide in Washington and Illinois, urban officials have generally supported more restrictions on gun ownership and the types of guns available, in an attempt to reduce violence involving guns. Cara Smith, chief of policy for Cook County Sheriff Tom Dart, who supported closing what he and others saw as loopholes in firearm laws, including the firearm owner's identification card process, said she does not recall anyone reaching out to Dart's office to pitch a sanctuary county resolution.[36]

They have been met by a furious reaction from rural counties. Nearly two-thirds of counties in Illinois have declared themselves gun sanctuaries, effectively denying that loose gun laws in rural Illinois compromise the safety of Cook County residents, local law enforcement notwithstanding.

The chief counsel for a leading U.S. gun-control group questioned the legality of the sanctuary movement, saying state legislatures make laws and courts interpret them, not sheriffs. With that in mind, New Mexico Governor Michelle Lujan Grisham (D) signed a bill that closed a federal loophole exempting unlicensed vendors and gun shows from a law requiring that all licensed arms dealers conduct background checks on potential buyers, effective July 2018.[37]

That brought New Mexico into agreement with twenty other states and Washington, DC, all of which have expanded criminal background checks on handgun sales. A 2017 study conducted by the Giffords Law Center to Prevent Gun Violence estimated that 22 percent of American gun owners had obtained their firearms without a background check, a number that amounts to millions of unvetted buyers of guns each year.[38]

Gun advocates discussed ways of ignoring the legislation, which they claim infringes on the constitutional rights of the state's citizens. When the background check bill passed, twenty-five of New Mexico's thirty-three counties already had approved so-called Second Amendment sanctuary ordinances—declarations signed by local law enforcement officers as part of a broader effort to indicate opposition to the gun-safety measures being proposed by the Democratic-controlled New Mexico state legislature.

For example, Cibola County Sheriff Tony Mace said that these declarations signaled sheriffs' unwillingness to carry out a law that he described as unenforceable—a "feel-good" measure aimed at appeasing the state's gun-reform activists. Mace was then president of the New Mexico Sheriffs' Association; he came up with the idea for the sanctuary resolutions one day while he was driving home from a particularly frustrating committee meeting for the background check bill, during which he says sheriffs' concerns had largely fallen on deaf ears.[39] The initiative, he said, was directly inspired by the immigration sanctuary movements that have been spearheaded in liberal communities throughout the country, in which certain jurisdictions direct state resources away from enforcing federal immigration laws or otherwise do not cooperate with federal immigration officers.

"There are whole sanctuary county, city, and state movements, and those are essentially saying 'Hey, we can shield immigrants from the federal law,'" Mace says. "They're picking and choosing which laws they want to follow as a state, so we're thinking as a county, why can't we take this back to our commissioners and say we're going to draft a resolution that says our counties are Second Amendment sanctuary counties."[40] Of course, under Dillon's Rule, counties are subservient to states, whereas states enjoy immunity from federal legislation in some areas of jurisdiction under the Tenth Amendment.

Indeed, the United States Supreme Court ruled in 1992 that states are not mere political subdivisions of the United States. Whatever the outer limits of state sovereignty, one thing is clear:

> The Federal Government may not compel the States to enact or administer a federal regulatory program. . . . The Constitution enables the Federal Government to pre-empt state regulation contrary to federal interests, and it permits the Federal Government to hold out incentives to the States as a means of encouraging them to adopt suggested regulatory schemes. It does not, however, authorize Congress simply to direct the States [to assist Federal agencies in carrying out their Constitutional responsibilities].[41]

In particular, the Supreme Court ruled that federal agencies may not "commandeer" state or local resources to enforce federal law or policy, nor may federal agencies dictate that state and local law enforcement officers must detain immigrants who may be in the United States illegally in local or county jails. This poses a problem for federal agencies like Immigration and Customs Enforcement, which typically do not have detention facilities of their own in every locality and depend on local and state police to detain illegal immigrants until such time as ICE may investigate possible violations of federal law.

Mace was not alone in his efforts: similar gun-sanctuary movements have arisen in at least four other states with Democratic-controlled legislatures, including Washington, Nevada, Oregon, and Illinois. In those states, as in New Mexico, the ideological schism between state government and local law enforcement highlights a widening gulf between the state's rural and metropolitan populations.[42]

In Oregon, Second Amendment preservation ordinances were on the ballot in ten counties in November 2019, giving residents an opportunity to vote to strengthen protections around their right to keep and bear arms while simultaneously preventing government resources from being earmarked for enforcing any laws that would impede those rights. As in New Mexico, the ordinances came in response to a push for stricter gun laws by the state's Democratic lawmakers—including a bill signed into effect by Oregon Governor Kate Brown in March 2018 that prevents convicted stalkers and violent domestic abusers from obtaining firearms.[43] The ordinances passed overwhelmingly in eight of the ten counties but may well violate Oregon state law establishing that only the state legislature can regulate firearms.[44]

That county-level movement is "the brainchild of Tom McKirgan, the southern Oregon coordinator for the Committee to Protect the Second Amendment and a member of the Three Percenters (the militia group responsible for a forty-one-day occupation of the Malheur National Wildlife Refuge in Eastern Oregon in 2016)."[45] Like Mace, McKirgan believes that the ordinances are legitimized by the fact that law enforcement officers already make discretionary interpretations of the law as a part of their work.

On the other hand, nearly half of Oregon's population resides in counties near Portland, that is, counties west of the Cascade Mountains, whereas opposition to gun laws is concentrated in thinly populated counties east of the Cascades. In spring 2019, the western-dominated legislature considered a suite of regulations that would have made Oregon a national leader in gun regulation.

The reality of what the new laws will look like when put into practice varies, depending on whom you ask. While some sheriffs have acknowledged that the ordinances amount to a purely symbolic "expression" of their discontent, others, like Mace, have said that they will refuse to enforce the law outright.[46] Nonetheless, sheriffs stand united in their unflagging belief that the law would run afoul of the Second Amendment.

To that point, Grisham's office is clear: the argument is a nonstarter and a "cynical exhibition" by gun-rights activists designed to drum up fear and outrage. "A symbolic rebuke to state law is not grounds for duly sworn law-enforcement officers to ignore it," says Tripp Stelnicki, Grisham's director of communications. "Resolutions have no weight of law behind them; they are purely statements of opinion. There is no concern.[47]

Mace believes the decision not to enforce the law would be covered by the fact that New Mexico is an "officer discretionary state," where it falls to a law enforcement officer's discretion to decide what to charge an individual with. (For example, in drug cases, an officer decides whether an individual is charged with possession or drug trafficking.)

"As the sheriff, if I see problems with these particulars and they become law, I don't have to use that law," Mace says.[48] On the other hand, New Mexico's state government has repeatedly reaffirmed that sheriffs cannot cherry-pick which state laws they choose to enforce.[49]

Stelnicki says that Grisham and her administration are unfazed by the attempts to repeal or not enforce the law and expressed similar confidence on their chances of success should a future legal challenge arise. "I can't speak for the sheriffs," he says. "But the proper remedy, for those few folks who have wrapped themselves in the 'constitution,' is the courts."[50]

Mace says he's already heard rumblings of support for such challenges, with certain groups and individuals already expressing willingness to file future lawsuits challenging the state law (although Mace also notes that the New

Mexico Sheriffs' Association will not be the group to file any such suit). "When somebody's right is denied or delayed, then you have grounds for a suit," Mace says. "There [are] people who are just waiting for that to happen so that they can bring that suit forth."[51]

Thus, we have officers operating under the cover of state law, declining to enforce certain state laws. It makes sense politically for sheriffs who are elected, but under Dillon's Rule it is unlikely to pass muster before state supreme courts, and it may trigger preemptive legislation from state legislatures and governors, especially in states where rural populations are much smaller than urban populations.

Joint Sanctuaries

Of course, local enforcement may be soft, in spite of anti-immigrant fervor, precisely because immigrant labor is a critical resource in some rural communities, especially in areas dominated by dairy farms or farms that specialize in growing vegetables, fruits, and nuts, which depend heavily on migrant labor to harvest the crops.[52] The economic power of these immigrants was amply demonstrated by the United Farms Workers of America, under the direction of Cesar Chavez, which boycotted farmers who did not accept the union's demands on wages, housing, and working conditions. Currently, there is a shortage of migrant workers on the Pacific coast.[53]

Farmers who depend on migrant labor can be a formidable force in some rural areas. They may not oppose gun regulations, but they can certainly dampen sheriffs' enthusiasm for cooperating with federal immigration authorities. This puts some sheriffs in the difficult position of favoring gun sanctuaries but resisting federal pressure to cooperate on immigration enforcement.

The point is that sheriffs, who are elected and who think their bosses are the people of the county in which they reside, must be attuned to the differences of opinion in their county and the relative strength of those differences. But they must also attend to state laws and policies, which, under Dillon's Rule, are binding. Federal policies do not bind them, however, unless they reflect the sheriff's own views.

This is the nexus of American federalism, as local units of governance presume they are in a federal relation with their state government, which is in a federal relation with the U.S. government. That is misleading, insofar as local actions, of whatever sort, may be regulated, or even outlawed, by state laws, under Dillon's Rule. On the other hand, the popularity of those who defy state law may be celebrated, until the state supreme court disappoints. Without a law that makes political appointees the natural successors to elected officials, the issue will not be resolved, though it ought to be under a judicial ruling.

In most cases counties that are both immigrant and gun sanctuaries are dominated by large cities that often include parts of several adjacent counties. For example, the Denver–Aurora–Lakewood Metropolitan Statistical Area in Colorado includes portions of ten Colorado counties: the City and County of

Denver, Arapahoe County, Jefferson County, Adams County, Douglas County, the City and County of Broomfield, Elbert County, Park County, Clear Creek County, and Gilpin County. Together this conurbation was home to 2,888,227 people on July 1, 2017, making it the nineteenth most populous metropolitan statistical area of the United States. Denver plus the counties of Arapahoe, Aurora, Jefferson are immigrant sanctuaries that account for 1,922,286 of the combined population.

Given the electoral importance of urban concentrations, some sheriffs support sanctuaries for immigrants. Charlotte, in Mecklenburg County, is North Carolina's largest city. The county sheriff, Garry McFadden, declines to cooperate with ICE, unless they present a criminal warrant for a prisoner in custody. This put him at odds with the North Carolina Sheriffs' Association, which endorsed legislation calling for the removal of sheriffs who fail to cooperate with ICE. The legislation was vetoed by Governor Roy Cooper, a Democrat, who deemed it unconstitutional under the state's constitution. It is in fact difficult to remove sheriffs in most of the nation's counties.[54]

That said, demography is working against rural areas, which are losing population (and hence representation in state legislatures, which might otherwise preempt local sanctuary declarations).[55] The American Community Survey is the only annual data set that produces a range of statistics for all the nation's 3,142 counties. For the three-fourths of all counties with populations too small to produce single-year statistics (2,323 counties), it is the only available data set.

"Rural areas cover 97 percent of the nation's land area but contain 19.3 percent of the population (about 60 million people)," Census Bureau Director John H. Thompson said. "By combining five years of survey responses, the American Community Survey provides unequaled insight into the state of every community, whether large or small, urban or rural."[56]

Researchers also compared rural residents in 704 completely rural counties—those whose entire populations lived in rural areas—with their rural counterparts in counties that were mostly rural and those that were mostly urban. Between 2011 and 2015, about 9 percent of the rural population in the United States (5.3 million) lived in these completely rural counties, compared with about 41 percent (24.6 million) in the 1,185 mostly rural counties and about 50 percent (30.1 million) in the 1,253 mostly urban counties.

Conclusion

These stories outline a growing problem for counties and states with deep political divides. Emerging patterns of preemption regarding gun and immigrant sanctuary declarations are reawakening the county–state divide as an arena of political battles. But the divide is shifting, demographically speaking, in ways that diminish rural counties' representation in state legislatures.

A study by the University of New Hampshire found that "in all, 746 counties representing 24 percent of all U.S. counties are depopulating, and nearly all of them—91 percent—are rural. Over one-third (35 percent) of all rural counties are depopulating. Today, only 6.2 million residents remain in these depopulating rural counties, a third fewer than resided there in 1950."[57] As rural counties decline in population, there is a question of whether people are seeing high-profile conflicts as further reasons to prefer cities. Either way, this trend is having (and will continue to have) serious economic ramifications that have already affected rural counties, which in some regions do not have a labor force big enough to supply the demand from local industries or to maintain community school systems.

One solution for this decline has been marketing these depopulating counties as destinations for immigrants. A demographic study done by Kenneth M. Johnson and Daniel T. Lichter found that "Hispanics contributed more than two-thirds of the rural population gain between 2000 and 2010. This cushioned non-Hispanic population losses in many rural counties. Hispanic growth was often the difference between overall population growth and decline."[58] For example, in Huron, South Dakota, a small town of roughly fourteen thousand residents, refugee populations from around the world have become the impetus for recent population and economic growth in the meatpacking and processing industry.[59] Immigrants constitute an important sector of the workforce for agricultural, forestry, and meat-processing industries.

However, because of the way that progun and anti-immigrant sentiments have been packaged as part of the mainstream conservative ideology, rural counties will have to carefully consider what message they want to send. There are serious trade-offs to weigh: being welcoming toward immigrants in order to keep economic development strong or shunning them at the risk of hurting local economies and accelerating depopulation. This presents unique incentives to sheriffs in rural counties, who may choose to emphasize their commitment to gun sanctuaries as an electoral issue but who also see the need to protect local industries by not emphasizing anti-immigrant policies or rhetoric. They may be politically pressured to publicly denounce illegal immigration but privately decide not to cooperate fully with ICE. But will immigrant communities continue to choose to move or live in communities who may provide them with a job but not support them when ICE decides to increase deportations and coordinate raids?

These clashes between counties and states may well represent a new era of politics in the United States and underscore the unique role of nearly 3,100 elected sheriffs. Whether it be local ordinances, discretionary power to interpret state law, or symbolic shows of disagreement, sheriffs highlight a kind of politics that connect some of the gaps between federal and local laws. Considering this, the role of state courts will also play an increasingly important role in settling these conflicts. Even though rural sheriffs may represent smaller populations, they still have the power to affect the enforcement of state and federal laws, and hence their viability.

CAREER PROFILE

Katharine Czarnecki

Senior Vice President, Community Development
Michigan Economic Development Corporation

The Michigan Economic Development Corporation (MEDC) works across Michigan to foster business growth and economic and community development. Katharine Czarnecki worked for MEDC from 2008 to 2019 and oversaw the community development staff and programs, with an emphasis on downtown development. Czarnecki explains, "Our first rung of customers are local units of government." Small communities have limited staff to manage economic development projects and planning, and these capacities are put under additional stress during economic recession. Czarnecki asks, "How can we help fill in some of those gaps for the communities until they are back up to full staff or until they see the revitalization to get them to a better financial state?" The MEDC's Redevelopment Ready Communities Program offers technical assistance to evaluate the development process, from master planning to marketing strategies, to aid business conditions in the community. As one example, MDEC worked with the city of Allegan to envision the redevelopment of their riverfront, including public infrastructure improvements to allow river access and new business development in the downtown area.

MEDC also collaborates with state agencies, such as the Michigan Department of Environment, Great Lakes, and Energy, a partner on brownfield redevelopment, the restoration and revitalization of contaminated properties. The Michigan State Housing Development Authority aids with the evaluation of housing needs when new businesses enter the state. The state's Department of Transportation is a partner when examining local infrastructure and transportation needs.

Czarnecki earned a Bachelor's of Business Administration from the University of Georgia. After a period of work in banking, she worked in economic development in the city of Midland, Michigan. She returned to Michigan State University for a master's degree in urban and regional planning and spent time working for a private planning firm and the Lansing Regional Chamber of Commerce before working for MEDC. Czarnecki advises students to volunteer and identify internship opportunities that provide experience in community development. Students should develop work experience in college, even if it is in unrelated areas, to illustrate their capacity to contribute to a business or an organization. A track record of good work qualities and strong references will aid students as they pursue new job opportunities.

Interview: September 5, 2019

Discussion Questions

1. Why can't the federal government compel states to enforce national policies on immigration, even though states can require cities and counties to enforce state laws on immigration?
2. Why are immigrant sanctuaries concentrated on the West Coast, whereas gun sanctuaries are more broadly distributed?
3. What motivates elected sheriffs to defy state laws they oppose, and does this undermine the rule of law or erode the prerogatives of state legislators?
4. How will impending demographic shifts alter the balance of power between urban and rural areas in state legislatures? What effect might this have on future sanctuary legislation?

Notes

[1] Melvin Delgado, *Sanctuary Cities, Communities, and Organizations: A Nation at a Crossroads* (Oxford: Oxford University Press, 2018).

[2] State governments in California, Colorado, Connecticut, Illinois, Massachusetts, and New Jersey have declared their entire states sanctuaries. Vermont has severely limited cooperation with ICE.

[3] Mark Johnson, "Scott Signs Bill "Not . . . Establishing a Sanctuary State," *VTDigger*, March 28, 2017, https://vtdigger.org/2017/03/28/scott-signs-bill-not-establishing-a-sanctuary-state/.

[4] Governments that have not declared themselves sanctuaries may, of course, be de facto sanctuaries, owing to existing policies or weak laws.

[5] Miriam Jordan, "8 Million People Are Workimg Illegally in the U.S.: Here's Why That's Unlikely to Change," *New York Times*, December 11, 2018, https://www.nytimes.com/2018/12/11/us/undocumented-immigrant-workers.html?auth=login-email&login=email.

[6] Conrad Wilson, "ICE Pays to Use 2 Oregon Jails Despite Sanctuary State Law," Oregon Public Broadcasting, June 21, 2018, https://www.opb.org/news/article/ice-jail-oregon-norcor-josephine-contract-sanctuary-state/.

[7] Kate Houston, "Josephine County Ends Contract with ICE," KDRV News, June 27, 2018, https://www.kdrv.com/content/news/Josephine-County-Sheriff-Issues-Statement-on-ICE-Contract-Ending-486719721.html.

[8] Jamie Parfitt, "Josephine County Sheriff Weighs in on 'Sanctuary Law' Repeal," KDRV News, August 18, 2018, https://www.kdrv.com/content/news/Josephine-County-Sheriff-Weighs-in-on-Sanctuary-Law-Repeal-491933451.html.

[9] Crime rates are not affected by sanctuary status, as shown by Benjamin Gonzalez O'Brien, Loren Collingwood, and Stephen Omar El-Khatib, "The Politics of Refuge: Sanctuary Cities, Crime and Undocumented Immigration," *Urban Affairs* 55, no. 1 (2019): 3–40.

[10] Tom K. Wong, "Sanctuary Cities Don't 'Breed Crime,' They Encourage People to Report Crime," *Washington Post*, March 24, 2018, https://www.washingtonpost.com/news/monkey-cage/wp/2018/04/24/sanctuary-cities-dont-breed-crime-they-encourage-people-to-report-crime/.

[11] Anna Flagg, "Illegal Immigration Crime Rates Research," *New York Times*, May 13, 2019, https://www.nytimes.com/2019/05/13/upshot/illegal-immigration-crime-rates-research.html.

[12] Oregon State Laws, "2013 ORS 181.850¹: Enforcement of Federal Immigration Laws," https://www.oregonlaws.org/ors/2013/181.850.

[13] Conrad Wilson, "30 Years Later, Oregon's 'Sanctuary State' Law Serves As A Model For Others," Oregon Public Broadcasting, May 31, 2018. https://www.opb.org/news/article/oregon-sanctuary-city-state-donald-trump-immigration/

[14] Amelia Templeton, "5 Insights from Multnomah County Sheriff's Internal ICE Investigation," Oregon Public Broadcasting, November 3, 2017, https://www.opb.org/news/article/multnomah-county-immigration-ice-investigation-mike-reese/.

15 Ericka Cruz Guevarra, "Portland Police Clarify Policy on Cooperation with ICE," Oregon Public Broadcasting, December 23, 2017, https://www.opb.org/news/article/portland-police -cooperate-ice-directive/.

16 Elise Foley, "Oregon 'Sanctuary State' Policy Survives as Voters Reject Fearmongering," *Huffington Post*, November 7, 2018, https://www.huffingtonpost.ca/entry/oregon-sanctuary-state _n_5be2d331e4b0769d24c78e00?ri18n=true.

17 Vote No on Measure 105, "Law Enforcement against Measure 105," https://www.youtube.com/ watch?v=K1L4UYD0S9g&feature=youtu.be.

18 Rachel Monahan, "Mayor-Elect Ted Wheeler Says Portland Will Be a Sanctuary City for Immigrants, Despite Donald Trump's Threats," *Willamette Week*, November 15, 2016, https://www .wweek.com/news/2016/11/15/mayor-elect-ted-wheeler-says-portland-will-be-a-sanctuary-city -for-immigrants-despite-donald-trumps-threats/.

19 Andrew Selskey, "Judge Rules for Oregon in Sanctuary City Case with Trump," *Komonews*, August 8, 2019, https://komonews.com/news/local/judge-rules-for-oregon-in-sanctuary-city -case-with-trump.

20 Ilya Somin, "Federalism, the Constitution, and Sanctuary Cities," *Washington Post*, November 26, 2016, https://www.washingtonpost.com/news/volokh-conspiracy/wp/2016/11/26/federalism -the-constitution-and-sanctuary-cities/.

21 F. Stockman and J. D. Goodman, "Immigration Policies Pose Conflict for Police in 'Sanctuary Cities,'" *New York Times*, February 25, 2017, A10.

22 Jeffrey S. Passel and D'vera Cohn, "20 Metro Areas Are Home to Six-in-Ten Unauthorized Immigrants in U.S.," Pew Research Center, March 11, 2019, https://www.pewresearch.org/ fact-tank/2019/03/11/us-metro-areas-unauthorized-immigrants/.

23 "Texas Governor Abbott Threatens Austin Sheriff over 'Sanctuary Cities' Policy with Immigrants," *CBS News*, January 24, 2017, https://www.cbsnews.com/news/texas-governor -abbott-threatens-austin-sheriff-sanctuary-cities-immigrants/

24 Margaret Downing, "'Cite and Release': New Houston Police Chief Wants Fewer Trips to Jail," *HoustonPress*, December 16, 2016, https://www.houstonpress.com/news/cite-and -release-new-houston-police-chief-wants-fewer-trips-to-jail-9031494.

25 Mary Tuma, "Hernandez to ICE Reversal Critics: 'This Is Not Over,'" *Austin Chronicle*, October 20, 2017, https://www.austinchronicle.com/news/2017-10-20/hernandez-to-ice-reversal -critics-this-is-not-over/.

26 Ibid.

27 Julian Aguilar, "Critics of Texas' 'Sanctuary Cities' Law Ask Federal Appeals Court to Reconsider Case," *Texas Tribune*, March 28, 2018, https://www.texastribune.org/2018/03/28/ critics-texas-sanctuary-cities-law-ask-federal-appeals-court-reconside/.

28 Erin Rubin, "Austin, Texas: If We Can't Be a Sanctuary City, How about a Freedom City," *Nonprofit Quarterly*, July 11, 2018, https://nonprofitquarterly.org/austin-texas-if-we-cant-be -a-sanctuary-city-how-about-a-freedom-city/.

29 Tuma, "Hernandez to ICE Reversal Critics."

30 Manny Fernandez, "Texas Banned 'Sanctuary Cities': Some Police Departments Didn't Get the Memo," *New York Times*, August 3, 2018, https://www.nytimes.com/2018/03/15/us/texas-sanc tuary-sb4-immigration.html?searchResultPosition=1.

31 Audie Cornish, "Houston Mayor Sylvester Turner Weighs in on Expected ICE Raids," NPR, July 11, 2019, https://www.npr.org/2019/07/11/740871260/houston-mayor-sylvester -turner-weighs-in-on-expected-ice-raids.

32 Cf. Robert Spitzer, *Guns across America: Reconciling Gun Rules and Rights* (Oxfod: Oxford University Press, 2015), for an excellent review of the politics of gun control in the United States.

33 See Washington State, Office of the Attorney General, "Initiative 1639," https://www.atg.wa .gov/initiative-1639.

34 Washington State, Office of the Attorney General, "AG Ferguson Issues Open Letter to Law Enforcement on I-1639," news release, February 12, 2019, https://www.atg.wa.gov/news/ news-releases/ag-ferguson-issues-open-letter-law-enforcement-i-1639.

35 Joshua Hersh, "This Washington Sheriff Is Refusing to Enforce His State's New Gun Control Law," VICE News, March 22, 2019, https://www.vice.com/en_us/article/gyaew4/this-washington -sheriff-is-refusing-to-enforce-his-states-new-gun-control-law.

[36] Katherine Rosenberg-Douglas, "Second Amendment 'Sanctuary County' Movement Expands as Organizers Take Aim at New Gun Laws," *Chicago Tribune*, April 17, 2019, https://www .chicagotribune.com/news/breaking/ct-met-second-amendment-sanctuary-county-movement-il linois-20190416-story.html.

[37] In this discussion, we borrow heavily from Brianna Provenzano, "What Happens If Sheriffs Refuse to Enforce State Gun Control Laws?" *Pacific Standard*, March 13, 2019, https://psmag .com/social-justice/what-happens-if-sheriffs-refuse-to-enforce-state-gun-control-laws.

[38] Giffords Law Center, "Universal Background Checks," https://lawcenter.giffords.org/gun-laws/ policy-areas/background-checks/universal-background-checks/.

[39] Provenzano, "What Happens If Sheriffs Refuse?"

[40] Ibid.

[41] *New York v. United States*, 488 U.S. 1041 (1992), a case in which national authorities pressed New York's Alleghany County to accept nuclear waste from federal facilities.

[42] Provenzano, "What Happens If Sheriffs Refuse?"

[43] Ibid.

[44] Ben Botkin, "Oregon Lawmakers Debate Multiple Bills to Make Gun Laws More Restrictive," *Statesman Journal*, February 12, 2019, https://www.statesmanjournal.com/story/ news/politics/2019/02/12/gun-control-legislation-oregon-lawmakers-bills-laws-more-restric tive/2774567002/.

[45] Provenzano, "What Happens If Sheriffs Refuse?"

[46] Ibid.

[47] Ibid.

[48] Ibid.

[49] Ibid.

[50] Ibid.

[51] Ibid.

[52] Jonathan H. Harsch, "California Leads Fight to Fix National Farm Labor Shortage," *Agri-Pulse*, September 26, 2019, https://www.agri-pulse.com/articles/12172-california-leads-fight -to-fix-national-farm-labor-shortage.

[53] David Bacon, "The Pacific Coast Farm-Worker Rebellion: From Baja California to Washington State, Indigenous Farm Workers Are Standing up for Their Rights," *Nation*, August 28, 2015, https://www.thenation.com/article/the-pacific-coast-farm-worker-rebellion/.

[54] In many states sheriffs are elected constitutional officer holders. Cf. Jessica Pishko, "Why Can't We Get Rid of Bad Sheriffs?," *New York Times*, September 26, 2019, https://www.nytimes .com/2019/09/26/opinion/sheriff-north-carolina-hitman.html.

[55] This may be a slow process, as Jonathan A. Rodden explains in *Why Cities Lose: The Deep Roots of the Urban-Rural Political Divide* (New York: Basic Books, 2019). The dispersion of Republican voters in suburbs, exurbs, and rural areas gives them a structural advantage over Democratic voters, who are concentrated in cities. On the other hand, millennials now outnumber baby boomers, and relatively few millennials are aligned with the GOP. Cf. Daniel J. McGraw, "The GOP Is Dying Off. Literally," *Politico*, May 17, 2015, https://www.politico.com/ magazine/story/2015/05/the-gop-is-dying-off-literally-118035.

[56] U.S. Census Bureau, "New Census Data Show Differences between Urban and Rural Populations," press release, December 8, 2016, https://www.census.gov/newsroom/press-releases/2016/ cb16-210.html.

[57] Kenneth M. Johnson and Daniel T. Lichter, "Rural Depopulation: Growth and Decline Processes over the Past Century," *Rural Sociology* 84, no. 1 (2019): 3–27.

[58] Kenneth M. Johnson and Daniel T. Lichter, "Diverging Demography: Hispanic and Non-Hispanic Contributions to US Population Redistribution and Diversity," *Population Research and Policy Review* 35, no. 5 (2016): 705–25.

[59] Daniel T. Lichter and Kenneth M. Johnson, "Immigrant Gateways and Hispanic Migration to New Destinations," *International Migration Review* 43, no. 3 (2009): 496–518.

CHAPTER 10

Franchising the Regulation of Fracking
Governance Solutions to Intergovernmental Coordination Dilemmas in U.S. States and Municipalities

Brian K. Collins, University of North Texas

State–local relations increasingly frame the regulatory environment of fracking in the United States. Hydraulic fracturing or "fracking" is a method of unconventional gas extraction from shale deposits found in the majority of U.S. states. State and local governments are attempting to balance competing interests and complex technological problems with uncertain societal outcomes. Fracking activities generate regulatory challenges for natural resource management, environmental protection, and economic development as well as hazards and residential nuisances for both state and local governments.

This chapter asks why state control over municipal authority to regulate fracking varies and what induces states to expand or to contract municipal authority. Much research examines state- or national-level determinants of fracking policy.[1] State–local relations are rarely developed in this policy arena,[2] and so this chapter applies an institutional analysis to explain the conflict and cooperation between states and municipalities. In particular, this analysis relies heavily on Whitford's franchise theory of governance organization to explain evolving state–local relations in the regulation of fracking.[3]

The chapter also compares fracking regulation in Texas and Colorado because both states have extensive natural resource extraction interests and vocal, varied groups that seek to restrict fracking activities.[4] Both states have strong state policies regulating fracking.[5] However, Texas and Colorado are moving in opposite directions regarding the extent to which local governments can exercise policy discretion over fracking regulation. Texas began with a substantial degree of municipal autonomy but moved to limit and even to remove municipal powers, while Colorado is marginally increasing municipal regulatory

Texas- moving towards State policy

powers.[6] These cases demonstrate two approaches to resolving state–local conflict in this and potentially other contentious policy arenas.

The Dilemmas of Fracking Regulation

Horizontal hydraulic fracturing, commonly known as fracking, presents two distinct but related sets of collective action dilemmas that provide an impetus for state and local government regulation. The first set of problems revolve around natural resource extraction for economic gain. Private actors extracting natural gas through fracking (i.e., drillers) have economic incentives to site too many extraction wells in any single geographic area.[7] In response to market competition, drillers will attempt to appropriate natural resources in a manner that is not financially sustainable for their individual firms. In seeking to maximize their individual profits, drillers will site wells so that revenues do not cover their break-even points. Consequently, drilling firms lose the incentive to extract natural gas, society loses access to a natural resource in demand, and state and local economies experience lost employment and growth.[8]

Governments can enhance social welfare through market coordination that mitigates the behavior of individual drilling firms. The two most common regulatory regimes are integration contracts and well spacing requirements.[9] Both of these regulatory instruments have a long history in conventional oil and gas drilling and have long been used to address potential economic waste in that context. Integration contracts are instruments that enable drillers to pool mineral or natural resource rights into a size that supports fiscally sustainable extraction.[10] Governments can aid the creation of these contracts through regulatory requirements that give drillers superseding property rights over other landowners or land uses. In addition, governments can also manage resource extraction through well spacing requirements that seek to maximize profitable natural resource extraction. Drillers are typically required to obtain permits that demonstrate a sufficient geographic dispersion relative to other firms. If governments optimize this dispersion, then in theory the number of financially sustainable firms can be optimized relative to the distribution of natural gas. Consequently, governments hope to minimize economic waste associated with the appropriation dilemma and maximize employment opportunities, economic growth, and tax bases. However, governments are also tasked with resolving another dilemma that may run counter to optimizing economic output.

This second problem centers on negative externalities associated with fracking processes at or near extraction points. Negative externalities are a cost imposed on society that producers or consumers do not pay, such as air pollution. In fracking, drillers generate negative externalities to the extent that fracking is linked to technological and natural hazards, nuisances, and unsustainable infrastructure demands. Fracking involves highly toxic chemical compounds and powerful physical processes that pose significant risks to human life, built environments, and the natural environment.[11] Research continues into potential linkages between fracking and systemic pollution of air and water, and evidence that fracking affects seismic activity continues to mount.[12] These hazards are

(margin annotations, handwritten):
• decreasing competition
• maximise individual profit
• creates jobs & taxes 4 areas

• minimize economic waste

present even if drillers operate accident free, but the potential for transportation hazards such as gas line explosions, chemical truck accidents, well-site explosions, and contaminated wastewater dumping pose additional risks. Fracking amplifies the risks in high-density urban populations.[13] Concordant with these populations, negative externalities arise in the form of nuisances such as traffic, noise and odors from drilling, and the concomitant loss of property value. These processes also increase demand for water and transportation infrastructure that often are not sustainable for localities.[14]

(margin, handwritten, right side:) Local area are more effected environmentally

Therefore, governments regulate drillers to internalize the costs of negative externalities, or at least mitigate the costs to third parties. For example, governments can mandate public disclosure of some or all chemicals used in fracking fluid, and permit fees support safety inspections or subsidize transportation infrastructure.[15] Zoning policies made through variance processes are critical tools.[16] When drillers request zoning variances, governments can extract concessions in the drilling process such as firm-provided ingress and egress to well pads or the use of walls and fences to mitigate noise and aesthetic nuisances.[17] Setbacks are one of the most common regulatory actions because setting a geographic buffer zone between the mixed land use of industrial fracking and residential or commercial uses is a low-transaction-cost resolution to the firms internalizing some of the negative externalities.[18] And, at the extreme, governments can ban fracking absolutely or when hazard triggers are activated. In any case, the potential benefits of limiting economic waste are likely to be diminished in whole or in part.

(margin, handwritten, right side:) environmental concerns are more important than are local concerns.

The tension between these two first-order collective action dilemmas highlights the importance and puzzle of second-order intergovernmental governance coordination: how do states and municipalities organize the allocation of policy authority and tools to coordinate solutions to the problems identified above?[19] Federal regulation of fracking is not well developed at this point, and so intergovernmental relations between state and local governments is the critical arena.[20] The two second-order problems are the vertical allocation of policy authority between states and local governments and the municipalities' resolution of horizontal coordination problems, such as competition for economic benefits or NIMBY (not in my backyard) actions. The next section explains and applies a franchise theory of government to explain potential solutions to these second-order problems that configure intergovernmental relations and why they may differ across states.[21]

Applying Franchise Theory to Fracking Regulation

A franchise theory of governance relies on a market analogy to explain the distribution of governance authority in the production of policy, goods, and services. Although several scholars have developed this framework,[22] this discussion relies heavily on Whitford's articulation and explanation.[23] As an economic governance structure, firms may choose a franchisor–franchisee relationship that involves the delegation of bounded authority and discretion to franchisees regarding production, prices, advertising, and quality controls, among other

[handwritten: State delegates power so that LA can enstill policy with meeting public demands & State interest]

factors. This system of governance should be effective because decentralization with boundaries maximizes the local information necessary for effective policymaking but forces local governments to keep state interest in mind. In theory, effective policymaking at the local level is also beneficial at the state level, but state governments want to prevent policies contrary to state interests. In other words, state governments (franchisors) will delegate powers to produce regulation to local governments (franchisees) in a way that will maximize the benefits to the state while giving local governments some discretion to meet local demands.

However, the benefits of franchising arise only if vertical and horizontal coordination dilemmas are resolved.[24] A critical vertical coordination dilemma presents as a double moral hazard between the franchisor and franchisee, respectively. Franchisors must ensure that franchisees do not shirk by cutting quality, local advertising effort, or royalty payments. Franchisees also face a vertical dilemma because they essentially delegate the enforcement of reputational protection and competition protection to the franchisor, who has incentives to extract rents by not enforcing horizontal equity among franchisees. Moreover, franchisees face the problem of a franchisor who cannot credibly commit to profit sharing over time or maintaining level quality standards. In addition to the vertical coordination problem, franchisees at the local level experience horizontal coordination problems because each depends on system-wide quality reputations, but individual franchisees may cut quality to free ride on the reputational good. Franchisees can also free ride on local advertising efforts of others. Consequently, franchisors and franchisees develop governance structures to mitigate these dilemmas so all parties can obtain or approach the desired outcome, which is typically a profitable economic enterprise for both franchisor and franchisee.

The analogue to fracking governance at the state and local level is instructive. State governments may decide to produce fracking regulation internally (state's scope of discretion), or they may franchise policy production to local governments, which includes, but is not limited to, municipalities and counties. If state actors want to maximize political and policy benefits, then geographically dispersed policy production presents opportunity. Designing effective policies is often contingent on localized information about the physical, cultural, and political environments. As the variation in these factors increases, the potential benefits of delegated local policy production increases. Local knowledge in a complex, varied, and geographically disparate context is likely to produce locally optimal policies that aggregate into greater state-level political support than suboptimal, generic policies from a distant central administration. Even if localized policy production does not generate effective policies, central governments (states) may delegate to hedge against the loss of political support in cases of highly controversial topics, such as fracking or abortion and some environmental regulation on a national level, for example. Such blame shifting or plausible deniability focuses political losses on the local policymakers rather than the state policymakers. Therefore, if policy effectiveness corresponds to

[handwritten: If LA is popular & successful than states give power to LA]

local conditions, then states have an incentive to franchise particular policy discretion to localities.

Fracking regulation is an interesting case because states face incentives to franchise some policy domains to local governments while retaining other policy domains for internal production. For example, the natural resource economics regulation of oil and gas production has long been the purview of state governments. Maximizing resource extraction is generally not contingent on local information, and policy benefits are generally diffuse even if distributions across a state are unequal.[25] In contrast, regulation of numerous and varied negative externalities are commonly highly localized in impact and policy response. For example, states provide local zoning authority to cities and counties to deal with local nuisances, public safety, and negative, but localized, environmental impacts. However, states also retain policy discretion over environmental regulations directly and indirectly related to fracking where policy impacts are more general and localized information is less useful. For example, policies about disclosure of fracking fluids are commonly found in the state arena.[26] Therefore, a franchise theory of governance can explain how to coordinate multidimensional policy space with varied governance arrangements.

In table 10.1, for example, four configurations of state–local regulatory relations are illustrated. The upper left quadrant indicates a state that franchises significant regulatory authority to local government in the negative externality space but retains regulatory authority in permitting to maximize economic gains. Although a franchise theory of governance suggests that this configuration should perhaps be an equilibrium outcome for fracking, states have chosen alternatives such as the lower left quadrant, in which states retain regulatory authority across policy domains. However, this multidimensional conceptualization of state–local relations also hints at potential trade-offs and the challenge of managing vertical and horizontal coordination problems if or when state governments franchise regulatory authority.

TABLE 10.1   Franchise Configurations for State–Local Fracking Regulation Coordination

Regulatory Arena	Economic Growth		
		Low demand for local information	High demand for local information
Negative Externalities	High demand for local information	Franchise, State *(NE) (EG)*	Franchise, Franchise
	Low demand for local information	State, State *(Dillion's Rule)*	State, Franchise *Balance*

[handwritten annotations: "St is handling that area" pointing to Low demand for local information; "local level has the autonomy on this level," ; "St. want to handle what they can, but want Local Gov to have authority to take some of the work"]

The strategic choice to franchise is contingent on the ability to manage the vertical and horizontal coordination problems. For example, states can experience a vertical coordination dilemma with localities if policy production at the state level supports wealth maximization but municipalities regulate to minimize negative externalities that weaken state regulatory objectives. A franchise arrangement also presents municipalities with horizontal coordination dilemmas if policies externalize pollution or noise to other jurisdictions without any environmental mitigation from the region or state. Both races to the bottom and races to the border exemplify such horizontal coordination problems. Yet, if local policy production can leverage benefits of localized information and policy production, and more distal and centralized policy production can be brought to bear as an overt or covert coordinator of policy production, then states can franchise to affect a preferred balance of policy production and societal outcomes. The question is how states organize the franchise arrangements to allocate policy production, to monitor policy production, and to restrain potential shirking in second-order relations (both vertical and horizontal).

Whitford suggests three general government franchise strategies that can be applied to arrange franchised fracking governance.[27] First, states can present a credible threat to internalize policy production, which is equivalent to rewriting the franchise contract and removing discretion from the franchisee. State preemption of local government is the actualization of this threat, but credible threats can substitute for actual preemption. Loss of local government autonomy in a policy space diminishes local political power and can reduce the effectiveness of policy responses to local problems. If local governments want to retain these powers, then they must structure policies that comply with explicit or implicit state boundaries. For example, if local governments regulate negative externalities in a manner that impedes wealth maximization, states may threaten to remove or actually preempt policy tools and discretion at the local level. Hence, municipalities either limit or forego negative externality mitigation.

States can also employ a dual distribution strategy to monitor and to enforce the explicit or implicit franchise contract with local governments.[28] If local governments are regulating fracking outside of state limitations within or across policy domains, then state governments can monitor policy opportunism through dual distribution of regulation. Dual distribution in governance can present as local governments with much less policy discretion and closer institutional ties with the state government, such as counties or regional governments in some states. If counties are regulating fracking within a certain range and municipalities are deviating substantially, then municipalities are signaled to maintain alignment or be subject to state constraints such as preemption. Similarly, state-level agencies can coproduce regulations that are applied to limited and specific geographies to check local governments. For example, the nationalization of civil rights litigation demonstrates a dual distribution of authority in response to local quality cutting.[29] States and local governments retain authority to address civil rights disputes, but the creation of the Civil Rights Division in the Department of Justice marked an important departure from previous reliance on state and local governments that did not meet minimum federal standards. The potential for similar dual distribution dynamics exists in fracking regulations if local governments do not meet minimum standards for state objectives in either wealth maximization or reduction of negative externalities (independently or concordantly).

A third coordination strategy involves franchisees offering bonds to ensure performance consistent with franchisor objectives.[30] In a private firm, for example, franchisees pay sunk cost fees and demonstrate capital reserves to signal the ability and intention to perform required tasks of production and delivery. Franchise contracts may also require franchisees to provide performance bonds to insure against failure to perform. The same holds in public–private networks when governments require private-sector partners to provide surety bonds. Other intergovernmental examples include matching funds for intergovernmental grants or financial penalties for compliance failures. In each case, both vertical and horizontal dilemmas are coordinated under threat of financial loss that is imposed ex post performance failure on detection and enforcement or ex ante through incentive design. Therefore, states can provide both ex ante and ex post financial requirements that effectively constrain municipalities from policy production that does not meet implicit or explicit state standards.

In sum, a franchise theory of fracking regulation provides a framework for analyzing the dynamics of fracking regulation. This framework recognizes that complex policies often present multiple, overlapping governance structures within a policy space and that specific policy arenas may mitigate or exacerbate intergovernmental regulatory conflict. The next section provides a brief comparative case study of Texas and Colorado to illustrate how state governments construct and adapt regulatory franchises for fracking.

A Comparative Case Study of Franchising Fracking Regulation

Texas and Colorado are the subjects of this narrative analysis, and their similarities and differences concerning fracking policy and politics have been reviewed extensively.[31] For this chapter, the similar economic reliance and saliency of oil and gas extraction is important to note. Both states have strong lobbies and activism in the oil and gas industry, but Colorado's more active environmental lobby and activism constitute an important difference. Such similarities and differences should result in similar narratives but also generate important differences in the structure and change in regulatory arrangements of fracking.

The policy domains in fracking are many, ranging from fluid disclosure to noise abatements, with permitting and property rights typically at the core.[32] These cases begin with the proposition that both design state–level fracking permitting systems, in large part to maximize the economic return on extraction activities. In contrast, states can employ many policy production tools and arrangements to address negative externalities associated with extraction (fracking or otherwise). These cases focus on the policy domain associated with zoning and land use regulation, which is commonly, but not exclusively, assigned to local governments for the promotion of public safety, reduction of negative

State-level regulation encourage to economic return [handwritten margin note]

externalities, and even maximizing of local economic welfare. Common examples include local permitting requirements for industrial activities, setback provisions for public safety and property value protection, and noise abatements. The land use regulatory domain presents a clear example of the dynamics associated with franchised regulation.

The short case studies highlight critical cross-sectional differences between Texas and Colorado but also an important convergence in governance structures. In each case, regulatory franchises developed to address traditional oil and gas extraction were applied to the innovation of fracking. However, both cases identify a franchise contract failure that is common to both states—namely, indeterminate moratoriums or local bans on fracking activity. Ultimately, the states diverge in response to these franchise failures with new governance relationships.

Texas: Franchise Failure and Adjustment

Texas uses a franchise regulatory structure for fracking in that the state government regulates permitting for economic return but delegates other policy authority to municipal governments through land use planning. At the state level, the Texas Railroad Commission (RRC) provides permits to regulate well spacing and to enforce integration contracts and pooling requirements. However, the RRC does not have jurisdiction over roads, traffic, noise, odors, and other negative externalities relevant to the geographically proximate residents or businesses near state-permitted wells. Regulation of these negative externalities is delegated to municipalities through a general grant of authority to govern land uses for the purposes of protecting public health, safety, and welfare.[33] The state does not specifically attach these powers to extraction technologies or activities, but they fall within the purview of home-rule municipalities without restrictions related to extraction industries. Accordingly, municipalities engage drillers in the zoning process through requests for variances. Municipalities also permit extraction but often after requiring buffer zones (setbacks), noise abatements at well pads, and fees to subsidize local safety inspections.[34] Texas does not delegate these powers to county governments.

This combination of state and local objectives and delegation of powers illustrates the vertical and horizontal coordination problems previously discussed. The dual moral hazard problem has been evident in concerns expressed by municipalities, the extraction industry, and the RRC. Municipalities are concerned that the state's pursuit of economic return is jeopardizing local health and well-being with fracking technologies that enable drilling in urban and more densely populated areas. State actors are concerned that local land use regulation is impeding extraction and the associated economic benefits. In terms of horizontal coordination, many municipalities essentially play a NIMBY game by increasing setbacks or making costly abatement requirements that drive extraction industries to site well pads just across borders in other municipalities or counties. However, as more municipalities play a NIMBY regulatory strategy, the economic costs of extraction can become cost prohibitive and reduce the aggregate economic return.

[handwritten margin note top: economic reasons why TX stepped in]

To preserve the benefits of this franchised regulatory regime, Texas employs both dual distribution and a form of bonding as a means of constraining policy production at the municipal level. For example, Texas employs a form of dual distribution through county governments. As agents of the state government in Texas, counties do not hold land use regulatory authority. Consequently, extraction firms can arbitrage policy differences by locating well pads in unincorporated areas that cannot restrict extraction activities, which supports the RRC objective of maximizing economic return. Like firm-operated production in a private franchise context, the state is able to induce competition and the revelation of local information about the economic costs of regulation in municipalities.

Another constraint is the potential financial penalty associated with a credible threat of regulatory takings lawsuits. The threat from extraction industries is that state court systems will hold municipalities liable for lost profits resulting from regulations that restrict or preclude access to duly owned mineral rights, known as regulatory takings. This threat is central in land use negotiations and credible to the extent that city attorneys and elected council members frequently identify the potential financial catastrophe should such suits be tried and lost. In sum, municipalities are informally bonded as state agents to allow fracking with reasonable restrictions or pay a severe financial penalty under the credible threat of court-supported regulatory takings threats.

These strategies have represented a largely stable franchise contract that accommodates different policy objectives, but clear conflict, resistance, and franchise contract failure has occurred. In 2014, the city of Denton banned fracking. After significant public pressure, citizen engagement, and debates among elected officials, the Denton City Council had rejected a proposed ban on fracking, but citizens organized an initiative that eventually received voter approval, even in the face of significant expenditures from the extraction industry and threats of regulatory takings lawsuits. Even though it was the first and only ban in Texas, it represented a clear franchise failure. A ban clearly undermined the state economic return objective but also posed problems for others. For example, no elected body in Texas, including Denton's, had ever violated the implicit contract constraints by banning fracking. Elected officials and professional staff expressed concern about regulatory takings suits and the credible threat that the state would "rewrite" the franchise contract to remove the land use discretion over fracking. The initiative ban highlighted a rift between concerned voters and their elected officials at the state and local levels and effectively signaled a failed regulatory franchise.

The state's response to the ban demonstrates two mechanisms for course correcting after franchise failure. First, the extraction industry immediately began regulatory takings proceedings against the City of Denton. However, in 2015 and before those suits could be heard, the state legislature statutorily rewrote the franchise contract through HB 40 and explicitly banned municipal authority to ban fracking. Municipalities retained franchised powers of land use regulation associated with fracking, but the state precluded banning as a policy tool in municipalities and preempted the Denton ban. Lawsuits were dismissed,

[handwritten margin notes right side: financial threat to Municipalities - If impose restrictions, corporations will sue]

[handwritten margin notes right side: TX banned Municipalities from banning Fracking]

and no other municipality has challenged the statute that bans bans. In sum, the state reset the franchise contract status quo to the pre-Denton ban conditions, and it remains a relatively stable governance structure.

Colorado: Franchise Failure and Marginal Mutual Adjustment

Colorado also uses a franchise regulatory structure for fracking but one that is structured very differently from Texas. Historically, Colorado has vested the authority to regulate oil and gas extraction in a state agency, the Colorado Oil and Gas Conservation Committee (COGCC). This agency's mandate is to promote economic returns associated with extraction industries, protect property rights, and mitigate environmental impacts. The COGCC engages in statewide permitting that seeks optimal well spacing and pooling of mineral rights. In addition, the COGCC has land use policy powers over roads, traffic, noise, odors, and other negative externalities near state-permitted wells. For example, the COGCC permits extraction, requires and defines setbacks and noise abatements at well pads, and assesses fees. In addition, home-rule municipalities hold regulatory power over negative externalities within the jurisdiction. According to the Colorado Supreme Court in *Voss v. Lundvall* in 1992, these powers can attach to fracking so long as regulations do not frustrate state intentions and coordinate with COGCC decisions.

Although Colorado faces coordination problems similar to Texas, they use a dual distribution strategy that has largely resolved horizontal coordination problems but seemingly exacerbated vertical coordination problems. Vesting the COGCC with the mission and the bulk of policy discretion and tools to maximize economic returns and mitigate environmental damage gives the state the ability to enact policies with consistent floors and ceilings across local jurisdictions (both municipal and county). Historically, localities have had powers that only marginally affect the local impact of COGCC regulation, and thus dual distribution effectively reduces NIMBY strategies at the local level. However, since the COGCC largely internalizes policy production to balance economic return and mitigation of negative externalities associated with horizontal coordination, dual distribution seemingly exacerbates vertical coordination.

Colorado's largely asymmetrical dual distribution strategy has clearly fomented franchise contract failure with the growth of fracking as an unconventional extraction methodology. As fracking in Colorado began to grow as an extraction methodology in the early 1990s and continued to encroach into more densely populated areas throughout the first fifteen years of the new century, the franchise arrangement buckled. In short, both municipalities and counties expressed concerns that the COGCC was cutting quality in the regulation of fracking-related negative externalities. Moreover, local governments lacked the discretion and policy space to redress local concerns. Consequently, in 2012 and 2013, local governments in Longmont City, Lafayette, Brownfield, Boulder, and Fort Collins passed ballot initiatives instituting fracking bans or five-year moratoriums. In 2014, Loveland considered but did not pass a ballot initiative for a two-year moratorium. Moreover, seven constitutional amendment

[handwritten margin note, left: COGCC has power over economic and negative externalities.]

[handwritten margin note, right: Make worse]

[handwritten note, bottom: Moving to increase municipal regulatory powers.]

initiatives were pursued but did not reach the ballot because Governor Hickenlooper brokered an agreement to review fracking regulation. In sum, clear signals of franchise contract failure presented.

It is important to note that each of the cities banning fracking relied on ballot initiatives. Like Texas, this observation speaks to informal bonding as a mechanism of vertical coordination a franchise contract. Local governments in Colorado were constrained by the potential litigation costs associated with preemption cases and the COGCC, as well as credible threats of regulatory takings litigation by the extraction industry. This offers some insight as to why governments and elected officials are not at the forefront of regulatory challenges. Elected officials can free ride off of citizen initiatives in their own jurisdictions, and more importantly, in other jurisdictions. By doing so, they minimize the cost of litigation but potentially gain regulatory discretion or a more favorable franchise contract.

In light of the franchise failure associated with the bans, Colorado protected the status quo from local governments with active citizens. In *City of Longmont v. COGCC*, the Colorado Supreme Court protected their dual distribution model when ruling that local fracking bans and indeterminate or unreasonably long moratoriums were unconstitutional because they interfered with state law. Then, Colorado voters approved Amendment 71, which set new constitutional standards for statewide initiatives associated with fracking. The standards make it more difficult for initiatives to be considered by the public. The judicial remedy supporting preemption stands in contrast to the legislative remedy used in Texas, but both illustrate how states internalized the production of banning policy, effectively removing it from the sphere of direct democracy.

Nevertheless, it is also fair to note that Colorado has made both formal and informal adjustments that invite greater local government policy participation. For example, in 1992 the COGCC promulgated rules to create local government designees (LGDs) to enhance local government communication in state permitting processes. Later innovations included the creation of local government liaisons (LGLs), employees of COGCC assigned to facilitate the communication more proactively. In 2005, the COGCC essentially overlooked the La Plata County memorandum of understanding (MOU) with an operator. The MOU established mutually agreed-upon drilling conditions that explicitly recognized the disputes about local/state control, but operators found the MOU useful because the county expedited local permitting with the understanding that the COGCC still held preemption vetoes. Since 2005, local governments and operators have established forty-five MOUs even though their legal standing is questionable. In the period of most significant local resistance (2011–2013), the COGCC made four intergovernmental agreements with local governments. These agreements generally focused on more formal communication and disclosure of operator information and plans at the local level. Moreover, in 2013, the COGCC promulgated rules that required operators to provide setback information and engage local governments on the issue. The content of these agreements and rules were precursors to several recommendations of the 2014 Colorado Oil and Gas Taskforce, which promised to address conflicts between the local and state governments. However, that taskforce rejected seven proposals that would reallocate policy production from the state to the local government. Instead, the taskforce approved two recommendations that formalized LGD participation in COGCC proceedings and required additional operator disclosures to local governments. The COGCC promulgated rules regarding these recommendations in 2016. In that same year, the COGCC entered into an agreement with Adams County that delegated inspection authority to the local government. In sum, the franchise contract in Colorado is stable but fraying at the edges as local governments demand more policy authority and the COGCC offers some accommodations at the margin.

The Dynamics of Intergovernmental Regulatory Arrangements

The intergovernmental relations in Texas and Colorado fracking regulation present some differences, but three areas of convergence are important to note. First, both states have developed an intergovernmental regulatory structure that is stable but susceptible to franchise contract failures that result from direct democracy challenges. Informal bonding and credible threats of losing local autonomy seem to provide effective constraints on local government officials (both elected and professional). However, the public, acting through direct democracy outlets, is less sensitive to the terms of franchise agreements. Direct democracy, therefore, becomes a destabilizing influence for intergovernmental regulation. Stable intergovernmental regulatory arrangements may or may not be in the public interest, but citizen initiatives clearly introduce dynamics that raise questions about the direction and consequence of regulatory regimes.

Hence, a second point of convergence among the case studies is the reaction function of the state to local signals that regulatory franchises have failed. Despite the direct democracy challenges in both Texas and Colorado, local governments retained status quo regulatory powers for basic land use and zoning powers. Perturbations in fracking regulation, such as initiative-based bans, were eliminated, but the previous fracking regulatory regimes were generally maintained. An effective franchise governance structure seeks to preserve a distribution of policy production that accommodates multiple policy objectives across diverse local conditions. The Texas legislature did not internalize local land use powers as related to fracking, and Colorado began discussions about extending more powers to local governments. Even though the taskforce did not recommend any greater delegation to localities, the COGCC has informally granted greater local discretion, as seen in the growing use of city/county–operator MOUs and intergovernmental agreements, with direct delegation of regulatory power to Adams County. One critical question for Colorado is whether the formalized local government participation in COGCC proceedings has a substantive effect on policy outputs, and if so, how those outputs would compare to other arrangements that enable direct local regulation (i.e., Texas). Comparative institutional analysis of specific policy outputs is needed to further our understanding regarding the configuration of the franchise arrangements and particular policies. In both cases, however, stable is not static, and change is negotiated within state-defined boundaries.

Third, reducing the phenomenon of intergovernmental coordination to the legal exercise of preemption obfuscates and oversimplifies the dynamics of adjusting regulatory arrangements. A franchise governance framework suggests that observable preemption is a last-resort mechanism of coordination that is costly to all parties. If formal preemption is the remedy for franchise contract failure, then other methods of coordination such as dual distribution, informal bonding, and threats of internalization have failed. In other words, coordination strategies present a type of "dark preemption" that may not be directly observable as an applied legal doctrine, but they have the same coordination effect as preemption without the legal enforcement costs. Whereas the legal doctrine of preemption assumes only a top-down vertical relationship, the double moral hazard problems suggest that dark preemption can conceptually capture local government efforts to prevent policy shirking at the state level. Even at the horizontal level, local government compliance may mask resistance to state-level policy production because local governments can free ride off the efforts of one or a few champions who are willing to bear the cost of preemption challenges. Hence, horizontal free riding can generate dark preemption that facilitates both vertical and horizontal coordination as an emergent property of a franchise governance arrangement.

Fundamentally, a franchise theory of fracking regulation demonstrates that policymaker interaction in intergovernmental relations can be characterized as bounded negotiation about regulatory discretion. Resolving complex vertical and horizontal coordination problems is a function of both state and local policymaker decisions. State policymakers have tools other than preemption to shape local government regulation, yet they have strong incentives to maximize local government discretion, subject to controls. Colorado illustrates this through their use of MOUs and negotiation between the governor and local interests regarding the balance between state and local regulatory powers. In contrast, local government policymakers must use discretion strategically, which means balancing local and state interests at the local level. Failure to do so can result in loss of regulatory powers and discretion, as the Texas case demonstrates. In both cases, a franchise framework provides a way to understand the scope of regulatory authority, potential triggers for change, and the configuration of new regulatory regimes.

In conclusion, fracking regulation is only one example of governance dilemmas that emerge with rapid technological changes, and unforeseen problems will continue to arise and directly affect environmental, economic, and public safety outcomes in an often highly charged political environment. As the national arena for problem solving becomes more contentious, state–local relations are increasingly important and potentially more effective regulatory arenas. Understanding how to franchise regulatory powers is an important tool in solving these complex governance and social problems.

John Tennert

Environmental Mitigation Manager
Regional Flood Control District, Clark County, Nevada

In many states, special district governments overlap other units of local government to provide narrow and specialized services. In Clark County, Nevada, John Tennert's work supports the planning and development of regional flood control facilities, ensuring that these facilities comply with various federal regulations. The Regional Flood Control District is a funding and planning agency, and the flood control facilities are owned by units of municipal government. Each unit of local government is represented on the board of the special district. Stormwater management is particularly important for the Las Vegas region because pollutants accumulate on roads and lands during extended periods without rain. The district's efforts to mitigate and manage stormwater reduce the amount of pollutants that reach the Las Vegas Wash and Lake Mead during periods of rainfall.

Intergovernmental communication is a regular feature of Tennert's work. Under the federal National Pollutant Discharge Elimination System (NPDES), the State of Nevada grants discharge permits to local governments, setting standards for compliance and improvement in stormwater quality. Tennert interacts with state regulators regarding the permit and local governments regarding project implementation. He explains, "We meet with them on a regular basis. . . . We have been meeting with them to discuss everything from water quality standards that they establish for the Las Vegas Wash and Lake Mead; we meet with them to discuss specific projects that we are implementing and whether or not they comply with our permit; so we interact with all levels of government on a regular basis."

Tennert completed a bachelor's degree in political science and a Ph.D. in public administration and policy at Virginia Tech. He moved to Las Vegas and began work with the Southern Nevada Water Authority and then for the county government's endangered species program before moving to the Flood Control District. For students in public administration and policy, Tennert recommends classes in environmental policy to learn more about this field. He also stresses the importance of developing strong communication skills. "Particularly in the environmental field . . . I spend the bulk of my time in the office reading and writing reports. . . . Everything you do, even if you are a biologist out in the field, you are spending a lot of your time writing up the results of the surveys that you are doing, or you are spending a lot of time in the office coordinating, reading . . . preparing environmental documents." Tennert emphasizes, "The ability to write is really critical to be able to communicate clearly to your audience."

Interview: September 13, 2019

Discussion Questions

1. What are the benefits and limitations of regulating fracking at the state level only? At the local level only? With some franchise arrangement of state and local regulation?

2. Consider new technological implications, such as autonomous vehicles. What are the benefits and limitations of regulating these at the state level only, local level only, or through some form of franchise arrangement? What would a franchise arrangement look like in such a case?

3. Local-level direct democracy has provoked state preemption in some, but not all, fracking cases. How would you advise local environmental activists regarding the efficacy and strategic implications of pursuing citizen initiatives to enact local-level environmental policies?

Notes

1   Tim Boersma and Corey Johnson, "The Shale Gas Revolution: U.S. And EU Policy and Research Agendas," *Review of Policy Research* 29, no. 4 (2012): 570–76; Charles Davis, "The Politics of 'Fracking': Regulating Natural Gas Drilling Practices in Colorado and Texas," *Review of Policy Research* 29, no. 2 (2012): 177–91; Charles Davis and Katherine Hoffer, "Federalizing Energy? Agenda Change and the Politics of Fracking," *Policy Sciences* 45, no. 3 (2012): 221–41; Dallas J. Elgin and Christopher M. Weible, "A Stakeholder Analysis of Colorado Climate and Energy Issues Using Policy Analytical Capacity and the Advocacy Coalition Framework," *Review of Policy Research* 30, no. 1 (2013): 114–33; Jonathan M. Fisk, "The Right to Know? State Politics of Fracking Disclosure," *Review of Policy Research* 30, no. 4 (2013): 345–64; Kyle E. Murray, "State-Scale Perspective on Water Use and Production Associated with Oil and Gas Operations, Oklahoma, U.S," *Environmental Science & Technology* 47, no. 9 (2013): 4918–25; Barry G. Rabe and Christopher Borick, "Conventional Politics for Unconventional Drilling? Lessons from Pennsylvania's Early Move into Fracking Policy Development," *Review of Policy Research* 30, no. 3 (2013): 321–40; Dianne Rahm, "Regulating Hydraulic Fracturing in Shale Gas Plays: The Case of Texas," *Energy Policy* 39, no. 5 (2011): 2974–81; Elvis Stephenson and Karena Shaw, "A Dilemma of Abundance: Governance Challenges of Reconciling Shale Gas Development and Climate Change Mitigation," *Sustainability* 5, no. 5 (2013): 2210–32.

2   Robert Holahan and Gwen Arnold, "An Institutional Theory of Hydraulic Fracturing Policy," *Ecological Economics* 94 (2013): 127–34.

3   Andrew B. Whitford, "Can Consolidation Preserve Local Autonomy? Mitigating Vertical and Horizonal Dilemmas," in *Self-Organizing Federalism: Collaborative Mechanisms to Mitigate Institutional Collective Action Dilemmas*, ed. R. Feiock and J. T. Scholz, 33–50 (Cambridge: Cambridge University Press, 2010).

4   Andrew T. Balthrop and Zackary Hawley, "I Can Hear My Neighbors' Fracking: The Effect of Natural Gas Production on Housing Values in Tarrant County, TX," *Energy Economics* 61 (2017): 351–62; Davis, "Politics of 'Fracking.'"

5   Yasminah Beebeejaun, "Exploring the Intersections between Local Knowledge and Environmental Regulation: A Study of Shale Gas Extraction in Texas and Lancashire," *Environment and Planning C: Politics and Space* 35, no. 3 (2016): 417–33; Davis, "Politics of 'Fracking.'"

6   Charles Davis, "Substate Federalism and Fracking Policies: Does State Regulatory Authority Trump Local Land Use Autonomy?," *Environmental Science and Technology* 48, no. 15 (2014): 8397–8403.

7   Rahm, "Regulating Hydraulic Fracturing."

8   Jeremy G. Weber, J. Wesley Burnett, and Irene M. Xiarchos, "Broadening Benefits from Natural Resource Extraction: Housing Values and Taxation of Natural Gas Wells as Property," *Journal of Policy Analysis and Management* 35, no. 3 (2016): 587–614.

9   Holahan and Arnold, "Institutional Theory of Hydraulic Fracturing Policy."
10 Stephenson and Shaw, "Dilemma of Abundance."
11 Benjamin D. Blair, Christopher M. Weible, Tanya Heikkila, and Larkin McCormack, "Certainty and Uncertainty in Framing the Risks and Benefits of Hydraulic Fracturing in the Colorado News Media," *Risk, Hazards & Crisis in Public Policy* 6, no. 3 (2015): 290–307; Matthew Fry, Adam Briggle, and Jordan Kincaid, "Fracking and Environmental (In)Justice in a Texas City," *Ecological Economics* 117 (2015): 97–107.
12 Blair et al., "Certainty and Uncertainty in Framing the Risks"; Jonathan M. Fisk, Charles Davis, and Benjamin Cole, "Who Is at 'Fault'? The Media and the Stories of Induced Seismicity," *Politics & Policy* 45, no. 1 (2017): 31–50.
13 Balthrop and Hawley, "I Can Hear My Neighbors' Fracking."
14 Ibid.
15 Davis, "Politics of 'Fracking.'"
16 Matthew Fry, "Urban Gas Drilling and Distance Ordinances in the Texas Barnett Shale," *Energy Policy* 62 (2013): 79–89; Fry, Briggle, and Kincaid, "Fracking and Environmental (In)Justice."
17 Fry, "Urban Gas Drilling."
18 Davis, "Politics of 'Fracking'"; Fry, "Urban Gas Drilling"; Rahm, "Regulating Hydraulic Fracturing."
19 Richard C. Feiock and John T. Scholz, eds., *Self-Organizing Federalism: Collaborative Mechanisms to Mitigate Institutional Collective Action* (Cambridge: Cambridge University Press, 2010).
20 Gwen Arnold and Robert Holahan, "The Federalism of Fracking: How the Locus of Policy-Making Authority Affects Civic Engagement," *Publius: The Journal of Federalism* 44, no. 2 (2014): 344–68; Deserai A. Crow, "Policy Punctuations in Colorado Water Law: The Breakdown of a Monopoly," *Review of Policy Research* 27, no. 2 (2010): 147–66; Fry, Briggle, and Kincaid, "Fracking and Environmental (In)Justice"; Ilia Murtazashvili, "Institutions and the Shale Boom," *Journal of Institutional Economics* 13, no. 1 (2016): 189–210.
21 Hilary Boudet, Christopher Clarke, Dylan Bugden, Edward Maibach, Connie Roser-Renouf, and Anthony Leiserowitz, "'Fracking' Controversy and Communication: Using National Survey Data to Understand Public Perceptions of Hydraulic Fracturing," *Energy Policy* 65 (2014): 57–67.
22 Jonathan R. Macey, "Federal Deference to Local Regulators and the Economic Theory of Regulation: Toward a Public-Choice Explanation of Federalism," *Virginia Law Review* 76, no. 2 (1990): 265–92; Vincent Ostrom, Charles M. Tiebout, and Robert Warren, "The Organization of Government in Metropolitan Areas: A Theoretical Inquiry," *American Political Science Review* 55, no. 4 (1961): 831–42.
23 Whitford, "Can Consolidation Preserve Local Autonomy?"
24 Ibid.
25 Holahan and Arnold, "Institutional Theory of Hydraulic Fracturing Policy."
26 Deserai A. Crow, Elizabeth A. Albright, and Elizabeth Koebele, "Environmental Rulemaking across States: Process, Procedural Access, and Regulatory Influence," *Environment and Planning C: Government and Policy* 34, no. 7 (2016): 1222–40; Fisk, "Right to Know?"
27 Whitford, "Can Consolidation Preserve Local Autonomy?"
28 Ibid.
29 Brian K. Landsberg, *Enforcing Civil Rights: Race Discrimination and the Department of Justice* (Lawrence: University Press of Kansas, 1997).
30 Whitford, "Can Consolidation Preserve Local Autonomy?"
31 Davis, "Politics of 'Fracking'"; Fry, Briggle, and Kincaid, "Fracking and Environmental (In)Justice"; Tanya Heikkila, Jonathan J. Pierce, Samuel Gallaher, Jennifer Kagan, Deserai A. Crow, and Christopher M. Weible, "Understanding a Period of Policy Change: The Case of Hydraulic Fracturing Disclosure Policy in Colorado," *Review of Policy Research* 31, no. 2 (2014): 65–87; Tanya Heikkila and Christopher M. Weible, "Unpacking the Intensity of Policy Conflict: A Study of Colorado's Oil and Gas Subsystem," *Policy Sciences* 50, no. 2 (2017): 179–93; Rahm, "Regulating Hydraulic Fracturing"; Sara Rinfret, Jeffrey J. Cook, and Michelle C. Pautz, "Understanding State Rulemaking Processes: Developing Fracking Rules in Colorado, New York, and Ohio,"

Review of Policy Research 31, no. 2 (2014): 88–104; Stacia S. Ryder, "Unconventional Regulation for Unconventional Energy in Northern Colorado? Municipalities as Strategic Actors and Innovators in the United States," *Energy Research & Social Science* 26 (2017): 23–33; Austin Shaffer, Skylar Zilliox, and Jessica Smith, "Memoranda of Understanding and the Social Licence to Operate in Colorado's Unconventional Energy Industry: A Study of Citizen Complaints," *Journal of Energy & Natural Resources Law* 35, no. 1 (2016): 69–85; Christopher M. Weible and Tanya Heikkila, "Comparing the Politics of Hydraulic Fracturing in New York, Colorado, and Texas," *Review of Policy Research* 33, no. 3 (2016): 232–50; Christopher M. Weible, Tanya Heikkila, and David P. Carter, "An Institutional and Opinion Analysis of Colorado's Hydraulic Fracturing Disclosure Policy," *Journal of Environmental Policy & Planning* 19, no. 2 (2017): 115–34; Skylar Zilliox and Jessica M. Smith, "Memorandums of Understanding and Public Trust in Local Government for Colorado's Unconventional Energy Industry," *Energy Policy* 107 (2017): 72–81.

32 Davis, "Politics of 'Fracking'"; Davis, "Substate Federalism and Fracking Policies"; Charles Davis, "Fracking and Environmental Protection: An Analysis of U.S. State Policies," *Extractive Industries and Society* 4, no. 1 (2017): 63–68; Charles Davis and Jonathan M. Fisk, "Mitigating Risks from Fracking-Related Earthquakes: Assessing State Regulatory Decisions," *Society & Natural Resources* 30, no. 8 (2017): 1009–25; Fisk, "Right to Know?"; Kate J. Neville and Erika Weinthal, "Scaling up Site Disputes: Strategies to Redefine 'Local' in the Fight against Fracking," *Environmental Politics* 25, no. 4 (2016): 569–92; Elena Pacheco, "It's a Fracking Conundrum: Environmental Justice and the Battle to Regulate Hydraulic Fracturing Annual Review of Environmental and Natural Resources Law," *Ecology Law Quarterly* 42, no. 2 (2015): 373–96.

33 Texas Local Government Code §211.01.

34 Riley W. Vanham, "A Shift in Power: Why Increased Urban Drilling Necessitates a Change in Regulatory Authority Comment," *St. Mary's Law Journal* 43, no. 1 (2011): 229–88.

PART III

Cooperation in State–Local Relations

CHAPTER 11

State Involvement and
Local Government Energy Policies

Jayce L. Farmer, University of Nevada, Las Vegas

States frequently interact with local governments to address a variety of policy issues. Within these interactions, states will either partner with or regulate cities and counties in their activities. As partners, states can work alongside local governments to enhance their service delivery. As regulators, they can limit the autonomy of local governments in their choices regarding local issues. Regardless of the nature of these interactions, state–local relationships often develop around the availability and provision of funding. Here, states will provide, dictate, or control monies that local governments use to implement policies. State–local relationships that evolve around monetary or financial resources are referred to as having state involvement in local fiscal affairs. In other instances, states will interact with local governments by way of laws or policy actions. In these situations, states will establish policies, rules, or laws (mandates) that dictate how local governments operate or behave. State–local relations that evolve around policy actions generally involves state-initiated laws being executed and enforced by local governments.

The purpose of this chapter is to explore state–local relations around fiscal and policy interactions within the context of energy sustainability. Here we define energy sustainability as the practice of energy use strategies that emphasize the preservation of resources for the environmental and human well-being of future generations.[1] This includes individuals, businesses, nonprofits, and government organizations alike using responsible energy-efficient practices to eliminate energy waste. Energy efficiency brings with it a variety of benefits, such as enhancing our overall environmental health, lowering energy cost, creating jobs, and increasing energy reliability.[2] This issue is so vital that it often transcends local and even state jurisdictional boundaries, therefore requiring state and local governments to work together to address mutually beneficial goals.

How city and county governments spend money to address and promote energy conservation is greatly affected by the fiscal and policy involvement of

interact either monetarily or by laws or policy

189

their states. State fiscal and programmatic involvement in local affairs shape local-level decisions. The autonomy (or governing authority) afforded to local governments, both fiscally and functionally, can greatly impact local behavior.[3] Given that states often promote sustainability policies and that their involvement can impact local affairs, it is appropriate to consider the intergovernmental dynamics of the state-and-local-government relationship. This chapter approaches this issue by first examining how state fiscal policy involvement affects local government efforts for sustainable energy programs. As we delve into this issue, we begin by exploring state–local government relations and outlining the implications of state-level fiscal and policy involvement in local affairs. Second, this chapter examines the impacts of state involvement from a functional perspective by analyzing how state regulatory policies impact city and county abilities to make financial investments in energy sustainability programs. As we explore some of the literature on local government sustainability, we evaluate implications involving the complex relationship between state and local governments. Finally, this chapter presents evidence from an analysis that links state funding and policy commitments for energy programs to local government sustainability endeavors. Specifically, we pay special attention to the interesting contrast between cities and counties in the nature of state fiscal and policy impacts.

State Fiscal Involvement in Local Affairs

Before we move further into our discussion of state–local relations around sustainability issues, we must first explore the more general dynamics of state fiscal intervention. State governments play a significant role in the way local governments carry out their affairs. This is especially true with state fiscal policies that can affect local government behavior.[4] For example, states can impose tax and expenditure limitations (TELs), which can directly affect the fiscal structure and autonomy of local governments. TELs are laws that restrict increases in revenues (tax collection) or spending by either capping them at fixed dollar amounts or limiting their rates of growth.[5] Such laws are usually put into place to prevent local governments from raising taxes too high too fast or from overspending their budgets.

TELs can affect how local units such as cities and counties manage their property taxes, accumulate debt, and generally carry out their budgetary decisions. While all TELs are not created equal, they do place a substantial amount of fiscal control within the hands of state governments.[6] Specific TELs can be nonbinding, which means local governments can evade tax limitations through alternative or altered tax collection methods (or what we call tax assessments; see Exhibit A).[7] On the other hand, TELs that are potentially binding may impose multiple restrictions coupled with stricter tax assessment limits (see Exhibit B). Such limitations on local government fiscal autonomy can have adverse effects on their abilities to generate revenue. Because constrained authority to generate revenue and expend tax dollars can restrict service provision abilities, local governments may be forced to find alternative ways to provide services.[8]

[handwritten: ↳ finding a way to hustle the law]

[handwritten left margin: If taxes get binded how do the LG decide who gets more money?]

- *Exhibit A—Nonbinding TELs:* A county in Florida can potentially overcome a limit on property tax rates through a reassessment of property values. Essentially, the tax collector for each county is charged with evaluating property values. A reassessment of property values would determine whether property values would rise or fall. Because the property taxes in the state are based on a percentage of the property value, an increased value in property would allow the county to levy a higher tax rate on the property in question. In this example, the nonbinding nature of the assessment limitation allowed the county to circumvent this taxation limit and increase property taxes.

- *Exhibit B—Binding TELs:* Property taxes in Texas are subject to specific rate increase limitations throughout the state. This means that all local governments within a county jurisdiction must adhere to a specific limitation throughout that county. For instance, if the tax rate in Hays County, Texas, was capped at a millage rate of 5 (five dollars for every one thousand dollars of assessed property value), then all local governments within that jurisdiction are limited to taxation that does not exceed this given rate. Therefore, if the local school district was taxing at a millage rate of 2, then a city within this county would be limited to a millage of 1, with the county itself being limited to a millage rate of 1, while the various special districts in this county would be forced to divide their taxation share within the remaining parameter of 1 millage rate. The accumulated taxation rate for all jurisdictions throughout the county would come to a total taxation rate of 5 (2 for the school district + 1 for the city + 1 for the county + 1 for the special districts). This tax limitation becomes even more binding as an increase in the millage rate for one jurisdiction would require an at-large citizen vote to increase the millage rate for all jurisdictions. Thus, the local jurisdictions themselves have little say regarding their tax increasing abilities.

State Policy Actions and Local Abilities

State participation in local affairs can come not only through fiscal involvement but also from policy actions. Policy actions implemented by the states can play a substantial role in local government behavior. These actions can function within a regulatory manner much like TELs and impose restrictions on local government functions. In some instances, restrictions can go hand in hand with grant-in-aid programs and require local governments to comply in order to maintain funding eligibility. Other regulatory policies can come in the form of social or protective regulation measures that provide devices to deal with social injustices or environmental hazards.[9]

An example of this was provided when Mauldin showed how economic regulation can be merged with social regulation when he illustrated how the State of Florida provided collaborative governance to support the expansion and creation of Black-owned businesses.[10] This was done through a collaborative agreement between Florida's Office of Tourism, Trade, and Economic Development and the Florida Black Business Investment Board. This agreement established policies that provided capitalization funds to regional business investment corporations, which in turn were mandated to give loans and loan guarantees to qualified underrepresented business owners. Cooperative regulations like this can reinforce the actions of local entities and provide substantiated support that enables local policy initiatives.

State Impacts on Local Sustainability Programs

The role of states in their relationships with local governments in the promotion of sustainability has been complex. On one hand, the regulatory role of the state has been to thwart efforts by local entities to promote sustainability. On the other, states have been cited as providing substantial support for local government efforts.[11] In some cases, the position of states to prevent sustainability has come in the form of fiscal regulation designed to discourage sustainability programming. Portney notes that a handful of states have made attempts to impose legislation that actively prevents the use of public funds to support policies and programs on sustainability.[12] Other more direct regulations speak clearly in regard to prohibiting sustainability policies. For instance, Alabama, along with Oklahoma, Kansas, and Arizona, imposed legislation making it illegal for the state and all political subdivisions to adopt sustainable development policies.[13] However, Arizona municipalities expressed opposition to their state's law with a campaign led by the mayor of Phoenix to overturn this regulation.

Meanwhile, not all states have come out in opposition to local efforts for sustainability. The American Council for an Energy-Efficient Economy (ACEEE) notes that states have demonstrated a growing interest in sustainability, especially in the area of energy efficiency.[14] Accordingly, states have made strides in advancing energy efficiency policies and programs. Between 2007 and 2009, state budgets for energy efficiency were almost doubled, increasing from $2.5 to $4.3 billion.[15] Likewise, the ACEEE found that at least twenty states have either adopted or made progress toward energy-saving building codes for homes and commercial properties. According to the Center for Climate and Energy Solutions (CCES), twenty-nine states require electric utilities to deliver a certain amount of electricity from renewable or alternative energy sources.[16] From a fiscal standpoint, several states actively encourage local sustainability efforts through the establishment of public benefit funds as a mechanism to support energy efficiency programs.[17]

Intergovernmental Connections: Policies and Resources

While much has been written regarding local government sustainability efforts, few studies have made the connection between this phenomenon and state influences. Those that do have placed an emphasis on resource dependency as a source of explanation.[18] The concept of resource dependency in this light suggests that local governments are dependent on the states for monetary resources to implement policies and programs. Saha used this concept to study reasons why local government enhanced its sustainability efforts.[19] Her findings made a direct connection between local government sustainable development and state involvement for land use policies. Here, states were seen as resources that provided centralized policy coordination among fragmented local governments in the face of regional issues. States that played a greater role were seen as providing more guidance in land use planning. Greater state involvement in local sustainable development issues was found to be a critical tool for enabling local sustainability planning efforts.[20]

Within a similar context, Hawkins linked the fiscal capacity of local governments with decisions to participate in state land use policy programs.[21] That is, local tax restrictions were seen as imposing external constraints that incentivized local governments to engage states in sustainable policy initiatives. The more a local government was constrained by state-imposed TELs, the more likely they were to participate in state growth policy programs. If state governments are fiscally engaged in sustainability initiatives, local governments will be encouraged to enhance their efforts for these types of programs. This can be realized through direct monetary investments from the states or through legislative policy initiatives that incentivize energy savings.[22] Such legislative initiatives can come in the form of energy efficiency resource standards that serve to encourage resourceful energy use. Scholarly research on this issue has suggested that state policies can highly influence the activities of local governments.[23] This is especially true in the area of sustainability.[24]

State Policies and Governing Authority

State grants of home-rule authority can be highly influential in local policy decisions.[25] Home-rule authority affords local governments wide-ranging powers that allow them to function with little state involvement.[26] States that limit home rule constrain local government discretion for programs due to their lack of autonomy to administer their functional and fiscal affairs. Earlier in this volume, León-Moreta and Totaro discussed how state laws impact local government functional autonomy (see chapter 7). As they asserted, states can shape the way local governments provide services, execute programs, and administer their daily functions. Fiscal autonomy, however, affords local governments the ability to alter their budgets with greater ease due to fewer or less stringent TELs. Local governments that reside within home-rule-granting states generally have greater abilities to spend on a broader variety of services.[27] Greater spending for more services can lead to less involvement from the states for functional and fiscal authority and more freedom to govern as independent local entities.

State enabling policies that guide program directions can go hand in hand with local government autonomy. While states can advance localities in their efforts to implement policy, heavy-handed state mandates can obstruct local abilities to function. State enabling policies for sustainability can potentially be hampered if those policies are offset by overbearing mandates that stifle local abilities to govern. Within the context of sustainability, public utility commissions serve as an example of how state legislative powers can affect local government programs. Public utility commissions are regulatory bodies established by state legislation that oversee and regulate the operations of public utilities. While most public utility commissions regulate utilities operated and owned by local governments, some, such as the Public Utility Commission of Nevada and the Idaho Utilities Commission, only regulate investor-owned utilities. Public utility commissions can establish energy efficiency standards in addition to other policies that dictate the way utilities are implemented (see the policy examples provided below in Exhibits C and D). Standards such as these can provide collaborative governance that empowers local efforts to pursue sustainability. However, such standards coupled with local governments lacking home rule can become constraining and preclude local entities from expanding their functions and service capacity beyond the minimum state requirements.

Exhibit C—Indiana Utility Regulatory Commission Policy: The Indiana Utility Regulatory Commission requires all local electric utility providers to submit three-year energy demand management plans for meeting energy savings goals as outlined by the commission. These demand management plans provide guidelines for providers to monitor energy consumption activities and encourage consumers to use energy more efficiently.[28]

Exhibit D—Arizona Corporation Commission Policy: In 2010, the Arizona Corporation Commission ordered that all investor-owned utility providers achieve a total annual savings from electricity usage of no less than 22 percent by 2020. This commission outlined energy savings targets that must be achieved each year beginning in 2011.[29]

Analysis of Local Energy Sustainability Programs

To illustrate the relationship between state-enabled policies for energy efficiency and local government energy sustainability activities, this chapter presents an abridged segment of a larger study on state and local relations around sustainability. In essence, the interest of this study was to see if state government policies had any effects on local government commitments to sustainability. This analysis used data from the International City/County Management Association's (ICMA) 2010 *Local Government Sustainability Policies and Programs.*[30] This data set was derived from survey responses from city and county officials regarding their sustainability activities. For the purposes of this analysis, only cities and counties that reported financial information within the U.S. Census of Governments' *Historical Finances of Individual Governments* for 2008 were included in the sample.[31] This resulted in a sample size of 1,914 local governments. The local governments included within this sample consisted of 1,614 cities and 300 counties throughout the United States.

Observing Local Government Energy Sustainability

The observation of interest is local government energy sustainability activities, which are measured through a rating based on the average score of the likeliness to implement an energy program or policy (policy tools). The ICMA's survey contained questions (items) that covered local government policy initiatives taken to reduce energy consumption within their internal operations and among business and residential consumers. Higher scores on a scale of 0 to 5 were assigned to lower percentage distributions, therefore denoting a greater commitment to sustainability. Because not all policy tools are easy or accessible to all local governments, programs that were more expensive, more difficult to implement, and occurred less frequently were deemed as requiring greater program commitments. The local government energy efficiency adoption ratings for this analysis ranged from 0 to 4.08, with an average of 0.59. The survey items and the adoption ratings are displayed in table 11.1.

TABLE 11.1   Local Government Sustainability Policy Tools

Energy Efficiency Policy Tools (Survey Items)	Percent Distribution of Energy Efficiency Policy Tools	Score
Policies for Internal Government Operations	Not Adopted	0
Established fuel efficiency targets for government vehicles	55% or higher	1
Purchased hybrid vehicles	45 to 54.9%	2
Installed charging stations for electric vehicles	30 to 44.9%	3
Installed energy management systems to control heating/cooling	15 to 29.9%	4
Established policy to purchase only Energy Star Equipment	1 to 14.9%	5
Upgraded or retrofitted facilities for energy efficiency		
Upgraded or retrofitted traffic signals and street lighting for efficiency		
Policies for Residential and Business Consumers		
Energy audit, individual—residents/businesses		
Weatherization, individual—residents/businesses		
Purchase of energy efficiency appliances—residents/businesses		
Installation of solar equipment—residents/businesses		

Source: ICMA, *Local Government Sustainability Policies and Programs, 2010* (Washington, DC: ICMA Press, 2010).

Note: For brevity, the policies above only include a limited sample of the items used within the analysis. A full listing of the analyzed survey items is available from the author upon request.

State Fiscal Involvement Measure

To study the effects of state policies on local sustainability initiatives, this analysis used various state-level measures to represent state policies that might affect local actions. The first measure used was one for state fiscal involvement that captured the level of commitment by a state to its state electric program budget for 2009. This metric consists of funding dedicated to ratepayer programs financed through charges within customer utility bills and collected within a state-administered public benefits fund. Data for this measure come from the ACEEE, which scored states on a scale of 0 to 5 based on the levels of energy efficiency budgets within states as a percent of utility revenues.[32] For the current analysis, state electricity program funding is represented by the score assigned to a state by the ACEEE. A higher score represents a greater financial commitment by a state for energy efficiency programs.

State Enabling Policies and Governing Authority Measures

The second and third measures use energy efficiency standards and home rule to capture the effects of state enabling policies and state grants of local governing authority. An energy efficiency standard sets a minimum amount of energy savings and allows utilities to choose how to best achieve those savings, whether by percentage form or by mega-, kilo-, or gigawatts.[33] The analysis uses 2009 data drawn from the Pew Center for Global Climate Change to assess whether states required some type of energy efficiency standard for local utility providers.[34] The home-rule measure captures whether states grant their local governments the ability to establish home rule. Data for this measure come from the National Association of Counties' 2010 *County Authority: A State by State Report*.[35] This measure also allows the analysis to examine how state policies affect local governments under conditions where local authority was more limited.

Differences between Cities and Counties

Before we proceed, it is important to acknowledge the distinctions between city and county governments. The institutional differences behind the inherent nature of cities and counties can bring varying effects regarding states laws. Cities are institutions voluntarily created by a body of citizens to pay for and overcome public service needs.[36] Because of the citizen-initiated or -incorporated nature of municipalities, they have more flexibility when it comes to services and programs. Counties, on the other hand, are involuntary entities created by state legislation and exist traditionally to function primarily as state administrative arms.[37] This traditional role requires counties to operate more intricately within state systems and to be the direct providers of vital state services (law enforcement, health, judicial, etc.).[38] Therefore, state laws prohibiting governing authority can more directly affect counties as their institutional makeup subjects them to more state control. Conversely, cities have more leeway in choosing their policy directions as their functions are generally not directly tethered to their states. As a result, home rule, or the lack thereof, can have heavier implications for counties. Because of this, the impacting effects of state policies are analyzed separately for city and county governments.

Summary of Findings

Using the provided data, the analyses suggested that increases in state fiscal budgets for energy funding led to greater local commitments for energy sustainability (see appendix for tables 11.2 to 11.4 with full results). This was found to be the case for both city and county governments. On average, an increase in a state's score for energy efficiency commitments caused an increase in the level of energy sustainability commitments for cities and counties alike. Energy efficiency standards, however, were only important for enhancing sustainability efforts within cities. Yet this was only the case where states permitted cities the power to establish home rule. Meanwhile, home-rule authority appeared to have a greater impact on county policy activities as opposed to cities. This means that counties are more likely to pursue energy sustainability initiatives if they reside in states that allow home rule. On the other hand, when states constrain the governing authority of counties, they are less likely to commit to sustainability altogether.

Lessons from the Analysis of State Policy and Local Energy Programs

Local governments' pursuit of sustainability can be tied to the policy constraints of states. This chapter highlighted important issues in local government sustainability efforts to explore how state-level policy directives affect local sustainability behavior. Specifically, it explored the funding efforts of states along with state policies set to enable sustainable policy initiatives. An overarching lesson to be gleaned from this chapter is that state government support for sustainability policies can encourage sustainability within local governments. This is because the resources and capabilities of states can have great influence over local policy directives. This is especially the case if state initiatives go hand in hand with local initiatives. This chapter sheds light on this perspective and provides three major lessons regarding the area of state financing efforts for energy sustainability and energy policy initiatives respective to local government autonomy.

Lesson 1: State Resources Can Enhance Local Energy Policy Efforts

The findings of the analysis spoke directly to state funding initiatives and their effect on local government programs. Consistently, the findings revealed that state electricity program funding plays a significant role in local government sustainability efforts. Evidence of an influential relationship between state energy funding and local sustainability initiatives was found for both cities and counties. That is, energy sustainability within cities and counties is heavily influenced by state program funding. While state program funding was not measured by raw dollar amounts, an assessment of the ACEEE's funding score-card suggested that greater financial commitments by states to energy efficiency leads to local government sustainability program activity. This finding coincides with prior studies in the state and local government relations literature in that state resources and involvement for sustainability stimulates local government sustainability.[39] From a broader fiscal federalism perspective, the current find-ings confirm how resources from higher-level centralized governments can be important for decisions and actions for lower-level fragmented governments.

Lesson 2: County Energy Policies Are Constrained Where States Prohibit Home Rule

Because local government abilities to self-govern play a major role in local deci-sions, the findings were observed considering the condition of whether states allowed home rule. Consistent with other findings, this finding revealed that state program funding plays a significant stimulating role. Interestingly, the findings indicate that state commitments to energy program funding encour-age local government sustainability efforts regardless of whether states enabled home-rule authority. This was especially the case for cities. For counties, we found that they tend to shy away from sustainability efforts when states con-strain home rule. Although much of the evidence points to state funding hav-ing a significant influence on county decisions, this conditional effect for home rule suggests that county governments have a higher sensitivity to state laws and state grants of authority than municipalities. This finding coincides with assumptions regarding the institutional differences between cities and counties and supports prior work that notes these differences.[40] This conclusion is espe-cially important for our understanding of state–local relations, as it furthers our recognition of how county governments are typically more constrained in their governing abilities than cities.

Lesson 3: Cities Afforded More Autonomy Will Promote State Energy Policies

On their own, energy efficiency policies such as energy efficiency standards had no effect on local government sustainability. However, when energy efficiency standards were observed under the condition of home rule, the findings pro-duced interesting results. Here, the energy efficiency standards measure was shown to have a positive effect, but only when states allowed home rule. This provided some support for the notion that the enabling effects of some state policies might be offset if states constrain local abilities to function. Given this result, and the fact that counties displayed no effects, one can infer that energy efficiency standards play a larger role within cities. However, this is only the case in states where cities are afforded home rule. This finding may speak to the institutional differences between cities and counties and may be a result of cities placing a heavier emphasis on development. Because energy efficiency standards generally include demand-side management incentives,[41] cities can use these as tax incentives to entice businesses to invest in their communities. Yet these tax incentives are only effective when cities have the functional autonomy to make business investment decisions. With this, we can conclude that state enabling policies coupled with grants of home-rule authority can provide cities the support and autonomy to pursue innovative initiatives that coincide with state policy directions.

Implications for State–Local Relations

Local policy decisions go hand in hand with state policy directions. While states have been cited as taking strides in implementing sustainability programs, local government efforts have been deemed as growing at a slower pace.[42] However, for those localities that have jumped on board, one must question the role of state involvement. This chapter attempted to address this issue by providing some evidence that suggests a link between state policy endeavors and local sustainability activity. If we were to put this question within the greater context of the state and local intergovernmental relationship or fiscal federalism, one might discern that local governments are highly reactive to state funding levels. State policies that encourage energy efficiency and promote local government authority are important, but only when observed conditionally. The given findings speak to states as promoters of sustainability, but only when local governments have the capacity to function as self-governing entities. In essence, the results presented within this chapter provided insight into the dynamics of state–local relations in their efforts to partner around energy sustainability. Within this context, increased state-level funding can actually tend to promote local programs. Conversely, states can also obstruct local activities when they rob localities of governing authority to address their fiscal and administrative affairs. States that restrict home rule might provide overbearing policy constraints, even if the state has goodwill that coincides with local policy directions.

For vital issues such as energy policy, opportunities exist for state–local relations to develop around collaborative partnerships. With the assistance of state resources, local governments can commit to addressing energy efficiency and sustainability in a manner that benefits the local community as well as the state environment as a whole. This advances the importance of understanding how sustainability can be promoted at multiple levels of government.[43] Moving forward, future work should consider this point and place a special emphasis on the implications of state resources in state–local partnerships around sustainability and energy efficiency. This chapter made an attempt at this by connecting state fiscal and policy resources with local government sustainability initiatives. However, it merely scratched the surface of the importance of the intergovernmental connection between local units and the states regarding sustainability. An in-depth integration of state–local relations with the multifaceted issue of energy policy can help state and local officials recognize opportunities to work together in their efforts to promote energy conservation and the overall environmental health of our communities.

James Leiman

Director, Economic Development and Finance
North Dakota Department of Commerce

State and local governments frequently cooperate in the field of economic development. In North Dakota, James Leiman is director of economic development and finance. He describes his work as offering the governor and state legislature "innovative and transformative ideas to take [North Dakota] to the next level, sector by sector . . . and then to also work with the legislature, other agencies and private industry on developing the requisite tool sets and infrastructure for the type of growth that we would like to achieve here." Before working for the state, Leiman was a city administrator and served in both the military and in intelligence. He completed a Ph.D. in logistics and supply chain management at North Dakota State University, an MPA from Evergreen State College, and a BA in political science and economics from Pacific Lutheran University.

"I work with local governments on a daily basis," explains Leiman, "because we are constantly trying to work with one another to team up to improve our capital situation." With over ninety local economic development officials across the state, the state helps local communities identify the best tools and strategies to pursue growth. This includes meeting directly with local officials, assessing local strengths, and explaining the return on investment that different approaches may bring. Having an understanding of economic strengths across the state's geography is important, such as North Dakota's emphasis on energy production in the west and agriculture in the east. Leiman is quick to highlight North Dakota's success in economic growth, including its position as the state with the nation's highest median income.

How can students prepare for this work? "Be innovative, be transformative, and outcompete your peers," advises Leiman. "Innovation is key." To develop this ability, students can watch private industry and study their business models, suggests Leiman. This prepares economic development professionals to work with private firms on a daily basis. An MPA degree can help students prepare for this type of work. Developing a strong understanding of state and municipal finance, macro- and microeconomics, and the public policy process prepares students for work in economic development at the state or local levels.

Interview: September 17, 2019

APPENDIX TABLE 11.2 Descriptions and Sources of Modeled Variables

	Mean	Stand. Deviation	Min.	Max.	Variable Description	Source
Variables						
State electricity program funding	1.74	1.707	0	5	Score for the percent of electricity program funding committed to energy efficiency (range from 0 to 5)	ACEEE 2009
State energy efficiency standards	0.579	0.494	0	1	Dichotomous measure indicating whether a state has energy efficiency requirements (prior to 2010; no = 0; yes = 1)	CCES 2017
Broad home rule granted within state	0.628	0.483	0	1	Dichotomous measure indicating whether a state permits local governments to adopt home-rule charter allowing broad home rule.	National Associations of Counties 2010; Krane, Rigos, and Hill 2000
State-mandated residential building codes	0.855	0.351	0	1	Dichotomous measure indicating whether a state has residential building energy codes (prior to 2010; no = 0; yes = 1)	CCES 2017
State mandate-commercial building codes	0.879	0.325	0	1	Dichotomous measure indicating whether a state has commercial building energy codes (prior to 2010; no = 0; yes = 1)	CCES 2017
Appointed executive official	0.657	0.474	0	1	Dichotomous measure indicating whether local government has an appointed executive head official (no = 0; yes = 1)	ICMA 2010

(continued)

APPENDIX TABLE 11.2 (continued)

	Mean	Stand. Deviation	Min.	Max.	Variable Description	Source
Council–manager	0.539	0.498	0	1	Dichotomous measure indicating whether city has the council–manager form of government (no = 0; yes = 1)	ICMA 2010
Commission–administrator	0.117	0.322	0	1	Dichotomous measure indicating whether county has the commission–administrator form of government (no = 0; yes = 1)	ICMA 2010
City government	0.843	0.363	0	1	Dichotomous measure indicating whether a local government is a city (no = 0; yes = 1)	ICMA 2010
Per capita taxes	1,755.79	1,339.77	85.15	14,037.20	Per capita tax revenue for a local government	U.S. Census 2006–2010 American Community Survey Five-Year Estimates
Log population	9.75	1.34	6.29	15.90	The natural log of the total population of a jurisdiction	U.S. Census 2006–2010 American Community Survey Five-Year Estimates
White non-Hispanic	0.811	0.169	0.058	1.000	Percent of the population White non-Hispanic	U.S. Census 2006–2010 American Community Survey Five-Year Estimates
Young adults	0.258	0.048	0.033	0.482	Percent of population twenty-five to forty-four	U.S. Census 2006–2010 American Community Survey Five-Year Estimates

	Mean	SD	Min	Max	Description	Source
GINI	0.424	0.051	0.285	0.606	The GINI coefficient of income inequality	U.S. Census 2006–2010 American Community Survey Five-Year Estimates
Median property values	242,389.00	431,165.00	4,000.00	8.41E-04	Median property values for a local jurisdiction	U.S. Census 2006–2010 American Community Survey Five-Year Estimates
Geographic region (dummies)	---	---	0	1	Dummy variables for U.S. geographic region	ICMA 2010
Midwest	0.358	0.479	0	1		
South	0.32	0.466	0	1		
West	0.231	0.421	0	1		

N = 1,914 (n Cities = 1,614; n Counties = 300)

APPENDIX TABLE 11.3 Estimates of City Energy Sustainability Policy Adoption

	Model 1	Model 2	Predictive Margins (min., max.)	First Difference
Key Independent Variables				
State electricity program funding	0.055*** (0.015)	0.095*** (0.035)	**0.494, 0.771**	**0.333**
State energy efficiency standards	0.074 (0.048)	−0.001 (0.077)	0.549, 0.623	0.619
Broad home rule granted within state	0.002 (0.048)	0.002 (0.068)	0.592, 0.594	0.012
Electricity funding x broad home rule		−0.049 (0.038)		
Energy efficiency standards x broad home rule		0.108 (0.095)		
Controls				
State-mandated residential building codes	0.0264 (0.111)	0.029 (0.113)		
State-mandated commercial building codes	−0.097 (.120)	−0.097 (0.120)		
Council-manager	0.054* (0.029)	0.054* (0.029)		
Per capita tax revenue	6.80E-05*** (1.00E-05)	6.70E-05*** (1.00E-05)		
Population (logged)	0.223*** (0.013)	0.224*** (0.013)		
Population density	−9.83E-06 (7.70E-06)	−1.01E-05 (7.71E-06)		
White non-Hispanic	0.016 (0.092)	0.016 (0.093)		
Young adults	−0.043 (0.308)	−0.046 (0.308)		
GINI coefficient	0.663** (0.280)	0.668** (0.281)		
Median property values	1.81E-09 (2.87E-08)	1.90E-09 (2.87E-08)		
Intercept	−2.03*** (0.224)	−2.042*** (0.224)		

Variance Between Groups

Geographic Region	1.20E-16 (3.01E-15)	2.17E-17 (5.29E-16)
State	0.009** (0.004)	0.008** (0.004)
Error term	0.253*** (0.009)	0.254*** (0.011)
Wald chi-square (*df*)	541.85 (13)***	550.20 (15)***
LR test vs. OLS: chi-square	16.87***	11.82***

Group Variables

N observations—Level 1	1,614	1,614
N States—Level 2	49	49
N Geographic Regions—Level 3	4	4

Note: Robust standard errors are in parentheses. Significance code: *p < .10; **p < .05; ***p < .01. Predictive margins and first difference observations are based on Model 1. All dichotomous variables were set to their maximum values, while all other variables were set to their means. First differences were calculated using Clarify, ver. 2.1 (Michael Tomz, Jason Wittenberg, and Gary King, "Clarify: Software for Interpreting and Presenting Statistical Results," *Journal of Statistical Software* 8, no. 1 [2003]: 1–30), with 1,000 Monte Carlo simulations. Significant postestimation values are in bold.

APPENDIX TABLE 11.4   Estimates of County Energy Sustainability Policy Adoption

	Model 1	Model 2	Predictive Margins (min., max.)	First Difference
Key Independent Variables				
State electricity program funding	0.075*** (0.023)	0.072 (0.053)	*0.511, 0.888*	*0.383*
State energy efficiency standards	−0.004 (0.069)	−0.172 (0.109)	*0.623, 0.618*	*−0.008*
Broad home rule granted within state	0.127** (0.063)	0.021 (0.091)	*0.542, 0.669*	*0.127*
Electricity funding x broad home rule		0.011 (0.061)		
Energy efficiency standards x broad home rule		0.275** (0.137)		
Controls				
State-mandated residential building codes	0.038 (0.199)	0.088 (0.199)		
State-mandated commercial building codes	−0.057 (0.214)	−0.100 (0.215)		
Commission–administrator	−0.127** (0.061)	−0.138** (0.061)		
Per capita tax revenue	0.0001*** (2.34E-05)	0.001*** (2.47E-05)		
Population (logged)	0.229*** (0.025)	0.227*** (0.025)		
Population density	2.20E-06 (4.91E-05)	1.13E-05 (4.93E-05)		
White non-Hispanic	−0.025 (0.218)	0.169 (0.221)		
Young adults	0.659 (0.915)	0.562 (0.915)		
GINI coefficient	1.48* (0.893)	1.15 (0.898)		
Median property values	9.17E-08 (1.04E-07)	9.73E-08 (1.03E-07)		

Intercept	−3.00*** (0.571)	−2.77*** (0.575)

Variance Between Groups

Geographic Region	7.86E-24 (2.15E-15)	6.16E-09 (1.76E-05)
State	9.42E-27 (6.31E-26)	1.10E-11 (8.66E-08)
Error term	0.198*** (0.017)	0.442*** (0.018)
Wald chi-square (*df*)	282.99*** (13)	292.92*** (15)
Prob > chi-square	0.000	0.000

Group Variables

N observations—Level 1	300	300
N States—Level 2	43	43
N Geographic Regions—Level 3	4	4

Note: Robust standard errors are in parentheses. Significance code: *p < .10 **p < .05; ***p < .01. Predictive margins and first difference observations are based on Model 1. All dichotomous variables were set to their maximum values, while all other variables were set to their means. First differences were calculated using Clarify, ver. 2.1 (Michael Tomz, Jason Wittenberg, and Gary King, "Clarify: Software for Interpreting and Presenting Statistical Results," *Journal of Statistical Software* 8, no. 1 [2003]: 1–30), with 1,000 Monte Carlo simulations. Significant postestimation values are in bold.

Discussion Questions

1. Do you see state policies as obstructing or promoting the ability of local governments to implement energy policies?
2. How do the institutional differences between cities and counties impact their abilities to carry out energy programs?
3. Why does understanding state law and home-rule provisions matter in addition to understanding specific energy policies or regulations?

Notes

[1] David L. Greene, *Measuring Energy Sustainability* (Oak Ridge, TN: Oak Ridge National Laboratory, 2009).

[2] Michael Sciortino, "How State Governments Enable Local Governments to Advance Energy Efficiency," ACEEE, May 11, 2011, https://aceee.org/white-paper/state-enabling-local-ee.

[3] Dale Krane, Platon N. Rigos, and Melvin Hill, eds., *Home Rule in America: A Fifty-State Handbook* (Washington, DC: CQ Press, 2001).

[4] Philip G. Joyce and Daniel R. Mullins, "The Changing Fiscal Structure of the State and Local Public Sector: The Impact of Tax and Expenditure Limitations," *Public Administration Review* 51, no. 3 (1990): 240–53.

[5] Tax Policy Center, "What Are Tax and Expenditure Limits?," Tax Policy Center's Briefing Book, June 2019, https://www.taxpolicycenter.org/briefing-book/what-are-tax-and-expenditure-limits.

[6] Daniel R. Mullins and Bruce A. Wallin, "Tax and Expenditure Limitations: Introduction and Overview," *Public Budgeting and Finance* 24, no. 4 (2004): 2–15.

[7] Ibid. Cf. Joyce and Mullins, "Changing Fiscal Structure."

[8] Jered B. Carr and Jayce Farmer, "Contingent Effects of Municipal and County TELs on Special District Usage in the United States," *Publius: The Journal of Federalism* 41, no. 4 (2011): 709–33. Cf. Jayce L. Farmer, "Factors Influencing Special Purpose Service Delivery among Counties," Public Performance & Management Review 33, no. 4 (2010): 535–54.

[9] Eugene Bardach, "Social Regulation as a Generic Policy Instrument," in *Beyond Privatization: The Tools of Government Action*, ed. L. M. Salamon and M. S. Lund, 197–222 (Washington, DC: Urban Institute Press, 1989).

[10] Marcus D. Mauldin, "A New Governance Explanation for the Creation of a Minority Economic Development Public-Private Partnership in Florida," *Public Performance and Management Review* 35, no. 4 (2012): 679–95.

[11] Sciortino, "How State Governments Enable," 5.

[12] Kent E. Portney, *Sustainability* (Cambridge, MA: MIT Press, 2015).

[13] Ibid., 58–61.

[14] ACEEE, *The 2010 State Energy Efficiency Scorecard* (Washington, DC: ACEEE, 2010).

[15] Ibid.

[16] CCES, "Public Benefit Funds," August 2018, https://www.c2es.org/document/public-benefit-funds/.

[17] Ibid.

[18] Christopher V. Hawkins, "Smart Growth Policy Choice: A Resource Dependency and Local Governance Explanation," *Policy Studies Journal* 39, no. 4 (2011): 679–707.

[19] Devashree Saha, "Factors Influencing Local Government Sustainability Efforts," *State and Local Government Review* 41, no. 1 (2009): 39–48.

[20] Ibid., 45–46.

[21] Hawkins, "Smart Growth Policy Choice," 680.

[22] ACEEE, *2010 State Energy Efficiency*. Also CCES, "Public Benefit Funds."

[23] James C. Clingermayer and Richard C. Feiock, *Institutional Constraints and Policy Choice: An Exploration of Local Governance* (Albany: State University of New York Press, 2001). Cf. David K. Hamilton, David Y. Miller, and Jerry Paytas, "Exploring the Horizontal and Vertical

Dimensions of the Government Metropolitan Regions," *Urban Affairs Review* 40, no. 2 (2004): 147–82.

[24] Portney, *Sustainability*, 57. Also Saha, "Factors Influencing," 42, and Hawkins, "Smart Growth Policy Choice," 681.

[25] Jered B. Carr, "Local Government Autonomy and State Reliance on Special District Governments: A Reassessment," *Political Research Quarterly* 59, no. 3 (2006): 481–92. Also see J. Edwin Benton, "County Service Delivery: Does Government Structure Matter?," *Public Administration Review* 62, no. 4 (2002): 471–79.

[26] Farmer, "Factors Influencing Special Purpose Service Delivery," 540. Also Krane, Rigos, and Hill, *Home Rule in America*, 59–60.

[27] Benton, "County Service Delivery," 475. Also Carr, "Local Government Autonomy," 482, and Jayce L. Farmer, "County Government Choices for Redistributive Services," *Urban Affairs Review* 47, no. 1 (2011): 60–83.

[28] ACEEE, "State and Local Policy Database," August 2019, https://database.aceee.org.

[29] Ibid.

[30] ICMA, *Local Government Sustainability Policies and Programs, 2010* (Washington, DC: ICMA Press, 2010).

[31] U.S. Bureau of the Census, *Historical Finances of Individual Governments* (Washington, DC: U.S. Department of Commerce, 2008).

[32] ACEEE, *2010 State Energy Efficiency*.

[33] CCES, "Public Benefit Funds."

[34] Pew Center for Global Climate Change, "Residential Building Energy Codes," 2009, https://digital.library.unt.edu/ark:/67531/metadc31154/#collections.

[35] Matthew Sellers and Jacqueline Byers, County Authority: A State By State Report, National Association of Counties, December 2010, http://www.nvnaco.org/wp-content/uploads/County-Authority-a-State-by-State-Report.pdf.

[36] Nancy Burns, *The Formation of American Local Governments: Private Values in Public Institutions* (New York: Oxford University Press, 2004).

[37] Benton, "County Service Delivery," 473.

[38] Ibid., 473.

[39] Saha, "Factors Influencing," 44, and Hawkins, "Smart Growth Policy Choice," 681–82.

[40] Benton, "County Service Delivery," 472, and J. Edwin Benton and D. C. Menzel, "County Services: The Emergence of Full-Service Governments," in *County Governments in an Era of Change*, ed. D. R. Berman, 53–69 (Westport, CT: Greenwood Press, 1993), as well as ICMA, *Local Government Sustainability Policies*.

[41] CCES, "Public Benefit Funds."

[42] ACEEE, *2010 State Energy Efficiency*, 12, and James H. Svara, Tanya C. Watt, and Hee Soun Jang, "How Are U.S. Cities Doing Sustainability? Who Is Getting on the Sustainability Train, and Why?," *Cityscape* 15, no. 1 (2012): 9–44.

[43] Nathan Francis and Richard C. Feiock, "A Guide for Local Government Executives on Energy Efficiency and Sustainability," IBM Center for the Business of Government, 2011, http://www.businessofgovernment.org/report/guide-local-government-executives-energy-efficiency-and-sustainability. Also Luke Fowler, "Intergovernmental Relations and Energy Policy: What We Know and What We Still Need to Learn," *State and Local Government Review* 50, no. 3 (2018): 203–12.

CHAPTER 12

Local Government Performance Transparency
The Impact of State Open Records Laws

Jie Tao, University of North Texas
Brian K. Collins, University of North Texas

Transparency is an essential democratic value that promotes a trustworthy, better performing, and accountable government.[1] Governments promote transparency by releasing performance information through both traditional (i.e., paper form) and digital platforms (i.e., social media, government websites). In the United States, promoting transparency by releasing performance indicators is crucial to holding the government accountable.[2] However, promoting transparency through information disclosure is not as simple as it seems because federal, state, and local governments have complex and different information disclosure regimes.

Since the introduction of the Freedom of Information Act (FOIA) in 1966 and the subsequent adoption of open records laws in the fifty states and Washington, DC, American governments have been offering transparency to a degree. Passage of the Electronic Freedom of Information Act (E-FOIA) further facilitates government transparency in the digital age and makes information easier to access by the assistance of information and communication technologies.[3] These endeavors were followed by the Obama administration's Open Government Initiative, which aimed at promoting transparency and accountability by proactively releasing information to citizens.[4]

In addition, state regulations (i.e., state open records laws) play substantial roles in facilitating state and local governments to release their information. Local governments release government information to comply with state open records laws rather than the federal-level FOIA. Different states have varied open records laws, which may ultimately cause different local government behaviors in the process of information disclosure. For example, the open records law in Massachusetts requires public officials to comply with the open

Transparency through government information release

[handwritten: Do st gov transparency laws apply to the state?]

record request within ten days, while the Alabama law does not have a specific time frame for the public records to be processed.[5] The question, then, becomes whether state government transparency laws affect local government transparency behaviors.

The focus of this chapter is to explain how state government policy affects local government transparency. The first section defines performance transparency and discusses its importance. The next section discusses the intergovernmental context of government transparency. The third section discusses the impact of the variation in state open records laws on local government performance information disclosure processes. The last section concludes the chapter by providing suggestions on promoting government transparency and accountability. We find that the severity of state open records law penalties significantly influences the probability of performance information disclosure from local governments. Further, local governments are more likely to release performance information when the performance indicators make them look good. These findings highlight the importance of state-level institutions in promoting transparency among different levels of governments.

Government Transparency and Its Importance

[handwritten in left margin: transparency = accountability]

In general, transparency is "the disclosure of information by an organization that enables external actors to monitor and assess its internal workings and performance."[6] Applying this definition to the government context, we define government transparency as the disclosure of governmental information for external monitoring and evaluation. Promoting government transparency has always been a hot topic in the realm of public administration because transparency is regarded as an essential democratic value that promotes trustworthy, high performing, and accountable government.[7] Scholars and practitioners have paid even more attention to it after the New Public Management (NPM) movement simply because promoting transparency became a means for citizens to engage in accountability.

As one of the most important intellectual heritages of the NPM movement, Osborne and Gaebler's famous book *Reinventing Government: How the Entrepreneurial Spirit Is Transforming the Public Sector* depicts the idea of decentralized and results-oriented government.[8] Specifically, higher-level governments are supposed to delegate more powers to lower-level ones while lower-level governments are encouraged to work with other sectors to further reduce the hierarchies. In addition, different levels of governments have to focus more on improving performance instead of solely following the rules. In this regard, holding government accountable becomes a concern for the new government arrangement under the NPM framework. In other words, holding a less hierarchical and results-oriented government accountable is harder because of the loss of authority based on the hierarchical structure. Therefore, promoting government transparency through the release of performance information directly to the public is necessary to achieve accountability.

[handwritten at bottom: US is hierarchical structure. Rather than take it away. Transparency is necessary to have accountability]

[handwritten: Obama = open gov't]   *[handwritten: p written record]*

A more recent call for promoting transparency was under the Obama administration. President Obama issued a memorandum on transparency and open government that explicitly directed proactive transparency, participation, and collaboration to achieve open government.[9] President Obama said, "My Administration is committed to creating an unprecedented level of openness in Government. We will work together to ensure the public trust and establish a system of transparency, public participation, and collaboration. Openness will strengthen our democracy and promote efficiency and effectiveness in Government."[10] Obama's transparency initiative requires federal agencies to disclose their information such as operation performance and policy decisions for public access. Participation goes a step further to encourage public engagement to improve information distribution. Collaboration advocates collective actions among governments, nonprofits, businesses, and individuals in promoting open and transparent government.

[handwritten: having more than 1 center]

Given the importance of transparency and the complexity of polycentric government, key questions include the following: (1) How can different levels of governments promote transparency? (2) Is there any relationship among different levels of government in the process of promoting transparency? (3) What is (are) the best level(s) of government(s) to promote transparency? To answer these questions, we present the intergovernmental context of government transparency in the next section.

The Intergovernmental Context of Government Transparency

One of the major mechanisms that promotes government transparency is legislative control of bureaucracy. Specifically, lawmakers make open records laws to regulate the disclosure of information from governments. With more severe penalties for bureaucrats, governments are more likely to release information and be more transparent. This process sounds extremely simple. Nonetheless, it is much more complicated than it seems under the U.S. intergovernmental context. One the one hand, there is no one overarching open records law that regulates different levels of governments. In other words, an open records law that is applicable at one level of government may or may not have legal authority to regulate another level. On the other hand, open records laws vary from one jurisdiction to another even among governments at the same level. To understand this complex process, we examine two major regulations regarding the disclosure of government information.

[handwritten, right margin: Not one law that regulates all levels of gov't]

Freedom of Information Act: Federal Law

The Freedom of Information Act (FOIA) offers the public access to any federal agency.[11] FOIA requires federal agencies to disclose any information requested except information related to personal privacy, national security, and law enforcement. In other words, FOIA creates the presumption in favor of public access, but the public must request information. The FOIA request process is relatively simple, only requiring a written description of the records through mail, web form, email, or fax. In addition, requesters can also specify the form in which they want to receive the records. Another important aspect of the FOIA is that it does not specify a fixed time limit for the agencies to respond to a request, and the response time varies based on the complexity of the request and the number of requests received at the agency. For example, a simple request may only need a few pages of a certain document, while a complex one may require search for different documents from different locations. The number of requests received by each federal agency also varies significantly. Among the fifteen executive departments, the Department of Energy received the lowest number of requests at 2,073 during FY 2018, while the Department of Homeland Security had the highest number of requests at 395,751.[12]

Although FOIA provides a legal foundation to promote transparency, it is significant to notice that the FOIA is limited in terms of its capacity to facilitate intergovernmental cooperation in the information disclosure process. The central issue is that the scope of FOIA is solely confined to federal-level executive agencies. In other words, "FOIA is not applicable to the records of the Federal legislative and judicial branches."[13] Moreover, FOIA is not applicable to state and local agencies. To address this issue, state lawmakers adopted transparency legislations typically called open records laws in Washington, DC, and all fifty states.[14] The next section introduces the state open records laws by incorporating examples from different states and discusses state–local relations in the process of complying with open records laws.

Overview of State Open Records Laws

The adoption of the FOIA raised awareness of government transparency at the federal level, but state open records laws promote transparency at both the state and local levels. In Texas, for example, the state open records law is typically called Texas Public Information Act (TPIA), and it was adopted in 1973.[15] The TPIA is codified at section 552.001 of the Government Code, which states:

> Under the fundamental philosophy of the American constitutional form of representative government that adheres to the principle that government is the servant and not the master of the people, it is the policy of this state that each person is entitled, unless otherwise expressly provided by law, at all times to complete information about the affairs of government and the official acts of public officials and employees. The people, in delegating authority, do not give their public servants the right to decide what is good for the people to know and what is not good for them to know. The people insist on remaining informed so that they may retain control over the instruments they have created. The provisions of this chapter shall be liberally construed to implement this policy.[16]

The intention of TPIA is to empower the public with legal protections to access government information. Based on the TPIA, it is important to know what entities are subjected to the act because it reflects state–local relations in the government information disclosure process. According to section 552.003 of the Government Code, the TPIA applies to the following governmental bodies:

1. a board, commission, department, committee, institution, agency, or office that is within or is created by the executive or legislative branch of state government and that is directed by one or more elected or appointed members;
2. a county commissioners court in the state;
3. a municipal governing body in the state;
4. a deliberative body that has rulemaking or quasi-judicial power and that is classified as a department, agency, or political subdivision of a county or municipality;
5. a school district board of trustees;
6. a county board of school trustees;
7. a county board of education;
8. the governing board of a special district;
9. the governing body of a nonprofit corporation organized under Chapter 67, Water Code, that provides a water supply or wastewater service, or both, and is exempt from ad valorem taxation under Section 11.30, Tax Code;
10. a local workforce development board created under Section 2308.253;
11. a nonprofit corporation that is eligible to receive funds under the federal community services block grant program and that is authorized by this state to serve a geographic area of the state; and
12. the part, section, or portion of an organization, corporation, commission, committee, institution, or agency that spends or that is supported in whole or in part by public funds.[17]

Holistically, TPIA regulates the information disclosure of state government, but it also requires local entities (e.g., counties, school districts, special districts, and municipal governments as well as nonprofits and other organizations receiving government funds) to release public information upon request. That is, local-level entities have to comply with the state laws in cases of information requests.

The TPIA makes clear how an open records law works in a single state. However, the fifty states have somewhat different open records laws, ranging from different requirements on processing time to different penalties for violations.[18] The major distinctions among these laws are the difficulty of compliance and the severity of penalties on violations. The difficulty of compliance determines how hard it is for public officials to release requested information. A good example is the processing time for information requests.

For example, Massachusetts's General Laws Section 10 requires "a records access officer appointed pursuant to section 6A, or a designee, shall at reasonable times and without unreasonable delay permit inspection or furnish a copy of any public record as defined in clause twenty-sixth of section 7 of chapter 4, or any segregable portion of a public record, not later than 10 business days following the receipt of the request."[19] The state of Texas puts a relatively

[Handwritten margin note: "Massachusetts puts a time limit"]

looser restriction on the processing time by stating that "an officer for public information of a governmental body shall promptly produce public information for inspection, duplication, or both on application by any person to the officer."[20] In this case, prompt response in Texas can be interpreted as less than ten days like what the state of Massachusetts does or longer than that because it is subjected to different interpretations. Thus, the difficulty for public officers to respond to information requests in Texas is relatively easier than it is in Massachusetts. However, public officials in Texas must notify the requestors about the receipt of the open records requests and set a reasonable time about when the information will be available if they cannot release the information within ten business days.[21] The Alabama law, however, has no specific response time.[22]

The severity of penalties for violation of state open records laws also varies across states. Most states rely on fines and jail time as two major tools to punish violations, and these mechanisms are commonly called the "teeth" of open records laws.[23] According to Stewart's study, twenty states have civil fines on the violation of open records laws, and the highest fine is five thousand dollars for a purposeful violation in Missouri.[24] Twenty-two states have criminal fines, in which judges have discretion to determine the fines because most of the states only set an upper limit for the fines. For example, the criminal fines cannot exceed one hundred dollars in states such as Arkansas, Colorado, Georgia, and Missouri while the cap is one thousand dollars in Maryland, Minnesota, Florida, and Connecticut. Jail time is also an adopted punishment for violators in sixteen states. The jail time ranges from days to years, where West Virginia has the least jail time, up to twenty days, while violators in Nevada may be locked up for one to five years.

From the intergovernmental relations perspective, variation of state open records laws may influence local government information disclosure. Specifically, local governments in a state with restrictive open records laws should be more likely to comply with state-level authority than local governments in states with weak open records laws. The next section empirically tests this proposition.

Local Government Performance Transparency

Based on our discussions on the intergovernmental context of government transparency, we propose that legal institutions at the state level may influence local government information disclosure. Under the regulation of state open records laws, local entities are required to disclose requested information. However, state open records laws also create a government transparency expectation that encourages local governments to disclose performance information in a proactive manner. The public does not need to request. As Stewart pointed out in his study, penalties for violations are the "teeth" of state open records laws.[25] States with strict laws create an expectation that local governments should be transparent. This can be observed when local governments disclose performance information proactively. This relationship between state laws and local performance transparency can be observed by collecting information on the variation of state open records laws and checking whether local governments release citizen satisfaction surveys.

We adapted Stewart's method of measuring severity of state open records laws by looking at the civil and criminal penalties for violations in all fifty states. These penalties include fines and jail time. Some states may only impose fines as penalties without instituting jail time while others have both. Accordingly, we assign scores to different states based on the severity of their open records laws, ranging from 1 (i.e., only imposing fines or jail time) to 4 (i.e., imposing both fines and jail time).

We collected data on local government disclosure of performance information. First, we selected National Citizen Survey (NCS) as the targeted performance information. NCS is conducted collectively by the International City/County Management Association (ICMA) and National Research Center. It collects public opinion on three aspects: community characteristics, governance, and participation. In this research, we utilized the governance perspective that captures perceived government performance as the quality of municipal goods and services. Second, we identified 186 local governments (i.e., only municipalities) by excluding counties and townships and narrowing the survey time period between 2013 and 2016. Last, we searched all 186 municipalities' websites during the summer of 2017 to see whether they proactively released their NCSs online. We made information requests to those municipalities that had not released the survey online during the summer of 2017. We collected 151 surveys (both online and after request) in total by October 2017. Thus, we measured the performance information disclosure by coding 1 if the municipality released the NCS either online or after request and 0 otherwise.

After summarizing the collected surveys, we noticed that most of the proactively released surveys online have relatively high citizen ratings on government performance. Is it possible that local governments' proactive disclosure online has something to do with high citizen ratings? In other words, local officials are like all other rational decision makers who choose the best option to maximize their utilities. In this case, local officials proactively released high performance information to avoid public criticism. Following this logic, we included perceived quality of services as a factor that may influence whether local governments release their performance information online. We captured this information by using the survey question "Overall, how would you rate the quality of the service provided by XX local government?" The answers are four-item Likert scales: excellent, good, fair, and poor. In this study, we operationalized it as the sum of the percentage of respondents who rate the overall service quality as "excellent" and "good." This operationalization is equivalent to the net promoter score, which is widely used in the private-sector literature to measure customer's overall satisfaction.[26] In addition, we coded the performance information disclosure online as 1 if the municipality released the NCS online and 0 otherwise.

Since performance information disclosure online is a subset of all the performance information disclosure, we employed a two-stage Heckman probit model to prevent the potential issue of sample bias.[27] The model has two equations: the selection equation and the outcome equation. In the selection equation, the two-stage Heckman probit model simply estimates the probability of government disclosure of performance information (both online and after request) as a function of the severity of state open records laws and control variables. Then, it predicts the probability of government disclosure of performance information online as a function of citizens' perceived government performance and control variables in the outcome equation.

To control for other potential factors that may influence local government information disclosure, we included several control variables in both selection and outcome equations. We included three control variables for the selection equation. Logged median household income is included because previous research finds that it has a positive relationship with the level of government transparency.[28] Government resources is the next variable and is measured by total municipal expenditures per capita (logged). We included it because municipalities with insufficient resources may have a lower priority to release the information.[29] Total population (logged) of each municipality is the last variable included, because Bearfield and Bowman find that transparency levels are different in large and small cities (i.e., measured by population size) in Texas.[30]

For the outcome equation, we included five control variables. Form of government is coded 1 if a local government is in council–manager form and 0 otherwise. Although its impact on performance transparency is not clear, we included it because the city manager is expected to promote government performance. As a result, better government performance may lead to a higher possibility to release performance-related documents (e.g., National Citizen Survey). We also took government resources and total population (logged) into account because sufficient government resources and larger population size may indicate the financial capacity of municipalities to utilize ICTs, which ultimately affect whether a local government releases performance information online. We operationalized government resources as the median home value (logged) instead of median household income (logged) because they are both indicators to show the fiscal resources of local government, which can be used interchangeably. Moreover, they are highly correlated with each other, and we have included median household income (logged) in the selection stage. Thus, we used median home value (logged) in the outcome model. We used another control variable, "low education levels," which is the percentage of population aged twenty-five and older with less than a ninth-grade education. Bearfield and Bowman argue that demands for information release from citizens may be a key factor for managers to release the information.[31] In other words, higher citizen demands lead to a higher likelihood of information disclosure. However, public preferences are contingent on education levels.[32] Thus, higher education levels may have a positive impact on performance transparency. Table 12.1 lists the descriptive statistics of the variables and their sources.

Table 12.2 reports results of the two-stage Heckman probit model. The Wald χ^2 test shows that the model is statistically significant (i.e., Wald $\chi^2 = 10.91$; p-value = .091). The likelihood ratio test for selection and outcome equations

TABLE 12.1 Descriptive Statistics and Data Sources

Variables	Concept	Obs.	Mean	Std. Error	Min.	Max.	Source
Selection:	NCS documents disclosure	186	0.81	0.39	0	1	Local government websites
Outcome:	NCS documents disclosure online	151	0.85	0.35	0	1	Local government websites
Other variables:	Severity of state open records laws	186	1.72	0.74	1	3	Stewart 2010
	Perceived government performance	151	74.78	12.93	27	94	2013–2016 National Citizen Survey
	Median household income (logged)	186	10.98	0.37	10.07	11.91	2010 Census Bureau
	Total population (logged)	186	10.54	1.05	7.43	13.76	2010 Census Bureau
	Median home value (logged)	186	12.41	0.58	11.09	13.82	2010 Census Bureau
	Expenditure per capita (logged)	186	7.55	0.62	6.34	9.46	2010 Census Bureau
	Low education levels	186	4.20	3.88	0	23.60	2010 Census Bureau
	Form of government	186	0.76	0.43	0	1	Local government websites

TABLE 12.2   **Heckman Probit Regression of Performance Transparency**

	Coefficient	Std. Error
Selection Equation (NCS documents disclosure)		
Severity of state open records law	0.35***	0.01
Median household income (logged)	0.48***	0.16
Expenditure per capita (logged)	0.06	0.16
Total population (logged)	0.01	0.09
Constant	−5.51***	2.13
Outcome equation (NCS documents disclosure online)		
Perceived government performance	0.01**	0.01
Form of government	−0.24***	0.08
Total population (logged)	0.06	0.09
Median home value (logged)	0.17	0.15
Expenditure per capita (logged)	0.22	0.17
Low education levels	0.02	0.02
Constant	−4.55*	2.54
N(uncersored)	186 (151)	
Log likelihood	−142.22	
Wald χ^2	10.91*	
LR χ^2	6.17**	

*p< .1; **p< .05; ***p< .01

is also significant (i.e., χ^2 = 6.17; p-value = .013), which verifies the use of the Heckman probit model to correct selection bias.

   In the selection equation, the severity of state open records laws has a significantly positive impact on the probability of performance information disclosure from municipalities. In other words, municipalities are more likely to disclose performance information (either online or after request) as the severity of state open records laws increases. This result also implies that municipalities in states with more severe penalties are more likely to release performance information than municipalities in states with weaker laws. The outcome equation also shows significant findings. As expected, higher perceived government performance is associated with an increase in the likelihood that municipalities release the NCS documents online. To interpret the substantive meaning of the relationship between perceived performance and online disclosure, we calculated marginal effects by holding other variables at their means. For example, if citizen ratings in a certain local government increase from 60 to 90 (i.e., 30 points), the probability for local officials to release the NCS documents online goes up by 12 percent.

Holistically, the findings support our propositions at both stages of the model. For the selection equation, we observed that local officials choose to release or withhold performance information based on the severity of the state open records laws. In other words, more severe penalties in the state open records laws lead to a higher probability for local officials to release the NCS documents. The results from outcome equation explain the disclosure of performance information in more detail by distinguishing information disclosure online and after request. It further confirms that local officials are more likely to proactively release performance information when ratings are higher.

Promoting Transparency and Accountability

Although FOIA and state open records laws have limitations in the scope of application and the consistency of penalties, they are fundamental legal institutions to ensure the public access to government information. This chapter provides a theoretical framework from the state–local relations' perspective to enhance our understanding of how state open records laws influence information disclosure among local governments. However, this is just a small step toward promoting society-wide transparency.

Promoting government transparency is not a simple process because it involves multiple actors interacting with each other under the context of multiple legal institutions at different levels of government. At the federal level, FOIA is the overarching legal authority to protect the public's access to federal government information. However, FOIA does not impose regulations on entities at state or local levels. The state open records laws fill this gap by regulating information disclosure for state and local entities. The state open records laws also create complex state–local relations in the process of information disclosure because the severity of penalties across states influences the proactive performance transparency of local governments.

Therefore, promoting government transparency is an endeavor that varies from one state to another in a manner consistent with constitutional federalism. It seems to make little sense to have huge differences in the severity of penalties for different states. For example, the maximum fines for unlawfully denied access to a record in Kansas City, Kansas, is five hundred dollars for a civil penalty, while a similar violation in Kansas City, Missouri (just across the border), is up to five thousand dollars.[33] Based on our theoretical model, Kansas City, Missouri, will have a higher possibility to release its government information than Kansas City, Kansas. This trend likely results in the unequal implementation of transparency between cities and states. Thus, revising the penalties of state open records laws toward a more consistent or uniform state legislation is a worthy consideration. More importantly, making more consistent state open records laws is in alignment with increasing demands for public accountability.

Finally, improving government transparency can improve performance. Based on our findings, local officials are also rational individuals who want to show their best images to the public. Thus, the better a local government performs, the more likely it will proactively release its performance information. In this sense, government officials may consider assigning more weight to promoting government performance because it is much easier to release "good results." The pressure is real and can affect social and service outcomes. The public can hold officials accountable for performance. They need transparency to do so.

■ CAREER PROFILE ■

Jennifer Groce
Director of Community Promotion
Northern Illinois University

State universities in communities across the United States operate at the interface of state–local relations. Because universities are large employers in their communities, and because they control large tracts of tax-exempt land, the relationship between a state university and its community may entail both conflict and cooperation. Often, state universities have offices responsible for constructive engagement with their home communities. At Northern Illinois University, Jennifer Groce is the director of community promotion, where she works to promote a positive, engaged relationship with the City of DeKalb, other local governments in the region, and area nonprofit organizations. What does this work entail? "It can be everything from positive brand building for the university and community; it can be encouraging diversity and inclusion; it can have linkages with business development and government strategic initiatives . . . but we are really now focused on strategic partnerships," explains Groce.

The university and local governments have different missions and have different languages for their work, asserts Groce. The key work of IGR involves understanding each side's mission and language. "Neither language is right or wrong; it's just challenging at times to learn what each other's focus is, mission is, and how we speak that to one another." Groce helps with this translation. Several recent initiatives exemplify this work. The bus systems serving Northern Illinois University and the surrounding community recently merged to provide more efficient service to both students and community members. This process took four years of planning to engage public input, integrate public funding, and plan an effective route system. Groce is also engaged in outreach with local diverse- and minority-owned businesses in the region to explain state purchasing procedures in order to expand the number of local businesses doing business with the university.

Students can prepare for work linking universities and communities by having a strong understanding of government and the public policy process, suggests Groce. Working in a local government or local nonprofit organization helps one learn about a community and how the community approaches local policy problems. "A Master's of Public Administration is invaluable because . . . those challenges of learning to speak different languages, learning to understanding each other's different budgeting processes or timelines, that gets address in that course development, and you put those into practice." Groce also suggests finding work in a university's applied research institute, alumni affairs, or community

outreach to develop an understanding of how a higher education institution works and interacts with the surrounding community. "Be involved," advises Groce. "You have to be curious and humble. . . . When you are responsible for helping an intersection between the state and local entity, you have to understand that you're not going to know all parts and all pieces of it. You have to be humble in that fact that you need to learn that."

Interview: September 3, 2019

Discussion Questions

1. Do you think having a universal open records law at all levels of government is a good way to promote transparency? What are the benefits and limitations of having a universal open records law that applies to all governments?
2. What factors cause variation in open records laws across states? What are some consequences of this variation?
3. If you were asked to improve the consistency of open records laws among different states, what would you do? How would you improve government transparency at the federal, state, and local levels?

Notes

[1] Christopher Hood, "Transparency in Historical Perspective," in *Transparency: The Key to Better Governance?*, ed. Christopher Hood and David Heald, 3–23 (Oxford: Oxford University Press, 2006).

[2] Christopher Pollitt and Geert Bouckaert, *Public Management Reform: A Comparative Analysis* (Oxford: Oxford University Press, 2004).

[3] Ben Wasike, "FoIA in the Age of 'Open. Gov': An Analysis of the Performance of the Freedom of Information Act under the Obama and Bush Administrations," *Government Information Quarterly* 33, no. 3 (2016): 417–26, https://doi.org/10.1016/j.giq.2016.05.001.

[4] Ibid.

[5] General Court of the Commonwealth of Massachusetts, *General Law, Title X, Chapter 66, Section 10: Inspection and Copies of Public Records; Written Responses; Extension of Time; Fees*, 1974, https://malegislature.gov/laws/generallaws/parti/titlex/chapter66/section10; Code of Alabama, *Statute Code § 36-12-40: Rights of Citizens to Inspect and Copy Public Writings; Exceptions*, 1975, http://alisondb.legislature.state.al.us/alison/CodeOfAlabama/1975/Coatoc.htm.

[6] Stephan Grimmelikhuijsen and Albert Meijer, "Effects of Transparency on the Perceived Trustworthiness of a Government Organization: Evidence from an Online Experiment," *Journal of Public Administration Research and Theory* 24, no. 1 (2012): 563, https://doi.org/10.1093/jopart/mus048.

[7] Hood, "Transparency in Historical Perspective"; Albert Meijer, "Understanding Modern Transparency," *International Review of Administrative Sciences* 75, no. 2 (2009): 255–69, https://doi

.org/10.1177/0020852309104175; Eric Welch, Charles C. Hinnant, and M. Jae Moon, "Linking Citizen Satisfaction with E-Government and Trust in Government," *Journal of Public Administration Research and Theory* 15, no. 3 (2005): 371–91, https://doi.org/10.1093/jopart/mui021.

8 David E. Osborne and Ted Gaebler, *Reinventing Government: How the Entrepreneurial Spirit Is Transforming the Public Sector* (New York: Penguin, 1992).

9 Barack Obama, "Memorandum for the Heads of Executive Departments and Agencies," *Presidential Studies Quarterly* 39, no. 3 (2009): 429.

10 White House Archives, "Open Government Initiative," 2009, https://obamawhitehouse.archives .gov/open.

11 FAOI.gov, "Freedom of Information Act Statute," https://www.foia.gov/foia-statute.html.

12 FAOI.gov, "Agency FOIA Data: Annual Data," https://www.foia.gov/data.html.

13 Harold C. Relyea, "Federal Freedom of Information Policy: Highlights of Recent Developments," *Government Information Quarterly* 26, no. 2 (2009): 314, https://doi.org/10.1016/j .giq.2008.12.001.

14 Shannon M. Oltmann, Emily J. M. Knox, Chris Peterson, and Shawn Musgrave, "Using Open Records Laws for Research Purposes," *Library & Information Science Research* 37, no. 4 (2015): 323–28, https://doi.org/10.1016/j.lisr.2015.11.006.

15 Office of the Attorney General of Texas, *Public Information Act Handbook 2018*, https://www .texasattorneygeneral.gov/sites/default/files/2018-06/PIA_handbook_2018_0.pdf.

16 Ibid., 173.

17 Ibid., 174–75.

18 Oltmann et al., "Using Open Records Laws"; Daxton R. "Chip" Stewart, "Let the Sunshine In, or Else: An Examination of the 'Teeth' of State and Federal Open Meetings and Open Records Laws," *Communication Law and Policy* 15, no. 3 (2010): 265–310, https://doi.org/10.1080/108 11680.2010.489858.

19 General Court of the Commonwealth of Massachusetts, *General Law, Title X, Chapter 66, Section 10*.

20 Office of the Attorney General of Texas, *Public Information Act Handbook*, 19.

21 Ibid., 36.

22 Oltmann et al., "Using Open Records Laws."

23 Ibid.; Stewart, "Let the Sunshine In."

24 Stewart, "Let the Sunshine In."

25 Ibid.

26 Frederick F. Reichheld and Stephen R. Covey, *The Ultimate Question: Driving Good Profits and True Growth* (Boston: Harvard Business School Press, 2006); Richard Owen and Laura L. Brooks, *Answering the Ultimate Question: How Net Promoter Can Transform Your Business* (San Francisco: John Wiley & Sons, 2008).

27 James J. Heckman, "The Common Structure of Statistical Models of Truncation, Sample Selection and Limited Dependent Variables and a Simple Estimator for Such Models," *Annals of Economic and Social Measurement* 5, no. 4 (1976): 475–92; James J. Heckman, "Sample Selection Bias as a Specification Error," *Econometrica* 47, no. 1 (1979): 153–61.

28 Domonic A. Bearfield and Ann O'M Bowman, "Can You Find It on the Web? An Assessment of Municipal E-Government Transparency," *American Review of Public Administration* 47, no. 2 (2017): 172–88, https://doi.org/10.1177/0275074015627694.

29 Ibid.

30 Ibid.

31 Ibid.

32 Aaron Whitman Smith, "Government Online: The Internet Gives Citizens New Paths to Government Services and Information," Pew Internet and American Life Project, April 27, 2010, https://www.pewinternet.org/2010/04/27/government-online/.

33 Stewart, "Let the Sunshine In."

CHAPTER 13

State Marijuana
Legalization and the Local Response

Russell L. Hanson, Indiana University Bloomington
Eric S. Zeemering, University of Georgia

Article I, Section 8, of the U.S. Constitution assigns Congress the authority to regulate interstate commerce. Congress generally interprets this power broadly, usually with the concurrence of the Supreme Court. For example, in 1970 Congress passed the Controlled Substances Act, which was signed into law by President Nixon. The act declared marijuana an illegal controlled substance, effectively preventing states from regulating its use, though they could still define penalties for possession and use of marijuana.

In 1973 the Texas legislature declared that possession of four ounces of marijuana or less was a misdemeanor offense. Oregon decriminalized cannabis that same year, imposing a fine of one hundred dollars for possession of up to one ounce of marijuana. Alaska, Maine, Colorado, California, and Ohio decriminalized possession of marijuana in 1975. Minnesota followed in 1976, as did Mississippi, New York, and North Carolina in 1977 and Nebraska in 1978.

Also in 1978, New Mexico passed the Controlled Substances Therapeutic Research Act, which recognized the therapeutic value of marijuana. A year later Virginia enacted legislation authorizing physicians to recommend cannabis for glaucoma and to treat the side effects of chemotherapy.

In 1996 Californians legalized medical marijuana by approving ballot proposition 215, with the assent of 55.6 percent of those who voted. Oregon, Washington, and Alaska did the same in 1978, also via ballot measures (which are expressly allowed under most western state constitutions). Maine followed suit in 1999, as did Nevada and Colorado in 2000 and Montana in 2004 (again, via ballot measures). State legislatures in Hawaii (2000), Vermont (2004), and Rhode Island (2006) also allowed physicians to prescribe marijuana for medical purposes.

Not surprisingly, the conflict between federal and state laws provoked a constitutional challenge, and in 2005 a majority of the U.S. Supreme Court ruled that Congress had the authority to regulate the use of marijuana grown in California, which could affect interstate commerce. Justice Clarence Thomas dissented, as the marijuana in question never crossed state lines and so had little or no impact on interstate commerce, in his view. Justice Sandra Day O'Connor also dissented, on the grounds that such a broad reading of interstate commerce would undermine federalism. Chief Justice William Rehnquist joined her dissent.

The split decision by the Supreme Court presaged a change in federal policy, which occurred after Barack Obama was elected president in November 2008. On October 19, 2009, Attorney General Eric Holder announced guidelines for federal prosecutors in states that authorized the use of marijuana for medical treatments. He explained, "It will not be a priority to use federal resources to prosecute patients with serious illnesses or their caregivers who are complying with state laws on medical marijuana, but we will not tolerate drug traffickers who hide behind claims of compliance with state law to mask activities that are clearly illegal. This balanced policy formalizes a sensible approach that the [Justice] Department has been following since January: effectively focus our resources on serious drug traffickers while taking into account state and local laws."[1]

Since then, the legalization and decriminalization of marijuana have accelerated in the states, as illustrated in figure 13.1, which displays marijuana policy in the states as of 2019. When discussing federalism and marijuana policy, most people think of the tension between the federal government and the states. As states chart a course apart from federal policy, state–local relations are also transformed. This chapter describes the evolving state policy environment for the regulation of marijuana and illuminates how state–local relations are also adapting the changing legal context.

Changes in State Laws

State policy on the regulation of marijuana is in a state of flux. Policies that regulate individual use of marijuana are changing, but these changes also bring about additional state policy action in public health and agriculture.

By 2019 marijuana was legally available for medical treatment and recreational use in ten states, plus the District of Columbia. It was available for medical use in thirty more, and in many of those states the penalties for possession of marijuana for recreational use had been reduced, or "decriminalized." For example, in 2019 New York's General Assembly, with Governor Andrew Cuomo's concurrence, reduced possession to a misdemeanor offense and expunged most previous convictions for possession of marijuana from individuals' criminal records.

Of course, those who use marijuana, either for medical reasons or for recreation, might still run afoul of state law if they drive while impaired. Law enforcement officers must prove impairment, whereas previously possession itself was enough to convict an offender. Nevertheless, legalization of marijuana goes much further than decriminalization, which still results in fines and

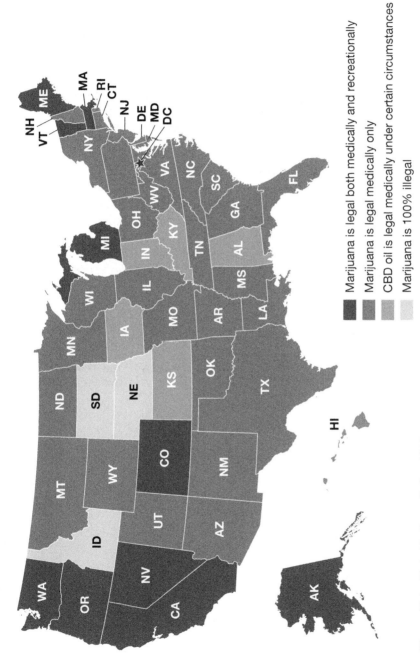

Figure 13.1 State Marijuana Policy, 2019

Source: Steve Fiorillo, "Is CBD Oil Legal in 2019? State-by-State and Future Legality," *Street*, May 22, 2019, https://www.thestreet.com/lifestyle/health/is-cbd-oil-legal-14802001

Marijuana is legal both medically and recreationally

Marijuana is legal medically only

CBD oil is legal medically under certain circumstances

Marijuana is 100% illegal

potentially a criminal record. Only three states—Nebraska, South Dakota, and Wyoming—consider marijuana illegal in all instances, including medical treatments.

Marijuana is derived from *Cannabis sativa*, an annual herbaceous plant that produces tetrahydrocannabinol, or THC, a psychoactive constituent responsible for the sensation of being high in concentrations at or above 0.3 percent. It is also a source for cannabidiol, or CBD, which typically has a THC concentration of 0.3 percent or less. Under federal law, CBD extracted from *Cannabis sativa* is illegal. Most CBD oil in the United States is extracted from the seeds of hemp plants. CBD is most commonly used for seizure disorder (epilepsy). It is also used for anxiety, pain, a muscle disorder called dystonia, Parkinson's disease, Crohn's disease, and many other conditions, although there is little scientific evidence to support these uses.[2] Perhaps the most common use of CBD in the United States is in vaping, the use of electronic cigarettes that provide the option of adding CBD to their chambers. In July 2019 about 9 percent of all American adults admitted to vaping occasionally or regularly.[3] But vaping rates are much higher among young adults, as illustrated in figure 13.2.

The proliferation of vaping contributed to the onset of vaping-related illnesses and several deaths.[4] According to the *Los Angeles Times*, the U.S. Centers for Disease Control and Prevention linked vaping to 1,479 cases of a deadly

[handwritten marginalia: a. What cannibis makes
b. What it is used for]

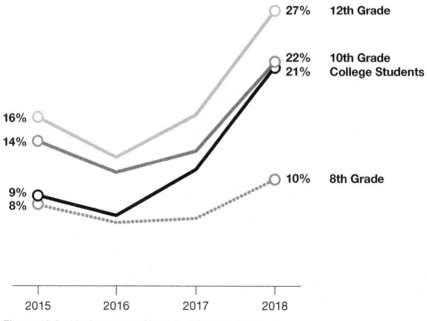

Figure 13.2   Vaping among K–12 and College Students

Note: Pre-2017 survey asked about "any vaping." Data after 2017 based on separate questions about vaporine nicotine, marijuana, and just flavoring.

Source: University of Michigan Monitoring the Future Survey, via Pew Research Center

new lung disease by late 2019, including thirty-three deaths. The vast majority of the cases occurred in adults aged thirty-five and younger, with 15 percent occurring in children under age eighteen. State and local governments have responded to this emerging health crisis with new bans on flavored tobacco and vaping products and an increase in the age to legally purchase tobacco products. These bans may be battled in state courts, so the regulatory landscape must be described as in flux.

[Vaping and other commercial uses of hemp led Congress to permit cultivation of hemp in its renewal of the 2018 Farm Bill.] State legislatures followed suit, and hemp production in the United States quadrupled, increasing from 27,424 acres in August 2018 to 128,320 acres in 2019.[5] Cultivation of hemp is uneven across the states, reflecting variations in state laws. Some states, such as Virginia, permit prescriptions for CBD for any condition diagnosed by a licensed doctor or practitioner. On the other hand, Wyoming only permits CBD prescriptions for patients with epilepsy that has not responded to other treatments.[6]

These differences aside, cultivation of hemp, mostly for the purpose of generating CBD, is widespread—even though the Food and Drug Administration has prohibited the sale of CBD in any unapproved health products, dietary supplements, or food, that is, everything except the drug Epidiolex. Enforcement of this rule is limited, however, and can be evaded by vendors who do not make any health claims about CBD.

Hemp growing is a boon for American agriculture, especially in the midst of a trade war with China, which has depressed prices for corn and soybeans. By some projections, the industrial hemp market might be worth $22 billion by 2022.[7] A few states, such as Wisconsin, now offer state technical support for hemp farmers.[8] The key is to raise hemp that does not exceed 0.3 percent THC. At that point, it becomes illegal and may be seized by the authorities. Indeed, a Minnesota farmer was recently charged with two counts of drug possession while transporting his crop to market; tests showed that the hemp contained ten times the legal limit of THC. Of course, hemp with that amount of THC commands a premium price. The market for CBD and something as potent as marijuana is robust. That explains why hemp is now widely grown in the United States, as illustrated in figure 13.3.

Local Impacts

The shifting regulatory landscape for marijuana has created new challenges for local governments in law enforcement, zoning and land use, and public health. These complications renew the need for state–local dialogue so that state policymakers can be aware of the challenges that emerge from implementing new state laws. Local government officials have also turned to their professional organizations and state associations of local government to learn and share information about how other local units of government have responded to policy change.

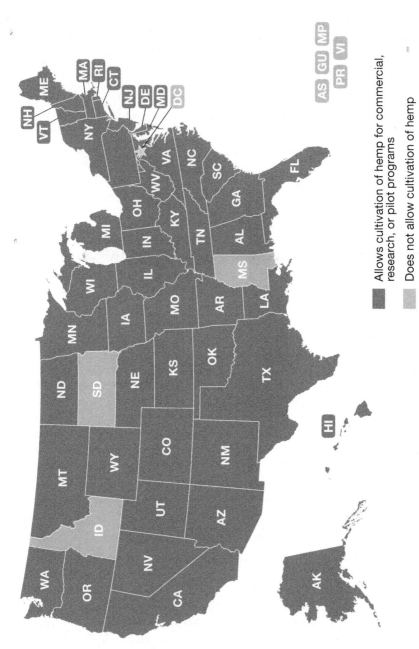

Figure 13.3 Hemp Cultivation in the United States

Source: National Conference of State Legislatures, "State Industrial Hemp Statutes," February 25, 2020, http://www.ncsl.org/research/agricul
ture-and-rural-development/state-industrial-hemp-statutes.aspx

Law Enforcement

First, state laws expanding access to marijuana, as well as CBD, have significant implications for county and municipal law enforcement. In some states, possession of marijuana is no longer sufficient grounds for arrest and prosecution, especially in states that permit small amounts of marijuana for recreational purposes. Prosecution will only succeed if the amount of marijuana exceeds the legal limit or the user is impaired to the point of violating other laws, such as those concerning impaired driving. Complicating matters further, there is no simple test that can determine if an impaired driver has ingested marijuana in one form or another. The situation is even more difficult in states that permit medical marijuana but not recreational use. Possession itself is not criminal if the user has a proper prescription for the drug. Because of this, police must authenticate prescriptions before proceeding to prosecution. This adds a step to the investigation.

The situation surrounding CBD is even more complicated, as there is no simple test that can determine if the oil falls below the 0.3 percent threshold.[9] "Law enforcement authorities from Texas to Florida have said they don't have tests that can differentiate between legal hemp and illegal marijuana, and the patchwork of testing standards is complicating the Farm Bill's goal of allowing nationwide commerce for the new crop."[10] Consequently, county prosecutors in Texas are declining to prosecute misdemeanor marijuana cases since they would need to show that the drug in question was marijuana and not a hemp product.[11] City and county prosecutors in Ohio are adopting this course of action, too.[12] The problem is that there is no agreed-upon testing protocol, and expensive machinery would be required to distinguish between a legal hemp product and illegal marijuana, where the dividing line is 0.3 percent THC. Even then, results might be long delayed, owing to the large volume of testing requests pending before state crime laboratories. Laboratories are underfunded in many states, creating backlogs or prioritization of work that makes timely prosecution of marijuana offenses difficult for local officials.

According to an expert panel organized by the National Highway Traffic Safety Administration (NHTSA), "Good preparation and report writing by the arresting officer go a long way toward supporting a conviction. Training and education (for prosecutors, law enforcement, and others) is critical to mount successful cases against defense arguments about marijuana and drug-impaired driving."[13] The panel argues prosecuting attorneys lack experience with new state regulations and the science of determining impairment. This highlights the need for state and local law enforcement officials to develop educational resources and implement training to ensure that all officials responsible for marijuana regulation in the state are up to speed on the implications of new state policies.

Not all law enforcement officials are eager to implement new marijuana laws, and some have even turned to the courts to resist these changes to state policy. When Colorado legalized recreational use of marijuana in 2014, several county sheriffs from Colorado and Kansas sought an injunction against the state to prevent implementation. The law enforcement officials argued that enforcing Colorado state law would violate their oath of office, which states they will support the U.S. Constitution and adhere to federal law. However, Kamin explains the federal government may not commandeer or require state or local officials to implement federal policy, which means the sheriffs faced no real dilemma with federal law. The legal structure of local government required them to adhere to state law.[14] While the legal dilemma in this case may be moot, the lawsuit illustrates a lack of enthusiasm by some local elected officials to embrace changes to state marijuana regulation. Understanding the political support or opposition of local law enforcement requires more attention by policy researchers in the future.

In summary, state policy changes have made cooperation between law enforcement and prosecutors both more important and more difficult. The role of state governments in providing crime laboratories and testing facilities to local governments means that effective state–local cooperation may facilitate or inhibit local action, depending on the adequate staffing and resourcing of state facilities. In many states, legislators may be unaware of the implementation difficulties facing local law enforcement and prosecutors as a result of state policy change. New marijuana policies require effective IGM among state and local law enforcement officials and prospectors, but also necessitate IGR so that legislators can learn about the difficulties associated with implementing these policies and respond with state resources or additional policy change to clarify obscure aspects of state law.

Land Use

Second, state legalization and decriminalizing of marijuana raise land use and zoning challenges for local governments. Zoning is a police power of local government, allowing cities and other local governments to regulate how land is used and what uses are allowed for various purposes. State laws may grant local governments discretion to regulate or ban certain aspects of marijuana in their communities. Local governments' authority to regulated marijuana varies from state to state. Florida, for instance, effectively preempts local regulation in favor of statewide controls. On the other hand, Colorado permits local governments to ban the sale and cultivation of marijuana within their jurisdictions. Most states expressly allow for local regulation, however, so long as it does not conflict with state law.[15] Local governments use their zoning authority to limit both retail establishments and medical marijuana dispensaries, as well as agriculture and cultivation of marijuana.

For example, in Colorado, local governments decide how to license local marijuana dispensaries or retail sale locations, which may include preventing or significantly constraining the number of sale locations within the community. Communities with significant concerns about law enforcement, and communities that voted in opposition to the state initiative that allowed recreational marijuana, appear to be more likely to ban the establishment of local retail operations.[16] In other states, local governments have attempted to prevent the establishment of dispensaries or retail sites through local nuisance ordinances, arguing that marijuana remains illegal under federal law, which may pose a nuisance to allowing the activity in the community.[17] Through zoning, local governments may regulate the distance between a marijuana dispensary and other land uses, including schools or residential properties. For example, Washington requires dispensaries to be at least one thousand feet from elementary and secondary schools, playgrounds, recreational centers, childcare centers, public parks, public transit hubs, and youth arcades. It also permits local governments to establish buffers for other entities. The city of Tacoma, Washington, requires dispensaries to be at least five hundred feet from correctional facilities, drug rehabilitation centers, libraries, and parks—but only in the downtown area. Of course, dispensaries must also comply with building codes, which may require separate facilities for manufacturing and retailing. Certain areas of cities may also be declared off-limits for dispensaries. Local governments may also impose fees for permits and licenses, and they may collect taxes on the sale of marijuana or CBD. Additionally, local sign or business ordinances may limit the visibility of these land uses within the community by restricting sign size or placement.

State and local governments must also confront agricultural activity. Because marijuana is illegal under the Controlled Substances Act, it may not be cultivated on federal lands of any sort, although these accessible and seldom-patrolled lands were once favored by those who raised marijuana illegally. With legalization and decriminalization, more private lands are being cultivated under state laws and local regulations. In principle, this promises stricter regulation of the growing process, including limits on pesticide usage, water pollution, wetland conversion, air pollution, and local land use laws. Water use is a salient concern, as each plant requires about six gallons of water per day over the ninety-day growing cycle.[18] Some local governments allow marijuana cultivation only in areas zoned for agricultural use. Others require specific security or safety features on properties. Colorado, for instance, requires a marijuana growing operation to include an investment of at least thirty-five thousand dollars with twenty-four-hour surveillance, "clearly indicating that there is something special about marijuana plants." Washington further distances marijuana cultivation from other forms of agriculture so as to deny marijuana cultivators access to agricultural protections and promotions.[19] Still other communities have granted conditional use permits to marijuana cultivators, which are subject to revocation. Of course, farmers, including marijuana cultivators, must adhere to local, state, and federal environmental laws, especially those regulating water usage, and antipollution regulations. In turn this creates new responsibilities for local authorities, compliments of state legislators who may not fully appreciate the consequences of legalizing or decriminalizing marijuana.

Hemp, the source of CBD, presents similar challenges to local authorities. In the first place, there are federal regulations on the cultivation of hemp, mostly bearing on the concentration of THC.[20] Within these regulations, "State policymakers have addressed various policy issues, including the definition of hemp, licensure of growers, seed regulation and certification, statewide commissions and legal protection of growers. State research programs include studying growing conditions—soil quality, season length, seed viability—and exploring the crop's economic and marketing potential."[21] Local officials must administer these regulations and programs. "While this new industry is likely to yield greater tax revenues, now local governments must confront some of the difficult challenges that come with regulating a new industry. Business need to be licensed, facilities and products need to be inspected, and enforcement operations must be improved so officers know how to detect the difference between hemp cannabis plants and recreational cannabis."[22]

In summary, state policy on marijuana has significant consequences for local governments because they are responsible for locating the sites at which marijuana is grown and distributed. Local planning and zoning officials have been forced to become familiar with new agricultural issues and understand the compatibility of marijuana with other land uses in their community. At times, this requires political sensitivity to discern how local residents view the state government's new policy positions, and local actors may find creative ways to use local zoning authority to limit the visible appearance of marijuana-related business or activities in their communities.

Public Health

With the expanded availability and accessibility of marijuana, state and local governments have also worked in partnership to develop appropriate public health responses. Some states began to plan for public health when they designed state policies. For example, Colorado, Oregon, and Washington, early adopters of recreational marijuana, all have provisions requiring revenue from marijuana sales to go to state and local public health, including substance abuse education and prevention.[23] Public health officials explain that legalized marijuana requires ongoing research. State and local governments must monitor the consequences of legalization for marijuana use, including potential health effects and substance abuse rates. Resources are also needed to provide the public with accurate information about marijuana use, as the State of Colorado has attempted through its website dedicated to the topic, GoodToKnowColorado.com.[24]

Local officials must also navigate the complexities that emerge from contradictory state and federal policy. For example, a briefing from the California School Board Association acknowledges local public schools may be required to allow students to use medical marijuana to appropriately accommodate their health and educational needs; however, the use of marijuana remains banned on school properties. To navigate these contradictions, parents may need to remove children from school property to allow use off-site before returning to class.[25] Local government officials are often on the front lines of balancing state and federal policy.

Conclusion

In the years ahead, marijuana regulation in the states will continue to be an evolving field of conflict and cooperation in intergovernmental relations. In the states that have relaxed marijuana regulation for medical or recreational use, state policymakers must be attentive to the implementation challenges that accompany new state law. Within the states, public officials working in law enforcement, land use planning, and public health will have distinct perspectives on the consequences of state policy. Effective IGR may require state governments to develop more robust feedback mechanisms so that state policymakers can hear about the challenges local officials confront in the field. Understanding local implementation challenges may be particularly important for how state policymakers think about the structure of marijuana taxation and the use of revenue from that source.

Moreover, state and local officials will continue to operate in a complicated landscape between federal prohibition and state authorization. While the federal government appears to have relaxed enforcement to allow state-level experimentation in recent years, this equilibrium may be disrupted at any point. Congress may direct more stringent federal enforcement, or may follow the lead of the states in relaxing marijuana regulation. As these dynamics unfold, understanding intergovernmental relations at all levels is critical.

■ CAREER PROFILE ■

Jessica Neuwirth
Retail Marijuana Education and Youth Prevention Coordinator
Colorado Department of Public Health and Environment

The shifting legal landscape for marijuana use has introduced new IGR pressures across the U.S. federal system. Jessica Neuwirth works for the Colorado Department of Health and Environment. Colorado voters supported the legalization of recreational marijuana in 2012. State agencies operate within a legal framework that allows marijuana use while also attending to potential public health implications. Neuwirth works with other state programs "to ensure that all of the known public health impacts and effects [are] communicated correctly across all the state agencies." Because marijuana has addictive properties, increased need for treatment was anticipated, so efforts to enhance treatment were coordinated with the Department of Human Services. Neuwirth works with the Department of Transportation to help them accurately communicate with the public about the impairments associated with marijuana use. Nonprofit organizations are also engaged in public health education. The state provides education materials and grant funding to support educational efforts at the community level. Finally, Neuwirth provides professional development and information about marijuana to local health departments, discussing potential community impacts and resources for the prevention of misuse by youth.

Neuwirth completed an MPA at the University of Colorado Denver with a focus in nonprofit management. Working in the nonprofit sector in community engagement prepared her for her current work. She underscores the importance of building trust with others, "including honoring local expertise." For a politically charged issue like marijuana, playing a neutral role and understanding diverse community perspectives is important. Neurwith explains, "Often my job is to provide information to them, but to approach it in a way that's useful for them—not to tell them how to use it . . . but, being able to say, I am a resource for you when you need it, and then continuing to show up, to continue to respond to inquiries and requests for information, as I have promised to build that trust."

Often, employees working in public health have an undergraduate or graduate background in public health; however, Neuwirth explains other academic backgrounds including social work and public administration can prepare students for positions like hers. Neuwirth advises students to engage in professional networking to identify new opportunities. "Show up well," she advises. This entails dressing professionally, representing your expertise and experience, and being open to learning new expertise. Internal relationship building in your own organizational also matters. "Everything you do is about prioritizing the work without sacrificing the relationships. How can you build relationships so that you all can work together to get innovative, or creative, or difficult work done in your community or in state government?" Government can be slow moving at times, but knowing the right people can help you implement change and make progress.

Interview: August 28, 2019

Discussion Questions

1. Compare the relationship between the federal government and the states on marijuana policy with the relationship between the states and their local governments. How are these different? What are the consequences of this difference for state–local relations?
2. If a local community opposes the state government's relaxation of marijuana regulation, what tools are at their disposal to resist state policy?
3. If you worked for a local public health department in a state that has just legalized the recreational use of marijuana, what steps might you take to work with other local government officials to understand the impact of state policy change on your community?

Notes

[1] Department of Justice, "Attorney General Announces Formal Medical Marijuana Guidelines," news release, October 19, 2009, https://www.justice.gov/opa/pr/attorney-general-announces -formal-medical-marijuana-guidelines.

[2] "Human studies have shown that taking CBD can cause liver problems, diarrhea, vomiting, and fatigue. Rodent research also suggests CBD can cause harm to male and female reproductive organs." Nsikan Akpan and Jamie Leventhal, "Is CBD Legal? Here's What You Need to Know,

according to Science," *PBS NewsHour*, July 12, 2019, https://www.pbs.org/newshour/science/is-cbd-legal-heres-what-you-need-to-know-according-to-science

[3] Katherine Schaeffer, "Before Recent Outbreak, Vaping Was on the Rise in U.S., Especially Among Young People," *Fact Tank*, September 26, 2019, https://www.pewresearch.org/fact-tank/2019/09/26/vaping-survey-data-roundup/#targetText=In%20a%20July%202018%20Gallup,among%20those%2065%20and%20older.

[4] https://www.vice.com/en_us/article/zmk55a/everything-we-know-about-the-health-risks-of-vaping-cbd

[5] Barely one thousand acres were devoted to hemp in 2015, though hemp was widely cultivated during World War II for naval purposes (especially ropes). Cf. the promotional film *Hemp for Victory*, made by the U.S Department of Agriculture and released in 1942.

[6] Steve Fiorillo, "Is CBD Oil Legal in 2019? State-by-State and Future Legality," *Street*, May 22, 2019, https://www.thestreet.com/lifestyle/health/is-cbd-oil-legal-14802001.

[7] Hemp Benchmarks, "Hemp-Derived CBD Market Could Reach $22 Billion by 2022," September 11, 2018, https://www.hempbenchmarks.com/hemp-derived-cbd-market-could-reach-22-billion-by-2022/.

[8] Caroline Li, "Hemp Industry Presents State Farmers with New Opportunities, yet Calls for Cautionary Approach amongst Growers," *Badger Herald*, October 22, 2019, https://badgerherald.com/news/2019/10/22/hemp-industry-presents-state-farmers-with-new-opportunities-yet-calls-for-cautionary-approach-amongst-growers/.

[9] Jon Schuppe, "'I Feel Lucky, for Real': How Legalizing Hemp Accidentally Helped Marijuana Suspects," NBC News, August 18, 2019, https://www.nbcnews.com/news/us-news/i-feel-lucky-real-how-legalizing-hemp-accidentally-helped-marijuana-n1043371.

[10] "USDA: National THC Test for Hemp 'as Challenging as You Think It Is,'" *Hemp Industry Daily*, August 19, 2019, https://hempindustrydaily.com/usda-national-thc-test-for-hemp-as-challenging-as-you-think-it-is/.

[11] Jolie McCullough, "Texas Has a Marijuana Problem after Hemp Legalization: Can It Be Fixed?," Governing.com, July 23, 2019, https://www.governing.com/topics/public-justice-safety/tt-texas-marijuana-problem.html.

[12] Scott McDonald, "Did Ohio Lawmakers Accidentally Pass a Law That Decriminalizes Marijuana? Law Enforcement Think So," *Newsweek*, August 9, 2019, https://www.newsweek.com/did-ohio-lawmakers-accidentally-pass-law-that-decriminalizes-marijuana-law-enforcement-think-so-1453617.

[13] NHTSA, "Impact of the Legalization and Decriminalization of Marijuana on the DWI System," June 2017, 6, https://www.nhtsa.gov/sites/nhtsa.dot.gov/files/documents/expert_dwi_panel.pdf.

[14] Sam Kamin, "The Battle of the Bulge: The Surprising Last Stand against State Marijuana Legalization," *Publius: The Journal of Federalism* 45, no. 3 (2015): 427–51.

[15] Martha Harrrell Chumbler, "Land Use Regulations of Marijuana Cultivation: What Authority Is Left to Local Government?," *Urban Lawyer* 49 (Summer 2017): 505–10. Also see Barry Malone, "Regulating Legalized Marijuana at the Local Level," *Municipal Law*, April 29, 2019.

[16] Tracy L. Johns. "Managing a Policy Experiment: Adopting and Implementing Recreational Marijuana Policies," *State and Local Government Review* 47, no. 3 (2015): 193–204.

[17] Patricia E. Salkin and Zachary Kansler, "Medical Marijuana Zoned Out: Local Regulation Meets State Acceptance and Federal Quiet Acquiescence," *Drake Journal of Agricultural Law* 16 (2011): 295–319.

[18] Jessica Owley, "Unforeseen Land Uses: The Effect of Marijuana Legalization on Land Conservation Programs," *University of California Davis Law Review* 51 (2018): 1673–1716, https://lawreview.law.ucdavis.edu/issues/51/4/Articles/51-4_Owley.pdf. Owley's essay reviews land use under federal bans as well as land use issues under deregulation.

[19] Ibid., 1700.

[20] Daniel A. Kracov, Evelina J. Norwinski, Raqiyyah Pippins, and Ryan D. White, "Agencies, States and Local Governments Respond to Congressional Legalization of Hemp (Non-psychoactive Cannabis)," Arnold & Porter, February 12, 2019, https://www.arnoldporter.com/en/perspectives/publications/2019/02/agencies-states-and-local-governments-respond.

238 Russell L. Hanson and Eric S. Zeemering

21 Mindy Bridges and Karmen Hanson, "Regulating Hemp and Cannabis-Based Products," National Conference of State Legislatures, October 2017, http://www.ncsl.org/research/agricul ture-and-rural-development/regulating-hemp-and-cannabis-based-products.aspx.

22 Accela, "What Legalized Hemp Means for Local Government," May 2, 2019, https://www .accela.com/accela-insights-blog/what-legalized-hemp-means-for-local-government/.

23 Jonathan M. Fisk, Joseph A. Vonasek, and Elvis Davis, "'Pot'reneurial Politics: The Budget-ary Highs and Lows of Recreational Marijuana Policy Innovation," *Politics & Policy* 46, no. 2 (2018): 189–208.

24 Tista Ghosh, Mike Van Dyke, Ali Maffey, Elizabeth Whitley, Laura Gillim-Ross, and Larry Wolk, "The Public Health Framework of Legalized Marijuana in Colorado," *American Journal of Public Health* 106, no. 1 (2016): 21–27.

25 Virgina Admas Simon, "Governance Brief: The Impact of Marijuana Legalization on K-12," California School Boards Association, November 2018, https://www.csba.org/-/media/CSBA/ Files/GovernanceResources/GovernanceBriefs/201811MarijuanaImpact-MarijUseInSchools .ashx?la=en&rev=7d86219f4f7c43269c79cf44dc782684.

CHAPTER 14

Not State, Not Local
Regional Intergovernmental Organizations

Jay Rickabaugh, Appalachian State University
George W. Dougherty Jr., University of Pittsburgh

When citizens, public officials, and scholars think about intergovernmental relations, they traditionally think of the relationship between the federal government and the fifty states. This makes sense given our nation's formation through colonial revolution, problems of governance under the Articles of Confederation, and the limited roles given to the national government in the U.S. Constitution in Article I, Section 8, and in the Tenth Amendment. These two levels of government have been haggling over their roles and powers from the beginning and continue to do so today.

However, to define intergovernmental relations as solely focused on state–federal relations would deny reality in the United States. There are approximately eighty-eight thousand governments in the United States, one of which is the federal government and fifty of which are states. The remainder are local governments like cities, towns, boroughs, and villages or school or special districts, all of which are chartered and regulated by states. If these local governments were distributed evenly among the states (they're not), each state would have to keep tabs on and regulate the affairs of approximately 1,760 local governments. States would also hear from the mayors, council presidents, and administrators of each local government unit on a wide variety of issues (crime, taxes, education, transportation, water/sewer infrastructure, environment, etc.). The result is a lot of energy, information, ideas, and potential for conflict between state and local government and among local governments.

Many of the issues that affect an individual local government (like economies, rivers, highways, poverty, and pollution) are beyond their control as they cross jurisdictional lines. Citizens who work, live, shop, worship, and play all within the same municipality are exceedingly rare. However, each citizen can only vote in local elections based on where they live. We frequently think of local elected officials (mayors, town council members, and county commissioners) as being responsible for the internal affairs of their local governments and responsive to their local voters. Being a responsible leader for the internal affairs of your government means you also have to address both the ways your residents and resources impact the region around you and the ways your region's residents and resources impact your locality.

Problems and opportunities that cross borders take coordination and cooperation; unfortunately, cooperation and coordination are not easy. Local governments within regions vary in population, budget, services offered, and the influence they have on other jurisdictions. Local governments often compete with one another to lure residential, commercial, and industrial development projects. Local governments also often use their legal authority to prevent unwanted land uses that can lower property values (landfills, wastewater treatment plants, public housing projects, halfway houses, etc.) from being sited in their jurisdictions, resulting in a big game of "not it." Coordinating all of this can be difficult.

To provide a forum to discuss and address these regional public policy concerns, most states either mandate or enable local governments to form Regional Intergovernmental Organizations (RIGOs). The federal and state governments frequently rely on RIGOs to develop regional plans and priorities for transportation, economic development, and human services consistent with federal and state interests. The higher forms of government sweeten the pot by providing block grants to RIGOs, on the condition that the local government members have to collectively consent to the regional plans for how they will spend the money. As a result of this negotiation and consensus building, the higher forms of government hope to encourage trust among local governments to solve additional regional issues.

This chapter introduces RIGOs that help federal, state, and local governments negotiate and coordinate public policy within regions. RIGOs are fascinating in that they are made up primarily of local government members but serve state and federal constituencies as well. Convening local governments into RIGOs provides the state with a consistent institution to manage concerns that are too big for one jurisdiction to handle alone but too geographically concentrated to require the full attention of the state. RIGOs also provide local governments a forum to make their collective voice heard on issues of state or federal policy. RIGOs are not the muscle or the bone of American government; they operate more like tendons and ligaments that allow muscle and bone to serve their intended purposes. In this chapter, we explain how RIGOs formed, their major purposes and policy areas, how they are governed, who serves in those governance roles, and the regions they serve.

What Are RIGOs?

There are a large number of "regional" or cross-jurisdictional organizations in the United States, but only 477 currently meet the criteria to be classified as a RIGO. First, an organization's membership must be made up primarily of general-purpose local governments (50 percent +1 of member institutions should be counties, cities, towns, boroughs, or villages). [Chambers of Commerce or Regional Business Councils whose primary focus is the private sector, while important in bringing a region together, do not qualify.] Second, RIGOs all engage multiple local governments across *multiple* policy areas. In some regions, freestanding single-policy bodies (like special districts) perform these functions; these are not RIGOs because they do not work across a breadth of policies. Third, the organization must be legitimate in the eyes of local, state, and federal agencies. RIGOs usually maintain some number of designations from the federal or their state governments. These designations usually are necessary to receive block grants; some of the most common federal designations are for the following (see box 14.1 for more details): metropolitan planning organizations (MPOs; urban transportation), economic development districts (EDDs), workforce investment boards (WIBs), and area agencies on aging (AAAs). Fourth, the organization should have the stated ambition of representing the region and creating a space for the region's governments to work together. Finally, an organization is considered a RIGO if it covers the largest area and population within its region. For example, the Pittsburgh region has multiple councils of government to which local governments can belong, but the Southwestern Pennsylvania Commission is much broader, covering a ten-county area with a combined population of over 2.4 million residents.

[handwritten margin note: Private cooperations → not allowed]

Box 14.1 Common RIGO Designations

[handwritten margin note: what are designations]

- MPO—Metropolitan Planning Organization: A policy board designated to carry out the federal transportation planning process in urbanized areas with a population over fifty thousand. MPOs certify that regional transportation improvement programs meet all federal requirements when submitted to state and federal transportation agencies.
- EDD—Economic Development District: A multijurisdictional organization that leads local economic development planning processes that include public, private, and nonprofit representatives. The planning process results in a comprehensive economic development strategy (CEDS) that serves as a blueprint for economic development efforts within a region.
- WIB—Workforce Investment Board: An agency designated to direct local, state, and federal funding for workforce development programs. These agencies: conduct research on local workforce needs; coordinate education, training, and employer efforts; and staff career centers.
- AAA—Area Agency on Aging: An agency designated to coordinate services for older citizens, allowing them to remain in their homes if they so desire.

RIGOs label themselves in a variety of ways and look slightly different from state to state, but all meet the five criteria just outlined. The Commonwealth of Virginia has carved up the state into a system of planning district

242 Jay Rickabaugh and George W. Dougherty Jr.

commissions with very specific functions outlined in state statutes. Indiana, by contrast, allows local governments to form their own organizations. These organizations label themselves differently even within the same state (council of governments, regional planning commission, regional coordinating council, etc.). Some counties and local governments (including most of the Indianapolis area) have elected not to form an organization or join an existing one. You can find the RIGOs in your area by visiting www.rigos.pitt.edu.

Regional Intergovernmental Organizations perform two crucial functions across the landscape of intergovernmental relations: they promote cooperation among local governments, and they ensure state/federal programs are implemented in concert with the priorities of local elected officials. Forty-seven states have local governments that belong to RIGOs; some RIGOs are almost entirely urban and others are entirely rural. RIGOs have substantial variation in both the geographic scale and the policy agendas they undertake. This chapter identifies a few broad trends in the way these organizations function.

This chapter begins by highlighting how RIGOs formed before outlining three key roles that RIGOs play at the nexus of local governments, state and federal government programs, and the civic- and private-sector stakeholders that bring regions together. First, we discuss RIGOs as conveners across territorial and sectoral boundaries. Second, RIGOs function as a legislative body to undertake programs and services on behalf of their members and in partnership with states and the federal government. Third, RIGOs can fulfill an important role reinforcing cooperation and partnership in bilateral relationships among local governments and holistically for the region.

Creating RIGOs

RIGOs owe their existence to state and federal government efforts to implement their policies in ways that meet local needs in the latter part of the twentieth century (Miller and Nelles 2019). Their genesis followed three broad patterns: creation by states to fit existing state agency regional service areas, expansion from federally designated agencies to serve additional policy areas, or as local attempts to grapple with multijurisdictional concerns.

State Service Regions

In some cases, the state identifies the boundaries of RIGOs through legislation or executive order. The state often draws these boundaries to align with the regions it determines are best for functions like the Department of Transportation or economic development planning. The Western Piedmont Council of Governments (Hickory, North Carolina) has boundaries that align with its MPO, EDD, AAA, and workforce development board (among other functions); this streamlines coordination among the local governments and between the local governments and the state. While the states across the Southeast generally organize themselves in this manner, there certainly are other examples across the country. The state compels local governments to become members of their assigned RIGO through access to funding and state resources, but this is not a mandate in most cases. This allows states to spread financial resources strategically among regions, reduce the number of direct interactions with local governments while funding regional priorities, and offload funding administration duties to RIGO staff. Occasionally, local governments will want to join a different RIGO (or a second RIGO) or make other alterations to their membership. In order for these changes to occur, they need the consent of the state government. The State of Maryland recently authorized Queen Anne County to join the Baltimore Metropolitan Council, and North Carolina recently approved the merger of two organizations that now form the Piedmont Triad Regional Council. Approval signifies state and local agreement on changes in economic or social patterns that require adjusting regional boundaries.

Federal Beginnings

In other cases, the state lets local governments decide for themselves if they want to form a RIGO and the membership determines for themselves if joining is in their best interest. In these states, these organizations may have formed initially as MPOs or EDDs to meet requirements to receive federal resources. These organizations expanded their missions over time into other areas like regional economic development, environmental planning, or public safety functions. As metropolitan areas expand through suburban development into new counties, membership in RIGOs often expands as well. Morrow County, Ohio, recently elected to join the Mid-Ohio Regional Planning Commission (Columbus) and, unlike the prior examples, did not require state approval to do so.

Local Needs

A handful of RIGOs have formed out of local efforts to solve local problems. When mayors from seven suburban Chicago counties sat down with the city's mayor, they slowly built trust with one another and formed the Chicago Metropolitan Mayors' Caucus. Their collective advocacy broke down silos in regional governance and created their RIGO, the Chicago Metropolitan Agency for Planning (Lindstrom 2010). A handful of states designated existing organizations as official regional actors. Many organizations in Arkansas, Iowa, Kentucky, and Maryland have grown from local efforts and now meet the criteria to be classified as RIGOs (Miller and Nelles 2019).

A few states and several major metropolitan areas do not have RIGOs but may accomplish some functions of RIGOs through other avenues. Rhode Island, Hawaii, and Delaware perform most of the functions of a RIGO through their respective state governments. This is mostly a function of their size and the relatively few number of local governments. A few New Jersey suburban local governments belong to the Philadelphia-area RIGO, the Delaware Valley Regional Planning Commission, but the Garden State largely lacks multipolicy forums like RIGOs. Several major metropolitan areas have MPOs to be eligible for federal transportation dollars, but these organizations do little if any convening beyond this function. New York City's, Buffalo's, and Indianapolis's metro areas are three examples where the MPO is the most substantial convener within the region but does not work on the breadth of policy issues to be considered a RIGO. Some rural areas, particularly those in the frontier areas of the interior West, may also choose not to belong to a RIGO.

RIGOs as Conveners

RIGOs operate as conveners for local governments in many of the same ways a chamber of commerce benefits business leaders or the ways an international organization supports its nation members, but with a few key differences to meet the interests of state and federal programs. Conveners are people or organizations that provide a neutral space for interested parties to have frank discussions, set group priorities, explore policy alternatives, and negotiate agreements. Just as a chamber of commerce brings together business leaders to build relationships and advocate for common interests, a RIGO can build similar networks among the elected and appointed officials within its territory. Also like a chamber of commerce, these local government members may choose to cooperate on some economic development opportunities and may compete against each other for other opportunities. If you wanted to engage a region's business leaders in conversations, you would go to the chamber of commerce. If you wanted to reach a region's local government leaders for similar conversations, you would go to the RIGO.

The membership size and characteristics of RIGOs vary widely across the United States. Some RIGOs bring together the municipalities within a county or two, while others represent hundreds of local governments across many counties, sometimes across multiple states. We discuss how these organizations make membership decisions later on in the chapter, but who has a seat at the table varies tremendously. States vary in how they regulate powers of municipal incorporation, patterns in growth, and the authority of local governments to join RIGOs. Variation in the membership of a RIGO is a direct outgrowth of those powers, patterns, and authorities. As a result, geographically large counties like Pima (Arizona, including Tucson) may constitute the RIGO for their region. Meanwhile, the Chicago Metropolitan Agency for Planning and the Atlanta Regional Commission cover hundreds of local governments across multiple counties.

While RIGOs primarily provide a forum for local governments, they often involve stakeholders from across the region and from other forms of government. The RIGO's multiple roles as an EDD or MPO or AAA or a rural broadband authority or a regional stormwater resource put it at the nexus of a wide variety of decisions that affect more than just the local governments of a region. To ensure these decisions are not made in a vacuum, RIGOs often invite the business community, major regional institutions like universities or military installations, Native American governments, regional philanthropic

[handwritten margin note: If across multiple state. What State agenda are they going off of.]

foundations, communities of color organizations like regional NAACP chapters, school districts, and other special districts to provide input.

The importance of RIGOs as conveners is highlighted with a familiar example. Imagine a major industrial employer is moving into City A. The highways that serve City A may need to be expanded in City B and County C so that employees can get to work and products can be shipped more easily. The community college (located in County D) may need to provide technical training to get future employees prepared to work there. Maybe the regional NAACP chapter and the local philanthropic community want to develop some scholarships to help communities of color access the training and jobs to improve regional equity. This kind of coordination happens because the right stakeholders are all in the same room, getting information, and realizing how they can contribute to the opportunity. RIGOs are forums for these discussions to occur among stakeholders that may be voting or nonvoting members of the RIGO.

example

In order to ensure conversations are informed and productive, RIGOs also hire professional staff to provide research and information so these representatives have more information about issues with which they may not be familiar. Because not all stakeholders will have expertise on every issue, RIGO staff is charged to provide technically sound, unbiased information to the board. Having confidence in the quality of this information gives local governments assurance that no municipality or county has an unfair advantage in decisions about economic development or transportation funding decisions. Professional staff may also serve as a regional resource, especially for smaller governments that lack staff expertise, analytic skills, or contacts and influence in state government. In many cases, RIGO professional staffs also are liaisons with the state and federal governments to ensure that the decisions the board makes also comply with the necessary regulations to receive resources.

As a result, the RIGO convenes a unique cross-section of the communities it represents to tackle the challenges the region faces. In some cases, these challenges are competitive regional opportunities like the bid process for Amazon HQ2 or threats that require regional responses, like climate crisis resilience planning or combating human trafficking. In other cases, RIGO conversations create regional solutions for challenges that local governments might face individually, like rural broadband access, weatherization for energy efficiency, disaster readiness information, or joint code enforcement. These solutions might become new functions for the RIGO professional staff to implement at the direction of the governing board, a new spun-off agency or organization with a new staff and governing board, or solutions implemented internally by the local governments.

Convening these conversations is only the first step of what RIGOs do. While planning and gathering feedback is important, RIGOs also take action and allocate substantial amounts of federal and state funding based on decisions of the local governments and the other stakeholders on the board. The next section tackles how RIGOs go about this process.

RIGOs as Decision Makers

In their role as MPOs, EDDs, or other state or federal designations, the governing boards of RIGOs have the authority to adopt plans and allocate funding for projects. The process for ratification, the representational rights of members, and who is permitted to represent local governments varies tremendously because the members themselves vary tremendously. Key characteristics include population, tax base, or historical significance to the region. RIGO leaders need to sort these characteristics in a way that is acceptable to or creates consensus among members.

The U.S. House and Senate make for a good analogy to explain the challenges of balancing the interests of the local governments in a region. The way these governance rules are developed could have a substantial impact on the decisions that are made. If House legislative districts were gerrymandered differently or Senate seats distributed in a different fashion, congressional decisions would be affected even though they represent the same people. At one extreme is a system that reflects population proportionality like the U.S. House. At the other extreme is a system that reflects each local government equally like the U.S. Senate. In most cases, RIGOs are somewhere in between.

RIGOs need to balance the needs of many types and sizes of local government to be effective. To have the confidence of the local government members and to achieve collective agreement over a sustained period of time, these organizations need to answer some key questions. Is a town of fifty thousand people entitled to five times as many board votes as a town with ten thousand people? If one county or municipality has more than 50 percent of the region's population, should they be allowed to unilaterally dominate the RIGO agenda? How should county populations be weighted compared to the municipalities inside those counties (or populations in unincorporated areas)? Who should serve on the executive committee and be responsible for setting the agenda on which the board votes? Should the mayors and council members represent their local governments, or should they appoint citizens from the municipality or county? These are just a few questions that need to be settled to effectively govern and build the trust of local governments.

State-Determined Representation

In some situations, the state prescribes these answers; this might be one particular formula applied statewide. All New Hampshire RIGOs follow a state statute (NH Rev Stat § 36:46 [2017]) that determines how many representatives each municipality can send: two representatives for every municipality under 10,000 people, three for those with 10,001–25,000 people, and four for those with more than 25,000 people. This formula provides towns with more population more representation, but some communities are substantially overrepresented by population and others substantially underrepresented. Manchester (2010 population: 109,627), Derry (33,109), and Francestown (1,546) are all members of their RIGO, the Southern New Hampshire Regional Planning Commission (SNHRPC). Manchester gets the same number of representatives as a town more than a third smaller (Derry) and twice as many representatives as the town seventy times smaller (Francestown). If you think this is unfair, consider this from a small town's perspective. There are fourteen communities in SNHRPC, but two of them (Manchester and Derry) together make up more than half of the regional population. If every vote was based on population, Manchester and Derry could pass everything they wanted without compromising with the other twelve towns. Creating a one-size-fits-all formula that balances the need for large local governments to have more representatives without crowding out the voices of smaller local governments is a real challenge.

Negotiated Representation

In other circumstances, the local government members themselves negotiate these provisions. North Carolina draws the boundaries for which local governments belong to which RIGO (council of governments) but allows members to determine representation and voting for themselves. A one-size-fits-all plan likely would be difficult to achieve in a state where Charlotte is the population-dominant city in its region but the "center city" status is split across local governments in other regions like Winston-Salem/Greensboro/High Point. Furthermore, there may be some rural regions of the state where the population is naturally more equal among all members. There may be additional challenges to negotiation when counties and the municipalities within those counties cannot agree on how to share representation.

Who Represents Local Governments

Even when the region's local governments come to a decision about which local governments get to vote and how many votes are to be allocated to each, they still need to decide who gets to cast those votes. Some federal and state programs set regulations to ensure broad representation, but these are generally low thresholds. Not every local government uses the same form of government, so not every RIGO board will look the same. Some counties have executives and others have commissioners; some municipalities have strong mayors with executive powers like a governor or strong councils where the mayor's powers are quite limited. In some cases, the RIGO bylaws stipulate that the local governments determine for themselves who can represent them (mayors, council members, professional staff, citizens, etc.). In other circumstances, bylaws may require some jurisdictions to send commissioners, others to send mayors, and still others to send managers or citizens. When a jurisdiction has multiple votes, it can be a mix of any of the above categories.

RIGOs often include nonlocal government organizations in their membership in an effort to better represent their regions and improve deliberations. Native American governments, which hold the status of sovereign nations while providing services similar to general-purpose local governments, are sometimes allotted membership rights equal to other local governments in the region. State and federal laws may also require membership for nongovernment representatives. In some states, the governor or speaker of the statehouse appoints citizens to RIGO boards. Similarly, RIGOs that serve as the federally designated EDD are required to include some combination of representatives of chambers of commerce, workforce investment boards, labor organizations, and other community interests.

Many RIGOs include representatives from outside local government without the prompting of state or federal government. Business interests, whether large employers, small-business owners, or chamber of commerce representatives, are commonly included on RIGO boards. Large, influential institutions such as universities, technical and community colleges, and military installations are also included on boards due to their roles as major employers or developers of the region's future workforce. Virginia state statutes specifically permit two RIGOs to include representatives from local universities on their boards.[1] Other RIGOs include "regional citizens" on their boards to provide broader representation, and some designate seats specifically for minority representatives. Finally, some RIGO bylaws include membership for representatives of state agencies with expertise in highways, civil aviation, or environmental protection.

Agendas and Voting Procedures

Who gets a seat at the table is not the only important decision RIGOs must make to ensure effectiveness and long-term viability. The governance structure of the organization can be critical. Officers and executive committees often determine the agenda, so local governments have strong interest in these positions as well. Whether the governance structure is determined by state law or internal negotiations, the leadership of the board usually reflects a mix of interests. These interests could ensure representatives from a mix of counties and municipalities, ensure the center city (or one of the center cities) holds a permanent leadership position, or ensure balanced geographic representation (north, east, south, west). In most cases, these leadership positions are protected in the bylaws to be held by elected officials.

How these boards approve policy and allocate federal or state funding for projects and programs also needs to balance each local government's individual interests with the good of the region as a whole. In some cases, convening the local governments together (sometimes with civic- and private-sector leaders) generates ideas that are adopted as policy and funded by the board. Examples of ideas RIGOs have adopted include projects to improve rural broadband access, addressing food deserts, and public information campaigns for emergency preparedness.

In other cases, federal or state governments provide funding through block grants that the board needs to allocate for projects and programs that meet certain requirements. Each RIGO receives a different amount of money (based on formulas), and these block grants support a different mix of policy areas. These funding programs authorize RIGOs to fund projects that improve transportation, environmental quality, economic or community development, services for the elderly, and public safety. Utilizing block grants allows states and the federal government to provide support for these regional and local needs but gives the RIGO flexibility to address the most pressing needs within given parameters. This gives local leaders discretion in the projects that affect their constituents directly, rather than a process more centrally directed through state and federal agencies. As a result, a municipality that has a strong manufacturing or commercial area might negotiate for higher levels of funding from a RIGO's role as an EDD. The neighboring community that is highly residential might be willing to give up their "fair share" of that economic development funding to get more funding for community development programs or transportation projects. As a result of this trade, both localities end up getting more of the funding that is beneficial to their community's goals.

The process an organization uses to make its decisions is a major factor in what decisions that organization ends up making. As noted above, this is one major reason why the U.S. Senate has a different agenda and makes different decisions than the U.S. House. Since RIGOs balance a lot of competing interests, deciding how they allocate votes and who gets to cast those votes is the result of complex negotiations. Making decisions regionally keeps some control local rather than in state government or Washington, DC, while still providing higher-level intergovernmental support for valuable programs and projects. RIGOs allow local leaders a say in how to allocate funding for federal projects and programs and solve regional problems, even if every decision does not go their way.

RIGOs as a Force for Cooperation or an Arena for Competition

RIGOs also operate as a space where trust can be built, tested, and diminished among local governments. Jurisdictions sign interlocal agreements (see chapter 15 for more on ILAs), engage in handshake agreements, and coordinate to make sure the roads and sewer pipes line up. The extent to which these interactions are fulfilled, revised, or reneged upon are all factors that determine how much local governments trust one another. Different officials within a local government may have different opinions about the same relationships; the mayor from Town A might trust Town B but the council president from Town A does not. These opinions and experiences come along with those representatives in their work with RIGOs, and the experiences they have in the RIGO informs future opinions and experiences working with other local governments.

Keeping all of these competing interests satisfied and building cooperative solutions requires diplomacy among RIGO members and from the professional staff. The "wish list" of projects each municipality and county wants to get funded through RIGO programs and block grants far exceeds the available money. As a result, tough choices need to be negotiated among local governments. One of the reasons to have a neutral technical staff that provides information and data to the RIGO representatives is so that every project can have its financial costs and benefits measured consistently. Not every project can be easily measured that way; the value of human services programs like assistance for the elderly is difficult to measure in dollars and cents. RIGOs also have to balance how much they should invest in projects with broad regional interest (e.g., improved highway access to an airport) or projects with benefits to only one or two communities (e.g., a trail that connects Town A's bike routes to Town B's bike routes). They also need to balance investing in growing communities to catalyze more growth with investing in struggling communities that need help.

RIGOs, Competition, and Inequity

Some scholars see these block grant funding programs combined with the governance of RIGOs as a contributing factor to urban sprawl or reinforcing racial and socioeconomic inequities. As mentioned above, the ways RIGOs make decisions vary tremendously either as a result of state law or from the negotiations among local governments themselves. When RIGOs allocate votes in ways that favor suburban interests over urban ones, these scholars believe that the boards are more likely to support projects that favor suburban interests over urban ones. These scholars see RIGOs as disproportionately funding infrastructure and economic development activities in suburbs and sprawling exurbs; these decisions perpetuate inequities between urban and suburban communities.

Second, these scholars believe RIGO boards will avoid putting crucial regional problems on the agenda that require collaboration with urban centers. Solutions for these regional problems (e.g., affordable housing) might direct resources away from more favored programs or require solutions unpalatable to suburban constituents. As a result, these scholars believe that issues that disproportionately affect large urban centers are not sufficiently addressed.

One reason a RIGO that wanted to curb urban sprawl and reduce racial or socioeconomic inequities would struggle to do so is that it cannot mandate local governments take certain actions. While the RIGO can allocate funds for transportation or economic development projects and incentivize certain land use priorities over others, most local governments have tremendous power over land use in their communities. If a community has sufficient interest from developers (residential, commercial, or industrial), the politics of growth and the promise of jobs is hard for most elected officials to vote against. They are not likely to vote differently as a member of a RIGO board.

The regional effects of local decisions can be quite severe. For example, if one local government provides minimal land zoned for multifamily housing, there may be enough of a regional market to pick up the slack. If too many local governments all provide minimal land zoned for multifamily housing, now there are too few apartments at too high a cost trying to serve too many renters. The result is one form of an affordable housing crisis. RIGOs like the Puget Sound Regional Council based in Seattle, Washington, may help coordinate regional-local approaches to housing to plan and build healthy, welcoming communities where all citizens can find appropriate housing.

RIGOs can be a forum where these issues are brought forward, but most RIGOs do not have the authority to resolve them single-handedly. There is much debate about if a RIGO is the right forum for addressing these issues, if RIGOs need more authority over land use, or if other changes should be made to how RIGOs function. Despite their utility for federal and state governments, some argue RIGOs undermine the principle of local self-determination and governance by promoting regional solutions over local concerns. While some argue regionalization undercuts growth by favoring urban core redevelopment over suburban growth, others claim the opposite is true. RIGOs must negotiate this complicated territory to support multiple constituencies to enjoy sustainable success and support. For more about these perspectives, see Rusk (2013), Orfield (1997), Hall (2009), and Kurtz (2012).

As a result, negotiations over how projects get funded sometimes require concessions to get impacted municipalities or counties on board. For example, allocating funding for an expanded highway may be a necessary step to relieve traffic congestion that impacts the whole region's connectivity. In addition, the regional air quality could improve by reducing the amount of time vehicles sit idle. Expanding a highway also requires local governments to agree to that land use and relocate the homes and businesses affected. These local governments may also need to respond to lower property values because of increased noise pollution and manage the social impacts of road construction on neighborhoods. Affected local governments may try to highlight the costs they are bearing for the region as leverage to get other projects or programs funded (maybe within the transportation budget, but this could also be through the EDD or other block grants the RIGO receives). Having multiple service areas within the RIGO allows local government officials to "expand the pie" by allowing negotiation across policies and programs.

Credit Claiming and Local Implementation

In their relationships with RIGOs, elected officials and appointed staff have different incentive structures that could affect these negotiations and the proposals on which RIGO boards vote. Elected officials seek to claim credit to be reelected or to win higher office. Because there are federal and state block grants to be distributed, local elected officials who negotiate for investment in their community get all the benefits of "bringing home the bacon" without the demonization of "pork barrel politics." RIGOs also provide a rare opportunity for a local elected official to credibly claim that they were instrumental in the delivery of a policy, program, or infrastructure project outside their home jurisdiction.

While local elected officials claim the credit, appointed county and municipal professional staff are responsible for implementation. Town, city, and county managers have professional norms and technical expertise in both seeing the project through to fruition and complying with complex state and federal regulations. A manager (or other appointed staff member) with a reputation for success in this regard will likely get opportunities for promotion or job offers from larger or wealthier local governments. Local-government-appointed staff serves at the pleasure of the elected officials who appoint them (council, mayor, commission, etc.); acquiring the funding for the project becomes a liability for an elected official when implementation flounders. In this circumstance, the appointed staff may be subject to termination, whether or not they bear responsibility for the shortcomings in implementation. For more information about the differences between elected and appointed officials, see Matkin and Frederickson (2009).

A successful RIGO can reinforce other forms of collaboration among local governments, and other forms of collaboration can improve success within the RIGO. In Kansas City, the RIGO (Mid-American Regional Council) has been instrumental in developing a culture of trust among its localities (across two states, no less) that the expectation of helping one another (via interlocal agreements, handshakes, memoranda of understanding) is so commonplace you need a reason *not* to do it. Thurmaier and Wood (2002) call this kind of culture "norms of reciprocity." Negative cycles can also be hard to reverse. The collapse of the Kalamazoo County Council of Governments exposed hard feelings that persisted for years (Visser 2004) and poisoned the well for a long time. The region began to reformulate organizations dedicated to working cross-boundary only recently (Klug 2012; Mitchell 2013).

Conclusion

Regional Intergovernmental Organizations are a fascinating and necessary component of modern American federalism. They bind together state and federal programs to be prioritized and implemented in local contexts and permit local leaders to make those determinations. How local officials make those determinations is influenced by the representation and voting rules they negotiate when establishing their RIGO. RIGOs also bring local governments to the table to discuss regional issues with other levels of government, civic institutions, and representatives of the private sector. The hope is that a broader coalition can provide a clearer understanding of regional issues and foster sustainable solutions. As such, RIGOs also can reinforce the importance of cooperation across boundaries that congeal the region's identity.

RIGOs play an important intermediary role and are one key to understanding state and local intergovernmental relations. RIGOs reduce the burden of intergovernmental relations on states by reducing the number of direct interactions with local governments and transferring administrative tasks to RIGO staff. Regions and local governments benefit by collectively approaching the state, having already discussed and potentially reached consensus on regional needs and priorities. RIGO staff provide expertise on their region to state officials and technical support to member local governments.

Grace Gallucci

Executive Director
Northeast Ohio Areawide Coordinating Agency

Regional Intergovernmental Organizations (RIGOs) come in a variety of forms, as described by Rickabaugh and Dougherty in chapter 14 of this book. Grace Gallucci serves as the executive director of the Northeast Ohio Areawide Coordinating Agency (NOACA), which is the metropolitan planning organization for the Cleveland, Ohio, region. With a forty-five-member board, NOACA covers an area of over two thousand square miles, which includes five counties, sixty-one cities, forty-five villages, and fifty-eight townships (NOACA, "About NOACA," https://www.noaca.org/about/about-noaca). According to Gallucci, the organization plays an important role in balancing local and regional needs in transportation planning and investment. Bringing local governments to the table to discuss regional transportation priorities came about in part because federal and state investments during the 1960s and 1970s often failed to engage community priorities, explains Gallucci. NOACA plays a role in planning and channeling federal funding, but the State of Ohio or local governments implement the transportation projects.

After completing an MPA at the University of Dayton, Gallucci went to work for Broward County, Florida, as a budget management analyst in the Office of Transportation. She continued to develop expertise in transportation policy through work at the Greater Cleveland Regional Transit Authority and then the Regional Transportation Authority of Northeastern Illinois before returning to Ohio as the executive director for NOACA. "All of my positions over the last thirty years have been public sector [and] have had a focus on transportation," explains Gallucci. Progressing through a series of jobs in transportation policy allowed Gallucci to develop street-level insight into transportations service delivery and land use planning while also developing a familiarity with how each level of government in the U.S. federal system had impact on different elements of metropolitan transportation systems.

Careers in transportation policy and planning can be rewarding. Gallucci explains, "It's very noble to be able to participate in the structuring of the civic involvement and really working toward the public good. I think that transportation offers a nice balance between some private-sector initiatives and public–private partnerships as well as true public policy work." Students considering this field can develop relevant skills in undergraduate political science, business, or land use planning programs. Entry-level jobs in local government provide one path, but students can also work for consultants or construction firms that work on transportation infrastructure. Gallucci also emphasizes the need to develop analytical thinking. "It's really important to be able to look at a multitude of situations, a multitude of people engaged, a multitude of problems and potential solutions, and really think about what is the best way forward." Students must also prepare to be mindful and respectful of the different viewpoints expressed during public participation processes.

Interview: October 14, 2019

Discussion Questions

1. Look at the map available at https://www.rigos.pitt.edu/data-visualizations/interactive-rigo-map and find the website for your region's RIGO (or one in a nearby or familiar location). How does this RIGO bring local governments together to address common concerns? How does this RIGO connect their local governments to state/federal agencies?
2. With so many different members representing so many different stakeholders, what kinds of challenges would you expect in the *process* of making decisions as a RIGO board?
3. How might RIGOs help facilitate cooperation between state and local government?

Note

1 VA Code § 15.2-4203 (2018) permits the New River Valley Regional Commission (District #4, including Virginia Tech) and the Commonwealth Regional Council (District #14, including Longwood University) to include "representatives from higher education institutions."

References

Hall, J. S. 2009. Who will govern american metropolitan regions, and how? In *Governing metropolitan regions in the 21st century*, ed. D. Phares, 54–78. Armonk, NY: M. E. Sharpe.

Klug, F. 2012. Kalamazoo County Council of Governments approves new bylaws, focusing on education. *Kalamazoo Gazette*, November 14.

Kurtz, S. 2012. *Spreading the wealth: How Obama is robbing the suburbs to pay for the cities*. New York: Sentinel.

Lindstrom, B. 2010. The Metropolitan Mayors Caucus: Institution building in a political fragmented metropolitan region. *Urban Affairs Review* 46 (1): 37–67. https://doi.org/10.1177/1078087410370670.

Matkin, D. S. T., and H. G. Frederickson. 2009. Metropolitan governance: Institutional roles and interjurisdictional cooperation. *Journal of Urban Affairs* 31 (1): 45–66.

Miller, D. Y., and J. Nelles. 2019. *Discovering American regionalism: An introduction to Regional Intergovernmental Organizations*. New York: Routledge.

Mitchell, A. 2013. Newly reformed Southcentral Michigan Planning Council gives presentation to Kalamazoo County Council of Governments. *Kalamazoo Gazette*, June 13.

NH Rev Stat § 36:46 (2017).

Orfield, M. 1997. *Metropolitics: A regional agenda for community and stability*. Washington, DC: Brookings Institution Press.

Rusk, D. 2013. *Cities without suburbs: A Census 2010 perspective*. Baltimore, MD: Johns Hopkins University Press.

Thurmaier, K., and C. Wood. 2002. Interlocal agreements as overlapping social networks: Picket-fence regionalism in metropolitan Kansas City. *Public Administration Review* 62 (5): 585–98. https://doi.org/10.1111/1540-6210.00239.

VA Code § 15.2-4203 (2018).

Visser, J. A. 2004. Voluntary regional councils and the new regionalism: Effective governance in the smaller metropolis. *Journal of Planning Education and Research* 24 (1): 51–63. https://doi.org/10.1177/0739456x04267180.

(Alamo Area Council of Governments
• Pop: 2,249,718
• 20th highest pop.

Marlon Brown - Michigan (LARA) - St. Job
  °City Council Member: Vice-President
   -Run my City manager ↳ elected
Mandates affecting funding - CARES Act helped
  - Significant impact - user fees non existing
  - Local residents have to take the reprocussions
  of the city revenue. City operations
 °Fiscal Reserves - Had to tap in
 °Open Meetings Act
    - making it accessible (remote = confusion)

interesting facts
expansion

CHAPTER 15

Balancing Local and Regional Interests
Thomas Skuzinski, Northern Illinois University

This chapter is about the space state governments create for cooperation among general-purpose local governments, and how the individuals working in local governments make decisions within that space. We will refer to the relationships among two or more local governments—the cities, towns, counties, and similar units that serve a broad, general purpose spanning many policy areas—as *interlocal relations* in the rest of this chapter. Local governments often work together to efficiently or effectively deliver public services or to solve complex policy problems. For example, several neighboring communities can adopt a joint strategy for attracting economic development to their region.[1] A large city might provide water treatment to several suburbs.[2] A group of coastal communities might work together to promote disaster resilience.[3]

While the focus throughout much of this book is on relationships among *governments*, these relationships must be formed and maintained by people. In other words, intergovernmental relations are human relations.[4] To help us understand these human relations in the interlocal context, we will be using a series of simple questions that we should use whenever we are trying to understand why cooperation occurs. Some of these questions will explore the attributes, preferences, and behaviors of the administrative staff and elected officials responsible for shaping intergovernmental relationships. Others will target the decision-making context in which they function.

The goal of the chapter is to use these questions and illustrative examples to develop a simple framework for making sense of cooperation among local governments. You should come away from reading it with two key insights, which we will revisit in the conclusion. The first is that the state plays a dominant role through its ability to define the limits of what local governments can and cannot do with regard to other local governments. If we want to understand the possibility for interlocal cooperation, we must first look to what state governments have said about these actions through provisions in state constitutions and state statutes. The second is that cooperation, to the extent a state has left that option open as a voluntary action by local governments, is never thoroughly predictable. For example, even if a state allows interlocal cooperation, and even if it seems like a sensible choice given the actors involved and the context in which they are making decisions, we still might find that it does not occur. If you work in or with local governments in your career, you are likely to encounter examples of cooperation flourishing among governments despite numerous obstacles, or failing despite seeming like an obvious and easy option. Because interlocal relations are human relations, they can often be messy and inexplicable. But the framework in this chapter should equip you with the tools and knowledge to make sense of most situations.

The chapter is organized around three big questions. First, we will ask, What does state law say about interlocal relations? We will look at how states can expressly enable cooperation, and how they can indirectly increase or decrease its potential. Second, we will consider, What are some of the contexts in which cooperation tends to happen? We will be thinking through the socio-economic, institutional, and organizational settings that tend to be favorable. Third, we will explore, What are the characteristics of the individuals who tend to support cooperation?, with primary attention given to distinctions between elected officials and administrative staff. In each section, we will walk through illustrative examples.

A note before moving forward: local governments also compete with one another. This is not surprising if we think about the nature of local government boundaries. These boundaries define where local governments have policy authority—that is, where the laws they adopt and implement can operate on individuals, households, and businesses—and also limit the people, land, and goods from which a local government can collect taxes and fees to fulfill its many public responsibilities. A common strategy for a local government is to try to compete successfully against other local governments for new households moving into the region, or for businesses shopping for a new location. Sometimes this takes the form of highly visible competition for international corporate activity, as was evident in the contest over the location of Amazon's HQ2.[5] A more commonplace example, though, is the decision to adopt zoning regulations that favor large, single-family homes over multifamily apartment complexes targeting middle- or lower-income households.[6] Local governments can also engage in what is commonly known as yardstick competition, in which they use peer local governments as comparisons—or "yardsticks"—against which to measure their tax rates and fees and the bundle of public goods and services they offer. Despite the commonness of competition as a strategy, you should not think of cooperation as exceptional. A recent study of more than 1,500 municipalities found that the average one provides about thirty-six services, and that about eight of these are provided through cooperation.[7] We single out cooperation in this chapter both because it is common and because it requires an intentional shift away from the default position in which local governments exist.

What Does State Law
Say about Interlocal Relations?

Each state uses its laws to define the types of local government (e.g., cities, towns, boroughs, villages), how they form, and how much power they have in various policy domains. These laws are not static: they change over time, and so too can the behavior of local governments in response to such changes. A 2010 study found that, on average, 20 percent of all state legislation concerned the form or function of local governments,[8] and that these vary in the extent to which they are empowering or restricting.[9] While no study has directly explored the share of this state activity targeted at influencing interlocal relations specifically, it is likely that much of it at least indirectly does by shaping the resources and autonomy with which decision makers can work. State laws can motivate cooperative interlocal relations in three ways: (1) by creating conditions in which a local government is responsible for producing or providing a service but may lack the fiscal capacity to do so effectively (at a high enough level of quality) or efficiently (at a low enough unit cost) on its own, (2) by limiting the ability of a local government to increase its territorial footprint to meet its policy goals, or (3) by expressly enabling interlocal cooperation.

Find a example of each one (margin annotation)

State governments articulate through laws the service responsibilities of local governments and the revenue streams these governments can potentially access to pay for these services. When resources are scarce, the capacity to directly produce and provide services may be constrained. There are many possible responses for this. If a local government opts to continue with direct production and provision, it may have to strategically reduce expenditures by lowering the quantity or quality of a service or increase the revenues flowing from that service by raising taxes or fees. But a local government might find that contracting with another entity is more efficient, whether that entity is a private contractor or another government. Cooperation is, therefore, one of a suite of responses to resource scarcity.[10]

Problems to how to Pay 4 services (margin annotation)

A local government that is constrained from growing its territorial footprint (i.e., from expanding its boundaries to encompass more land) might also be more likely to cooperate with neighboring local governments to meet policy goals, though no research has been undertaken to support this reasoning. Consistent with this logic, though, some researchers have found that having more neighboring local governments—those with adjacent boundaries—can increase the likelihood of cooperation. Such territorial shifts can occur through the process of annexation or—less commonly—through the merger or consolidation of two or more units of government.[11] The processes through which these structural changes occur are defined by the state and can vary quite a bit. Under the most lenient form, a local government can unilaterally take unincorporated land—that which is not part of an incorporated municipality already—with minimal state involvement. Under more restrictive forms, the government acquiring new land and the one giving it must mutually agree to the transfer, and the state must approve of it under stringent requirements. In North Carolina, local governments had for decades the ability to easily annex land outside

Annexing land Cooperation (margin annotation)

Why 13 How did Charlotte grow this much?

Sounds like a Rigo

their current boundaries, and they still retain much of this ability. Charlotte grew in size from about 19 square miles (50 square kilometers) in 1940 to 140 square miles (362 square kilometers) in 1980, to nearly 298 square miles (about 770 square kilometers) in 2010.[12] The increase in size means an increase in population and an increase in both the service responsibilities and the revenue-generating potential of the city. In the 1990s, 53 percent of Charlotte's population growth—in one of the fastest-growing cities in the United States—came through annexation of 68 square miles of land (176 square kilometers).[13]

Lastly, state legislative bodies can pass laws that speak directly about cooperation. For example, in 2003 Michigan adopted the Joint Municipal Planning Act (JMPA), which allowed all general-purpose local governments in the state—counties, cities, townships, and villages—to work together formally to adopt joint comprehensive plans and zoning codes. Together, these plans and codes form the legal foundation for how a local government controls the use of land within its boundaries.[14] If two or more governments chose to cooperate under the JMPA, each would ratify an agreement specifying the terms of its involvement, such as representation on any joint bodies and the imposition of any penalties for exit. With the coordination of land use, several local governments could more effectively leverage the economic and social benefits flowing from a shared natural resource (e.g., a lake, a watershed, a forest), or direct where new commercial or industrial growth occurs, or better match the locations of jobs to housing in an economic region. Interestingly, the local governments in Michigan already had, at least implicitly, the legal ability to cooperate with regard to their planning and zoning activities. In general, most local governments in Michigan have broad powers under the state's home-rule grant. The JMPA, however, provided a clearer signal about the legality of land use cooperation that had not previously existed. Such legal signals about cooperation—or about any powers—can be especially important in states in which the powers of local government are not certain due to the combination of unclear or ambiguous enabling legislation and the use of Dillon's Rule by state courts in interpreting such laws.[15] We will revisit the JMPA at the start of the next section to learn how local government leaders responded to it.

When Dillion's rule in play it is more important to have legal signals 4 cooperation.

Why Does Cooperation Only Sometimes Happen?

Even if a state empowers local governments to cooperate, such behavior remains voluntary. It may be incentivized or encouraged, but it is not mandated. Although the state of Michigan anticipated cooperative land use planning and regulation would occur among many of the state's nearly two thousand cities, townships, and villages in the wake of the passage of the JMPA in 2003 (described in the previous section), such activity was exceedingly rare. What this section, and the next, will help us think through is *why*. What were the characteristics of the targeted policy domain (land use planning and regulation), of the local governments in Michigan, and of the local elected officials and administrative staff negotiating cooperation that made its adoption and endurance so uncommon?

We can begin by considering two conceptual lenses that have dominated the study of variation in interlocal cooperation in recent decades. One is the *logic of collective action.*[16] In the simplest terms, the most important component of the logic of collective action is that working together will be more likely, where that effort can secure joint gains or benefits that could not otherwise be realized. More plainly, the whole must be greater than the sum of its parts. Beyond the joint gains, selective gains—those that flow to each participant in a cooperative endeavor—would also make collective action more likely. In the case of the JMPA, every story of cooperation began with a well-defined problem that could only be solved through joint work. *when everyone gets something out of cooperation.*

In Grand Traverse County, in the far north of Michigan's lower peninsula, land slated for large-scale redevelopment—and positioned to provide economic benefit to the region—was located in both Traverse City and Garfield Township, on the site of a former state hospital.[17] In the city of Marshall and Marshall Township in the south central part of the state, a new expressway interchange likely to draw intensive commercial development similarly straddled land in two neighboring communities. In the southwestern communities of Washtenaw County, several townships and a city were facing how best to absorb growth spreading outward from Detroit and Ann Arbor suburbs while still preserving open space and leveraging existing infrastructure assets.[18] Each of these three situations presented the potential for joint gains by ensuring a comprehensive and orderly approach to development and growth management that would likely be more successful than a haphazard one. However, the possibility of selective benefits—those that would flow directly to each participant local government—was unclear since revenues from property taxes and fees would only flow to one of the participant communities. No ready mechanism for revenue sharing existed. Moreover, many communities throughout the state were facing similar problems and opportunities as those just described but opted not to cooperate. While the potential for joint gains seemed to be a *necessary* precursor to cooperation, the geography of cooperation suggests these gains were not *sufficient* alone to make it happen.

The logic of collective action helps us start to understand the story of interlocal relations, but we also need to think about the actual act of negotiating a cooperative endeavor. This brings us to a second conceptual lens through which interlocal relations are examined: *transaction cost economics.*[19] We can think about economics as being broadly concerned with the act of exchange, or transaction, between producers and consumers. Transaction cost economics is concerned with the costs of such transaction, and with how economic activity is organized in response to variation in these costs. It originally focused on businesses, or firms, and whether they would seek a good or service from another firm in a marketplace of them or simply bring that activity "in house," and the interaction of firms provides a useful metaphor for understanding how transaction costs work among local governments considering cooperation. General Motors, a major automotive manufacturer, needs a variety of parts in the manufacturing process. It could bring the production of any given part within its own corporate organization or seek that part in the marketplace of automotive

Could explain more in depth.

suppliers. Each part would have a cost associated with it—reflected either in the price available on the market or in the marginal in-house production cost. But there is also a cost to the market transaction itself—the real and opportunity costs of negotiating, maintaining, and enforcing a contract with an automotive supplier. When the marketplace transaction costs plus the product cost of a given part outweigh the in-house production costs for it, we would expect General Motors to choose in-house production. Otherwise, it should enter the marketplace and contract with an outside supplier. The decision by General Motors about how to organize its economic activity should be similar to the decision by a local government to pursue interlocal cooperation.

Transaction cost logic asks us to consider how the parties to interlocal cooperation and the environment in which it happens can make the bargaining process easier. As one might intuitively suspect, cooperation tends to be more likely where positive norms of reciprocity—the idea of "tit-for-tat" exchange—and trust exist from a history of successful cooperation between two local governments or the officials representing them. Reciprocity can diminish opportunism and foster cooperation through predictability and repeated exchanges, and trust can help diminish perceptions of risk.[20] The treatment of interlocal agreements through a social network metaphor is reflective of the importance of relationships in understanding patterns of cooperation.[21]

Cooperation also seems to be more likely when the local governments considering undertaking it are very similar demographically, socioeconomically, fiscally, or even politically.[22] The size of the pool of potential partners could conceivably affect information gathering, bargaining over the division of gains, and monitoring or enforcing behavior, although having more available partners has been viewed as both an aid[23] and a challenge[24] to interlocal cooperation. And, lastly, some goods and services are more likely targets of cooperation, and this can also be explained through transaction cost logic. For example, if a service is highly meterable—that is, its fixed and variable costs are well known, as is true for many local services like solid waste management[25]—then we expect negotiation over its contract price and subsequent monitoring to be easier.[26]

What we can glean from this discussion of transaction costs is that even when interlocal cooperation is made explicitly legal by a state and may hold the promise of joint gains, it still might not happen. Again returning to the example of the Joint Municipal Planning Act, we can use transaction cost logic to explain why cooperative planning and zoning were so rare immediately following the law's passage and why they continue to be exceptional. Land use as a public good or service is not highly meterable, and the bargaining process, revolving not around finding an optimal contract price but rather around defining shared goals and objectives, can be notoriously difficult. Even if one community has more fiscal and infrastructural capacity to handle new land development while another is less able to accommodate such activity, disagreement may exist over the extent to which growth should be directed to one community—especially if it creates a windfall for it.

While many communities in Michigan had a history of working together, these relationships typically extended through municipal managers and their

[margin handwritten note: Those with successful intergovernment cooperation are more likely to get more offers]

[margin handwritten note: More people need it More cooperation]

staff as they negotiated basic service maintenance functions—functions that would not translate easily into land use policymaking. Land use planning and zoning processes would often involve commentary from neighboring communities, but the notion of jointly crafting a comprehensive plan or allowing a joint board of zoning appeals to make important decisions was a step well beyond this. It required not merely welcoming feedback, which could be easily and lawfully ignored, but rather allowing actors from another local government to have potential veto power over important decisions. The reciprocity and trust regarded as key to lowering transaction costs—and that are intrinsic to the notion of intergovernmental relations as human relations mentioned at the start of this chapter—could not be developed incrementally. Not surprisingly, most of the agreements under the JMPA were facilitated by a preexisting regional body, such as a council of governments, with assistance from an outside entity providing funding and expertise.[27]

One could also see in land use a tension between joint gains and homogeneity. The two key benefits of collective action in planning and zoning are cost savings (e.g., the savings from preparing one comprehensive plan, drafting one zoning ordinance, and sharing administrative staff) and, over the longer term, a growing tax base from increased property values. These benefits would be most likely and most attractive for struggling communities—those that have historically lost out in the competition for growth (described briefly in the introductory section)—who would seek out more prosperous and fiscally stable neighboring communities. But communities that are already faring well would have little reason to find cooperation desirable. Why give up autonomy and independence in a policy domain being managed successfully already in exchange for benefits that are either small or uncertain? The resistance to a loss of autonomy is shown well in attempts at joint municipal planning and zoning in Michigan: only in one were the original local planning and zoning bodies and regulations dissolved and replaced completely by their joint counterparts.[28] All others were merely advisory or coordinative.

The problems with land use as a target of cooperation are simply not present for solid waste management, wastewater treatment, snow plowing, and other functions. Some of the goods and services local governments provide, therefore, are much more susceptible to cooperation.[29] The key takeaway from the preceding discussion is that a state can ensure that cooperation is a legal option among local governments, but it is likely only to flourish for *some* goods and services in *some* decision-making contexts. What we have not discussed directly yet are the decision makers who come to the cooperative bargaining table. We consider them in the next section.

What Are the Characteristics of the Individuals Who Tend to Support Cooperation?

The individual already made a minor appearance in the last section, as one node in the interpersonal relationships that may carry the trust needed to motivate and sustain cooperation. The individual can also matter, though, because of their own attributes—the interests they have because of the position they occupy in local government, as well as their own political and cultural preferences.

An extension of the collective action and transaction costs logic outlined above is the model of the individual as a rational economic actor, and this model can provide us some insights into why some people are more inclined to cooperation than others. Rational action is simply selection by actors among alternative courses of action in accordance with the maximization of self-interested, material utility. Material utility could be financial—that is, monetary gain—but it could also come in the form of reputation, reelection, or career advancement. The general proposition—to return to the logic of collective action described earlier—is that selective benefits matter: the larger the political incentives and career incentives from favoring cooperation, the greater the likelihood of cooperation. Whereas we focused earlier at the local government level on the treatment of joint and selective benefits, here we are concerned with the economic, political, and other gains of the individual. In other words, we must distinguish between benefits that are public and private.[30]

Interlocal cooperation can flow through individuals who are elected—such as mayors, county sheriffs, city commissions, and town council members[31]—as well as administrative staff such as city managers and town planners. Typically, we regard the primary private benefits for public elected officials as the interest in political power and reelection, and for administrative employees the corresponding interests are in job security and decision-making autonomy.[32] These individual costs and benefits that accrue to individuals and groups are often more able than collective costs and benefits (such as efficiency or scale economies) to explain interlocal cooperation.

One obvious way that the desire for reelection would manifest is in acting in a way viewed as responsive to the local voting public's needs and desires. What makes the local government setting unique is that relatively few local elected officials outside of those from large cities are career politicians who are actively seeking promotion to higher offices at the state or federal level. Many have long tenures and are often from small communities where incurring the wrath of even a few voters may be enough to lose their position on a city council or township board, or simply make their social interactions in the community less pleasant. The small size of local governments in the United States is often overlooked due to the high profile of larger cities. In Michigan, only thirty of the state's nearly two thousand local governments meet a population threshold of fifty thousand. Set the threshold at twenty thousand, and the number of included localities only grows to about one hundred. The same is true for most states. Less than 4 percent of New York's local governments have fifty thousand people. In Missouri, the figure is only about 1 percent. In Florida, the number pushes up to about 15 percent. Even in highly urbanized California, the corresponding figure is just over one-third. Interlocal cooperation in policy areas requiring adjacency and contiguity (as most do) would by necessity engage "small town" political actors.

[margin handwritten note:] greater incentives from favoring cooperation, the greater likelihood of cooperation

[margin handwritten note:] few local officials want to move up

The potential for a strong social mechanism in small towns may even make up for the lack of monetary reward from interest groups and low electoral turnout.[33] Of course, a more politically active public may have little opinion anyway about interlocal cooperation, which is not typically a hot-button issue (except, perhaps, when it targets land use planning and regulation) and may not even be on the political radars of constituents. A study of Michigan local elected officials found, in part, that officials reported receiving no public input about more than two-fifths of the projects subject to interlocal service arrangements.[34] About a third of the efforts received positive feedback, and another quarter received negative feedback.[35] While this general apathy about governance may suggest that local elected officials perceive an opportunity to exercise their own discretion, nevertheless the risk of reprisal at the voting booth by even a small but motivated group could be problematic. But even if regional benefits from cooperation do occur, they may not allow for credit claiming, the mechanism that leads elected officials to prefer projects that have visible benefits directed at the short-term interests of their general constituency or a specific interest group.[36] Another possibility is that policies might be decided according to partisanship—that local elected officials will choose the alternative most in line with what they think is the prevailing political ideology of constituents. A recent study found that variation in city policies tends to align with the variation in policy conservatism among residents of the cities.[37] But the partisan lines on interlocal cooperation generally are not well understood.[38]

The administrative employee is generally thought to have a longer time horizon than the elected official, and to find more career value in regionalizing activity such as interlocal cooperation. These actors also tend to exist in well-connected networks with one another across local boundaries, creating the opportunity for administrative conjunctions to form along which information and trust can flow, or even simply imparting professional ideals consistent with the pursuit of interlocal cooperation.[39] Administrative actors also tend to have a strong public-service ethos, perhaps making them more open to searching for alternative modes of service delivery in the pursuit of efficiency or effectiveness. We tend to think, based on all of the above reasons, that the council–manager form of government is more hospitable to cooperative endeavors.[40]

A final consideration with regard to any actor—whether political or administrative—involved in decision making about cooperation is whether that actor might simply be predisposed to working together with others. For example, some might have a cultural worldview that consistently suggests cooperation is a good idea—irrespective of whether it affords clear joint or selective benefits to them as individuals or to their communities.[41] Recent studies of interlocal cooperation have increasingly noted the possibility of behaviors that are not motivated by self-interest, such as a simple interest in helping a neighboring community.[42] The difficulty with cultural worldviews, though, is that they are very hard to discern and do not even consistently travel with outward signals such as partisan identity.

Returning a final time to the example of joint land use planning and regulation in Michigan, we can use this section to glean some final insights about its lack of uptake by local governments. Whereas most targets of cooperation are apolitical, land use can be a notoriously political battleground. But this battleground tends to be over what happens within local boundaries in the placement of unwanted or undesirable land uses. With regard to the cooperative, regional pursuit of land use planning, the evidence is decidedly mixed.[43] The outcomes in Michigan, though, suggest that land use cooperation either carried no political reward or that at least some members of the voting public were concerned about any loss of independence and autonomy in making land use decisions. While administrative staff may have been attracted by the efficiency gains from working together and by the appeal of claiming career credit for a successful regional comprehensive plan or zoning ordinance, many communities in Michigan have high turnover in their planning and zoning units or do not have full-time planning staff and instead rely on outside consultants for these needs.

Conclusion

In this chapter, we have explored the legal spaces that states create for interlocal cooperation among counties, cities, towns, and other general-purpose local governments. We discussed how state governments can and do use legislation to expressly enable cooperation in a wide array of policy domains—from wastewater treatment and snow plowing to land use and economic development. We also reviewed how states can indirectly influence the likelihood of cooperation versus competition by shaping the service responsibilities of local governments, the revenues available to them, and their ability to extend their boundaries through annexation. After explaining the cooperative space that states shape, we spent some time thinking through how the environment within which decision making about cooperation happens, and the decision makers working in it, can influence whether cooperation actually does happen or not. We looked at the importance of joint and selective gains from cooperation, and treated at length how the costs of the cooperative transaction balance against these. We finished by thinking about the material incentives of decision makers, whether political, careerist, or cultural.

The three questions that motivated this chapter—*What does state law say about interlocal relations? What are some of the contexts in which cooperation tends to happen? What are the characteristics of the individuals who tend to support cooperation?*—can be viewed as basic guideposts for you in a professional career. If you work in local government, you are now aware that cooperation is often a very real possibility, and you can be thoughtful about who you target as a potential partner or collaborator and how you can construct a space that is more amenable to cooperation. For example, you might work to create interlocal interpersonal relationships that allow the development of norms of reciprocity and trust, starting with smaller and less risky cooperative efforts before tackling more difficult ones. Or you might make an effort to persuade the public of the advantages of cooperation, if these do exist, to ensure they are politically supportive of it when needed. These are not panaceas that will guarantee cooperation flourishes, but evidence suggests they will be helpful. If you work in state government, you will also be more aware now of how laws can influence the competitive and cooperative impulses of local governments and that simply enabling cooperation is likely not enough to secure it as an outcome. Incentives may be needed in the short term to serve as a clear selective gain for governments participating in cooperation, or educational efforts may need to be undertaken.

Discussion Questions

1. Think about the laws in your home state and about the county, city, or other local government in which you live. Is your community able to cooperate with its neighbors? Which policy areas can this happen in? You may need to explore your state's compiled laws to find the answer.
2. Assume your home community can cooperate in any policy area in which it already has the authority to act. Think of one or two policy areas—land use, economic development, affordable housing, stormwater management, road maintenance, or any other—in which cooperation would be beneficial. Articulate what both the joint gains (those that arise from working together) and the selective benefits (those that flow to your community and to the individuals working in it) would be.
3. Imagine you are able to structure the cooperative decision-making process for question 2, from the actors involved to the nature of meetings, voting, and the like. What would it look like and why?

Notes

[1] Christopher V. Hawkins, "Competition and Cooperation: Local Government Joint Ventures for Economic Development," *Journal of Urban Affairs* 32, no. 2 (2010): 253–75.

[2] Anna Rossi, "Regionalizing the Detroit Water and Sewerage Department, the Effects of Privatization on Metro Detroit Residents and the Importance of Community Control," *Journal of Law and Society* 17, no. 2 (2015): 59–85.

[3] Kiki Caruson and Susan A. MacManus, "Disaster Vulnerabilities: How Strong a Push toward Regionalism and Intergovernmental Cooperation?," *American Review of Public Administration* 38, no. 3 (2008): 286–306.

[4] Deil S. Wright, "Intergovernmental Relations: An Analytical Overview," *Annals of the American Academy of Political and Social Science* 416, no. 1 (1974): 1–16.

[5] Adams B. Nager, Allison S. Lowe Reed, and W. Scott Langford, "Catching the Whale: A Comparison of Place Promotion Strategies through the Lens of Amazon HQ2," *Geography Compass* 13, no. 9 (2019): e12462.

[6] Rolf Pendall, "Local Land Use Regulation and the Chain of Exclusion," *Journal of the American Planning Association* 66, no. 2 (2000): 125–42.

[7] Yunji Kim and Mildred E. Warner, "Pragmatic Municipalism: Local Government Service Delivery after the Great Recession," *Public Administration* 94, no. 3 (2016): 789–805.

[8] Gerald Gamm and Thad Kousser, "Broad Bills or Particularistic Policy? Historical Patterns in American State Legislatures," *American Political Science Review* 104, no. 1 (2010): 151–70.

[9] Ann O'M. Bowman and Richard C. Kearney, "Are US Cities Losing Power and Authority? Perceptions of Local Government Actors," *Urban Affairs Review* 48, no. 4 (2012): 528–46.

[10] Mildred E. Warner, "Local Government Restructuring in a Time of Fiscal Stress," in *Public Jobs and Political Agendas: The Public Sector in an Era of Economic Stress*, ed. Daniel J. B. Mitchell, 41–58 (Champaign, IL: Labor and Employment Relations Association, 2012).

[11] Jered B. Carr and Richard C. Feiock, eds., *City-County Consolidation and Its Alternatives: Reshaping the Local Government Landscape* (London: Routledge, 2016).

[12] U.S. Census Bureau, "Census of Governments," 2019, https://www.census.gov/govs.

[13] Gerald Ingalls and Gary Rassel, "Political Fragmentation, Municipal Incorporation and Annexation in a High Growth Urban Area: The Case of Charlotte, North Carolina," *North Carolina Geographer* 13 (2005): 17–30.

[14] Thomas Skuzinski, *The Risk of Regional Governance: Cultural Theory and Interlocal Cooperation* (New York: Routledge, 2017).

[15] Jesse J. Richardson Jr., "Dillon's Rule Is from Mars, Home Rule Is from Venus: Local Government Autonomy and the Rules of Statutory Construction," *Publius: The Journal of Federalism* 41, no. 4 (2011): 662–85.

[16] Mancur Olson, *The Logic of Collective Action* (Cambridge, MA: Harvard University Press, 2009).

[17] Skuzinski, *Risk of Regional Governance*.

[18] Ibid.

[19] Oliver E. Williamson, "Transaction Cost Economics: The Natural Progression," *American Economic Review* 100, no. 3 (2010): 673–90.

[20] Manoj K. Shrestha and Richard C. Feiock, "Transaction Cost, Exchange Embeddedness, and Interlocal Cooperation in Local Public Goods Supply," *Political Research Quarterly* 64, no. 3 (2011): 573–87.

[21] Kurt Thurmaier and Curtis Wood, "Interlocal Agreements as Overlapping Social Networks: Picket-Fence Regionalism in Metropolitan Kansas City," *Public Administration Review* 62, no. 5 (2002): 585–98.

[22] Minsun Song, Hyung Jun Park, and Kyujin Jung, "Do Political Similarities Facilitate Interlocal Collaboration?," *Public Administration Review* 78, no. 2 (2018): 261–69.

[23] Richard C. Feiock, Annette Steinacker, and Hyung Jun Park, "Institutional Collective Action and Economic Development Joint Ventures," *Public Administration Review* 69, no. 2 (2009): 256–70.

[24] Manoj K. Shrestha and Richard C. Feiock, "Governing US Metropolitan Areas: Self-Organizing and Multiplex Service Networks," *American Politics Research* 37, no. 5 (2009): 801–23.

[25] Hugo Consciência Silvestre, Rui Cunha Marques, and Ricardo Corrêa Gomes, "Joined-Up Government of Utilities: A Meta-Review on a Public–Public Partnership and Inter-municipal Cooperation in the Water and Wastewater Industries," *Public Management Review* 20, no. 4 (2018): 607–31.

[26] Trevor L. Brown and Matthew Potoski, "Transaction Costs and Institutional Explanations for Government Service Production Decisions," *Journal of Public Administration Research and Theory* 13, no. 4 (2003): 441–68.

[27] Skuzinski, *Risk of Regional Governance*.

[28] Ibid.

[29] Germà Bel and Mildred E. Warner, "Factors Explaining Inter-municipal Cooperation in Service Delivery: A Meta-Regression Analysis." *Journal of Economic Policy Reform* 19, no. 2 (2016): 91–115.

[30] Richard C. Feiock, "Rational Choice and Regional Governance," *Journal of Urban Affairs* 29, no. 1 (2007): 47–63.

[31] Eric S. Zeemering, "Governing Interlocal Cooperation: City Council Interests and the Implications for Public Management," *Public Administration Review* 68, no. 4 (2008): 731–41.

[32] Richard C. Feiock and Jered B. Carr, "Incentives, Entrepreneurs, and Boundary Change: A Collective Action Framework," *Urban Affairs Review* 36, no. 3 (2001): 382–405.

[33] Ronald J. Oakerson, "The Study of Metropolitan Governance," in *Metropolitan Governance: Conflict, Competition, and Cooperation*, ed. Richard C. Feiock, 17–45 (Washington, DC: Georgetown University Press, 2004).

[34] Zeemering, "Governing Interlocal Cooperation."

[35] Ibid.

[36] Richard C. Feiock, Moon-Gi Jeong, and Jaehoon Kim, "Credible Commitment and Council-Manager Government: Implications for Policy Instrument Choices," *Public Administration Review* 63, no. 5 (2003): 616–25.

[37] Chris Tausanovitch and Christopher Warshaw, "Representation in Municipal Government," *American Political Science Review* 108, no. 3 (2014): 605–41.

[38] Skuzinski, *Risk of Regional Governance.*

[39] H. George Frederickson, "The Repositioning of American Public Administration," *PS: Political Science & Politics* 32, no. 4 (1999): 701–12.

[40] Jered B. Carr, Kelly LeRoux, and Manoj Shrestha, "Institutional Ties, Transaction Costs, and External Service Production," *Urban Affairs Review* 44, no. 3 (2009): 403–27.

[41] Skuzinski, *Risk of Regional Governance.*

[42] Austin M. Aldag and Mildred Warner, "Cooperation, not Cost Savings: Explaining Duration of Shared Service Agreements," *Local Government Studies* 44, no. 3 (2018): 350–70.

[43] Robert W. Wassmer and Edward L. Lascher Jr., "Who Supports Local Growth and Regional Planning to Deal with Its Consequences?," *Urban Affairs Review* 41, no. 5 (2006): 621–45.

CHAPTER 16

State–Local Relations and the COVID-19 Pandemic

Cali Curley, University of Miami
Peter Stanley Federman, Indiana University Purdue University Indianapolis
Eric S. Zeemering, University of Georgia

In March 2020, social interaction and economic activity in communities across the United States came to a near halt. The COVID-19 disease caused by the SARS-CoV-2 virus was identified in the United States after its emergence in China and its spread around the globe.[1] State and local officials, concerned about the rapid spread of the virus and its potential to overwhelm the healthcare system, put in place a variety of public health measures. Workplaces closed, shifting employees to telework or issuing layoffs. Restaurants ceased operations or transitioned to takeout-only service. Schools and universities pivoted to online classes. Public health messages encouraged the public to *social distance*, or stay at least six feet apart, to reduce the transmission of the disease. Face masks were encouraged or required by state and local governments or by large corporations in the absence of a federal mandate. Data from cellular telephone companies illustrated a dramatic reduction in travel by Americans, suggesting that many in the country heeded public health guidelines and stayed at home.[2] However, the details of stay-at-home orders and public health actions varied across the states, and even across local communities. The COVID-19 pandemic illustrates the complex dynamics of state–local conflict and cooperation discussed throughout this book.

The design of American federalism and the importance of state and local government provide context for thinking about how subnational governments responded to the COVID-19 public health crisis. In the early months of the government response to COVID-19, President Trump frequently pointed to state governors as the ones responsible for the pandemic response, shifting public attention away from Washington, DC.[3] Indeed, state governments have significant authority and responsibility to provide public health services and to manage emergencies. When a crisis impacts the entire country rather than a single

272 Cali Curley, Peter Stanley Federman, and Eric S. Zeemering

state, tensions can emerge in the federal system. COVID-19, impacting the entire country, put governors in competition with one another for personal protective equipment and resources to respond to the pandemic.[4] Some observers noted states led by Republican governors put in place more limited restrictions, in line with the Trump administration's concern about protecting jobs and the economy, while Democratic governors took more restrictive public health actions.[5] Cities, too, pursued a range of policy response. Some cities drew on their experiences with natural disasters to mobilize a local public health response.[6] When local governments took action inconsistent with their states, such as adopting more restrictive stay-at-home orders, conflict erupted between mayors and governors.[7] The tension and policy disputes were highlighted in media coverage of the pandemic response, but the true operation of American federalism during this crisis is more nuanced. Careful observers of state–local relations will see both conflict and cooperation as cities and states governed through the crisis.

The pages ahead discuss three dimensions of the state–local response to the COVID-19 pandemic. First, the prominence of state government action is discussed, with exploration of the actions taken by governors and state public health agencies. Second, the reactions of local government officials are conveyed through illustrations from a survey of cities in Georgia, conducted during the early months of the pandemic. While this survey data comes from a single state, nationwide surveys and examples from the media point to similar local sentiment around the nation. Third, the federal infusion of funding through the Coronavirus Aid, Relief, and Economic Security (CARES) Act, passed by Congress in March 2020, sent limited funding to state and local governments to assist the pandemic response. The importance of this financial transfer for the conduct of state–local relations is considered. The chapter concludes by encouraging readers to consider action necessary in the months ahead, and even suggests some students will want to pursue public service careers, aiding the nation's health and economic recovery.

For matters of public health, a healthy state–local relationship is critical. Moreover, the financial turmoil wrought by COVID-19, which pushed unemployment up between 5 and 10 percent in many states, will require a coordinated state–local response in the months and years ahead.[8] In 2020, some state and local leaders coordinated to meet these challenges while others wrestled for authority, resources, and policy control. For those who seek to help the United States recover from the COVID-19 pandemic in the fields of public health, human services, or economic recovery, understanding state–local relations will be critical.

The State Response to COVID-19

State governments are at the forefront of the response to the COVID-19 pandemic in the United States. The relationship between state and local governments, which is already often complicated, can become even more difficult to navigate during a crisis.[9] Over the course of the COVID-19 pandemic, state governments have taken varied approaches to addressing questions of power and jurisdiction, particularly as pertaining to the relationship between the state executive and local governments. States have taken different approaches with regard to their response to COVID-19, in terms of both the type of statewide orders they have instituted and the manner in which they have done so.

In particular, two main types of statewide orders have been identified: restrictions, such as nonessential business closures and stay-at-home orders, and suspensions, such as extending deadlines or providing more accessible public benefits. These orders also include authorizations made by state governments that provide powers to state agency directors, activate the national guard, authorize emergency funds to be accessed, and other actions. While most orders contain fairly similar substantive content in terms of actions, the strategies or approaches taken to handling the crisis vary across the states. There appear to be three commonly used approaches to instituting these orders: governor led, with the state executive issuing many of these orders through their office; agency led, where the state executive has allowed state agency heads to take the lead in issuing and instituting orders; and diffusive, where power has been distributed not only to agency heads but to local governments as well. These distinctions clarify how state governments have allotted, restricted, and distributed power to local governments and state agencies across the country.[10]

In an effort to better understand the strategies taken by states to govern the COVID-19 crisis, over one thousand executive orders adopted at the state level have been collected and coded.[11] This coding process was completed using inductive thematic analysis, paired with some preset themes based on the types of restrictions that had been popularized in the media, including business and school closures and stay-at-home orders, in a hybrid approach consistent with a thematic analysis.[12] A series of categories were created prior to coding, but the category construction was flexible and allowed for common themes to emerge. This process also captured the content of unique orders to make it possible to undertake a second round of coding to develop a more robust and inclusive coding scheme.

In the following sections, examples of actions taken in the context of the executive orders to restrict, allow, and guide local government activity are laid out as determined by this coding process. These orders, like many of those issued during the pandemic, take the form of preemptions, authorizations, and directives of coordination. While each state utilizes slightly different tools and language to define the legal and administrative boundaries of their executive power, the approaches fall into three main categories, as described here. Each concept is explained and discussed in the context of the state-level executive orders responding to COVID-19. It should be noted that these three descriptions are not intended to provide insight as to the specific utility of one approach over another but merely to delineate how states and state executives have approached this crisis from distinct angles.

Preemption

Several states have issued *preemption* orders, which explicitly restrict power at the local level. Preemptions can take many different forms, ranging from broad

broad

declarations that local governments cannot issue an ordinance of any kind that might contradict a state-level order to narrower constraints preventing localities from passing specific rules. Preemptions, regardless of their scope, are explicit, direct, and indicative of an approach that seeks to centralize power to address the crisis in the state executive.

Broad Preemptions: These preemptions offer a blanket statement intended to prevent local actors from taking significant action that might interfere with or contradict state-level orders. One example of a broad preemption is contained within Executive Order 202.3 from New York Governor Andrew Cuomo on March 16:

> No local government or political subdivision shall issue any local emergency order or declaration of emergency or disaster inconsistent with, conflicting with or superseding the foregoing directives, or any other executive order issued under Section 24 of the Executive Law and any local emergency order or any local administrative codes, charters, laws, rules or regulations, are hereby suspended with respect to any such order issued under such authority different or in conflict with Executive directives.

In this specific example, the preemption requires that states and local governments address the crisis in identical manners. Not only are local governments told they cannot do less than the state, they are also told that they cannot do more.

Narrow Preemptions: Narrow preemptions are often issued to prevent a certain type of activity. This allows local governments some flexibility still to act outside of the scope of the preemption but limits and restricts their rights to act in certain ways. One example of a narrow preemption is contained within Executive Order 7S, issued by Connecticut Governor Ned Lamont on April 1:

> The Commissioner of Economic and Community Development, in consultation with the Commissioner of Public Health, shall issue mandatory statewide rules prescribing such additional protective measures no later than 11:59 p.m. on April 1, 2020. Such rules shall be mandatory throughout the state and shall supersede and preempt any current or future municipal order and shall supersede the requirements of Executive Order No. 7N, Sec. 3, providing that nothing in this order shall eliminate or reduce the requirements of Executive Order No. 7N, Sec. 3 regarding firearms transactions.

In this example, local governments are denied the authority to restrict firearms transactions. This demonstrates that preemptions may be used to protect specific rights of the public. Narrow preemptions may be motivated by political or constitutional concerns and may impact smaller segments of the population or limited categories of businesses and organizations.

Authorization — *diffuse power to LG*

On the other hand, *authorization* can offer a range of powers to a range of actors. Authorizations, which tend to give power to local officials, can vary in what they authorize local governments to do and to whom they give power.

The actors authorized at the local level by these orders may include county or municipal governing actors, local public health actors, and local law enforcement. The orders authorize them to, or even explicitly recommend that they, supersede state-level orders if they deem such action necessary. This type of approach is less common and is perhaps more indicative of an approach that seeks to diffuse power throughout the state. In addition, this approach allows local governments to adjust their restrictions of movement and commerce or suspensions of certain regulations as they deem appropriate.

Narrow Authorizations: One example of a *narrow authorization*, which provides circumscribed discretionary power to specific actors, includes this directive to public safety officials given in a proclamation issued by Alabama Governor Kay Ivey on March 26: "A county or municipality may authorize law enforcement officers to issue a summons and complaint in lieu of custodial arrest for any violation or misdemeanor except as provided below." This order provides local law enforcement the discretion to issue summonses or complaints in lieu of arrests, an example of relatively limited additional powers granted to a single type of actor. However, these actions would be beyond their abilities if it were not for the order allowing them.

Broad Authorizations: An example of a broad authorization, granting wider discretionary powers to specific actors, comes from Executive Order D-2020-017 of March 25 from Governor Jared Polis in the state of Colorado: "Nothing in this Executive Order prevents a local public health authority from issuing an order more protective of the public than this Executive Order. For clarity, any stay at home or similar order issued by a local jurisdiction remains in full force and effect." This executive order authorizes public health authorities to go beyond state guidelines in providing guidance around COVID-19. This authorization provides a single actor with broad discretion to adopt and implement a wide range of potential policies, so long as the state minimum is met.

Coordination

Finally, some states took a *coordination* approach, wherein the state executive requires the county and state to respond together, simultaneously granting power to specific local officials, with certain caveats, exclusions, or provisos.

One example of such an approach was the adoption of the following language by Colorado Governor Jared Polis in Executive Order D-2020-003 of March 11, declaring a state of emergency: "I also verbally authorized employing the Colorado National Guard to support and provide planning resources to State and local authorities as they respond to the presence of COVID-19 in the State." This order, authorizing the state National Guard to work with state resources and local authorities to address the crisis, demonstrates one approach to the goal of coordination between levels of government.

Another form of coordination directive was authored by Florida Governor Ron DeSantis in Executive Order 20-70: "The Broward County Administrator and the Palm Beach County Administrator shall have the ability to enforce, relax, modify or remove these closures, as warranted, pursuant to the directives and parameters as set forth in Executive Order 20-68." This second type of directive clearly demonstrates that the state is adopting specific closures for the county level but offers certain county administrators the explicit right to modify those closures. This order grants power to local actors, in part to demonstrate that the state government is working with the interest of local government in mind.

Dynamism in Preemption, Authorization, and Coordination

→ vigorous activity and progress

While these strategies may appear stagnant, their categorization is far from the whole picture. States have also found ways to accommodate changes to the role of local governments over the course of the crisis, adding a temporal dimension to how these orders impact state governance. This includes entirely rescinding previous coordination approaches, overseeing authorizations, and exempting preemptions.

• *Rescinding Coordination:* In the case of Florida, a coordination approach where state executive orders granted powers to the county administrator was taken in the early response to the crisis; however, as the crisis escalated, this coordination approach seems to have been rolled back. Governor DeSantis issued further orders that restricted certain policies and restrained local government officials, including Executive Order 20-91 of March 30, which ordered "Miami-Dade County, Broward County, Palm Beach County and Monroe County to restrict public access to businesses and facilities deemed nonessential," which amended previous orders granting authority to those actors to determine their own internal closures. In light of this, it is safe to say that Florida's approach to intergovernmental relationships has changed over time, evolving with the ongoing nature of the crisis.

Overseeing Authorization: There are also clear examples of authorizations that contain caveats and provisos, including in the state of Alabama. Governor Kay Ivey issued an order to give power to the state health officer to make determinations about actions required to address the crisis. In State Health Officer Scott Harris's initial order, he "authorizes a County Health Officer to 'institute immediate measures to prevent the spread' of diseases so designated by the State Board of Health" on March 17. Three days later, on March 20, the state health officer created additional oversight for the initial authorization, determining that "the Jefferson and Mobile County Health Officers are authorized, after approval by the State Health Officer, to implement more stringent measures as local circumstances require." This suggests that even the broadest authorizations to local authorities can come with strings attached, or have further strings attached to them after their issuance.

Exempting Preemptions: Similarly, preemptions may not be as ironclad in some states as they initially seem. One example of this is Connecticut's Governor Ned Lamont, who issued a preemption (Executive Order 7H) on March 20, reading in part that "no municipal chief executive officer or designee may enact or enforce any order that conflicts with any provision of any of my Executive Orders," but providing a clause within the very same section for local

[handwritten margin note: Florida change their direction in policies]

governments to "first seek and receive written permission from the Department of Emergency Services and Public Protection" if they sought to adopt more stringent actions than the state executive orders demanded. Such an order, while at first glance a definitive preemption, in fact contains a fairly significant loophole that could allow many local governments to skirt the preemption with state agency permission.

Summarizing the State Role

This categorization of state action in the wake of the pandemic points to the pressing need to understand ramifications of intergovernmental interactions during times of crisis. These different strategies (preemption, authorization, and coordination) likely vary in their effectiveness, with implications for future interactions between state and local government. Steps must also be taken to understand public opinion about state action. The COVID-19 pandemic will undoubtedly be studied for a long time, and part of this exploration should include an understanding of the causes that influenced these different approaches to state–local relations. In the context of the COVID-19 pandemic, the variation in power given to local governments may be informed by the history of disaster in particular states, preexisting interpersonal and interorganizational dynamics, politics, and many other potential impactful elements. In order to explore these causal arguments, there must be a concerted empirical effort to catalog activities being taken across state and local governments. Seeing how conflict and cooperation play out in the midst of a pandemic only strengthens the argument for why government and intergovernmental relations matter for the future of the United States.

The Local Response to COVID-19

Most Americans have access to public health services through a local unit of government, though this does not mean that all, or even most, units of local government have expertise in public health. Local health departments are organized in many different ways and frequently engage with nonprofit organizations and private-sector health providers, as well as state and federal government agencies, as they deliver service to the public.[13] While these units exist to play a role in a public health crisis, their more routine work centers on public health education and interventions, mitigation of broad public health problems, and monitoring for problems including waterborne disease. The complexity of public health services, including regulation and funding from multiple levels of government, led political scientist Morton Grodzins to describe the *county sanitarian*, or public health officer, as the quintessential intergovernmental employee.[14] A public health official may work for a local unit of government, but the programs they provide may be authorized and funded through a mix of state and federal action. In large cities, sophisticated public health departments design interventions to promote positive health practices, provide preventive medical care, and prepare for emergencies like the COVID-19 pandemic.[15] Yet many units of local government have little interaction or experience with public health. In many states, county governments play the leading role in public health, while cities undertake no direct responsibility. Some local governments approached COVID-19 with detailed pandemic response plans and expertise on staff, but many units of local government had limited experience or public health capacity in early 2020 as they began to respond to COVID-19.

Local governments had frontline responsibility for implementing public health measures and maintaining critical services from water to policing. Using data from the National League of Cities (NLC), McDonald, Goodman, and Hatch find that in many states local action in response to the pandemic predated the start of state action.[16] A survey of city government in Georgia illustrates the range of action taken by local governments at the onset of the COVID-19 pandemic in early 2020.[17] In Georgia, county public health departments coordinate with the Georgia Department of Public Health in a regional structure of 18 public health districts across the state. This means city governments, as general-purpose units, are not extensively engaged in public health. Still, pandemic response is listed in the State of Georgia Emergency Operations Plan, which means cities should have considered how their city would need to respond to a pandemic in their emergency planning efforts. At the beginning of March 2020, 76 percent of cities in Georgia reported they did *not* have a written plan in place to respond to the pandemic. This is a critical, but unsurprising, gap in local preparation for a major public health crisis.[18] While local officials believed cities had an important role to play in the response to the pandemic, only 38 percent somewhat or strongly agreed that they had the necessary staff expertise to respond to the pandemic. Local officials described the pandemic as a novel problem that required a high level of innovation and adaptation.

What, specifically, did cities in Georgia do in the earliest days of the pandemic? The city-level response can be divided into two categories—internal management and public health actions. Internally, city governments reacted like many other workplaces, transitioning employees to telework, modifying sick leave policies, providing employees with personal protective equipment, increasing office cleanings, and providing employees with guidance on social distancing. Cities also reduced or modified access to services through facility closures, with 83 percent reporting city hall closure, 61 percent reporting recreation facility closure, and 67 percent reporting municipal court closure. Because the local government workforce has frequent, direct interaction with the public, these actions to protect employees were critical to the continuity of local government service delivery.

Beyond these management steps, many cities undertook new public health actions. City governments became public health promoters and information brokers, sharing information on city websites and social media accounts to inform the public about the importance of mask wearing, the availability of testing, and the availability of economic assistance.[19] About 20 percent of cities in Georgia developed specialized websites to share information about the city's response to the pandemic. In addition to outreach, cities modified their approaches to service delivery. Libraries and recreation centers moved programming and classes online. Common across the nation was the decision to suspend utility shutoffs, and 61 percent of Georgia cities took this action. Water is necessary for sanitation. If a family is not able to pay a water bill due to employment loss during the pandemic, a water shutoff might increase their risk for illness. Frequent hand washing would not be possible without running water. Finally, cities took ground-level responsibility for limiting the occupation of businesses and public spaces through temporary business closures, curfews, the cancelation of public events, and restrictions on gatherings. These examples illustrate that in the earliest days of the pandemic, cities in Georgia were rethinking their standard services, identifying new ways to inform and support their communities, and promoting social distancing through both education and enforcement.

While many cities lack public health experience and expertise, the COVID-19 pandemic illustrates how intergovernmental relations help fill this void. Cities came up to speed quickly, and membership organizations like the Georgia Municipal Association, the National League of Cities, and the International City/County Management Association quickly deployed informational resources to their members to assist local action. Cooperation, particularly through the exchange of information, helped local governments take informed action during a time of uncertainty. In the early months of the pandemic, 42 percent of cities in Georgia reported at least weekly communication with the Georgia Department of Public Health. About 47 percent of cities reported at least weekly communication with their county health department. About 70 percent of cities described the response of state agencies as adequate, and over 82 percent said the same about their county's response. In contrast, only 20 percent of cities report at least weekly communication with the U.S. Department of Health and Human Services, and 19 percent report the same level of communication with the U.S. Centers for Disease Control and Prevention. Still, about 72 percent of cities assessed the federal response as adequate. For city governments in Georgia, coordination within the state, horizontally and vertically, was common in the early days of the COVID-19 pandemic. Georgia was not the only state in which survey evidence shows high levels of interaction among local government officials. A survey of local government leaders in Michigan reveals a fairly positive assessment of the effectiveness of local coordination in response to the pandemic, though these leaders appeared more critical of their interactions with the federal government.[20]

Studying local action in response to the COVID-19 pandemic provides an important contrast to media coverage of the crisis, which often emphasized partisan politics and tensions between mayors and governors. Certainly, these tensions existed. Mayors across the country expressed discontent as their governors moved to ease restrictions on business and economic activity by the late spring of 2020.[21] While some local governments push for more stringent restrictions and health measures, others push to loosen the same constraints. For example, in early 2021, officials in Baraga County, Michigan, issued a manifesto refusing to implement or comply with many of the pandemic orders issued by Governor Gretchen Whitmer and the Michigan Department of Health and

Human Services.[22] While these tensions grab media headlines, the methodical work of state and local government officials cooperating to provide services and manage the pandemic often go unnoticed. A full understanding of American federalism requires attention to both dynamics. Scholars studying political science and public administration could assist our future understanding of state–local relations by investigating the consequences of divided public sentiment for effective coordination between state and local government during the COVID-19 pandemic.

The CARES Act and Future Support for State and Local Government

During the COVID-19 pandemic, state and local governments bore significant new costs while also suffering reduced tax revenue. The impact on state and local budgets is shaped not only by the condition of the economy but also by how governments tax to raise money. Different taxes suffer different weaknesses during periods of economic stress. States and some local governments are highly dependent on sales tax, so as economic activity slowed, revenues also slowed. Most local governments rely more heavily upon property taxes. These revenue streams are more stable in the short term but may see volatility in the future if the pandemic has consequences for property values and transactions. This scenario may come about if commercial property values decline as some companies shift toward longer-term models of telework for their employees, reducing their need for office space. Because of the complexity of state and local revenue streams, no quick or easy answer can be offered to understand the local financial impact of COVID-19.[23] One estimate from Brookings, a Washington, DC, think-tank, projects $155 billion in state and local revenue losses in 2020.[24] Yet these projections are difficult to make. An analysis by the Federal Reserve Bank of Dallas points to volatility across revenue sources in Texas, projecting uncertainty for the year ahead. The briefing explains that under these conditions "lawmakers must make fiscal adjustments to close the gap between expected revenues and necessary expenditures, often with distinct consequences for those dependent on local government services and for the taxpayers who fund the services."[25]

Revenue reductions are not the only problem for state and local government. The modifications to the government workplace described above come with significant costs. Not only are state and local governments purchasing masks, hand sanitizer, office cleaning supplies, and other personal protective equipment, they are also upgrading their information technology infrastructure. Governments find themselves paying for new online services and platforms to maintain public access to government services. School districts, in particular, have grappled with problems of online access for students now required to learn from home. State and local leaders have documented these expenses and taken their case to policymakers in Washington, DC, to press for support.

When state and local governments face unanticipated economic shocks, the federal government may provide aid to maintain public services or to stimulate the economy. Most recently, the American Recovery and Reinvestment Act (ARRA) of 2009 sent funds to "shovel ready" projects across the country, helping state and local governments spend money quickly on infrastructure, energy retrofits, and preplanned projects that just needed funding. This stimulus aided in recovery from economic recession. For the federal government, crafting aid in response to the COVID-19 pandemic is more complex. Federal policymakers may seek to address both the health and economic consequences of the pandemic, and these goals may require spending on different types of activities. Divided opinions in Washington on where to target aid have left state and local governments out of many relief discussions, despite mobilization and lobbying by state and local officials and their interest groups.

The first major relief bill in response to COVID-19, the CARES Act, passed Congress in March 2020. This package provided $150 billion in aid to state, local, and tribal governments, with funds targeted at expenses related to pandemic response. Direct aid was sent to local units of government over 500,000 in population. Smaller local units had to wait for their states to "pass through" aid based on state priorities. The CARES Act provided targeted assistance for specific problems that might also assist local governments, such as homelessness assistance. Investigations of CARES Act implementation have raised concern about the slow pace at which funds have moved from Washington, DC, through the states, and to local programs in need of assistance. For example, one investigative journalist found the Department of Housing and Urban Development had only completed grant agreements for less than 30 percent of homelessness assistance funds by August 2020.[26] Thus, even though aid was allocated in March, many local governments are navigating the costs of the pandemic without timely federal assistance.

When Congress passed another $900 billion of aid in December 2020, state and local governments were not included. The inauguration of the Biden administration and the switch to Democratic control of Congress in January 2021 raised the prospect of a new round of stimulus that might contain support for state and local government. In the months ahead, the design and allocation of federal aid to assist state and local governments with health efforts and economic recovery from COVID-19 will be a critical challenge for policymakers and public managers. Models from the past, such as the General Revenue Sharing Program of the 1970s, might be resurrected to widely distribute federal aid to assist in recovery. These solutions hinge on effective policy negotiations among federal, state, and local leaders in the American federal system, and on the recognition that state and local governments have played a critical role on the front lines of the nation's response to the pandemic.

COVID-19 and the Future of State–Local Relations

The disruptions caused by the COVID-19 pandemic will continue to reverberate through state and local government. The early months of 2021 bring optimism that public health conditions will improve. Yet, for state and local government, challenges will continue in the months ahead. State and local leaders will navigate the financial consequences of extended business closures and restrained economic activity. State–local relations have been strained in places due to conflicting views on the appropriateness of business closures and public health restrictions. Ongoing conflict is not the only possible outcome from these tensions. State and local leaders can look to areas of cooperation during the pandemic, including the sharing of public health information and expertise across levels of government. State leaders can assist local governments with future public health efforts, building from the successful foundations of emergency management partnerships. Local governments can provide input on new state legislative priorities, including technology investments to assist transformed public-sector workplaces and public access to government services. Public managers can look to lessons from the implementation of ARRA to think through effective state–local partnerships for the distribution of economic assistance. State policymakers can join local officials in coordinated lobbying of Congress, requesting that aid be designed in a manner that maximizes the flexibility of the decentralized administrative structure of American federalism.

Finally, the COVID-19 pandemic underscores the critical need for professional public servants who are prepared to work across organizational boundaries to improve public service delivery and response to unanticipated events. Whether student observers of the COVID-19 pandemic have concern for human health and well-being or the economic struggles of businesses and communities, there is important work to be done, helping state and local governments move into the post-COVID-19 era. Continued education in public administration or policy can help equip students with the analytical and managerial skills necessary to work effectively across organizational boundaries and resolve the tensions described in this chapter and in the book more broadly. The future of state–local relations is promising, and the potential for partnership is great, because dedicated elected officials and government employees understand the benefits that can come from cooperation between our states and their local communities.

■ CAREER PROFILE ■

Dr. Sandra Elizabeth Ford
District Health Director, DeKalb County, Georgia
Chief Executive Officer, DeKalb County Board of Health

"When you do things right in public health, you impact millions," explains Dr. Sandra Elizabeth Ford. Public health has always required coordination across levels of government, but the COVID-19 pandemic brought new importance to intergovernmental coordination. Dr. Ford leads public health efforts in DeKalb County, Georgia, as district health director and chief executive officer for the DeKalb County Board of

Health. In these roles, Dr. Ford is responsible for all public health services in DeKalb County, Georgia, the state's fourth most populous county, which includes parts of the City of Atlanta.

Dr. Ford's role illustrates the state–local design of public health services in Georgia. As a state government employee, she reports to the commissioner of the Georgia Department of Public Health, but as the executive officer for the county's public health efforts, she also reports to the county's board of public health. In this role, Dr. Ford serves as a bridge between state and local health efforts. For example, as the DeKalb County Board of Health began to establish and operate sites for COVID-19 testing in early 2020, Dr. Ford needed a new site with specific characteristics. She reported this need through a phone call to the county executive, and two hours later she had the new site. "That's cooperation at its finest," explains Dr. Ford. "In crises, this is what you need. You don't need a whole lot of bureaucracy and paperwork. You need to have trust and relationships established so that when you ask for something, it gets done quickly."

What skills are necessary for students seeking a career in public health? Dr. Ford explains medical training may be necessary for some positions, while others will require a master's of public health, master's of public administration, or master's of business administration. Dr. Ford completed a BA in psychology at Stanford University and then earned MD and MBA degrees from Howard University. Before her current position, Dr. Ford worked in pediatrics and became interested in the management of health organizations. She served as deputy secretary for children's medical services in the Florida Department of Public Health. She moved on to become acting director for the Division of Health in the Georgia Department of Human Resources and served in several other positions in state and local government.

In addition to her medical training, Dr. Ford points to the basics of managing people, budgets, and communication as critical for success in a public health career. "The ability to explain complicated concepts in a simple way that people can understand is critical; but also, as a manager, or as a leader, providing feedback in a way that can be received is also critical." The COVID-19 pandemic illustrates state and local governments need professional public servants, like Dr. Ford, to navigate intergovernmental relations in the field of public health.

Interview: May 11, 2020

Discussion Questions

1. Compare the categories of state responses to COVID-19 presented in this chapter. How did your state respond? Investigate media coverage in your state to learn more about the state and local actions taken in response to the pandemic.

2. Would you argue for or against state preemption of local authority in response to the COVID-19 pandemic? Why?

3. Imagine you are preparing to meet with your member of Congress to discuss a new federal relief bill in response to the COVID-19 pandemic. Would you suggest financial aid be targeted at the state government, local

government, or some combination of both? What are the consequences for state–local relations?

4. If you had the opportunity to meet with a public health official in your city, county, or state government, what questions would you ask them about government coordination during the COVID-19 pandemic?

Notes

The authors of this chapter are listed alphabetically. The editors thank Dr. Curley and Dr. Federman for contributing their work on state executive orders. This book on state–local relations was complete before the outbreak of the COVID-19 pandemic in the United States. This chapter was added to the volume in January 2021, before publication but after the other contributors had completed their work. The pandemic illuminates the dynamics of conflict and cooperation central to this book, a fitting conclusion to the volume.

1. Anthony S. Fauci, H. Clifford Lane, and Robert R. Redfield, "Covid-19—Navigating the Uncharted." *New England Journal of Medicine* 382, no. 13 (2020): 1268–69.
2. S. Gao et al., "Association of Mobile Phone Location Data Indications of Travel and Stay-at-Home Mandates with COVID-19 Infection Rates in the US," *JAMA Network Open* 3, no. 9 (2020): e2020485, doi:10.1001/jamanetworkopen.2020.20485.
3. Jennifer Selin, "Trump versus the States: What Federalism Means for the Coronavirus Response," *Conversation*, April 17, 2020, https://theconversation.com/trump-versus-the-states-what -federalism-means-for-the-coronavirus-response-136361.
4. Ann O'M. Bowman and James H. McKenzie, "Managing the Pandemic at a Less Than Global Scale: Governors Take the Lead," *American Review of Public Administration* 50, nos. 6–7 (2020): 551–59.
5. Michael K. Gusmano, Edward Alan Miller, Pamela Nadash, and Elizabeth J. Simpson, "Partisanship in Initial State Responses to the Covid-19 Pandemic," *World Medical & Health Policy* 12, no. 4 (2020): 380–89.
6. Komla D. Dzigbede, Sarah Beth Gehl, and Katherine Willoughby, "Disaster Resiliency of U.S. Local Governments: Insights to Strengthen Local Response and Recovery from the Covid-19 Pandemic," *Public Administration Review* 80, no. 4 (2020): 634–43.
7. Sheila R. Foster, "As COVID-19 Proliferates Mayors Take Response Lead, Sometimes in Conflicts with Their Governors," Georgetown Project on State and Local Government Policy and Law, https://www.law.georgetown.edu/salpal/as-covid-19-proliferates-mayors-take-response -lead-sometimes-in-conflicts-with-their-governors/.
8. Marios Karabarbounis, Reiko Laski, and Nicholas Trachter, "The Effect of Lockdown Measures on Unemployment," Federal Reserve Bank of Richmond, September 4, 2020, https://www.rich mondfed.org/publications/research/coronavirus/economic_impact_covid-19_09-04-20.
9. K. Caruson and S. A. MacManus, "Mandates and Management Challenges in the Trenches: An Intergovernmental Perspective on Homeland Security," *Public Administration Review* 66, no. 4 (2006): 522–36; L. K. Comfort, "Crisis Management in Hindsight: Cognition, Communication, Coordination, and Control," *Public Administration Review*, 67 (2007): 189–97.
10. C. Curley and P. S. Federman, "State Executive Orders: Nuance in Restrictions, Revealing Suspensions, and Decisions to Enforce," *Public Administration Review* 80, no. 4 (2020): 623–28, https://doi.org/10.1111/puar.13250.
11. Leslie Wells, "Understanding the Impact of COVID-19 Executive Orders," *Making a Difference: News and Notes from the O'Neill School at IUPUI*, April 29, 2020, https://blog.oneill.iupui .edu/2020/04/29/covid-19-executive-orders/.
12. J. Fereday and E. Muir-Cochrane, "Demonstrating Rigor Using Thematic Analysis: A Hybrid Approach of Inductive and Deductive Coding and Theme Development," *International Journal of Qualitative Methods* 5, no. 1 (2006): 80–92.

[13] Jacqueline Merrill, Jonathan W. Keeling, and Kathleen M. Carley, "A Comparative Study of 11 Local Health Department Organizational Networks," *Journal of Public Health Management and Practice* 16, no. 6 (2010): 564–76, doi:10.1097/PHH.0b013e3181e31cee; Aaron Wachhaus, "Building Health Communities: Local Health Care Networks in Maryland," *American Review of Public Administration* 50, no. 1 (2020): 62–76.

[14] Morton Grodzins, *The American System: A New View of Government in the United States* (New York: Rand McNally, 1966).

[15] Bruce F. Berg, *Healing Gotham: New York City's Public Health Policies for the Twenty-First Century* (Baltimore, MD: Johns Hopkins University Press, 2015).

[16] Bruce D. McDonald, Christopher B. Goodman, and Megan E. Hatch, "Tensions in State–Local Intergovernmental Response to Emergencies: The Case of COVID-19," *State and Local Government Review* (December 2021), https://doi.org/10.1177/0160323X20979826.

[17] Eric S. Zeemering, "Georgia Cities and COVID-19: Engaging the Pandemic Challenge—Survey Overview," April 24, 2020, https://medium.com/@eric.zeemering/georgia-cities-and-covid-19-engaging-the-pandemic-challenge-survey-overview-256adeeaad44.

[18] P. Edward French and Eric S. Raymond, "Pandemic Influenza Planning: An Extraordinary Ethical Dilemma for Local Government Officials," *Public Administration Review* 69, no. 5 (2009): 823–30.

[19] Eric S. Zeemering, "Functional Fragmentation in City Hall and Twitter Communication during the Covid-19 Pandemic: Evidence from Atlanta, San Francisco, and Washington, DC," *Government Information Quarterly* 38, no. 1 (2021): 101539.

[20] Center for Local, State and Urban Policy, "The Initial Impact of the COVID-19 Pandemic on Michigan Communities and Local Governments," Gerald R. Ford School of Public Policy, June 24, 2020, http://closup.umich.edu/michigan-public-policy-survey/80/the-initial-impact-of-the-covid-19-pandemic-on-michigan-communities-and-local-governments.

[21] Jaweed Kaleem, "'There Will Be a Coronavirus in the Fall': As Mayors Battle Governors on Reopening, Experts Warn of Reviving Outbreak," *Los Angeles Times*, April 22, 2020, https://www.latimes.com/world-nation/story/2020-04-22/coronavirus-stay-at-home-reopening-trump.

[22] Slone Terranella, "U.P. County Is Refusing to Enforce COVID-19 Restrictions from Whitmer," *Detroit Free Press*, January 12, 2021, https://www.freep.com/story/news/local/michigan/2021/01/12/michigan-baraga-county-covid-19-restrictions/6636896002/.

[23] Michael A. Pagano and Christiana K. McFarland, "When Will Your City Feel the Fiscal Impact of COVID-19?," *Brookings: The Avenue*, March 31, 2020, https://www.brookings.edu/blog/the-avenue/2020/03/31/when-will-your-city-feel-the-fiscal-impact-of-covid-19/.

[24] Louise Sheiner and Sophia Campbell, "How Much Is COVID-19 Hurting State and Local Revenues?" *Brookings: Up Front*, September 24, 2020, https://www.brookings.edu/blog/up-front/2020/09/24/how-much-is-covid-19-hurting-state-and-local-revenues/.

[25] Jason Saving, "COVID-19's Fiscal Ills: Busted Texas Budgets, Critical Local Choices," *Southwest Economy*, Third Quarter 2020, Federal Reserve Bank of Dallas, https://www.dallasfed.org/research/swe/2020/swe2003/swe2003b.aspx.

[26] Katie Surma, "Months after the CARES Act, Communities Still Await Federal Homeless Aid," *USA Today*, August 28, 2020, https://www.usatoday.com/story/news/investigations/2020/08/28/covid-19-cares-act-communities-still-await-federal-homeless-aid/5641210002/.

Index

Page numbers followed by *b* refer to boxes, *f* to figures, and *t* to tables.

Made in United States
North Haven, CT
11 January 2022

14574001R00174